THE NORMANS AND EMPIRE

The Normans and Empire

The Ford Lectures delivered in the University of Oxford during Hilary Term 2010

DAVID BATES

UNIVERSITY PRESS

OXFORD
UNIVERSITY PRESS

Great Clarendon Street, Oxford, OX2 6DP,
United Kingdom

Oxford University Press is a department of the University of Oxford.
It furthers the University's objective of excellence in research, scholarship,
and education by publishing worldwide. Oxford is a registered trade mark of
Oxford University Press in the UK and in certain other countries

© David Bates 2013

The moral rights of the author have been asserted

First Edition published in 2013

Impression: 1

All rights reserved. No part of this publication may be reproduced, stored in
a retrieval system, or transmitted, in any form or by any means, without the
prior permission in writing of Oxford University Press, or as expressly permitted
by law, by licence or under terms agreed with the appropriate reprographics
rights organization. Enquiries concerning reproduction outside the scope of the
above should be sent to the Rights Department, Oxford University Press, at the
address above

You must not circulate this work in any other form
and you must impose this same condition on any acquirer

Published in the United States of America by Oxford University Press
198 Madison Avenue, New York, NY 10016, United States of America

British Library Cataloguing in Publication Data
Data available

Library of Congress Control Number: 2013945610

ISBN 978–0–19–967441–1

As printed and bound by
CPI Group (UK) Ltd, Croydon, CR0 4YY

Links to third party websites are provided by Oxford in good faith and
for information only. Oxford disclaims any responsibility for the materials
contained in any third party website referenced in this work.

In Memory of Phyllis Jacobs

Preface

The invitation to deliver the Ford Lectures in the University of Oxford in the Hilary Term of the academic year 2009–10, received in a letter dated 5 December 2006, came as a great surprise. Once calm reflection became possible, it swiftly became clear to me that I must devote the six lectures to a topic that has occupied my thoughts since almost the start of my career as a professional historian, namely the cross-Channel polity created by the conquest of England in 1066 and brought to an end by Philip Augustus's conquest of the duchy of Normandy in 1204. I have a vivid memory of a conversation in Henry Loyn's office in the former Arts Building of the then University College, Cardiff, during which he passed to me a copy of John Le Patourel's recently published 1970 Stenton Lecture *Normandy and England 1066–1144*. I was instantly fascinated by its theme and, in the arrogance of youth, was somewhat critical of the argument. I was soon teaching a two-term Optional Course entitled 'Normandy and England, 1066–1204', which was taken by many excellent students. By 1976, I was hard at work tracing and reading charters in the archives and libraries of Normandy and northern France and in the late 1970s, by this time seriously launched on research into cross-Channel history, I acquired two exceptional research students, David Crouch and Kathleen Thompson, both of whom have gone on to make contributions of outstanding importance in the field. I am deeply indebted to both of them and to all the other postgraduates I have supervised. I have learnt an enormous amount from all of them, and from all who have shared my enthusiasm for this book's subject.

I first met John Le Patourel, if memory serves me right, at the IHR at an Anglo-American Conference. He greeted me by saying that he was pleased to meet Odo of Bayeux, who was the subject of my doctoral thesis and of such publications I had produced by that time. Thereafter, he was consistently and warmly encouraging until his death in 1981, encouragement that included passing to me in 1977 a personally dedicated copy of John Horace Round's *Calendar of Documents preserved in France*. Although my interest in cross-Channel matters remained a consistent one throughout the following forty years, both the nature of this interest and my commitment to it have inevitably fluctuated. There have been distractions in the shape of other projects and of important managerial positions in three of the five universities that have chosen to employ me. Although I always regarded the articles I published in 1989 and 1994 as unfinished business, it was often unclear to me how—or indeed whether—I would produce the statement that I knew ought to follow. The Electors to the Ford Lectures put an end to indecision.

My time at all of the five of the universities I have worked for has contributed significantly to the lectures as given and to the book that has now emerged. It was at Cardiff that the interest was first nurtured and where the subject played a central role in my teaching and research. My colleagues at the University of Glasgow helped me to broaden my horizons and introduced me to new methodologies. More than thirty years spent living and working in Wales and Scotland led to the development of a sympathetic knowledge of the national historiographies of the two countries which has, I hope, informed this book sufficiently to meet the demands of specialists in those fields. That I was a colleague of Rees Davies in the University of Wales was also of immeasurable benefit to me. The Institute of Historical Research has always been my favourite place to work and its seminars have always been a stimulus to thought; it played a part in my early career, to which I will return. My years as Director of the Institute helped me to think about this book's theme from perspectives that were not simply those of a medieval historian. From 2008, the University of East Anglia, by creating the post that has enabled me to write this book, has provided a supportive and stimulating environment and introduced me to themes and ideas that have profoundly influenced my thinking. I am as good as certain that this book could not have been written without the generosity of UEA colleagues and, above all, without the faith in me shown by John Charmley and Nicholas Vincent. Between 2009 and 2012 I held a Chaire d'Excellence at the Université de Caen Basse-Normandie financed by the Conseil Régional de la Basse-Normandie. This gave me indispensable access to the university's unique libraries and to seminars at a university with which I have long been closely associated, and of which I am honoured to hold a Doctorate *honoris causa*. Special thanks are due to Pierre Bauduin and Véronique Gazeau for making all this possible and to colleagues in Caen who have welcomed me so warmly. I must also add that, since 2003, the Faculty of History of the University of Cambridge, Clare Hall (of which I was elected a Life Member with the support of the late Marjorie Chibnall), and Cambridge University Library have provided support, stimulus, and working conditions that have also been indispensable to the development of this book.

While the majority of secondary material cited in this book is either Anglophone or Francophone, I am very aware that it ultimately draws on a massive scholarship written in many languages. Since this book is ultimately an essay with an argument rather than a monograph that seeks to establish definitively a particular point, it is inevitable that the citations in the footnotes cannot do full justice to everyone. It sets out to engage with many historiographies and to argue for new perspectives on familiar subjects. It is for the reader to judge the validity of my reference to 'disconnected historiographies' (see Chapter 1). It is also my hope that any apparent omissions in my large Bibliography of secondary literature will be treated tolerantly and kindly. The overriding objective is to set out an argument for critical appraisal. I have largely retained the organization of the lectures as given in January and February 2010, and the titles of the six chapters are those of the lectures given. As those patient enough to attend the lectures will, however, recognize, the content and argument have both changed significantly in several places. That I end the book by saying that the material required for a definitive statement of my thesis is not yet available is intended as an appeal for further work to be undertaken. I make some suggestions as to the form that it might take.

A book of this kind written at a relatively advanced stage in a career inevitably draws on the stimulus derived from colleagues and contemporaries, some of whom are no longer with us. All who consult it will, I hope, recognize how they have contributed in the pages that follow and will forgive disagreements where they are expressed. From the time that I was invited to give the lectures, I have talked to what feels like an almost infinite number of people about the arguments that have emerged in this book. It is, therefore, likely that I will have omitted names where my memory has failed to retain a specific record of an important conversation; to those omitted from the following list, I must apologize profusely. Those who have certainly given help are Lesley Abrams, Richard Allen, Mathieu Arnoux, Sir John Baker, Robert Bartlett, Martin Brett, Joe Canning, David Carpenter, Stephen Church, Peter Crooks, David Crouch, David Ditchburn, Sir John Elliot, Eric Fernie, Jean-Hervé Foulon, Elizabeth Friend-Smith, George Garnett, Brian Golding, Lindy Grant, Judith Green, Claire Hanusse, Sandy Heslop, Leonie Hicks, John Hudson, Edward Impey, Susan Johns, Ewan Johnson, Lars Kjaer, Catherine Letouzey-Réti, Tom Licence, Robert Liddiard, Stephen Marritt, Peter Marshall, Henry Mayr-Harting, Nicholas Morton, Daniel Power, Susan Raich, Susan Reynolds, Miri Rubin, Ian Short, Hélène Sirantoine, Julia Smith, Pauline Stafford, Keith Stringer, and Colin Young. I have given lectures and seminars on the themes of this book at the universities of Caen Basse-Normandie (several times), Cambridge (twice), East Anglia (twice), Rennes-II, Trinity College Dublin, and Nottingham Trent, at the London Society for Medieval Studies, the Cambridge and Nuneaton branches of the Historical Association, and the Leeds International Medieval Congress, at a 'Norman Edge' conference at the University of Lancaster, and at a conference in London in honour of my Cardiff colleague Peter Edbury. During my many weeks in Caen away from home and family, the staff of the Hôtel des Quatrans and the Restaurant ArchiDona provided friendship and support which must receive a special mention. Anna Asbury gave generous and indispensable assistance with the compilation of the Bibliography. At OUP, Stephanie Ireland skilfully negotiated the commissioning process and gave good advice, Cathryn Steele guided me through the first steps towards production and publication, and Emma Barber has efficiently and sympathetically supported me through all the subsequent stages that have led to publication.

Much of the manuscript of this book has been read by Elisabeth van Houts, for whose comments and advice I am deeply grateful, as well as for the encouragement derived from our long-standing shared commitment to setting the subject of this book in its European context. Sections of the book have been read by Stuart Airlie, Pierre Bauduin, Alice Taylor, and Kathleen Thompson. All provided invaluable advice. My children, Jonathan Bates-Kawachi and Rachel Bates, have provided much encouragement. My greatest personal debt by far is to my wife, Helen. Not only has she had to tolerate a husband who habitually disappeared to France for significant periods of time, she has talked with me about all the ideas in this book, and she has read and commented hugely to its benefit on all of it. The book is, however, dedicated to someone whom I first met at the IHR in the summer of 1968 during a period of work in London that effectively made me a serious historian. Without her support for me from that time until her death on 17 July 2011 at the age of ninety-six, whatever I have achieved during my professional life just would not have been possible.

Contents

List of Abbreviations	xiii
1. The Normans and Empire	1
2. The Experience of Empire	28
3. William the Conqueror as Maker of Empire	64
4. Hegemony	93
5. Core, Periphery, and Networks	128
6. Empire: From Beginning to End	160
Bibliography	191
Index	227

List of Abbreviations

1204	Anne-Marie Flambard Héricher and Véronique Gazeau (eds), *1204: la Normandie entre Plantagenêts et Capétiens* (Caen, 2007)
AN	*Annales de Normandie*
ANS	*Anglo-Norman Studies*
ASC	Anglo-Saxon Chronicle, cited by year (corrected in square brackets if necessary) and manuscript; unless otherwise stated the edition is *Two of the Saxon Chronicles Parallel*, ed. Charles Plummer, 2 vols (Oxford, 1892–9)
ASE	*Anglo-Saxon England*
(BI)HR	*(Bulletin of the Institute of) Historical Research*
CDF	*Calendar of Documents preserved in France Illustrative of the History of Great Britain and Ireland*, ed. J. H. Round (London, 1899)
Chronicles	*Chronicles of the Reigns of Stephen, Henry II, and Richard I*, 4 vols, ed. Richard Howlett, Rolls Series (London, 1884–9)
DB	*Domesday Book, seu Liber Censualis Willelmi primi regis Angliae*, ed. Abraham Farley, 2 vols (London, 1783)
DD	K. S. B. Keats-Rohan, *Domesday Descendants: A Prosopography of Persons Occurring in English Documents 1066–1166* (Woodbridge, 2002)
DP	K. S. B. Keats-Rohan, *Domesday People: A Prosopography of Persons Occurring in English Documents, 1066–1166*, 1: *Domesday Book* (Woodbridge, 1999)
EHR	*English Historical Review*
EME	*Early Medieval Europe*
England and Normandy	David Bates and Anne Curry (eds), *England and Normandy in the Middle Ages* (London and Rio Grande, 1994)
Feudal Empires	John Le Patourel, *Feudal Empires: Norman and Plantagenet*, ed. Michael Jones (London, 1984)
GG	*The Gesta Guillelmi of William of Poitiers*, ed. and trans. R. H. C. Davis and Marjorie Chibnall, OMT (Oxford, 1998)
GND	*The Gesta Normannorum Ducum of William of Jumièges, Orderic Vitalis, and Robert of Torigni*, ed. and trans. Elisabeth M. C. van Houts, 2 vols, OMT (Oxford, 1992–5)
GP	William of Malmesbury, *Gesta pontificum Anglorum: The History of the English Bishops*, ed. and trans. M. Winterbottom and R. M. Thomson, 2 vols, OMT (Oxford, 2007)

GR	William of Malmesbury, *Gesta regum Anglorum: The History of the English Kings*, ed. and trans. R. A. B. Mynors, M. Winterbottom, and R. M. Thomson, 2 vols, OMT (Oxford, 1998–9)
HH	Henry, Archdeacon of Huntingdon, *Historia Anglorum: The History of the English People*, ed. and trans. Diana Greenway, OMT (Oxford, 1996)
HSJ	*Haskins Society Journal*
JEH	*Journal of Ecclesiastical History*
JMH	*Journal of Medieval History*
JW	*The Chronicle of John of Worcester*, ed. R. R. Darlington and P. McGurk, vols 2 and 3, OMT (Oxford, 1995–8)
MGH	Monumenta Germaniae Historica
Monarchy and Magnates	C. W. Hollister, *Monarchy, Magnates and Institutions in the Anglo-Norman World* (London and Ronceverte, 1986)
Normandie et Angleterre	Pierre Bouet and Véronique Gazeau (eds), *La Normandie et l'Angleterre au Moyen Age* (Caen, 2003)
Normandy and Neighbours	David Crouch and Kathleen Thompson (eds), *Normandy and Its Neighbours, 900–1250: Essays for David Bates* (Turnhout, 2011)
Normans in Europe	*The Normans in Europe*, ed. and trans. Elisabeth van Houts, Manchester Medieval Sources (Manchester and New York, 2000)
ODNB	*Oxford Dictionary of National Biography*
OMT	Oxford Medieval Texts
OV	*The Ecclesiastical History of Orderic Vitalis*, ed. and trans. Marjorie Chibnall, 6 vols, OMT (Oxford, 1969–80)
P&P	*Past and Present*
PBA	*Proceedings of the British Academy*
PL	*Patrologia cursus completus, series Latina*, ed. J.-P. Migne, 221 vols (Paris, 1844–65)
RADN	*Recueil des actes des ducs de Normandie de 911 à 1066*, ed. Marie Fauroux, Mémoires de la Société des Antiquaires de Normandie 36 (Caen, 1961)
Regesta	*Regesta Regum Anglo-Normannorum: The Acta of William I (1066–1087)*, ed. David Bates (Oxford, 1998)
Roman de Rou	*The History of the Norman People: Wace's Roman de Rou*, trans. Glyn S. Burgess (Woodbridge, 2004)
RRAN	*Regesta Regum Anglo-Normannorum, 1066–1154*, 3 vols (i, ed. H. W. C. Davis (Oxford, 1913); ii, ed. Charles Johnson and H. A. Cronne (Oxford, 1956); iii, ed. H. A. Cronne and R. H. C. Davis (Oxford, 1968))
RT (D)	*Chronique de Robert de Torigni, abbé du Mont-Saint-Michel, suivie de divers opuscules historiques de cet auteur et de plusieurs religieux de la même abbaye*, ed. Léopold Delisle, 2 vols, Société de l'Histoire de Normandie (Rouen, 1872–3)

List of Abbreviations

RT (H)	*The Chronicle of Robert of Torigni, Abbot of the Monastery of St Michael-in-Peril-of the Sea*, ed. Richard Howlett, in *Chronicles*, vol. iv
The English	John Gillingham, *The English in the Twelfth Century: Imperialism, National Identity and Political Values* (Woodbridge, 2000)
Tinchebray	Véronique Gazeau and Judith Green (eds), *Tinchebray 1106–2006: Actes du colloque de Tinchebray (28–30 septembre 2006)*, Le Pays Bas-Normand (Flers, 2009)
TRHS	*Transactions of the Royal Historical Society*

1

The Normans and Empire

Since the publication of John Le Patourel's *The Norman Empire* in 1976, the term 'empire' has featured prominently to describe the cross-Channel polity created by William the Conqueror in Anglophone historiography.[1] But, with a few notable exceptions, the usage has simply been one deployed to describe the combination under a single ruler or ruling family of Normandy, England, and, when appropriate, other conquered political units with a distinct identity, such as Maine and parts of Wales. It is also a usage that has not been universally accepted.[2] Since 1976, there has also been a multitude of publications on subjects as diverse as politics and property, individual and collective identity, and ecclesiastical architecture that have stressed diversity, difference, and, at times, disruptiveness, as features of the history of the cross-Channel world that the events of the year 1066 brought into existence.[3] Interestingly, these were developments and criticisms of his work that John Le Patourel had privately anticipated.[4]

At the start of another attempt to employ the term empire to analyse the history of the Normans in north-western Europe, it is essential to take note of Brian Golding's observation that neither John Le Patourel nor my critique of *The Norman Empire* that was published in 1989 truly addressed issues of definition.[5] The late Marjorie Chibnall correctly warned that 'any historian who draws

---

[1] John Le Patourel, *The Norman Empire* (Oxford, 1976).

[2] For the main critical assessments of *The Norman Empire*, David Bates, 'Normandy and England after 1066', *EHR*, civ (1989), 851–80; Judith A. Green, 'Unity and Disunity in the Anglo-Norman State', *HR*, lxii (1989), 115–34; Emily Zack Tabuteau, 'The Role of Law in the Succession to Normandy and England', *HSJ*, iii (1991), 141–69, at 142; David Crouch, 'Normans and Anglo-Normans: A Divided Aristocracy?', in *England and Normandy*, 51–67; Brian Golding, *Conquest and Colonisation: The Normans in Britain, 1066–1100* (London, 1994; rev. edn., 2001), 177–93; Francis J. West, 'The Colonial History of the Norman Conquest', *History*, lxxxiv (1999), 219–36. For a recent survey, Pierre Bauduin, 'Les modèles anglo-normands en questions', in *Nascita di un regno. Poteri signorili, istituzioni feudali e strutture sociali nel Mezzogiorno normanno (1130–1194)*, ed. Raffaele Licinio and Francesco Violante (Bari, 2008), 51–97.

[3] Note, especially, J. C. Holt, 'Politics and Property in Early Medieval England', *P&P*, no. 57 (1972), 3–52, at 19, 44 (reprinted in, J. C. Holt, *Colonial England, 1066–1215* (London, 1997), 113–59, at 127, 148) ('Rules of succession were applied in political circumstances quite unsuited to them' and 'The tenurial crisis of the Anglo-Norman period arose not because there was no law governing title and inheritance, or because kings flouted it, but because of the difficulties they encountered and created in applying it'); *DP*, Chap. 2 ('Provenance and the Past: Territorial Descriptors and Domesday Prosopography'); Lindy Grant, 'Architectural Relationships between England and Normandy, 1100–1204', in *England and Normandy*, 117–29, and *Architecture and Society in Normandy, 1120–1270* (New Haven, CT, 2005), 43–95, and see esp. 55–6.

[4] J. C. Holt, 'John Le Patourel 1909–81', *PBA*, lxxi (1985), 583–96, at 596.

[5] Golding, *Conquest and Colonisation*, 178.

comparisons needs to start by carefully defining what he means by "empire" or "colony"'.[6] In other historical fields, it has been observed that the term empire is sometimes carelessly used.[7] But with the phenomenon of empire having, in the words of Dominic Lieven in 2005, in his Elie Kedourie Lecture to the British Academy, 'returned to the centre of the academic agenda', and Lindy Colley having spoken in similar terms at an Anglo-American Conference, it is surely time to return to the subject.[8] This book is a discussion of the applicability of the frameworks associated with this renaissance of interest to the eleventh- and twelfth-century history—and histories—of the Normans. Its main argument is that through intellectual cross-fertilization from the political and social sciences and from the writings of historians working on other periods, we can re-frame and reassess some familiar subjects. Its arguments cover the whole period from 1066 to 1204, but its concentration is primarily on the years between 1066 and 1154.

It is crucial to my argument that a new terminology and set of analytical tools have reshaped from the 1980s onwards the study of the whole phenomenon of empire. In particular, Michael Mann's categorization of social power as military, political, economic, and ideological is an important landmark. From the same decade, Paul Kennedy's study of the rise and fall of great powers (for which now read empires) initiated debates that are also of central importance.[9] And even if the language of the social and political sciences is not deployed directly by historians of empire, those who write about the subject do so in notably subtle terms, taking account of what is often called informal power and recognizing the complexity of empire for all who took part.[10]

To my knowledge, the phrase 'The Norman Empire' was first used by Charles Homer Haskins as the title of Chapter 4 of *The Normans in European History*, published in 1916.[11] Also, although he made his argument for cross-Channel unity and uniformity without using the word empire, a similar thesis to Le Patourel's was developed by Warren Hollister in the 1970s.[12] There is a Francophone tradition whose principal product, written by the canon lawyer Pierre Andrieu-Guitrancourt, used the word empire to cover as a single process Norman

---

[6] Marjorie Chibnall, *The Debate on the Norman Conquest* (Manchester, 1999), 122.

[7] J. N. Hillgarth, *The Problem of a Catalan Mediterranean Empire, 1229–1324*, EHR Supplement, no. 8 (London, 1975), and especially at 1–2, 52; Michael Mann, *Incoherent Empire* (London, 2003), 15 ('the enemies of the United States are wrong to see it as the Great Satan or the Evil Empire. It is not that well organized').

[8] Dominic Lieven, 'Empire, History and the Contemporary Global Order', *PBA*, cxxxi (2005), 127–56, at 127; Linda Colley, 'The Difficulties of Empire: Present, Past and Future', *HR*, lxxix (2006), 367–82, at 367–8.

[9] Michael Mann, *The Sources of Social Power*: I. *A History of Power from the Beginning to 1760 AD*; II. *The Rise of Classes and Nation States, 1760–1914* (Cambridge, 1986–93); Paul Kennedy, *The Rise and Fall of the Great Powers: Economic Change and Military Conflict from 1500 to 2000* (London, 1988).

[10] P. J. Marshall, *The Making and Unmaking of Empires: Britain, India and America, c.1750–1783* (Oxford, 2005), 1–12.

[11] C. H. Haskins, *The Normans in European History* (London, 1916).

[12] Above all, C. W. Hollister, 'Normandy, France and the Anglo-Norman *regnum*', *Speculum*, li (1976), 202–42 (*Monarchy and Magnates*, 17–57).

activity in northern and southern Europe. It can largely be left to one side because, although the southern European conquests do feature in my argument, on any definition now current, an empire must have a single ultimate source of authority.[13] However, among French-speaking historians of the Normans, the publications of the late Professor Lucien Musset are most definitely relevant, since he both used the term empire and accepted and explored Le Patourel's ideas.[14]

Haskins's and Le Patourel's approaches to the subject of empire were hugely different. So different indeed were they that *The Norman Empire* made no reference to *The Normans in European History* and did not even include it in its bibliography. This, I would suggest, not only reflects the differing interests of the two historians, but also the fact that over the past century interest in empire in all intellectual disciplines and among the public at large has been episodic, and that the terms of reference of analysis have changed. Haskins's book was fundamentally a study of a people and a civilization and Le Patourel's, in comparison, a narrower one devoted primarily to domination, power, and colonization; the flavour of the difference is succinctly conveyed by Haskins's statement that Normandy was 'the mother of a greater Normandy in England, Sicily, and in America'.[15] The Normans for him were one of the great creative forces in European—and on his terms—world civilization, a civilization that he believed to be in peril of extinction when, in 1915, he gave the two series of lectures on which *The Normans in European History* was based.[16] Le Patourel's rationale for writing was also idealistic, but in a different way. The basis of his argument was that his upbringing in the Channel Islands gave him a special insight into matters cross-Channel and therefore into the state created by the conquest of England in 1066. He also believed that we should not be trapped into an excessively narrow concentration on national histories.[17]

The scale of modern interest in the phenomenon of empire is such that it has not only inspired a multitude of publications, but also television programmes by the likes of Niall Ferguson, Simon Schama, and Jeremy Paxman.[18] Interest and debate

---

[13] Pierre Andrieu-Guitrancourt, *Histoire de l'Empire normand et de sa civilisation* (Paris, 1952). Note, also, Pierre Aubé, *Les Empires normands d'Orient, XIe–XIIIe siècle* (Paris, 1985; 2nd. edn., Paris, 1991), a popular work written without footnotes.

[14] Lucien Musset, 'Un empire à cheval sur la mer: les périls de mer dans l'Etat anglo-normand d'après les chartes, les chroniques et les miracles', in Alain Lottin, Jean-Claude Hocquet, and Stéphane Lebecq (eds), *Les Hommes et la Mer dans l'Europe du Nord-Ouest de l'Antiquité à nos jours*, Revue du Nord, numéro 1 spécial hors série—collection Histoire (1986), 413–24. See further, Chap. 2.

[15] Haskins, *The Normans in European History*, 3.

[16] For Haskins's life and influence, Sally N. Vaughn, 'Charles Homer Haskins', in Clyde N. Wilson (ed.), *The Dictionary of Literary Biography*, vol. 47: *American Historians, 1866–1912* (Detroit, 1986), 122–44; 'Charles Homer Haskins (1870–1937)', in Helen Damico and Joseph B. Zadavil (eds), *Medieval Scholarship: Biographical Studies on the Formation of a Discipline*, vol. 1: *History* (New York, 1995), 169–84.

[17] 'Yet we (ie, the Channel Islanders) are perhaps more deeply involved, historically, in the relationship of Normandy and England created as a result of Duke William's conquest than either the English or the French'; John Le Patourel, *Normandy and England, 1066–1144*, The Stenton Lecture 1970 (University of Reading, 1971), 3 (*Feudal Empires*, Chap. 7, p. 3).

[18] Of recent publications, note, for example, Timothy H. Parsons, *The Rule of Empires: Those Who Built Them, Those Who Endured Them, and Why They Always Fall* (Oxford, 2010); Jane Burbank and Frederick Cooper, *Empires in World History: Power and the Politics of Difference* (Princeton, 2010);

have undoubtedly acquired a new intensity in the aftermath of the terrible events of 11 September 2001, with extreme positions sometimes being taken up and an interest in why empires and nations fail proliferating.[19] The two evocative phrases, 'hard power' and 'soft power', coined by Joseph Nye, and now assimilated into discourse beyond the world of academe, have given a vivid expression to the practice of power by focusing attention on the way that superior military and economic power are combined with the civilizing mission that many empires claim for themselves.[20] Such processes are observable even in the history of an empire such as the appalling and short-lived Third Reich.

The phrases hard and soft power also put the spotlight on the fact that empires, for all that they usually claim to have a civilizing mission, have been, and remain, for many people the manifestation of an immoral phenomenon, namely, the exercise of power without consent.[21] With the proclaimed moral and military superiority of the Normans being both regularly enunciated themes and hotly contested ones in the eleventh and twelfth centuries, the relevance of this framework of analysis to my subject is obvious. Hence, as part of my efforts to argue that cross-fertilization from the work of historians of other periods is a valuable exercise, it is irresistible not to suggest that the reader place alongside each other as parallel texts the writings of Niall Ferguson and William of Malmesbury, the first a proponent of a civilizing and economically productive role for the British Empire and the West, and the second a historian to whom the late Sir Rees Davies attributed an 'ardent and fawning Francophilia'.[22]

Inextricably associated with my subject is the fact that the topic of empire has been placed firmly on the agenda for historians of medieval Britain by Rees Davies's published 1998 Ford Lectures, *The First English Empire*, with the argument for extending the same forms of analysis into the Later Middle Ages having been set out by Peter Crooks.[23] It is especially helpful to this book's argument that, while Rees Davies never announced that he was making use of social science modelling, both he and Peter Crooks actually use a social science framework similar, but not

---

Kwasi Kwarteng, *Ghosts of Empire: Britain's Legacies in the Modern World* (London, 2011); Niall Ferguson, *Civilization: The West and the Rest* (London, 2011).

[19] See, recently, Daron Acemoglu and James A. Robinson, *Why Nations Fail: The Origins of Power, Prosperity and Poverty* (London, 2012). For examples of the extremes of controversy, Niall Ferguson, *Empire: How Britain Made the Modern World* (London, 2003); Mann, *Incoherent Empire*. For a succinct survey of many issues, Bernard Porter, 'Cutting the British Empire Down to Size', *History Today*, lxii, no. 10 (2012), 22–9.

[20] For the general issues, Joseph S. Nye, Jnr., *Soft Power: The Means to Success in World Politics* (New York, 2004).

[21] For a flavour of the debate, Stephen Howe, 'The Slow Death and Strange Rebirths of Imperial History', *Journal of Imperial and Commonwealth History*, xxix (2001), 131–41, with comment on the shift away from national to imperial history at 138–9.

[22] Ferguson, *Empire: How Britain Made the Modern World*, xii–xxv, 358–72; John Gillingham, 'The Beginnings of English Imperialism', in *The English*, 3–18; R. R. Davies, *The Matter of Britain and the Matter of England: An Inaugural Lecture Delivered before the University of Oxford on 29 February 1996* (Oxford, 1996), 10.

[23] R. R. Davies, *The First English Empire: Power and Identities in the British Isles, 1093–1343* (Oxford, 2000); Peter Crooks, 'State of the Union: Perspectives on English Imperialism in the Late Middle Ages', *P&P*, no. 212 (2011), 3–42.

identical, to mine; conceptual cross-referencing is therefore relatively easy.[24] However, with the Norman Empire, the Anglo-Norman Empire, and the Angevin or Plantagenet Empire also very much in play historiographically, one obvious issue raised for my argument by *The First English Empire* is whether there can be multiple, chronologically overlapping, empires.[25] Another is to wonder how an English empire could begin in what Rees Davies called the *annus horribilis* of 1093 when, twenty-seven years earlier, the *gens Anglorum* had suffered a catastrophic defeat and, in 1093 and for decades afterwards, was manifestly still continuing to suffer its consequences. And another is that, while Robin Frame's book on the medieval history of the British Isles did bring in the continental dimension that is largely lacking from *The First English Empire*, he also offered the opinion that the continental empires strengthened the power within Britain of the English kings, a proposition with which Keith Stringer, by alluding to 'imperial overstretch', appears to disagree.[26] These are issues to which I will return. Suffice to say for now that there are too many disconnected historiographies around for comfort and historical debates that ought to happen, but have not. And to spell out here for the first time that Normandy is of absolutely fundamental importance to the whole subject, even for those whose principal concern is the history of the British Isles.[27]

At an early stage in the development of his ideas, Le Patourel wrote in terms of the need for 'almost a sociological study of the Norman families'.[28] That he also saw clearly the benefits to be drawn from engagement with the social sciences has been a considerable stimulus to the development of my argument. If, over fifty years later, the ideal he wished for is undoubtedly closer to being realized because of the enormous advances in knowledge and understanding that have occurred in the form of books, articles, and several large prosopographical projects, and through the massive accumulated learning of the *Oxford Dictionary of National Biography*, it remains in the last resort unfulfilled on the terms in which he proposed it.[29]

---

[24] It is noteworthy that while the discussion at *The First English Empire*, 32, does not use the categorizations of 'hegemony', 'core', or 'periphery', it could very easily be re-cast in those terms. The statement in an earlier book that 'domination was often in effect secured, as in all periods, by tactics in which the kid glove rather than the mailed fist was to the fore' (R. R. Davies, *Domination and Conquest: The Experience of Ireland, Scotland and Wales, 1100–1300* (Cambridge, 1990), 6) anticipates the subsequently formulated concepts of soft and informal power.

[25] On these, see Chap. 6.

[26] Robin Frame, *The Political Development of the British Isles, 1100–1400* (Oxford, 1990), 20–44, 50–6; Keith J. Stringer, *The Reign of Stephen: Kingship, Warfare and Government in Twelfth-Century England* (London, 1993), 10, 11.

[27] For my argument, the parallel with Peter Crooks's observation about 'a bifurcated [late medieval] historiography that tends to treat "British" history and Anglo-French history as discrete subjects' ('State of the Union', 9) is a very telling one.

[28] J. Le Patourel, *Norman Barons* (Hastings and Bexhill Branch of the Historical Association, 1966), 28 (*Feudal Empires*, Chap. 6, p. 28).

[29] Diana E. Greenway et al. (eds), *John Le Neve: Fasti ecclesiae Anglicanae, 1066–1300*, 10 vols (London, 1968–2005); Dom. David Knowles, C. N. L. Brooke, and Vera London (eds), *The Heads of Religious Houses: England and Wales, 940–1216* (Cambridge, 1972); L.-R. Ménager, 'Pesanteur et étiologie de la colonisation normande de l'Italie', 'Appendice: Inventaire des familles normandes et franques émigrés en Italie mériodionale et en Sicile (XIe–XIIe siècles)', and 'Additions à l'inventaire des familles normandes et franques émigrés en Italie mériodionale et en Sicile', in L.-R. Ménager, *Hommes et institutions de l'Italie normande* (London, 1981), Chap. 4; K. S. B. Keats-Rohan, *DP* and *DD*; David

In addition, as Daniel Power has pointed out, a massive lacuna is the absence of any significant proposopographical treatment of the secular elites of the Angevin/Plantagenet Empire.[30] This and the coordination and expansion of all these current and completed research projects would be a much to be desired outcome of this book. One of my purposes is to set out the kind of sociological approach that is needed.

The publication of Ralph Davis's *The Normans and their Myth* in the same year as Le Patourel's *Norman Empire* was something of a remarkable coincidence.[31] In arguing against the whole notion of a single unified Norman world that had animated historians up until that time, as epitomized by the near-contemporary publications of David Douglas and R. Allen Brown, it reflected broader intellectual currents that were starting to demolish the, largely assumed, link between national identity and ethnic character.[32] There has since been a proliferation of books devoted to the subject of identity that have arguably produced something of a bifurcation in the historiography, with identity often becoming almost a separate area of enquiry and the books and articles dealing with it often concentrating on so-called narrative sources. At times indeed they have concentrated on histories written only on one side or the other of the Channel.[33] An extraordinarily woolly word

---

S. Spear, *The Personnel of the Norman Cathedrals during the Ducal Period, 911–1204* (London, 2006); Véronique Gazeau, *Normannia Monastica: Prosopographie des abbés bénédictins (Xe–XIIe siècle)* (Caen, 2007); 'The Paradox of Medieval Scotland, 1093–1286' (<http://paradox.poms.ac.uk>); 'Prosopography of Anglo-Saxon England' (<http://www.pase.ac.uk>); 'Domesday—Prosopography of Anglo-Saxon England' (<http://www.domesday.pase.ac.uk>); 'The "Lands of the Normans" in England (1204–1244)' (<http://www.hrionline.ac.uk/normans>). See also 'The Norman Edge: Identity and State-Formation on the Frontiers of Europe' (<http://www.lancs.ac.uk/normanedge>).

[30] Daniel Power, 'Henry, Duke of the Normans (1149/50–1189)', in Christopher Harper-Bill and Nicholas Vincent (eds), *Henry II: New Interpretations* (Woodbridge, 2007), 85–128, at 96.

[31] R. H. C. Davis, *The Normans and Their Myth* (London, 1976), *passim*, with the basic thesis set out at pp. 12–15. As a critique of Davis's book, Graham Loud, 'The *Gens Normannorum*—Myth or Reality', *ANS*, iv (1982), 104–16, 204–9 (reprinted in *Conquerors and Churchmen in Norman Italy* (Aldershot, 1999), Chap. 1), remains fundamental.

[32] Cf. David C. Douglas, *The Norman Achievement* (London, 1969), 5 ('a vast movement of interrelated endeavour which should be studied as a unity') and *The Norman Fate, 1100–1154* (London, 1976), 3 ('it deserves emphasis that they formed part of a single Norman endeavour which must be studied as a unity'). Both books were re-printed, but largely without footnotes, with a valuable introduction by Michael Clanchy, as David C. Douglas, *The Normans* (London, 2002). R. Allen Brown, *The Normans* (Woodbridge, 1984), 19–20, adopted a similar position in his references to a unique spirit and particular qualities that were characteristic of the Norman people, but expresses himself differently in relation to ethnicity in a way that has some parallels with the arguments of this book ('the inimitable spirit of *Normanitas* defined' and 'If, therefore, it is to be asked at the outset "Who were the Normans?", the answer can only be, those who, whether by birth or adoption, saw themselves and were accepted as members of that society'; and at pp. 61–2, 'the characteristic Norman gift for seizing opportunities and bending circumstances to their will').

[33] See, especially, Gillingham, *The English*; Leah Shopkow, *History and Community: Norman Historical Writing in the Eleventh and Twelfth Centuries* (Washington, DC, 1997); Emily Albu, *The Normans in Their Histories: Propaganda, Myth and Subversion* (Woodbridge, 2001); Nick Webber, *The Evolution of Norman Identity, 911–1154* (Woodbridge, 2005); Laura Ashe, *Fiction and History in England, 1066–1200* (Cambridge, 2007). Hugh M. Thomas, *The English and the Normans: Ethnic Hostility, Assimilation, and Identity, 1066–c.1220* (Oxford, 2003) does set its analysis of literary sources within a framework of individual lives and the history of communities, but does so exclusively within England. Ann Williams, *The English and the Norman Conquest* (Woodbridge, 1995) was published

Normanitas (sometimes spelt *Normannitas*) has also become part of the discourse, without apparently much critical examination of what it might mean. It has become so popular that it has crossed linguistic frontiers.[34] Ultimately, as I and many others would argue, identity cannot be understood without reference to the history of power and without undertaking an extensive analysis of life histories.[35] On these terms *Normanitas* becomes so vague a word that it must be immediately abandoned.

EMPIRE AND THE NORMANS

On the most basic of all definitions, the power of an empire is of a kind that transcends that of the nation-state.[36] It usually involves the dominance of one people or state over others, at the start often exercised by force and without the consent of those subjected to it. It also usually combines military and cultural power in ways felt both within and beyond the territorial borders of the lands where direct rule was exercised; in other words, through the media of hard and soft power. Although, in terms of the typology of empires, the subject of this book is manifestly a case study of power imposed by violence on mostly non-consenting peoples, a central theme, as, for example, is also the case in relation to the eighteenth-century British Empire, must be the response of the people living within the empire or around its peripheries.[37] Also relevant to my subject is the phenomenon that a frequent consequence of the proclaimed civilizing mission, obviously manifested in the cases of the Roman, Carolingian, and British Empires, and in the ongoing debates over the subsequent centuries about the significance of the impact of the Normans on the British Isles, is that an empire can have a long afterlife.

---

before most of the explosion of studies of identity and ethnicity. For her comments on these discussions of identity, see Chap. 2.

[34] I have made no serious attempt to trace the evolution of this neologism. It was used in the 1980s by Graham Loud ('The *Gens Normannorum*', 104, and Brown, *The Normans*, 19 ('the inimitable spirit of *Normanitas*')). I suspect that it was invented during the social life of one of the early Battle Conferences. Note: 'la *Normannitas* (o la *Apulitas*)', *Radulphi Cadomensis Tancredus*, ed. Edoardo d'Angelo, Corpus Christianorum, Continuatio mediaevalis, vol. 231 (Turnhout, 2011), li.

[35] Among recent general treatments of the Normans, Marjorie Chibnall's statement that 'up to the middle of the twelfth century, however, Norman traditions remained strong in the territories that historians have called either "the Norman empire" or "the Anglo-Norman realm"' (*The Normans* (Oxford, 2000), 64) might be construed as deliberate fence-sitting, except when her comments, cited earlier in this chapter, are taken into account. François Neveux, *L'Aventure des Normands (VIIIᵉ–XIIIᵉ siècle)* (Paris, 2006) (English translation as *A Brief History of the Normans: The Conquests that Changed the Face of Europe*, trans. Howard Curtis (London, 2008), 195), offers 'What truly unites these "Norman" protagonists, in the broadest sense, is the spirit of adventure'. David Crouch, *The Normans: The History of a Dynasty* (London, 2002), is full of stimulating biographical and cultural insights, but does not tackle the subject within the framework proposed here.

[36] The validity of the term 'nation-state' for the Middle Ages is, of course, controversial. This sentence was written with an approximate equivalence between *natio* and nation-state in mind as a means to avoid becoming embroiled in discussions that are not central to my argument at this point.

[37] Marshall, *Making and Unmaking of Empires*, 1–12.

Like the slippery word *imperium* from which it derives, empire is an imprecise term. So much so indeed that, as Julia Smith has put it for earlier times, 'empire and emperors were often in the eye of the beholder'.[38] Subjectivity is involved; it is possible for a polity to announce that it is an empire and be taken seriously. Also, as Susan Reynolds has concluded from a comparative analysis of the semantic problems of the language used to describe power that transcended the sort of power implied by the words *natio* and *gens* (translated loosely as 'nation' and 'the ethnically defined identity of a people'), it is essential to concentrate on phenomena rather than words. In other words—and this is the foundation of this book's arguments—the term empire can be used when certain phenomena are present.[39] That no one in the eleventh and twelfth centuries actually called the cross-Channel territorial complex an empire is therefore not a barrier to tackling the Normans on those terms. It is, of course, one of the supreme ironies of the whole subject that both the United States of America and the former Soviet Union, whose founding ethos was in both cases anti-imperial, can now find themselves so analysed.

Empire's apparent derivative, imperialism, is a largely meaningless word that I am not going to use at all. Having become detached in political science from its root in the nineteenth century and come to signify the expansionary expression of nationalism and the nation-state, it no longer has a sufficiently precise meaning to be treated in association with the phenomenon of empire.[40] Another long-established word that will feature only occasionally is 'colonization'. In an Anglophone historiography it does have value in relation to the process of the installation of new elites in the British Isles, but it comes nowhere near to encompassing the social and cultural dynamic operating in *both* directions across the Channel that is the theme of this book. The modern debates about whether Henry I abandoned the imperialism of his predecessors provide a straightforward illustration of this point. On my argument, if it is justified to use the term empire and imperialism is treated as a derivative of empire, then, as the ruler of an empire, Henry could not possibly abandon imperialism. If, on the other hand, the word is treated as indicating the expansionary expression of nationalism and the nation-state, then the debate is irrelevant to my argument.[41]

The abandonment of these two woolly and overworked words means that we must turn to other analytical tools deployed in the social sciences, most notably

---

[38] Julia M. H. Smith, *Europe after Rome: A New Cultural History* (Oxford, 2005), 275.

[39] Susan Reynolds, 'Empires: A Problem of Comparative History', *HR*, lxxix (2006), 151–65, with *imperium* and the problem of language discussed at 153–6. For similar pragmatic arguments, Martin Aurell, *The Plantagenet Empire, 1154–1224*, trans. David Crouch (Harlow, 2007), 1–3, although the treatment of *imperium* is not convincing.

[40] Golding, *Conquest and Colonisation*, 178; Wolfgang J. Mommsen, *Theories of Imperialism* (London, 1981), 3–8; Herfried Münkler, *Empires: The Logic of World Domination from Ancient Rome to the United States* (Cambridge and Malden, MA, 2007), 8; Parsons, *Rule of Empires*, 8–9.

[41] See, for example, C. Warren Hollister and T. K. Keefe, 'The Making of the Angevin Empire', *Journal of British Studies*, xii (1973), 1–25, at 3 (*Monarchy and Magnates*, 247–71, at 249); Judith A. Green, *Henry I, King of England and Duke of Normandy* (Cambridge, 2006), 18–19. See also C. W. Hollister, *Henry I*, edited and completed by A. Clark Frost (New Haven, CT, 2001), 497, where the same point is made without use of the word 'imperialism'.

social constructionism, ethnography, and network analysis. It is also crucial to bring into play the concept of diaspora, especially since it is nowadays deployed in harness with the term empire, its primary association with the traumatic suffering at the heart of the Jewish diaspora having become located within a broader analysis.[42] As they are used in analyses of other empires, all of them involve the use of narrative life-stories, a point that will be developed in Chapter 2. The concept of diaspora will enable me to extend the argument to the southern European conquests of the Normans where it is appropriate to do so.[43] A further point is that many developments in the modern historiography of the eleventh and twelfth centuries have shifted the discussion away from a specific focus on the local and regional and towards globalizing change, most notably through Robert Bartlett's notion of 'European change' and the development of literatures around subjects such as chivalry, lordship, and ecclesiastical reform.[44] Among other things, these developments introduce a significant element of counter-factuality into the discussion. If the changes we are dealing with were indeed global, then presumably some form of them would have influenced England and the British Isles if 1066 had not happened. They therefore call into question the use of concepts like 'Normanization' and 'Anglicization', and require that the terms of reference of cultural labelling are meticulously defined.[45] In similar vein, Eric Fernie has described Anglo-Norman as 'a most treacherous term' and, for Ian Short, it is a less exact description of the version of French written and spoken in England than 'Insular French'.[46] All this also requires a reassessment of the role of the duchy of Normandy, since it becomes a part of the globalizing processes and not the *fons et origo* of change across the empire.[47]

[42] Edward Larkin, 'Diaspora and Empire: Towards a New Synthesis?', *Diasporas: A Journal of Transnational Studies*, xv (2010, for 2006), 167–84, and esp. 179–83.

[43] See Chaps. 2, 6.

[44] Robert Bartlett, *The Making of Europe: Conquest, Colonisation and Cultural Change, 950–1350* (London, 1994), *passim*, with the central arguments at pp. 1–3. Among the many other important studies, see, David Crouch, 'From Stenton to McFarlane: Models of Societies of the Twelfth and Thirteenth Centuries', *TRHS*, 6th. ser., v (1995), 179–200, and his *The Birth of Nobility: Constructing Aristocracy in England and France, 900–1300* (Harlow, 2005), *passim*; Matthew Strickland, *War and Chivalry: The Conduct and Perception of War in England and Normandy, 1066–1217* (Cambridge, 1996); Paul R. Hyams, *Rancor and Reconciliation in Medieval England* (Ithaca, NY, 2003); Thomas N. Bisson, *The Crisis of the Twelfth Century: Power, Lordship and the Origins of European Government* (Princeton, 2009); Donald Matthew, *Britain and the Continent, 1000–1300* (London, 2005), 60–78, 95–125.

[45] Among stimulating reflections on this topic, Huw Pryce, 'Welsh Rulers and European Change, *c*.1100–1282', in Huw Pryce and John Watts (eds), *Power and Identity in the Middle Ages: Essays in Memory of Rees Davies* (Oxford, 2007), 37–51, at 38–40, with the neat insertion of the word 'perhaps' into a variant of one of Rees Davies's statements at p. 39 (cf. Davies, *First English Empire*, 170: 'Anglicization may be interpreted as the distinctively insular version of this process of Europeanization').

[46] Eric Fernie, *The Architecture of Norman England* (Oxford, 2000), 317–18; Ian Short, *Manual of Anglo-Norman*, Anglo-Norman Text Society, Occasional Publications Series no. 7, (London, 2007), 11 n. 2.

[47] This was of course one of the central arguments in David Bates, *Normandy before 1066* (London, 1982), even if I certainly would not now use the *mutationiste* framework on which I then relied.

An argument against using the term empire that I once used myself is that Normandy and England were for roughly fifty years of the period between 1066 and 1154 under a single ruler, but under different ones for roughly thirty-eight years of that same period.[48] That the succession to Normandy and England was so often unclear and/or undisputed is indeed important, as also is the fact that its history was fuelled not only by power struggles, but also by the consequences of accidents and tragic deaths. William of Malmesbury's observation that the moment when the White Ship hit the rocks off Barfleur on 25 November 1120, ending prematurely the lives of Henry I's only legitimate son and of many others, seemed to change everything is a remarkable and uncanny parallel with the rhetoric of the modern American empire.[49] Yet a side glance at the turbulent histories of two phenomena that we call empires without any qualms, namely the Roman and the Carolingian Empires, ought instantly to quell anxieties that succession disputes and civil wars are obstacles to the validity of an argument in favour of empire. Above all, it is notable that the rhetoric deployed throughout the civil wars that took place between 1087 and 1106, and 1135 and 1154, was one of continuation and that the conflicts throughout the whole period were confined within one family.[50]

Another argument, elegantly set out exactly one hundred years ago in Sir Maurice Powicke's *The Loss of Normandy*, is that Normandy and England were drifting apart in the twelfth century, with the creation of the Angevin/Plantagenet Empire in 1154 being an event that fundamentally changed the pre-existing relationship.[51] A more extreme version of this argument, set out by Lucien Musset, is that Normandy came to be so dominated by the larger England that it not only ceased to be the driving force of empire, but effectively became an appendage of an English empire.[52] If I am eventually going to reject this last argument in such a stark form, it does, however, pose two obvious questions. First of all, how close were Normandy and England in the first place and how close did they become over the course of the history of the cross-Channel empire? And second, how far do the

---

[48] Bates, 'Normandy and England', 871–2.
[49] *GR*, i, 762–3 (*Iuuenculi ergo morte cognita res mirum in modum mutatae*). Most recently, Hollister, *Henry I*, 276–9; Green, *Henry I*, 164–7.
[50] See Chap. 4 for these themes.
[51] F. M. Powicke, *The Loss of Normandy, 1189–1204: Studies in the History of the Angevin Empire*, 2nd edn. (Manchester, 1961), 297–307. See further, J. C. Holt, 'The End of the Anglo-Norman Realm', *PBA*, lxi (1975), 223–65, at 226, 245–54 (reprinted in J. C. Holt, *Magna Carta and Medieval Government*, 23–65, at 26, 45–54); David Crouch, *The Reign of King Stephen, 1135–1154* (Harlow, 2000), 325; Aurell, *Plantagenet Empire*, 207–11; Grant, *Architecture and Society*, 12–16; Mathieu Arnoux, 'L'événement et la conjuncture. Hypothèses sur les conditions économiques de la conquête de 1204', in *1204*, 227–38, at 234–7.
[52] Lucien Musset, 'Quelques problèmes posés par l'annexion de la Normandie au domain royal français', in R.-H. Bautier et al. (eds), *La France de Philippe Auguste* (Paris, 1982), 291–309, at 292–4. Note in particular, 'l'équilibre ancien entre Angleterre et Normandie se reverse complètement, au bénéfice de l'Angleterre' (p. 294). The argument is also clearly set out in Roger Jouet, *Et la Normandie devint française* (Paris, 1983), 17–19 (nb, 'c'est la dilution progressive au sein d'un empire dont elle n'est plus l'inspiratrice unique', at p. 19), with the arguments repeated in 'Avant-propos: Faut-il commémorer 1204?', in *1204*, 3–8. The argument was also one of the pillars of Davis, *Normans and Their Myth*, 122–5, with statements such as 'Once England had become the principal residence of most Normans' (p. 123).

norms of medieval society and of the logistics of long-standing communications effectively predetermine the predominance of the local and the regional over the national and international in ordinary lives while, at the same time, an empire is sustained by the dominant hard power of an imperial elite? To deploy the term empire as is done nowadays enables me to construct an argument in favour of an organic evolution that takes account of these questions. It is a crucial aspect of this evolutionary process that all empires at some point stop expanding.

When it comes to the language most commonly used to describe power in the eleventh and twelfth centuries, notions of how to define the exceptional power involved in rule over multiple *gentes* had passed through significant mutations in the three centuries immediately prior to the period that is the subject of this book. This Carolingian solution matters to my argument because it permits a polity that was born plural to be called an empire, since it set out to legitimize the inclusion of several peoples within a single unit of power.[53] One result, as Henry Mayr-Harting has pointed out, was that to use imperial language gave both legitimacy to hegemonic power and a status that flattered and integrated the periphery.[54] George Molyneaux has identified exactly the same pattern whereby power defined by using imperial language enhanced the status of the supposedly inferior periphery within the tenth-century *imperium* over the British Isles of the kings of the English.[55]

The duchy of Normandy, as it evolved during the tenth and eleventh centuries, undoubtedly possessed the cultural resources necessary to the creation of empire on the terms set out above. The many controversies about specific aspects of Normandy's early history notwithstanding, the consensus, expressed most fully in the publications of Pierre Bauduin, sees its evolution as fluctuating and, in broad terms, as the steadily advancing hegemonic control of the counts of Rouen/dukes of Normandy over the territory that became the duchy.[56] What happened is, also, within a post-Carolingian evolutionary process, typical of the development of all the successful French principalities of the tenth and eleventh centuries.[57] Hence, although historians might disagree about the extent and nature of power exercised in the west of what became the duchy, Normandy was unquestionably by the early eleventh century shaping into a well-organized and territorial principality, that is, a

---

[53] Robert Folz, *The Concept of Empire in Western Europe from the Fifth to the Fourteenth Century*, trans. Sheila Ann Ogilvie (London, 1969), 40–4, 53–8; Janet L. Nelson, 'Kingship and Empire in the Carolingian World', in Rosamond McKitterick (ed.), *Carolingian Culture: Emulation and Renovation* (Cambridge, 1994), 52–87, and see esp. 69–77. On titles and the long-term influence of Isidore of Seville, see David Crouch, *The Image of Aristocracy in Britain, 1000–1300* (London, 1992), 27–38, 43–4.

[54] Henry Mayr-Harting, 'Charlemagne, the Saxons, and the Imperial Coronation of 800', *EHR*, cxi (1996), 1113–33, and esp. 1113–17; Henry Mayr-Harting, 'Liudprand of Cremona's Account of His Legation to Constantinople (968) and Ottonian Imperial Strategy', *EHR*, cxvi (2001), 539–56, at 540–1.

[55] George Molyneaux, 'Why Were Some Tenth-Century Kings Presented as Rulers of Britain?', *TRHS*, 6th. ser., xxi (2011), 59–91, at 65–77.

[56] Pierre Bauduin, *La première Normandie (X^e–XIe siècles). Sur les frontières de la haute Normandie: identité et construction d'une principauté* (Caen, 2004), 25–141. See also Eleanor Searle, *Predatory Kinship and the Creation of Norman Power, 840–1066* (Berkeley, CA, 1988), 68–97.

[57] In general, Florian Mazel, *Féodalités, 888–1180* (Paris, 2010), 38–53.

regnum, with a clear association between the *gens* and customary law.[58] This process also created a political identity that emphasized the singularity of the Norman *gens* within Normandy built around a strong selective memory of a Viking past and a well-nigh standard Christian version of ethnogenesis that was mostly constructed from the basic texts available at the time.[59]

That modern identity theory is complex hardly needs to be said, except to add that, since, observably, so too are all actual forms of identity, this is to be expected.[60] It is therefore crucial to make clear that the guiding principles of analysis for my treatment of identity have been succinctly summed up by Patrick Geary:

> Thus, after almost two centuries of attempts to map ethnicity linguistically, archaeologically, and historically, one must conclude that all of these programs have failed. The fundamental reason is that ethnicity exists first and last in people's minds. Yet ethnicity's locus in people's minds does not make it ephemeral; on the contrary, it is all the more powerful as a result. A creation of the human will, it is impervious to mere rational disproof.[61]

Or, as Peter Heather puts it at the end of a survey of anthropological scholarship devoted to identity in relation to the migration movements, 'this work transports us a million miles' from assumptions that have long governed assumptions about identity.[62]

On a subject not far away historically from this book's, Helmut Reimitz has commented that 'the competition of these versions of Frankish identity often go unnoticed (that is, by modern historians), which is also due to the effort to write a *single* history of the Franks'. And Jinty Nelson has expressed the hope that 'I have left you in a similar state of uncertainty, or ambiguity, about what Frankishness meant in the empire of Charlemagne'.[63] Within this book's area of interest, Robert

---

[58] Most recently, Mark Hagger, 'Secular Law and Custom in Ducal Normandy, c.1000–1144', *Speculum*, lxxxv (2010), 827–67, at 831–2. On *gens* and *lex* in general, Susan Reynolds, *Kingdoms and Communities in Western Europe* (Oxford, 1984), 18–21, 256–67.

[59] There is a huge literature, some of which takes account of the situational constructionism, and some of which does not. Note, in particular, Pierre Bouet, 'Les Normands, le nouveau peuple élu', in Pierre Bouet and François Neveux (eds), *Les Normands en Méditerranée dans le sillage des Tancrède* (Caen, 1994), 239–52; Cassandra Potts, '*Atque unum et diversis gentibus populum effecit*: Historical Tradition and Norman Identity', *ANS*, xviii (1996), 139–52; Albu, *The Normans in Their Histories*, 7–105; Webber, *The Evolution of Norman Identity*, 18–39; Alheydis Plassmann, '*Origo gentis*': Identitäts- und Legitimitätsstiftung in früh- und hochmittelalterlichen Herkunftserzählunge (Berlin, 2006), 243–64. See further, Chaps. 2, 6.

[60] In relation to the Normans, the evolution of theory has been surveyed in Webber, *The Evolution of Norman Identity*, 2–9.

[61] Patrick J. Geary, *The Myth of Nations: The Medieval Origins of Europe* (Princeton, 2002), 40.

[62] Peter Heather, *Empires and Barbarians: Migration, Development and the Birth of Europe* (London, 2009), 11–15.

[63] Helmut Reimitz, '*Omnes Franci*: Identifications and Identities of the Early Medieval Franks', in Ildar H. Garipzanov, Patrick J. Geary, and Przemyslaw Urbanczyk (eds), *Franks, Northmen and Slavs: Identities and State Formation in Early Medieval Europe* (Turnhout, 2008), 51–68, at 62; Janet L. Nelson, 'Frankish Identity in Charlemagne's Empire', in *Franks, Northmen and Slavs*, 71–83, at 83. See also Peter J. Heather, 'Ethnicity, Group Identity and Social Status in the Migration Period', in *Franks, Northmen and Slavs*, 17–49.

Bartlett's study of Gerald of Wales supplies an example both of the flexibility of an individual's identity and of how collective and individual identities could change and be manipulated.[64] The comment by Ann Williams to the effect that it is necessary to remember that in the twelfth century, the prime, and perhaps sole, place of residence may have been the prime determinant of personal identity as much as, or perhaps in preference to, ancestry or place of origin is also pertinent; *natio* and *patria* are just as important to the discussion as *gens*.[65] And in a formulation that relates directly to the subject of this book, Ewan Johnson has observed that 'it is clearly absurd to talk about one Norman ethnicity in this period'.[66] The notion that there was such a thing as a universally accepted Norman identity, a 'Norman myth' that was accepted by all, is also now being specifically rejected in recent publications devoted to southern Italy.[67]

After 1066, the consequence of the formation of new relationships and communities in England in the aftermath of the violent creation of empire means that at that moment many individual identities instantly become diverse and multiple. For some, it would have been a clear-cut situation, and for others, a chaotic one. Laura Ashe's reference to 'the apparent paradox' of 'a post-Conquest crisis in Norman identity' sums up the situation quite effectively, even if her terms of analysis differ from mine. It is, in fact, hard to see what is paradoxical, especially since the personal and collective identities of the creators of empire were multiple and flexible in the first place, and because large-scale change of residence and lifestyle was logically bound to lead to changes of identity.[68]

On this basis, the situation in England is best analysed in terms of historical parallels that have involved unpredicted and sudden collapse and subsequent occupation, with France in 1940 coming immediately to mind, rather than in terms of ethnic hostility or the supposed gradual emergence of a new English nation.[69] In focusing, as much modern literature does, on a supposed long-term process in England of ethnic assimilation and social change over a century and a half after 1066, human behaviour is made into more of an abstraction than it actually is.[70] Although it is not entirely appropriate to the circumstances I am writing

---

[64] Robert Bartlett, *Gerald of Wales, 1146–1223* (Oxford, 1982), 9–27, 178–94; Patrick J. Geary, 'Ethnic Identity as a Situational Construct in the Early Middle Ages', *Mitteilungen der Anthropologischen Gesellschaft in Wien*, cxiii (1983), 15–26.

[65] Ann Williams, 'Henry I and the English', in Donald F. Fleming and Janet M. Pope (eds), *Henry I and the Anglo-Norman World: Studies in Memory of C. Warren Hollister, HSJ*, special volume, xvii (2006), 27–38, at 36–7.

[66] Ewan Johnson, 'Origin Myth and the Construction of Medieval Identities: Norman Chronicles, 1000–1100', in Richard Corradini, Rob Meens, Christina Pössel, and Philip Shaw (eds), *Texts and Identities in the Early Middle Ages*, Forschungen zur Geschichte des Mittelalters (Vienna, 2006), 153–64, at 164.

[67] See, for example, Rosa Canosa, *Etnogenesi normanne e identità variabili. Il retroterra culturale dei Normanni d'Italia fra Scandinavia e Normandia* (Turin, 2009), 21, referring to 'una sorta di specchi che si limitano a riflettere una realtà data, bensì come espressione di strategie culturali di costruzione di un'origine legittimante ogni volta potenzialmente diversa'.

[68] Ashe, *Fiction and History*, 7, 78.

[69] Cf. '*Gradually* [my italics] a new nationality and local society formed to replace the old'; D. A. Carpenter, *The Struggle for Mastery: Britain, 1066–1284* (Oxford, 2003), 80.

[70] Ann Williams's work on the prosopography of the English is a notable exception. See Chap. 2.

about—the sheer scale of the takeover of power and the economic sources of wealth after 1066 was well-nigh unique—a commentary from a modern historian of empire says a lot that needs to be said:

> The poor, the angry, and the blatantly opportunistic often have reason to cooperate with the new political order. The initial anarchy of imperial rule offered at least some people an opportunity to preserve or even improve their status by making themselves useful to the new regime.[71]

Where trauma is concerned, some recover rapidly, others do not, and there are many variants in between. 'Traumatic growth' has its place in the clinical language of psychology alongside 'post-traumatic stress'.[72] While Hugh Thomas argued that 'the brutality of the conquest furthered the cause of ethnic harmony and assimilation in the long term, even as it poisoned relations in the short term', there are surely compelling reasons to think both that a great deal of assimilation occurred in the short term and that a great deal of it was so long term that it did not happen—and indeed could not begin to happen—until after 1204, and in many respects beyond that date.[73] We are dealing with human beings seeking to make their individual and collective routes out of a human catastrophe. Nor was the situation straightforward for the victors.

My treatment of literary sources will be informed by Sir Richard Southern's dictum of almost forty years ago that 'the mistake is often made of looking for evidence of a historical revival only in the histories it produces', which was followed by a call to take into account every type of evidence.[74] While arguably no individual can be as eclectic as Southern proposed, as already indicated, his ideal of a multi-disciplinary synthesis is implicit to all analysis of empires. It is also at this point irresistible not to remark—in the expectation that the humour will be recognized—that John Gillingham's collected essays *The English in the Twelfth Century* and Hugh Thomas's *The English and the Normans*, both works that concentrate solely on England, and which have been a great inspiration to me, can at times seem in relation to the homeland of Normandy like a modern Anglophone transposed variant of George Orwell's famous remark about the English (*sic*) not knowing they had an empire.[75] In reading John Gillingham's statement to justify his choice of narrative sources—'all were Englishmen or were writing for audiences in England'—it almost feels as if the eleventh- and twelfth-century inhabitants of Normandy should be regarded as 'Absent-Minded Imperialists', to borrow the title of Bernard Porter's book on the British Empire, and ultimately to glance back to Sir John Seeley's famous words, apparently first uttered in lectures to Cambridge

---

[71] Parsons, *The Rule of Empires*, 13.

[72] A pioneering study in the psychology of the English defeat is Elisabeth van Houts's 'The Trauma of 1066', *History Today*, xlvi, no. 10 (1996), 9–15. See further, Chaps. 2, 3, 6.

[73] Thomas, *English and Normans*, 61; see Chap. 6 in this volume.

[74] R. W. Southern, 'Aspects of the European Tradition of Historical Writing: 4. The Sense of the Past', *TRHS*, 5th. ser., xxiii (1973), 246–63, at 249 (reprinted in Robert Bartlett (ed.), *History and Historians: Selected Papers of R. W. Southern* (Oxford, 2004), 66–83, at 72).

[75] The Orwell quotation is cited in Colley, 'Difficulties', 375–6; Gillingham, *The English*, xv–xxii, with the quotation at p. xvi; Thomas, *English and Normans*, *passim*.

undergraduates in 1881–2 ('We seem, as it were, to have conquered and peopled half the world in a fit of absence of mind').[76] When it comes to the selection of literary sources by which we must be informed, the list must include Orderic, Robert of Torigni, and Wace. And, in relation to the way the literary sources are read, Emily Albu's observation that all were aware that 'the Normans' realm, like all empires, must fall in its turn' correctly highlights that they were writing with a moral purpose and a broad historical perspective in mind. In consequence, we should be cautious about the way we interpret what they wrote.[77]

A CASE STUDY

To illustrate the way in which this book's argument is now going to develop, a case study based on a single charter is inserted that seemingly interrupts the flow of the argument. This is done because, early on in the process of the writing of the lectures on which this book is based, this particular case convinced me that old pastures had to be re-visited. More than almost any other of the life-stories that I constructed in the book's preparation, it illuminates the almost infinite number of forces that influenced the course of the empire's history. It therefore demonstrates how discussion needs to be broadened out to get away from a traditional focus on issues such as government, politics, institutions, and identity.

The charter concerned is a record that, at a date between 1142 and June 1155, and therefore, in all probability, at some point during the civil war between King Stephen and the Empress Matilda, Adeliza Peverel, widow of Richard de Reviers, granted Woolley in Berkshire to the abbey of Montebourg in the north of the Cotentin peninsula.[78] It tells us that Adeliza made the grant for the souls of her mother and father at a family gathering in the chapter house at Montebourg in the presence of three of her sons, her brother, and three of her grandsons. The gift was subsequently confirmed at Carisbrooke on the Isle of Wight, one of the two great centres of the family's power in England, the other being Devon. The charter's preservation, until its destruction along with most of the contents of the Archives Départementales of La Manche in 1944, in the cartulary of the priory of Loders in Dorset, a priory of Montebourg established in the early twelfth century, suggests it contributed to the priory's endowment. A second shorter confirmation exists in Montebourg's own cartulary, which is preserved in the Bibliothèque Nationale de France.[79]

Adeliza's husband had served Henry I so well in the Cotentin after the latter had obtained it in 1088 from his oldest brother, Duke Robert Curthose, that after 1100

---

[76] Bernard Porter, *Absent-Minded Imperialists: Empire, Society and Culture in Britain* (Oxford, 2004); J. R. Seeley, *The Expansion of England*, ed., with an introduction by John Gross (Chicago, 1971), 12.
[77] Albu, *The Normans in Their Histories*, 218.
[78] *Charters of the Redvers Family and the Earldom of Devon, 1090–1217*, ed. Robert Bearman, Devon and Cornwall Record Society, new series, vol. 37 (Exeter, 1994), no. 8.
[79] *Charters of the Redvers Family*, no. 9.

Henry had made him into a man of very great power in England.[80] Not a significant beneficiary of the post-1066 share-out of English lands, he rose on the back of empire, so-to-speak. His exploitation of opportunity illustrates immediately the dynamic that sustained the cross-Channel empire at the social level below the rulers in the generation after that of the conquerors; it also brings into the open the apparent paradox that cross-Channel civil war could contribute to the strengthening of the infrastructure of empire. The charter's interest increases further when we realize that Richard had died in 1107 and that, despite his massive acquisitions in England, he was brought home to rest in Normandy at Montebourg, the small religious community that he and his family had taken on in the late eleventh century and patronized very generously.[81] Adeliza's return to her husband's grave forty or so years later immediately invites reflections on the power of place as a factor in the history of the cross-Channel empire: home, the homeland, the burial place of a renowned ancestor were all a powerful magnet. But there is much more.

Adeliza had in all probability borne Richard six children, the three sons already mentioned, another two sons, and a daughter, making it a certainty both that she had been born during the lifetime of William the Conqueror and that she lived on into that of his great-grandson Henry II.[82] In terms of personal experiences we would like to know more about, Adeliza is surely someone we really would like to have been able to talk to! Her eldest son, Baldwin, inherited her husband's English lands and lived a seemingly undistinguished life for the rest of Henry I's reign, suddenly bursting into dramatic action after Stephen's coup in 1135 when, unlike almost everyone else, for reasons that are not entirely explicable, he refused homage to the new king and set out to fight him. Defeated, he was driven into exile in Normandy in 1136 and thereafter became an unyielding supporter of Henry I's daughter, the Empress Matilda, and her husband, Count Geoffrey of Anjou. He accompanied Matilda's invasion of England in 1139 and was made earl of Devon by her in 1141. His brothers, in contrast, inherited and probably augmented the family's Norman lands, with the older, William, inheriting the family estates around Néhou and Vernon, and the other, Robert de Sainte-Mère-Eglise, receiving land around the family's core estates in the north of the Cotentin. One certainty is surely that hardly any of these people unequivocally described themselves as 'Norman' or 'English'; Adeliza and Baldwin, above all, were most certainly fully signed up participants in empire.

---

[80] *Charters of the Redvers Family*, pp. 1–17, for an account of the family's history.
[81] For the Reviers family and Montebourg, Eric van Torhoudt, 'L' "énigme" des origines de l'abbaye de Montebourg: une question de methode?', in Pierre Bouet et al. (eds), *De Part et d'Autre de la Normandie médiévale: Recueil d'études en hommage à François Neveux*, Cahiers des Annales de Normandie (Caen, 2009), 331–46, and esp. 345–6.
[82] For Adeliza's survival into Henry II's reign, *Charters of the Redvers Family*, no. 10. For the family, Daniel Power, *The Norman Frontier in the Twelfth and Thirteenth Centuries* (Cambridge, 2004), 206–7, 287, 527–8; for Baldwin, Richard Bearman, 'Baldwin de Redvers: Some Aspects of a Baronial Career in the Reign of King Stephen', *ANS*, xviii (1996), 17–45, and 'Revières, Baldwin de, earl of Devon (c.1095–1155)', *ODNB*.

A further point is that the family get-together took place against the background of civil war, a statement that applies even though we cannot be entirely certain of the circumstances in which Adeliza made her grant because we cannot date the charter very closely. If the grant was made at an early date within the dating limits, it might be a demonstration of how familial considerations could cut across the territorialization of the civil war, since the property was in an area where King Stephen had support to an abbey equally secure under the control of his opponents. On the other hand, if later, it would fit into the pacification of the late 1140s and early 1150s. Whatever way, it illustrates how family and religious networks operated and continued to operate during the civil war, even if we cannot be entirely certain in this case of their strength and significance. In the end, because we cannot know whether the get-together was a one-off, a sentimental reunion after years of separation or of strong and continuous kinship and devotional links, we must not push its significance too hard. But it should at the least make us think about the world beyond the political; or rather about the cultural and social world that shaped the political and which, taken together, were the crucial determinants of the history of power. On this showing, there were clearly a range of practical and emotional cements in existence that assisted individuals and families to manage times of transition.

However interpreted, the charter unquestionably brings to the surface the importance of examining in depth personal experience and individual lives. It also introduces gender and religious history into the discussion, with, as Elisabeth van Houts would emphasize, the widow/mother being important as the repository of family memory and the instigator of continued association between family members.[83] It might suggest that loyalty to patrimony and to the family centre of religious devotion outweighed in significance the immediacies of political disorder and the frequent practice of dividing family lands situated on the two sides of the Channel; it certainly was part of the process whereby the family maintained its interest in the unity of cross-Channel lands over generations.[84] The survival of two differing versions of the charter opens up the further subject of the management of cross-Channel lands.[85] In short, there were a host of factors sustaining the cross-Channel world. Any analysis must do its best to look beneath the surface of every document to find the factors influencing its participants. Yet, since the foundations of empire were based on violence and conquest, it is now necessary to pick up again the threads of general argument in, I hope, some awareness of the multiple identities and agencies that were involved in the life of the cross-Channel empire.

---

[83] Elisabeth van Houts, 'The Memory of 1066 in Written and Oral Traditions', *ANS*, xix (1997), 167–79, with memory in Normandy discussed at pp. 174–8; *Memory and Gender in Medieval Europe, 900–1200* (Basingstoke, 1999), 123–42 and *passim* for numerous important insights into the issues raised by this charter.
[84] Holt, 'Politics and Property', 8–17 (Holt, *Colonial England*, at 118–28).
[85] See Chap. 5.

HARD POWER

The extreme nature of the violence employed by the conquerors at the Battle of Hastings and during the campaigns of the period from 1066 to 1070 now has the status of an historical orthodoxy.[86] If, perhaps, excessively rhetorical, Dominique Barthélemy's statement that the violence involved was on a scale scarcely practised before 1914, except perhaps by Napoleon Bonaparte ('C'est d'une sauvagerie rare, inconnue généralement des Romains, digne déjà de Napoléon: une horreur qu'on a aura du mal à dépasser avant 1914'), does bring the subject into focus in a thought-provoking way.[87] A second central modern orthodoxy is encapsulated in John Gillingham's comment that the takeover of land in England after 1066 should be seen as 'an event unparalleled in European history'.[88] Although earlier empires such as the Carolingian had intruded an imperial aristocracy into local and regional societies through the lands they had conquered, no takeover had been as comprehensive as the one that took place in England after 1066.[89] This comprehensiveness is appositely symbolized by the presence of only four significant English tenants-in-chief in Domesday Book and the survival in office by 1087 of only a single bishop of English birth, the remarkable Wulfstan, bishop of Worcester.[90] The long-term results are encapsulated in William of Malmesbury's bleak statement that in c.1125 no Englishman was an earl, bishop, or abbot, and that everywhere foreigners enjoyed England's riches and gnawed at her intestines, with there being no hope of the miserable state of affairs ever coming to an end. To this he also added his personal historical perspective by remarking on the contrast between William the Conqueror and Cnut, England's earlier eleventh-century conqueror; for William of Malmesbury, the savagery of the Conqueror was very different from Cnut's easy-going ways that had allowed the defeated to keep their rights and positions intact.[91]

A case study, first set out with characteristic vigour and clarity by John Horace Round, is provided by the activities of William the Conqueror's close friend William fitz Osbern in Herefordshire and Gwent, with his death in early 1071

---

[86] Thomas, *English and Normans*, 56–67; Dominique Barthélemy, *La chevalerie* (Paris, 2007), 193–6; John Gillingham, 'Holding to the Rules of War (*Bellica Iura Tenentes*): Right Conduct before, during, and after Battle in the Eleventh Century', *ANS*, xxix (2007), 1–15; Matthew Strickland, *War and Chivalry: The Conduct and Perception of War in England and Normandy, 1066–1217* (Cambridge, 1996), 3–7; Matthew Strickland, 'Killing or Clemency? Ransom, Chivalry and Changing Attitudes to Defeated Opponents in Britain and Northern France, 7–12th centuries', in Hans-Henning Kortüm (ed.), *Krieg im Mittelalter* (Berlin, 2001), 93–122, at 120–1.

[87] Barthélemy, *La chevalerie*, 193.

[88] John Gillingham, 'Problems of Integration within the Lands Ruled by the Norman and Angevin Kings of England', in Werner Maleczek (ed.), *Fragen der Politischen Integration in Mittelalterlichen Europa*, Vorträge und Forschungen, vol. lxiii (Ostfildern, 2005), 85–135, at 85.

[89] For a commentary on a huge literature, Stuart Airlie, 'The Aristocracy', in Rosamond McKitterick (ed.), *The New Cambridge Medieval History*, vol. ii: *c.700–c.900* (Cambridge, 1995), 431–50, at 432–3 ('Regional aristocracies survived').

[90] Williams, *The English and the Norman Conquest*, 98–9, identifies a total of thirteen English tenants-in-chief in 1066, but regards only four as holding estates that Sir Frank Stenton would have identified as being 'of baronial dimensions'.

[91] *GR*, i, 414–17, 470–1.

supplying a demarcation line at which to assess development within a little over four years of the Battle of Hastings. It shows that fitz Osbern, a man at first sight seemingly contradictorily described by Orderic as 'the bravest of the Normans, renowned for his generosity, ready wit, and outstanding integrity' and 'the first and greatest oppressor of the English', had already introduced tenants from his lands in Normandy into the region, had made grants of land there to the religious houses he had founded and patronized in Normandy, and had selected Chepstow as the site for the remarkable hall that we can still see.[92] In addition, the possibility that he confirmed a charter in England for the great Ile-de-France abbey of Saint-Denis dealing exclusively with the abbey's property in Normandy points to the rapid evolution of transmarine communication; monks of Saint-Denis must surely have crossed the Channel specially to secure the confirmation, if, as is suggested, it was confirmed in England.[93]

This one case study illustrates how John Le Patourel's process of colonization can be re-positioned, using the language of hard and soft power. While his magisterial focus on the centrality of castle-building and new monastic foundations needs no repetition, it is entirely logical to think of the construction of the hall and the patronage of the religious houses as demonstrative of a believed superior way of life, and of atonement, as well as of domination.[94] A further point to emphasize is that, while recent analyses of Domesday Book have produced notably different interpretations of the cultural and legal processes involved in the takeover of land in England, the rapidity and intensity thereof is common ground for all; the interpretative differences generally focus on the extent to which pre-existing tenurial patterns did, or did not, determine the nature of the new settlement.[95] Another frequent phenomenon of these times was the many acts of local violence and intimidation associated with the newcomers, with sheriffs often being identified as the greatest culprits; in other words, it was the very agents of the imperial power who were its most zealous proponents.[96] What the rapidity of the installation of the tenants and monastic landholders and of the choice of site for the hall also shows is that the process of the creation of empire was, if not culturally predetermined, then at least powerfully driven by norms and scripts familiar to the new elite.

---

[92] OV, ii, 282–3, 318–21; J. H. Round, 'The Family of Ballon and the Conquest of South Wales', in *Studies in Peerage and Family History* (Westminster, 1901), 181–215, at 183–7. More recently, Robin Fleming, *Kings and Lords in Conquest England* (Cambridge, 1991), 171; David Bates, 'William the Conqueror, William fitz Osbern and Chepstow Castle', in Rick Turner and Andy Johnson (eds), *Chepstow Castle: Its History and Buildings* (Logaston Press, 2006), 15–22, 274–5. For Orderic's apparent contradiction, see Chap. 2.

[93] Rolf Grosse, *Saint-Denis zwischen Adel und König: Die Zeit vor Suger (1053–1122)* (Stuttgart, 2002), 239–40 (Urkundenanhang, no. 2); Bauduin, *La première Normandie*, 382–3 (Annexe II: Dossier de Textes, no. 13).

[94] Le Patourel, *The Norman Empire*, Chap. 8.

[95] For different perspectives, David Roffe, 'From Thegnage to Barony: Sake and Soke, Titles and Tenants-in-Chief', *ANS*, xii (1990), 157–76; Fleming, *Kings and Lords*, 107–214; Judith A. Green, *The Aristocracy of Norman England* (Cambridge, 1997), 48–99.

[96] Fleming, *Kings and Lords*, 183–214; Richard Abels, 'Sheriffs, Lord-Seeking and the Norman Settlement of the South-East Midlands', *ANS*, xix (1997), 21–50, at 32–40.

The much discussed creation in England after 1066 of a framework by which the new regime set out to establish its legitimacy and legality can immediately be identified as a generic feature of empire. In medieval terms, it must be seen as another example of the constant searches for legitimacy associated with the many new regimes established in western Europe from the fall of Rome onwards; what happened after 1066 was no more than a variant of cultures and structures that had long been hard-wired into the history of the medieval West.[97] To this, it needs, of course, to be added that, for all that a variant of standard processes of legitimation was followed, above all through William the Conqueror's coronation on 25 December 1066 by the Englishman Ealdred, archbishop of York, the events that followed were a takeover achieved through violence that had, at most, limited genuine consent, even if there was soon to be the acquiescence and collaboration aplenty that normally follows the creation of an empire.[98] A further feature of these times was the seizure of treasure and the transfer of precious books to Normandy and other parts of France, an act that—at first sight paradoxically—might have been justifiable in terms of a proclaimed civilizing mission, because the sinful English were no longer thought fit to possess them, a point that was actually made at the time. In terms of the history of empires, however, it also conforms to a behavioural norm, something readily grasped through a walk around the British Museum, the Louvre, or the Acropolis Museum in Athens, for example.[99]

Subsequent displays of hard power intimidated England's neighbours. In 1072 when William sailed a fleet into the Forth and marched an army north from there, he was the first king of the English to do this since Æthelstan in 934.[100] Likewise, the crown-wearings that took place at Gloucester at Christmas when William was in England made his presence felt close to Wales, and in 1081 he marched an army through South Wales to St David's. These progresses can reasonably be seen as consolidating for the future the basic framework of empire within the British Isles, but, like the process of legitimation and the distribution of land, they did not come out of nowhere. Harold Godwineson had intervened in Wales as recently as 1063 to remove the threat from Gruffudd ap Llywelyn, who had established hegemonic power over most of Wales and campaigned with such savagery there that the manifestations could still be seen over one hundred years later. And the fortunes of Mac Bethad mac Findlaích (Macbeth), king of Scots, had recently been decisively influenced by the intervention from England of Siward, earl of Northumbria. As with the process of legitimation, some variants contingent on the specific circumstances notwithstanding, William and those around him were actually playing to scripts that they accepted as creative of context and values.

[97] For some general remarks on legitimacy and authority, see Susan Reynolds, 'Secular Power and Authority in the Middle Ages', in Pryce and Watts (eds), *Power and Identity*, 11–22. See also among a great deal of relevant material, Matthew Innes, 'Land, Freedom and the Making of the Medieval West', *TRHS*, 6th. ser., xvi (2006), 39–74, and esp. at 46–63. See further, Chap. 3.

[98] See Chaps. 2 and 3.

[99] David N. Dumville, 'Anglo-Saxon Books: Treasure in Norman Hands?', *ANS*, xvi (1994), 83–99. On this subject, see further, Chap. 2.

[100] Most recently, Sarah Foot, *Æthelstan, The First King of England* (New Haven, CT, 2011), 164–7.

Twelfth-century writers in the British Isles often wrote about the hard power of the conquerors and what was seen as the divinely ordained fate of the English and, subsequently, of the Welsh, in language that at first acquaintance make truly shocking reading. Henry of Huntingdon, for example, wrote that God had chosen the Normans to exterminate the English.[101] It is, however, crucial to recognize that Henry was not writing about genocide as we would understand it in terms of the UN Convention on the Prevention and Punishment of the Crime of Genocide, or even necessarily of physical slaughter, but of ethnic degradation and the loss of the characteristics that had previously been the unique property the English as a *gens*.[102] The same applies to the use of the language of extermination by Welsh writers.[103] Thus, the author of the *Brut y Twysygion*, now identified as a contemporary source, wrote that Henry I's 1114 three-pronged invasion of Wales was intended as a campaign of extermination, even though the author who wrote this would have known that the expedition petered out into peace-making with various Welsh rulers.[104]

While these authors apparently write of the most savage violence, they also praise the rulers of the cross-Channel empire. Thus, the author of the *Brut* wrote in the most evocative terms of how Henry I's hegemonic power could enhance the prestige of Welsh rulers.[105] And Henry of Huntingdon even placed William the Conqueror on the ultimate pedestal, sitting on the right hand of God, a place he reserved among kings otherwise only for a truly imperial figure, Charlemagne, and later, in his *Contemptu mundi*, for Henry I. He also stated that William was greater than all the kings that had preceded him.[106] The interpretation of these, at first sight, apparently contradictory statements, which are of a kind that also appear in William of Malmesbury, must ultimately take into account the educative purpose that the historians took upon themselves and of a form of literary and

---

[101] HH, 402–3 (*Elegerat enim Deus Normannos ad Anglorum gentem exterminandam*).

[102] In general, Len Scales, 'Bread, Cheese and Genocide: Imagining the Destruction of Peoples in Medieval Western Europe', *History*, xcii (2007), 284–300, and esp. 289–90 and 296–7; James E. Fraser, 'Early Medieval Europe: The Case of Britain and Ireland', in D. Bloxham and A. D. Moses (eds), *The Oxford Handbook of Genocide Studies* (Oxford, 2010), 259–79, and esp. at 268–70, 274–6. See also David N. Dumville, 'Celtic-Latin Texts in Northern England, *c*.1150–*c*.1250', in David N. Dumville, *Histories and Pseudo-Histories of the Insular Middle Ages* (Aldershot, 1990), Chap. 11, pp. 24–6.

[103] For several Welsh writers' reactions, see the passages cited in John Reuben Davies, 'Aspects of Church Reform in Wales, *c*.1093–*c*.1223', *ANS*, xxx (2008), 85–99, at 85–6; also, *Vita Griffini filii Conani: The Medieval Life of Gruffudd ap Cynan*, ed. Paul Russell (Cardiff, 2005), 78–9, 86–7.

[104] *Brut y Tywysogyon or the Chronicle of the Princes, Peniarth MS 20 Version*, trans. Thomas Jones (Cardiff, 1952), 38; *Brut y Tywysogyon or the Chronicle of the Princes, Red Book of Hergest Version*, ed. and trans. Thomas Jones (Cardiff, 1955), 81. For the *Brut* as a contemporary source, David Stephenson, 'The "Resurgence" of Powys in the Late Eleventh and Early Twelfth Centuries', *ANS*, xxx (2008), 182–95, at 184–8. For the 1114 campaign, Hollister, *Henry I*, 235–8; Green, *Henry I*, 132–3; Robert Babcock, 'The Irish Sea Province and the Accession of Henry I', in Fleming and Pope (eds), *Henry I and the Anglo-Norman World*, 39–62, at 54–8.

[105] See Chap. 4.

[106] HH, 394–5, 410–11, 594–5; Wendy Marie Hoofnagle, 'Charlemagne's Legacy and Anglo-Norman *Imperium* in Henry of Huntingdon's *Historia Anglorum*', in *The Legend of Charlemagne in the Middle Ages: Power, Faith and Crusade*, ed. Matthew Gabriele and Jane Stuckey (New York, 2008), 77–94, at 81, 87.

cultural conditioning that ran from the Old Testament through Bede and several classical authors. Henry, for example, might echo Boethius in saying that his history was a consolation for grief, but he was also using it to draw attention to the past sins of the English and their rulers in the hope that lessons would be learnt.[107] That these dramatic descriptions of violence are not the exclusive monopoly of insular writers further puts them into their cultural context; when wishing, for example, to provide an analogy for the disorder in Normandy in the year 1136, Orderic compared it to the anticipated violence of the Last Judgement and subsequently presented in the most lurid terms the invasion of Normandy later in the same year by the Empress Matilda's husband, Count Geoffrey of Anjou.[108] The ultimate source in this case may be the Book of Revelations rather than the Old Testament; it is, however, a warning to be aware that all our writers will describe the world in terms of the models available to them and that we should read them with this in mind. Fundamentally, it can be observed for now that even so obvious a devotee of hard power as William Rufus calculated his moves according to achievable objectives.[109] In this case, as always, even the apparently hardest hard power had its limitations.

What the dramatic language does do is draw attention to the ultimate superiority in the British Isles of the military power that might be deployed by the newcomers; despite all the well-known commentaries on, for example, the problems of campaigning with cavalry in Wales and a re-evaluation of the balance of military power within Wales, in the background there was always an awareness of the massively superior force that the newcomers could potentially bring to bear.[110] While Welsh rulers skilfully employed the strategy of tactical avoidance and the practices of guerrilla warfare, even managing three small victories over the imperial power immediately after 1135, the fate of King David I's army at the Battle of the Standard in 1138 must surely have been a warning to all that to join battle on a large scale was not likely to succeed.[111] The fate of the king of Scots, William the Lion, taken in 1174 from the far north of England to Normandy, to be imprisoned at Caen and Falaise, illustrates the continuation after 1154 of the same kind of hegemonic power, with his reinstatement after the so-called Treaty of Falaise (1174) showing that the ultimate objective was to re-establish a relationship of coexistence. But the multiple failure of the eleventh-century campaigns into Maine

---

[107] Thus, Diana Greenway, 'Authority, Convention and Observation in Henry of Huntingdon's *Historia Anglorum*', *ANS*, xviii (1996), 105–21; Matthew Kempshall, *Rhetoric and the Writing of History, 400–1500* (Manchester, 2011), 81, 138–71, 229–64.

[108] OV, vi, 458–9, 466–74.

[109] For Rufus, see Chap. 4.

[110] F. C. Suppe, *Military Institutions on the Welsh Marches: Shropshire, AD 1066–1300* (Woodbridge, 1994), 7–33; Sean Davies, *Welsh Military Institutions, 633–1283* (Cardiff, 2004), *passim*.

[111] For a powerful statement of this case, Matthew Strickland, 'Securing the North: Invasion and the Strategy of Defence in Twelfth-Century Anglo-Scottish Warfare', *ANS*, xii (1990), 177–98 (reprinted in Matthew Strickland (ed.), *Anglo-Norman Warfare: Studies in Late Anglo-Saxon and Anglo-Norman Military Organisation and Warfare* (Woodbridge, 1992), 208–29). Note esp. at p. 178 (*Anglo-Norman Warfare*, 209): 'For them (i.e., the kings of Scots), the caution in committing troops to battle displayed by many contemporary commanders was not a choice, but a necessity'.

is also every bit as much a factor in the history of empire. In that part of the world there was no superiority of hard power.[112] We are back to notions of 'imperial overstretch' and unresolved conflicting historiographies.[113]

LANGUAGE AND IMAGERY

The language and images associated with empire are on extensive display in the art, poetry, architecture, and charters of the period after 1066. The *Gesta Guillelmi Ducis Normannorum et Regis Anglorum* of William of Poitiers, a heavily classicizing work with many comparative references to William the Conqueror's superiority over his Roman predecessors, is an obvious starting point; too obvious a one perhaps, because the *Gesta*'s extravagance and its particular nature might be thought to make it untypical.[114] From the same immediately post-Conquest period, however, there is also the imperial imagery in the Bayeux Tapestry and the language in the poetry addressed to William the Conqueror and his children and the obituaries of the Conqueror.[115] In terms of the latter, it is also striking that a lot of this poetry was composed by authors writing outside Normandy and England.

Imperial language associated with claims to rule over the British Isles that had been a feature of tenth- and eleventh-century English kingship also continued to be used after 1066.[116] Thus, the author of the *Encomium Emmae Reginae* before 1066 had described Cnut as an *imperator* who ruled over five *regna* and after 1066 there were such dramatic flourishes as Goscelin of Saint-Bertin's description of England as 'an imperial kingdom ruled augustly by the Caesars, who boasted that they had their seat as much here as in Rome'.[117] Imperial language also appears in post-1066 diplomas and in the mid-twelfth century in both Normandy and England in, for example, the preface of *Quadripartitus*, Robert of Torigni's interpolations into the *Gesta Normannorum Ducum*, and the Abingdon *Historia*.[118] Most notably,

---

[112] On some general issues, Stephen Morillo, 'A General Typology of Transcultural Wars—The Early Middle Ages and Beyond', in H.-H. Kortüm (ed.), *Transcultural Wars from the Middle Ages to the 21st Century* (Berlin, 2006), 29–42.

[113] See the remarks in the introductory section to this chapter.

[114] On the *Gesta Guillelmi*, see Chap. 3.

[115] T. A. Heslop, 'Regarding the Spectators of the Bayeux Tapestry: Bishop Odo and His Circle', *Art History*, xxxii (2009), 223–49, at 237–40. For the poetry and obituaries, Elisabeth van Houts, 'Latin Poetry and the Anglo-Norman Court 1066–1135: the *Carmen de Hastingae Proelio*', *JMH*, xv (1989), 103–32 (reprinted in *History and Family Traditions in England and the Continent, 1000–1200*, Chap. 9); see also Frank Barlow, *William Rufus*, 2nd edn. (New Haven, CT), 51–2.

[116] Molyneaux, 'Why Were Some Tenth-Century Kings?', 59–91.

[117] *Encomium Emmae Reginae*, ed. Alistair Campbell, with a supplementary introduction by Simon Keynes, Camden Classic Reprints, 4 (Cambridge, 1998), 34–5; Goscelin, *Historia maior sancti Augustini*, Acta Sanctorum, May, vi (1688), 378 (c.2) (cit., Martin Brett, 'Gundulf and the Cathedral Communities of Canterbury and Rochester', in Richard Eales and Richard Sharpe (eds), *Canterbury and the Norman Conquest: Churches, Saints and Scholars, 1066–1109* (London, 1995), 15–25 at 20): Regnum est imperiale, Romanis caesaribus augustaliter regnatum, qui se tam quam Romae gloriabantur rerum habere solium.

[118] *Regesta*, nos. 138, 159, 181; regis tamen et Normannorum ducis, augusti domini nostri Caesaris Henrici, magni Willelmi regis filii, *Die Gesetze der Angelsachsen*, ed. F. Liebermann, 3 vols (Halle,

24   *The Normans and Empire*

it occurs in the anonymous mid-twelfth-century poem written in the late 1140s for the Angevin conqueror of the duchy of Normandy, the Empress Matilda's husband, Count Geoffrey Plantagenet, with a portrayal of Rouen as the new Rome served by conquered Britain with the English, Scots, and Welsh bringing gifts to her (I have simplified the translation somewhat).[119] The poet's focus on a city that was arguably at the very core of empire emphasizes the enduring usage of imperial language and the expectation that the cross-Channel empire that it symbolized would be continued under Geoffrey's rule (and, by implication, his son Henry's). It brings into the open a theme that will feature strongly in the later chapters of this book, namely what I regard as the sustained commitment of the Normans to empire.

It is important to grasp that, on their own, all this language and the imagery to which I will turn soon do not make the case for the use of the word empire. They demonstrate undoubted components of the phenomenon, namely triumphalism, a self-awareness of extraordinary power, and a proclamation of moral superiority. But the case I am arguing rests on a political science model to which they make no more than a contribution. In this case, what we are dealing with constitutes a combination of conventional language and of universally known concepts of political *imperium* that had been constantly recycled throughout the medieval West since classical times; to call William the Conqueror and Henry I 'Caesar' was not to propose promotion for them, but to flatter them and portray them as a superior type of king.[120] The pan-European conventionality of language can be illustrated for the eleventh and twelfth centuries by a host of examples. The Iberian Peninsula is especially fertile ground, with the title *imperator* appearing regularly in charters of the eleventh and twelfth centuries in a way which is not common in Normandy and England. Yet, the latest studies of the subject have shown that the usage was pragmatic and associated with conquest and hegemonic power over multiple *regna* in ways that closely parallel the language and imagery deployed in northern Europe; this special usage was actually set out in exactly these terms by Robert of Torigni.[121] Even the Conqueror's contemporary Capetian king Philip I, who is not someone who impresses historians

---

1903–16), i, 533 (translated, Richard Sharpe, 'The Prefaces of "Quadripartitus"', in George Garnett and John Hudson (eds), *Law and Government in Medieval England and Normandy: Essays in Honour of Sir James Holt* (Cambridge, 1994), 165); *inclitus augustus* (referring to Henry I), *GND*, ii, 236–7; *ut imperiali decreto, Historia Ecclesie Abbendonensis: The History of the Church of Abingdon*, vol. ii, ed. and trans. John Hudson, OMT (Oxford, 2002), 50–1.

[119] C. Richard, 'Notice sur l'ancienne bibliothèque des Echevins de la ville de Rouen', in *Précis Analytique des Travaux de l'Académie Royale des Sciences, Belles-Lettres et Arts de Rouen* (Rouen, 1845), 127–82, at 163. The first part of the poem is printed in Haskins, *Norman Institutions*, 144 n. 72. For a new text and translation, Elisabeth van Houts, 'Rouen as Another Rome in the Twelfth Century', in Leonie V. Hicks and Elma Brenner (eds), *Society and Culture in Medieval Rouen, 911–c.1300* (Turnhout, 2013), 101–24, at 119.

[120] For the general point, Smith, *Europe after Rome*, 272–7.

[121] See now Hélène Sirantoine, 'Memoria construida, memoria destruida: La identidad monárquica a través del recuerdo de los emperadores de *Hispania* en los diplomas de los soberanos castellanos y leoneses (1065–1230)', in José Antonio Jara Fuente, Georges Martin, and Isabel Alfonso Antón (eds), *Construir la identidad en la Edad Media. Poder y memoria en la Castilla de los siglos VII al XV* (Cuenca, 2010), 225–47. Her arguments have now been set out in detail in Hélène Sirantoine, *Imperator Hispaniae*: les idéologies impériales dans le royaume de León (IXe–XIIe siècles) (Madrid, 2012); RT (D), ii, 282; (H), 178 (*Caput regni huius regis civitas est Toletum; quem, quia principatur regulis*

greatly, could toy with the language of empire.[122] That the cross-Channel empire's rulers used titles in their charters that stressed that they ruled the distinct territories of Normandy, England, and, sometimes, elsewhere demonstrates immediately the conventionality that underpinned the practice of power.[123]

In a similar vein, as is well known, a significant number of buildings were erected in England in the half-century or so after 1066 that were on a scale unrivalled elsewhere in contemporary western Europe; Westminster Hall, Canterbury, Winchester, Norwich, and Durham cathedrals, and abbey churches of Ely, Bury St Edmunds, and St Albans are the best known examples.[124] The most poignant among them must surely have been the new cathedral at York built by Archbishop Thomas of Bayeux, of which almost nothing now survives above ground. A vast building, in the 1070s when it was started, much larger than anything then existing in either Normandy or England, it would have dwarfed the neighbouring burnt-out remains of the pre-1066 cathedral, severely damaged in William the Conqueror's attack on the city in 1068.[125] The early date of its construction underlines that the explicit articulation of extraordinary power through architectural language was present from the earliest times; the borrowings from Speyer cathedral of the even larger, but only slightly later, cathedral at Winchester is a further expression of the same point.[126] Size is not, however, the whole of this topic, because these and other buildings also contain a great deal of self-consciously imperial imagery: the White Tower of London, for example, is at the corner of the city's Roman walls, the new cathedral at York was located on a Roman site and used a great deal of Roman masonry, and the keep of Colchester was on the site of a Claudian temple used as a palace by Anglo-Saxon kings.[127]

All this fits with the general theme that imitation of Rome and the construction of grand buildings were an expression of moral superiority and of a higher civilization.[128] However, as with the literary evidence, architectural borrowing presents interpretative problems, as in even the case where the two seem to work together in

---

Arragonum et Galliciae, imperatorem Hispaniarum appellant), with comment on his accurate appreciation of the usage in Sirantoine, *Imperator Hispaniae*, 360–1. I am grateful to Dr Sirantoine for sending me a copy of her article in advance of publication and of her book on publication.

[122] Matthew Gabriele, 'The Provenance of the *Descriptio qualiter Karolus Magnus*: Remembering the Carolingians in the Entourage of King Philip I (1060–1108) before the First Crusade', *Viator*, xxxix (2008), 93–117, and esp. 96, 108–10, 111.

[123] Bates, 'Normandy and England', 862–4.

[124] For recent surveys, Fernie, *Architecture of Norman England, passim*, and esp. 24–49; Richard Plant, 'Ecclesiastical Architecture c.1050 to c.1200', in Christopher Harper-Bill and Elisabeth van Houts (eds), *A Companion to the Anglo-Norman World* (Woodbridge, 2003), 215–53, at 228–40.

[125] Christopher Norton, *Archbishop Thomas of Bayeux and the Norman Cathedral at York*, Borthwick Papers, no. 100 (York, 2001), 14–33.

[126] Eric Fernie, 'Three Romanesque Great Churches in Germany, France and England, and the Discipline of Architectural History', *Architectural History*, liv (2011), 1–22, and esp. 11–17. For a revised dating of the start of construction at York, Stuart Harrison and Christopher Norton, 'Lastingham and the Architecture of the Benedictine Revival in Northumbria', *ANS*, xxxiv (2012), 63–103, at 68–9.

[127] T. A. Heslop, *Norwich Castle Keep* (Norwich, 1994), 56–66.

[128] Leonie V. Hicks, 'Coming and Going: The Use of Outdoor Space in Norman and Anglo-Norman Chronicles', *ANS*, xxxii (2010), 40–56, at 46–9.

our favour, namely, William of Malmesbury's statement that Robert the Lotharingian (1079–95), bishop of Hereford, built a chapel near his cathedral modelled on a basilica at Aachen that might be thought to be Charlemagne's imperial chapel.[129] Similarly, Tadhg O'Keeffe's tentative suggestion that the gatehouse of Exeter castle drew inspiration from the entrance to the palace chapel at Aachen is also not necessarily convincing because the presence of the one single great arch is probably an insufficiently specific parallel.[130] As with language, imperial imagery of an analogous kind appears elsewhere. For example, although their interpretation is not straightforward, the western transepts of the abbey of Kelso supply a potential example from Scotland of imperial imagery, and may illustrate how King David I dipped into the same well.[131] Sicily and southern Italy, of course, provide many manifestations that often draw on Byzantine exemplars, with the most celebrated image being that in the church in Palermo, founded by King Roger II's chief minister George of Antioch, depicting the king in the ceremonial dress of a Byzantine emperor.[132] King William II of Sicily's Monreale is a magnificent expression of perceived extraordinary power, but as a phenomenon it fulfilled the same purpose as the examples I have drawn attention to.[133]

When the great post-Conquest churches and the smaller local churches of East Anglia are analysed in depth, it is clear that much of the inspiration did not come from Normandy. The elevation of Saint Etienne of Caen and other influences from Normandy and northern France are often present in the great churches, but exchanges across the North Sea are of great importance. Thus, while the western block still partly visible at Ely cannot necessarily be thought of as a straightforward early borrowing from the churches of the empire, it is beyond doubt that they were the sources on which it and other major churches were drawing, and that some aspects of the design had links with old St Peter's in Rome.[134] At a less elevated

---

[129] *GP*, i, 458–9. On the general influence of Aachen, see Richard Plant, 'Architectural Developments in the Empire North of the Alps: The Patronage of the Imperial Court', in Nigel Hiscock (ed.), *The White Mantle of Churches: Architecture, Liturgy, and Art around the Millennium* (Turnhout, 2003), 29–56. On the Hereford chapel, Christopher Wilson, 'Abbot Serlo's Church at Gloucester, 1089–1100: Its Place in Romanesque Architecture', in *Medieval Art and Architecture at Gloucester and Tewkesbury*, British Art and Archaeological Association Conference Transactions, vii, ed. T. A. Heslop and V. A. Sekules (1985), 52–83, at 55–6; Richard Gem, 'The Bishop's Chapel at Hereford: The Roles of Patron and Craftsman', in *Art and Patronage in the English Romanesque*, ed. Sarah Macready and F. H. Thompson, Society of Antiquaries of London, Occasional Paper (new series), viii (1986), 87–96; Hans J. Böker, 'The Bishop's Chapel at Hereford Cathedral and the Question of Architectural Copies in the Middle Ages', *Gesta*, xxxvii (1998), 44–54.

[130] Tadgh O'Keeffe, *Romanesque Ireland: Architecture and Ideology of the Twelfth Century* (Dublin, 2003), 24–5.

[131] For Kelso, Richard Fawcett, *The Architecture of the Scottish Medieval Church, 1100–1560* (New Haven, 2011), 33–5.

[132] Hubert Houben, *Roger II of Sicily: A Ruler between East and West*, trans. Graham A. Loud and Diane Milburn (Cambridge, 2002), 113–35.

[133] For Monreale analysed in these terms, G. A. Loud, *The Latin Church in Norman Italy* (Cambridge, 2007), 329–39, and esp. 337–9.

[134] See Richard Plant, 'Romanesque East Anglia and the Empire', in David Bates and Robert Liddiard (eds), *East Anglia and Its North Sea World in the Middle Ages* (Woodbridge, 2013), 270–86. For the general thesis of England's greater openness, Grant, 'Architectural Relationships', 121–6; Fernie, *Architecture of Norman England*, 120–4.

level, the origin of the famous round towers of the parish churches of Norfolk and Suffolk may draw partly on the new cathedral at Norwich and the abbey church of Bury St Edmunds, but what is certain is that such towers proliferated around the peripheries of the North Sea, and nowhere else, in the twelfth century.[135]

It surely cannot be an accident that the earliest example of the transfer to Normandy of what is nowadays seen as a type of domestic hall built in the style of pre-1066 English aristocratic residences is found in the so-called Salle de l'Echiquier at Caen. Normally thought to have been built for Henry I (an earlier date is actually possible), it is within the ramparts of the castle founded by his father, William the Conqueror, at a site from which the western towers of the abbey of Saint-Etienne are visible. As such it was a permanent reminder that this was the place founded by the maker of empire and of the link with the church where he was buried.[136] To say that the other early example of such a building is at Westminster within a stone's throw of where William was crowned as king, a hall that was among the largest buildings in Christendom, yet which its founder, William Rufus, thought was not big enough, is probably to invent symbolism where none exists; it is, however, irresistible not to propose it.

That some of the imperial language in the written sources and what became a style of building that occurs across the cross-Channel empire can be seen as a continuation of English practice might even lead to the suggestion that the empire of the Normans was made in England. This is to go too far. But there is absolutely no reason why the new imperial culture should not borrow from the world of the defeated, especially when victory had made the empire's ruler a king, a promotion to which poets had repeatedly drawn attention. Exactly the same thing did after all happen in southern Italy. These magnificent buildings do, however, also surely evoke more forcefully than anything else can the moral ambivalence that attends the phenomenon of empire. A consequence of violence and an expression of triumph and of a proclaimed civilizing mission that many found offensive, they also show that empires can be notably creative. Manifestly, however, the inspirations for this creativity cannot be labelled simply as either Norman or English. They demonstrate the inadequacy of identity as a form of analysis in the way in which it has traditionally—and often still is—used. The next stage in the argument is to set out how the phenomenon of empire can be analysed through the medium of life histories.

---

[135] Stephen Heywood, 'Stone Building in Romanesque East Anglia', in Bates and Liddiard (eds), *East Anglia and its North Sea World*, 256–69.
[136] For what follows, Edward Impey and John McNeill, 'La grande salle des ducs de Normandie à Caen', in G. Meirion-Jones (ed.), *La demeure seigneuriale du monde plantagenêt (XIe–XVIe siècles): salles, chambres et tours* (Rennes, 2013), 95–131.

2
The Experience of Empire

An extreme post-modernist and post-colonial position would argue that the study of personal experience is a more legitimate form of history than the focus on politics and power that has traditionally characterized the study of empires.[1] An intellectual middle ground is that since phenomena other than power and ethnicity influence lives, we are better able to explain both of them and many others of the subjects involved in the multifaceted world of empire through a focus on individual narratives.[2] Such an approach has recently been at the core of a book on the British Empire in the early modern period and has also been seen by Linda Colley as the basis for what she has called 'connexity', that is, the identification of the multiplicity of networks and links that existed across space and peoples.[3] Writing about the eighteenth century, Emma Rothschild has observed that:

> The history of empires, or the history of enlightenment, is itself, in this sense, a history of the inner life. To describe the circumstances of individuals in the past, and to imagine how they thought about these circumstances, is to describe the history of values.[4]

Although to write books and articles about personal letters and diaries as our modern colleagues do is usually not possible for the eleventh and twelfth centuries, narrative histories, charters, letters, and miracle stories supply eminently usable material and non-written evidence often provides vivid evidence of the lives of those who created it; the case study of the Reviers family already set out in Chapter 1, for example, is ultimately a study of networks and values. With the construction of life-histories also having a central place in certain types of archaeological analysis, it could be said that what I am doing is no more than foregrounding the arguments for the use of a methodology widely accepted elsewhere.[5] It is nonetheless important to observe that the telling of life-stories differs from prosopography in deliberately setting out to create a narrative, but that it is less ambitious than biography because it does not attempt to re-create personality. On these terms, the construction of

---

[1] For references, Patrick Joyce, 'The Return of History: Post-Modernism and the Politics of Academic History in Britain', *P&P*, no. 158 (1998), 207–35.
[2] For a cogent statement of this argument, C. A. Bayly, *The Birth of the Modern World, 1780–1914* (Oxford, 2004), 8–9.
[3] Miles Ogborn, *Global Lives: Britain and the World, 1550–1800* (Cambridge, 2008), 9; Linda Colley, 'What Is Imperial History Now?', in David Cannadine (ed.), *What Is History Now?* (Basingstoke, 2002), 132–47, at 138.
[4] Emma Rothschild, *The Inner Life of Empires: An Eighteenth-Century History* (Princeton, 2011), 300.
[5] See the statement in Roberta Gilchrist, *Medieval Life: Archaeology and the Life Course* (Woodbridge, 2012), 11–13.

life-stories consciously or unconsciously already plays a major part in the work of a good number of scholars working on the history of the Normans. Hence, ultimately what I am doing is making explicit the argument that—purposefully employed—this approach can open up many new vistas.

The social constructionist frameworks already mentioned immediately come into play within the analytical framework of empire because the telling of life-stories relates individual experience and behaviour to political and social culture and norms.[6] It makes it possible to locate lives within the overarching hegemonic power of the cross-Channel empire and its multiple systems and structures. Some aspects of what I am doing can be described as ethnography, although in this particular case, its application often involves an awareness of literary genre and, at times, the use of quantitative analysis.[7] Further, the study of 'mobilities' prompts reflection on the infrastructure that sustained the cross-Channel world and the dynamic that drove it, as well as on the evidence for the structures of 'movement, mobility and social order' (movement and mobility are, of course, different).[8] To bring in Robin Cohen's formulation of a Weberian 'ideal type' for the analysis of diasporas supplies another analytical framework, with the 'ideal' features relevant in varying ways to the subject of the Normans and empire being dispersal from an original homeland (or rather, in this case, a mixture of dispersal and expansion), a collective memory or myth about the homeland, a strong group consciousness of a common history, a troubled relationship with host societies, a sense of empathy and co-responsibility with co-ethnic members across the countries of settlement even when the home has become vestigial, and the possibility of a distinctive and creative enriching life in the countries of settlement involving cultural pluralism.[9] In particular, it allows for the complexities of personal identity and gets the whole discussion off the hook of needing to define everything as 'English', 'Norman', or 'Anglo-Norman', or even of such carefully crafted terms as 'English Normans', 'insular Normans', and 'continental Normans'.[10] Within these frameworks, the telling of life-histories is the very foundation of this book's argument because they often make us look at many things in a different way. For this reason, much of this chapter is deliberately descriptive. It does argue for the continuing resilience and dynamism of imperial values, ideas, and structures. But in doing so, it also aims to show the sheer diversity of lives as they were lived.

That the sea was not a barrier to political unity was one of John Le Patourel's most influential arguments, with the section of *The Norman Empire* devoted to

---

[6] See Chap. 1. On social constructionism, Vivien Burr, *Social Constructionism*, 2nd edn. (London, 2003); Kenneth J. Gergen, *An Invitation to Social Constructionism*, 2nd edn. (London, 2008), with some pertinent points for my argument on agency and identity at pp. 104–25.
[7] For guidance, Martyn Hammersley and Paul Atkinson, *Ethnography: Principles and Practice*, 3rd edn. (London, 2007), 1–19, 191–208.
[8] John Urry, *Mobilities* (Cambridge, 2007), with the quotation at p. 9.
[9] Thus, Robin Cohen, *Global Diasporas: An Introduction*, 2nd edn. (London, 2008), 16–17. For this approach taken for an earlier historical period, Lesley Abrams, 'Diaspora and Identity in the Viking Age', *EME*, xx (2012), 17–38.
[10] For all these terms, Grant, *Architecture and Society*, 13.

rulers' sea-crossings a contribution of enduring importance. It is also noteworthy that Haskins emphasized that communication over sea was often more rapid than communication over land.[11] It is worth reflecting that a man such as William the Conqueror in all likelihood crossed the Channel nineteen times between 1066 and 1087, and then to ponder on the scale of the fleets and organization on both sides of the Channel that were involved in this operation.[12] However, as an article by Lucien Musset reminded us, the sea was dangerous and the Channel was (and is) an especially turbulent stretch of water.[13] The wreck of the White Ship, a routine voyage that turned into a disaster partly because of the complacency of those who were setting out to make the crossing, and the wreck that is central to grasping the business-like nature of the commerce in Caen stone that features later in this chapter, epitomize the same themes; the normality of what was being undertaken, and the perils of the sea's unpredictability.[14] For Orderic, the sea was a changeable and uncertain place, a metaphor for life itself.[15]

In terms of the inner life of empire, the sea must have been either consciously or unconsciously present in many minds for much of the time and must have constituted a source of anxiety for many. John of Worcester told the story that a rough crossing of the Channel in 1131 led Henry I—a man, of course, whose psyche is as good as certain to have been scarred by awareness of what the sea could do—to promise to abandon danegeld for seven years and to seek the special protection of St Edmund, a saint who had become notable for performing miracles at sea.[16] The anxiety associated with the sea could, however, also provoke bravado; Henry's older brother, William Rufus, for example, when others counselled caution, in a story reproduced by several contemporary historians, famously dismissed their fears and announced that he knew of no king who had died at sea and therefore set off across the Channel in the summer of 1099.[17] Its role in other lives can be illustrated with many narratives, of which two, chosen from a potentially large number, involve the monks of Le Bec receiving supplies at a time when provisions were running short, as if the arrival of ships from England was a matter of routine, and a Norman noble anxiously visiting the same abbey to ask St Anselm for his prayers before setting out to cross the Channel.[18] Piracy was also a problem,

---

[11] Le Patourel, *Norman Empire*, 163–72; Haskins, *Normans in European History*, 87–8 ('it was quite as easy to go from London to Rouen as from London to York').

[12] *Regesta*, 78–80. There are in fact some uncertainties about the number of crossings William made because we are reliant on sources that usually refer to where he was, rather than stating the dates when he crossed the Channel. The statistic does, however, make the necessary point.

[13] Musset, 'Un empire à cheval sur la mer', *passim*. See further, Mark Gardiner, 'Shipping and Trade between England and the Continent during the Eleventh Century', *ANS*, xxii (2000), 71–93; Elisabeth Ridel, *Les navires de la Conquête: construction navale et navigation en Normandie à l'époque de Guillaume le Conquérant* (Cully, 2010).

[14] See Chaps. 1 and 4.

[15] *OV*, ii, 302–3; cf, Amanda Jane Hingst, *The Written Word: Past and Place in the Work of Orderic Vitalis* (Notre-Dame, IN, 2009), 125.

[16] JW, iii, 202–3; Hollister, *Henry I*, 353; Green, *Henry I*, 312.

[17] *GR*, i, 564–7. For the various accounts, Barlow, *William Rufus*, 403.

[18] *The Life of St Anselm by Eadmer*, ed. and trans. R. W. Southern, OMT (Oxford, 1972), 25–6, 47–8.

with the Abingdon *Historia* telling us of the mutilation of a knight by pirates and a consequent act of kindness by William the Conqueror, and the *Life* of Bernard of Tiron, of pirates, their captives, and their loot being driven ashore on the Chausey Islands after a battle at sea.[19]

For all this, the many routine Channel crossings led to the emergence of Barfleur, Caen-Ouistreham, Dieppe, Southampton, Hastings, and Dover as the main cross-Channel ports. In the case of Barfleur, it appears as if the cross-Channel empire was actually the making of the place; again, therefore, we are dealing with lives changed by empire.[20] All also invites reflection on an idea strongly argued by historians of modern empires, namely that maritime empires are intrinsically weaker than land-based ones.[21]

INDIVIDUAL LIVES

While the history of the dominant cross-Channel secular and clerical elites is in all probability the history that ultimately determined the beginning and end of empire, their lives cannot be treated as impervious to other influences.[22] To understand the currents that flowed beneath the surface and that often erupted on to it, it is necessary to turn to other lives. And, for all my expressed caution about the way we use the great twelfth-century historians, Orderic's epilogue to the *Historia Ecclesiastica*, written in 1141 in the seventh decade of his life as he contemplated death, is the only possible starting point for such an analysis, a remarkable statement from an extraordinary man from an ordinary background:

> And so, as a boy of ten, I crossed the British sea and came into Normandy as an exile, unknown to all, knowing no one. Like Joseph in Egypt, I heard a language which I did not understand.[23]

Born of a mixed marriage in 1075 in a relatively remote region of the English kingdom, and growing up speaking his mother's language, English, he was unquestionably a child of empire, a product of the new societies and relationships created by it. He is also surely an illustration of personal resilience and of how genius can thrive against the odds.

In the epilogue, after mentioning the shock of the change forced on him, he went on to say that he found 'nothing but kindness and friendship among strangers'.

---

[19] *Historia Ecclesie Abbendonensis*, 8–9; Geoffrey Grossus, 'Vita Beati Bernardi Tironiensis', *PL*, clxii, cols. 1384–5 (*The Life of the Blessed Bernard of Tiron/Geoffrey Grossus*, trans. Ruth Harwood Cline (Washington, DC, 2009), 35–6).
[20] Lucien Musset, 'Barfleur, plaque tournante de l'Etat anglo-normand', *Annuaire des cinq départements de la Normandie*, cxli (1983), 51–7, at 51.
[21] Colley, 'Difficulties', 371–4 (nb, 'if an overland empire prospers, people may well cease to regard it as an empire', at p. 372).
[22] In narrowing the wealth gap between the topmost Domesday elite and the rest, J. J. N. Palmer, 'The Wealth of the Secular Aristocracy in 1086', *ANS*, xxii (2000), 279–91, strengthens my arguments.
[23] For the epilogue, OV, vi, 550–7.

Yet despite finding the circumstances at Saint-Evroult congenial, and although he lived almost all his adult life in Normandy and at the start of Book V of the *Historia* declared that his objective was to write a history of the Normans for the Normans, he called himself *Ordricus angligena*, emphasizing to the end of his life his English descent from his mother, and subsequently being entered in Saint-Evroult's calendar under his English name.[24] His stated subject notwithstanding, he manifestly empathized profoundly throughout his life with the humiliation of the people among whom he had spent his childhood. His self-identity and the values that shaped his inner life might therefore be thought to have differed radically from the public responsibilities he believed he had to undertake as a historian. He thereby provides an instant warning against thinking that either values or identity can be treated in a simplified way when we turn to the many thousands of lives touched by the cross-Channel empire.

Unlike most of the other great twelfth-century historians discussed later in this chapter, Orderic had no mighty aristocratic patrons in mind. Indeed, to take him at face value, which would be a mistake, it is doubtful whether he thought of himself as having any audience beyond a few monks of his abbey.[25] In terms of my argument, however, this makes him more valuable because through him and because of his arguable isolation from some of the pressures of the wider world, we come as close to the private as we are ever likely to come. Ultimately an observer of a flawed and deteriorating world that he believed was close to its end, his astonishing curiosity makes his history a treasure trove of life-stories concerning the neighbours and patrons of Saint-Evroult and individuals from far and wide, to which I will frequently return. The Norman *gens* was for him a turbulent and self-destructive people who had at certain times and under certain conditions risen to greatness.[26]

When it comes to the fate of the English after 1066, an extensive historiography, with the work of Ann Williams being of central importance, has set before us many life-stories; the development of several major prosopographical projects will, in due course, deepen knowledge further.[27] Nothing, however, can fully compensate for

---

[24] OV, iii, 6–9 (*inspirante Deo Normannorum gesta et euentus Normannis promere scripto sum conatus*); Marjorie Chibnall, *The World of Orderic Vitalis* (Oxford, 1984), 3 n. 2. See further, Thomas, *English and Normans*, 81–2, 153–4. I am not convinced by the suggestion in Webber, *Norman Identity*, 143, that the passage *casus guerrae pacisque nostratuum ueraci stilo copiose dilucidabo* (OV, iv, 360) means that Orderic was 'presenting himself as a Norman' because it is too far removed from any context of ethnicity to make it certain that Orderic was being so specific. See also Nick Webber, 'England and the Norman Myth', in Julia Barrow and Andrew Wareham (eds), *Myth, Rulership, Church and Charters: Essays in Honour of Nicholas Brooks* (Aldershot, 2008), 211–28, at 223. On Orderic's childhood, Chibnall, *The World*, 3–11. For the calendar, Bibliothèque Nationale de France, ms. lat. 10062, fo. 19ᵛ; cit, Hingst, *The Written Word*, xix.

[25] OV, iii, 6–7 (*quod aliquibus in domo Domini fidelibus prosit seu placeat*).

[26] Thus, OV, iii, 98–9, 104–9; iv, 82–3, 226–9; v, 24–7, vi, 456–7. See further, Chap. 4.

[27] Williams, *The English and the Norman Conquest*, Chaps. 4 ('Survivors') and 5 ('The Service of the King') are the foundations of all study of this subject. For recent life-narratives, see, for example, Ann Williams, 'Little Domesday and the English: The Hundred of Colneis in Suffolk', in Elizabeth Hallam and David Bates (eds), *Domesday Book* (Stroud, 2001), 103–20; Sébastien Daniélo, 'Land, Family and

the near-total absence of information about the names of the English who died at Hastings; manifestly, the huge numbers of mostly male casualties would have brought misery to many people and family dislocation on a massive scale. We do know that women fled to religious houses to escape rape and forced marriage.[28] Statistics derived from Domesday Book demonstrate unequivocally that thousands of peasants carried heavier burdens and suffered a reduction of status after 1066.[29] And, despite the differing interpretations of other Domesday statistics, it is likely that the so-called 'Harrying of the North', famously condemned by Orderic as brutal slaughter that would not go unpunished, may have displaced as many as 150,000 people in Yorkshire.[30]

For my argument, the largely unnamed voices behind statistics such as these need to be kept constantly in mind; their ghostly presence is a reminder of what was unquestionably a human catastrophe. Unsurprisingly, however, it is about the minority of the elite of the old regime who came to terms with the newcomers that we know most. Thus, as early as 1068, Bishop Giso of Wells—admittedly a Lotharingian and one of the bishops from overseas appointed by Edward the Confessor—achieved a result in a land dispute at William the Conqueror's court that he certainly would not have achieved had Harold won the Battle of Hastings: his basic argument was that the estate had been taken by Harold 'inflamed by greed' and it ought, therefore, to be returned to his church; as it was.[31] Of fundamental importance to the way in which we interpret the whole situation is that, for all that Archbishop Lanfranc of Canterbury either in late 1072 or in 1073 might express anxiety about the future, and that there were occasional rumblings of invasions from Scandinavia that either turned into damp squibs or never happened at all, pretty well all must have acknowledged by 1072 that there was no way back for the defeated English; many had evidently recognized this much earlier.[32]

In this scenario, the composition of the *Vita Ædwardi Regis* for Queen Edith, Earl Godwine of Wessex's daughter and Edward the Confessor's widow, four of whose brothers had met violent deaths in 1066, and a fifth of whom was to be held

---

Depredation: The Case of St Benet of Holme's Manor of Little Melton', *ANS*, xxxi (2009), 49–63, at 54–60; David Roffe, 'Hidden Lives: English Lords in Post-Conquest Lincolnshire and Beyond', in David Roffe (ed.), *The English and Their Legacy, 900–1200: Essays in Honour of Ann Williams* (Woodbridge, 2012), 205–28. For the several prosopographical projects, see Chap. 1.

[28] For rape and forced marriage, Elisabeth van Houts, 'Intermarriage in Eleventh-Century England', in *Normandy and Neighbours*, 237–70, at 250–6.

[29] The basic point is well made in Stephen Baxter, 'Lordship and Labour', in Julia Crick and Elisabeth van Houts (eds), *A Social History of England, 900–1200* (Cambridge, 2011), 98–114, at 104–7.

[30] OV, ii, 232–3; J. J. N. Palmer, 'War and Domesday Waste', in Matthew Strickland (ed.), *Armies, Chivalry and Warfare in Medieval Britain and France* (Stamford, 1998), 256–75, at 273–4.

[31] *Regesta*, no. 286; David Bates, *Re-ordering the Past and Negotiating the Present in Stenton's 'First Century'*, The Stenton Lecture 1999 (University of Reading, 2000), 9; Simon Keynes, 'Giso, Bishop of Wells', *ANS*, xix (1997), 203–71, at 242–3.

[32] *The Letters of Lanfranc, Archbishop of Canterbury*, ed. and trans. Helen Clover and Margaret Gibson, OMT (Oxford, 1979), 34–5 no. 1.

in permanent captivity by William the Conqueror and his sons, is readily identifiable as a narrative constructed to shape the past in order to try to take control of the future, differences of opinion around its date of composition in the late 1060s notwithstanding. As a rapid response to crisis, it is a truly remarkable text, an attempt to negotiate traumatic change and integrate its patron and her family's history into the new world. That it largely failed in this objective, or is at best only one narrative of the multiple narratives that evolved out of 1066, is only part of the story.[33] Its account of the dying Confessor's prophecy of the green tree certainly did influence the future, as also did its portrayal of the pious King Edward, with the former later taken up by William of Malmesbury and Ailred of Rievaulx as a metaphor for the long-term subjugation inflicted on the English and becoming a central theme in the history of empire because of its idealistic prediction that the peoples of the empire would one day live harmoniously together.[34] Its message was to have permanent significance. But its attempt to rescue the reputations of a divided and, for many, discredited elite could not be taken at face value in the context of the times.

Bishop Wulfstan of Worcester (1062–95), the one long-term survivor among the episcopate of English birth, was manifestly a man of both remarkable personal religious qualities and considerable worldly acumen; the other-worldly saint presented to us by William of Malmesbury on the basis of Coleman's lost Old English *Vita* and Prior Nicholas's memories should not be taken entirely at face value.[35] We do at times in Malmesbury's accounts of his life hear voices that seem to regret the passing of a better previous age, most notably in Wulfstan's unhistorical lament as he supervised the construction of a grand new-style cathedral to replace the smaller one built in the later tenth century by his predecessor, St Oswald.[36] He undoubtedly did exert himself to preserve some things English, but it is a moot point as to whether his contribution was exceptional. His adjustment to the post-1066 world is demonstrated by the very fact that the cathedral was built and by his vigorous defence of his church's lands, and by his reported prophetic preaching that the English practice of wearing hair long had been an inevitable prelude to a terrible punishment, surely every bit as good a justification for the proclaimed civilizing mission of the new empire as any that the newcomers could have thought up, and also a good tactic to distance himself from

---

[33] *The Life of King Edward who rests at Westminster, attributed to a monk of Saint-Bertin*, ed. Frank Barlow, 2nd edn., OMT (Oxford, 1992), *passim*; Pauline Stafford, *Queen Emma and Queen Edith* (Oxford, 1997), 40–52 (nb: 'It was concerned to explain the Norman Conquest in ways which flattered rather than blamed Edith', p.45); Simon Keynes and Rosalind Love, 'Earl Godwine's Ship', *ASE*, xxxviii (2009), 185–223, at 199–202. For other references to discussion, Richard Mortimer (ed.), *Edward the Confessor: The Man and the Legend* (Woodbridge, 2009).

[34] See further later in this chapter and in Chap. 6.

[35] See in particular, Ann Williams, 'The cunning of the dove: Wulfstan and the politics of accommodation', in Julia S. Barrow and N. P. Brooks (eds.), *St Wulfstan and his World* (Aldershot and Burlington VT, 2005), 23–38; also, Stephen Baxter, 'The Representation of Lordship and Land Tenure in Domesday Book', in Hallam and Bates (eds.), *Domesday Book*, 73–102, at 81–92; Emma Mason, *St Wulfstan of Worcester, c.1008–1095* (Oxford, 1990), 108–55, 196–232.

[36] *GP*, i, 428–31.

King Harold II, to whom he had given overt support.[37] Since the sins of the English were one of William of Malmesbury's favourite themes, we cannot be entirely sure whether it is his or Wulfstan's voice we are listening to in some of this; the theme of atonement for sin is, however, present in other more contemporary sources.[38] Whether this counselling of a self-flagellating acceptance of blame or the rank opportunism of some of Wulfstan's compatriots are more or less attractive as responses to defeat and conquest is one of those endlessly debatable moral questions. Both have an infinite number of parallels in the history of empires.

Among the lay aristocracy, Edward of Salisbury, sheriff of Wiltshire under William the Conqueror and one of those four major tenants-in-chief of English birth mentioned in Chapter 1, was also able to resist the tsunami of the takeover. Marrying a woman from a Norman family, he founded a line that acquired some land in Normandy and thereby joined the cross-Channel elite. In 1144 his grandson was made earl of Salisbury, the first man of English descent to obtain that dignity since before 1066.[39] However, at the social levels below the topmost elite, the general point that some of the English prospered is a well-known one.[40] What, nonetheless, needs great emphasis is the almost instantaneous creation of new relationships and activities in response to the overwhelmingly dominant hard power of empire. Alongside the obvious, but very complex and notably creative, example of the making of Domesday Book, witness the suggestion that English memories were necessary to the writing of the *Carmen de Hastingae Proelio*, a collaboration that must have taken place at a very early date, and the English contribution to those many small churches that combine so-called Anglo-Saxon and Norman features ('the Saxo-Norman overlap').[41] One group, some of whom apparently integrated rapidly, were the warriors recruited through existing systems of obligation to fight the wars of the new elite. The anonymous authors of the 'D' and 'E' versions of the Anglo-Saxon Chronicle both told with manifest relish of the damage done by the English troops who were taken across the Channel to take part in William the Conqueror's campaign in Maine in 1073. Later in the same decade, an Englishman, Toki, son of Wigod of Wallingford, gave indispensable assistance to William in battle, losing his life in the process.[42] Although, in this first generation, intermarriage was extremely rare in the upper echelons of aristocratic society, Orderic's testimony—as well as that of others—does suggest that it must have been widespread at the social levels rarely touched on in the written sources; Little

---

[37] *William of Malmesbury: Saints' Lives*, ed. and trans. M. Winterbottom and R. M. Thomson, OMT (Oxford, 2002), 58–9.
[38] Below, Chap. 3.
[39] For Edward and his descendants, Williams, *The English and the Norman Conquest*, 105–7; David Crouch, *William Marshal*, 2nd edn. (Harlow, 2002), 23 and n. 18.
[40] Hugh M. Thomas, 'The Significance and Fate of the Native English Landholders of 1086', *EHR*, cxviii (2003), 303–33, and see esp. 305–14; Thomas, *English and Normans*, 61–9. See also John Blair, *Anglo-Saxon Oxfordshire* (Stroud, 1995), 171–85; Roffe, 'Hidden Lives', 205–7.
[41] For Domesday Book, Stephen Baxter, 'The Making of Domesday Book and the Languages of Lordship in Conquered England', in Elizabeth M. Tyler (ed.), *Conceptualizing Multilingualism in Medieval England, c.800–c.1250* (Turnhout, 2011), 271–308; for possible input into the *Carmen*, van Houts, *Memory and Gender*, 133; for 'the Saxo-Norman Overlap', Fernie, *The Architecture of Norman England*, 209–19.
[42] ASC, 'D', 1074 (*recte* 1073), 'E', 1073; 'D', 1079.

Domesday Book, in one of its narrative passages, mentions the case of a Breton who fell in love with an unnamed English woman living in Norfolk and married her.[43]

In another narrative passage, Little Domesday describes the new settlement established at Norwich as being for the *Franci de Norwic*. Of the indigenous population it says: 'those fleeing and the others remaining have been entirely ruined', another hearing for the largely silent voices behind the disruption associated with change, this time as a consequence of castle-building in towns.[44] Yet, when a longer term view is taken, within a quarter of a century of 1086, the urban area that made up Norwich had increased by thirty per cent and signs of prosperity were so manifest that James Campbell has written that 'these may well have been boom times'; the opportunities for enrichment thereby created were, of course, mostly to the benefit of the conquerors, but not entirely so.[45] A parallel case study is provided by 'the fall and rise of Oxford'.[46] However, while all this manifestly epitomizes the grandeur of the imperial architectural language and planning of the first fifty years of empire, it is also immediately clear that the changes that took place in Norwich cannot be described culturally as 'Norman'. The process that made Norwich into a cathedral city was worked out in England, with the city being the second choice for the episcopal church of the bishops of Thetford after they had failed to locate to Bury St Edmunds and to the monastery that housed the relics of a saint who himself rapidly became a participant in empire.[47]

When we turn to the victors and their descendants, Orderic's account of Richard Basset, one of Henry I's 'new men', 'swollen with the spoils of England' (*tumens opulentia*), building a splendid castle on 'the small fee' (*in paruo feodo*) he had inherited in Normandy is arguably the sort of story we would expect to find; it illustrates magnificently the nouveau riche imperial administrator returning home to show off to his former peers.[48] Since the Basset family estates in Normandy were modest in size, the story also highlights how large quantities of money crossed from England into Normandy during the decades after 1066 to finance such projects. Others were also clearly impressed by the promotion that empire gave them. The two brothers Hamelin and Winebald de Ballon, aristocrats from Maine installed on

---

[43] OV, ii, 256–7; *DB*, ii, fo. 232ʳ. In general, see van Houts, 'Intermarriage in Eleventh-Century England', 245–59.

[44] *DB*, ii, fo. 116ᵛ–18ʳ.

[45] Brian Ayers, 'The Urban Landscape', in Carole Rawcliffe and Richard Wilson (eds), *Medieval Norwich* (London, 2004), 1–28, at 13–19; James Campbell, 'Norwich before 1300', in Rawcliffe and Wilson (eds), *Medieval Norwich*, 29–48, with the Conquest discussed at pp. 39–45 and the quotation at p. 41.

[46] Blair, *Anglo-Saxon Oxfordshire*, 177.

[47] Most recently, Tom Licence, 'Herbert Losinga's Trip to Rome and the Bishopric of Bury St Edmunds', *ANS*, xxxiv (2012), 151–68, and esp. at 155–7. For Edmund as an imperial saint, see later in this chapter and Chap. 4.

[48] OV, vi, 468–9; Judith A. Green, *The Government of England under Henry I* (Cambridge, 1986), 231–2; *Basset Charters, c.1120 to 1250*, ed. William T. Reedy, Pipe Roll Society, new ser., l (London, 1995, for 1989–91), x–xii, xxxii.

the border of England and Wales by William Rufus, could not resist describing themselves, respectively, as 'a noble and most wise man . . . endowed, because of his industrious qualities, with the most generous gifts and honours by King William son of the renowned King William' and 'one of the greatest of King Henry I's barons' in charters in their names for the abbeys of Saint-Vincent of Le Mans and St Peter's, Gloucester.[49] Then there is Vitalis of Canterbury, the great Caen stone entrepreneur, whose life in Normandy before 1066 is completely unknown to us, and who has probably been immortalized by the Bayeux Tapestry. In due course he adopted an English self-image through his toponym and established a dynasty that continued to reside and thrive in twelfth-century Canterbury after his death. A more atypical investor in the new cross-Channel world of empire it would be hard to find; he takes on many trappings of Englishness while remaining centrally involved in the life of his birthplace.[50]

These three lives epitomize those of the multitude who used their wits to profit from the new cross-Channel empire. A story that illustrates how the humbler might seek to profit is provided by the tale of a certain Richard, ceremonially placing a branch of a rose tree and a knife on the altar of the abbey of Saint-Pierre de Préaux to hand over to the monks on an indeterminate lease land he had recently inherited, in return for a payment of eight shillings in English money to be delivered to him by a monk named Warin (presumably) in England. This narrative, dating probably from the first quarter of the twelfth century, demonstrates the existence of a system for providing cross-Channel financial support that in this case functioned even though the abbey had no conventual priory in England. That, in the event of his return to Normandy, the payment of eight shillings sterling was to be replaced by one of twenty shillings of Rouen money might even be thought to provide evidence of a cross-Channel currency exchange rate; but this is certainly pushing the evidence too hard.[51] Richard's story looks to be that of a fortune-hunter carefully taking out an insurance policy, although this may, of course, be a misreading of the narrative and, sadly, we do not know the outcome. Another much more dramatic tale of a rise in wealth and status resulting from a personal investment is that of Payn Peverel, in all probability a landless younger son, who, having distinguished himself in Robert Curthose's service on the First Crusade, was promptly recruited by Henry I into his military household, and then subsequently endowed with land in England. That he thereafter became a local figure known principally for his enlargement of the priory of Barnwell at Cambridge might make him seem to be

---

[49] *Cartulaire de l'abbaye de Saint-Vincent du Mans*, ed. R. Charles and M. le vicomte Menjot d'Elbenne (Le Mans, 1913), no. 832; *Historia et Cartularium monasterii sancti Petri Gloucestriae*, ed. W. H. Hart, 3 vols, Rolls Series (London, 1863–7), i, 61; Round, 'The Family of Ballon', 189–98.

[50] William Urry, 'The Normans in Canterbury', *AN*, viii (1958), 119–38, at 131–5; William Urry, *Canterbury under the Angevin Kings* (London, 1967), 51–3, 63–4. See the two paragraphs that follow the next one for more on Vitalis and Caen stone.

[51] *Le Cartulaire de l'abbaye bénédictine de Saint-Pierre-de-Préaux (1034–1227)*, ed. Dominique Rouet (Paris, 2005), 51–3 (A46) (*CDF*, no. 327). See further, Dominique Rouet, 'Le patrimoine anglais et l'Angleterre vus à travers les actes du cartulaire de Saint-Pierre de Préaux', in *Normandie et Angleterre*, 99–116, at 102, suggesting that the transaction took place in either 1104 or 1123. On the transfer of money from England to Normandy, see Chap. 4.

someone who renounced the world of empire after some extraordinary experiences. Yet the fact that his son and heir took part in the Second Crusade puts him firmly within another historiography, that of families with an emotional attachment to the Crusade; together they are a reminder of one of my central themes, namely that the near-silence of the sources is no demonstration that an individual ceased to be a participant in the wider world of empire and of pan-European events.[52]

Another feature of Norwich's history in this period is the shipment into the city of vast quantities of Caen stone for the great construction projects that were started in the 1090s. It was massively used elsewhere in, for example, the reconstruction of Canterbury cathedral and St Augustine's abbey at Canterbury, Westminster Hall, and at many other places besides. It was the stone of choice for the Conqueror's talismanic English foundation at Battle. It is also certain that it was not used in England before 1066; we, therefore, unquestionably have here an industry whose size expanded hugely as a result of the empire and whose scale has produced some dramatic, although not unreasonable, assessments of the quantities involved: Brian Ayers, for example, refers to 'colossal' quantities of stone coming into Norwich and Lucien Musset, in relation to England as a whole, refers to quantities of unimaginable size.[53] An immediate, albeit unsophisticated, response to these comments is that someone must have been making a lot of money out of the business, and that many of the people doing it must have lived in Caen.

Goscelin of Saint-Bertin's account of a fleet of fifteen ships sailing to England laden with stone, and of the tragic end of fourteen of them, supplies good late-eleventh-century evidence of how the transportation was managed. It shows the aforementioned Vitalis of Canterbury at the heart of a business of transporting stone from Caen to Westminster and Canterbury. The activity involved agreeing a price with the masters of all fifteen ships, which was then set down in sealed contracts.[54] This use of a very special stone can be treated as a display of cultural superiority typical of imperialists and a piece of job creation that must have benefitted many in Normandy. Yet there are also hints that this great industrial expansion was the cause of social tension in Caen; the poet Serlo of Bayeux, for

[52] Susan Edgington, 'Pagan Peverell: An Anglo-Norman Crusader', in P. W. Edbury (ed.), *Crusade and Settlement: Papers Read at the First Conference for the Study of the Crusades and the Latin East, and Presented to R. C. Smail* (Cardiff, 1985), 90–3. In general, Jonathan Riley-Smith, *The First Crusaders, 1095–1131* (Cambridge, 1997), 85–105.

[53] Brian Ayers, 'Building A Fine City: The Provision of Flint, Mortar and Freestone in Medieval Norwich', in David Parsons (ed.), *Stone: Quarrying and Building in England, AD 43–1525* (Chichester, 1990), 217–28, at 223 (that the statement is inclusive of Barnack and Caen does not detract from its force); Lucien Musset, 'La pierre de Caen: extraction et commerce, XIe–XVe siècles', in Odette Chapelot and Paul Benoit (eds), *Pierre et métal dans le bâtiment au Moyen Age* (Paris, 1985; repr., 2001), 219–35, at 223 ('Au total, le volume de pierre exporté dès le XIe siècle confond l'imagination'). On the use of Caen stone in England, Tim Tatton-Brown, 'La pierre de Caen en Angleterre', in Maylis Baylé (ed.), *L'architecture normande au Moyen Age*, 2 vols (Caen and Condé-sur-Noireau, 1997), i, 305–14.

[54] Richard Gem, 'Canterbury and the Cushion Capital: A Commentary on Passages from Goscelin's *De Miraculis Sancti Augustini*', in Neil Stratford (ed.), *Romanesque and Gothic: Essays for George Zarnecki*, 2 vols (Woodbridge, 1987), 83–101, at 83–5, 88–93, 98–9.

example, complained that he was being denied access to what had formerly been a communal quarry by Gilbert, abbot of Saint-Etienne of Caen.[55]

The new world of empire did not bring simple enjoyment of newfound wealth to all who crossed the Channel. Some indeed rejected it. One well-known case is that of Reinfrid, a knight in William the Conqueror's army that carried out the Harrying of the North, who, according to Stephen of Whitby's account, was so sickened by the violence and so inspired by northern England's great Christian past, that he became a monk, firstly at Evesham and then at the re-founded house of Jarrow, and ultimately became prior of the re-founded monastery at Whitby where he had first lived as a hermit in the ruins of the long-abandoned abbey.[56] A story of attachment to the homeland is that of Alvred d'Epaignes, a minor Norman landowner who profited massively from the conquest of England to become by 1086 a tenant-in-chief in five English counties, but who nonetheless made a grant of one hundred shillings to the Norman abbey of Saint-Pierre de Préaux to enable his body to be brought back to Préaux for burial should he die overseas (that is, presumably, in England).[57] For others, a new cross-Channel life might have provided release from unwelcome constraints. A letter of St Anselm mentions a monk of Le Bec who had to be prohibited from drinking with the locals in taverns at St Neots and the careful arrangements for maintaining monastic discipline that Anselm did his best to put in place to put a stop to his socializing.[58] Here we might think was either someone who had no difficulty whatsoever integrating into new surroundings or someone for whom the move away from familiar places brought on a sustained bout of inappropriate displacement activity.

It is ultimately easy to construct a case for the creation of empire having been problematic for some, perhaps many, among the victors. The so-called Penitential Ordinance and the complaints of wives left behind in Normandy mentioned by Orderic show this clearly; also, although the comment is rather unspecific, Orderic did write that ill-fortune held victors and vanquished in its grip.[59] The competition for reward and, for the scrupulous, anxieties about the consequences for the fate of their souls must have fuelled the sense of trauma that afflicted many. According to William of Malmesbury, Roger de Beaumont, one of the greatest magnates of the Conquest generation, whom Malmesbury thought to be a man with old-fashioned

---

[55] Serlo of Bayeux, *Quae monachi quaerunt*, in *The Anglo-Latin Satirical Poets and Epigrammists of the Twelfth Century*, 2 vols, ed. T. H. Wright, Rolls Series (London, 1872), ii, 207. For the attribution of the poem to Serlo, A. Boutemy, 'Deux poèmes inconnus de Serlon de Bayeux et une copie nouvelle de son poème contre les moines de Caen', *Le Moyen Age*, xlviii (1938), 241–69, and esp. at 260–9.

[56] *Cartularium Abbathiae de Whiteby*, ed. J. C. Atkinson, 2 vols, Surtees Society, lxix, lxii (1879–81), i, 1–2. For Reinfrid's life and significance, Janet Burton, *The Monastic Order in Yorkshire, 1069–1215* (Cambridge, 1999), 13–14, 32–9.

[57] *Le Cartulaire de Saint-Pierre-de-Préaux*, 19–21 (A11).

[58] *Sancti Anselmi Opera Omnia*, ed. F. S. Schmitt, 6 vols (Edinburgh, 1938–51), iii, no. 96; Marjorie Chibnall, 'The Relations of Saint Anselm with the English Dependencies of the Abbey of Bec, 1079–1093', *Spicilegium Beccense I. Le Bec-Hellouin and Paris, 1959*, 521–30, at 526–7 (reprinted in *Piety, Power and History in Medieval England and Normandy* (Aldershot, 2000), Chap. 9).

[59] *Councils and Synods, with Other Documents Relating to the English Church, I: A.D. 871–1204*, ed. D. Whitelock, M. Brett, and C. N. L. Brooke, 2 vols (Oxford, 1981), I, pt. ii, 581–4; OV, ii, 218–21 (*Aduersa fortuna miseros tam uictos quam uictores muscipula sua irretituit*).

principles, refused land in England on moral grounds; however his reticence is actually to be explained, there is no doubt that, while remaining influential with William the Conqueror after 1066, he did not receive the landed estates that might have been anticipated from his political prominence.[60] And there is the story of the monk Guitmund who, if Orderic is to be believed, lectured the Conqueror that England represented the spoils of robbery, before departing for a career in southern Italy that culminated in appointment to the bishopric of Aversa.[61] Problems for some, opportunities for others, the universal themes of the history of empires.

The number of northern French who obtained land and wealth in the British Isles after 1066 cannot be accurately estimated. Katharine Keats-Rohan's *Domesday People* includes the names of slightly fewer than two thousand landholders from northern France.[62] Given that Domesday Book deals only with the topmost elite and that names are concealed or difficult to isolate, the overall total must be higher; a multiplier needs to take account not just of the many unnamed *milites* and clergy in Domesday Book (around four hundred of the former according to Donald Fleming, with many appropriate caveats), but also women and children and the complexities of various forms of social mobility; John Palmer has suggested that the total of landholders for Domesday England may be close to eight thousand, to which a further multiplier then presumably needs to be applied.[63] Since the two earliest plausible population estimates for Normandy derive from late-twelfth- and early-thirteenth-century sources and produce figures for the duchy's population between limits of three-quarters of a million and one-and-a-half million, they can only be regarded as the broadest of interpretative guidelines. Taken alongside the certainty of steady population growth across the eleventh and twelfth centuries, they do, however, at least make the point that the vast majority of the inhabitants of Normandy did not cross the Channel in the decades after 1066.[64]

Whatever the numbers involved, we immediately must confront the question of what the consequences of such major change in personal circumstances was for individuals who had obtained land in England. A new cross-Channel lifestyle? Or a permanent move to a new home? Or something in-between? Although we rarely have evidence as explicit as the autobiographical material supplied by Orderic, we can make considerable progress in establishing other narratives. One route is to point out that, where they exist, studies of the patterns of enfeoffment on the largest

---

[60] *GR*, i, 736–7. For the argument that Roger's cross-Channel lands were more extensive than is immediately apparent from Domesday Book, see David Crouch, *The Beaumont Twins: The Roots and Branches of Power in the Twelfth Century* (Cambridge, 1986), 10 n. 33, 116–19.

[61] OV, ii, 270–81.

[62] *DP*, 23–4.

[63] Donald F. Fleming, 'Landholding by *milites* in Domesday Book: a Revision', *ANS*, xiii (1991), 83–98, at 87; Palmer, 'Wealth', 286.

[64] Lucien Musset, 'Essai sur le peuplement de la Normandie (VIe–XIIe siècle)', in Lucien Musset, *Nordica et Normannica: Recueil d'études sur la Scandinavie ancienne et médiévale, les expéditions des Vikings et la fondation de la Normandie* (Paris, 1997), 389–402, at 401–2; John Gillingham, *The Angevin Empire*, 2nd edn. (London, 2001), 59–60.

Domesday honours suggest that only a small elite of subtenants acquired possessions across the whole of the biggest estates.[65] These individuals were undoubtedly likely to travel and to be expected to be cross-Channel commuters. When, however, we turn to those of lesser wealth and status, a regional and local concentration of landholding was certainly a norm in England from immediately after 1066. And when we come to the unnamed *milites* of Domesday Book and their successors, the warriors who were the bedrock of the power of the conquerors, it is arguably reasonable to assume that many settled permanently in England, except when military responsibilities required otherwise; in other words, that they acquired a new local identity in England, but were also participants in empire and, for this reason alone, their 'Englishness' is of a qualified kind.

The names of the jurors who appear in the so-called 'satellites' of Domesday Book, although a limited set of evidence, demonstrate that the majority of lower status male settlers mentioned had adopted English toponyms before 1086— Geoffrey of Chelsfield, to choose a name at random, illustrates this—and that the scale of their landholdings was roughly the same as their pre-1066 English counterparts.[66] Many of the secular clergy who became members of the cathedral chapters of the English kingdom presumably also settled almost permanently on this side of the Channel; the historian Henry of Huntingdon and the mixed marriage of his parents illustrates this point very well.[67] That there is a contrast with the ratio of French to English toponyms in use at the level of the more powerful, which is heavily tilted in favour of a French usage, is, of course, very important. They, it would appear, wished to sustain a memory of their Norman and French past and their continuing present connections; we seem to be in the presence of some kind of indicator of how each individual located themselves within the world of the cross-Channel empire.[68]

However, for all that this might seem to be evidence of apparent early integration of the less elevated into new places and societies, there are lives accessible to us that show how politics, war, and attendance on an itinerant lord kept many such individuals involved in the life of the cross-Channel empire, there being several relevant stories in the *Historia* of the abbey of Abingdon. Thus, William of Seacourt, son of a man who fell foul of William Rufus, and of a woman who, after outliving her husband, became one of the mistresses of the future King Henry I, in due course both suffered and profited from the wider world of empire, since Henry's

---

[65] J. F. A. Mason, 'Barons and Their Officials in the Later Eleventh Century', *ANS*, xiii (1991), 243–62, at 249–53; Richard Mortimer, 'The Beginnings of the Honour of Clare', *ANS*, iii (1981), 119–41, 220–1, at 135–7; Green, *Aristocracy*, 160–9, while noting that 'the tenurial geography of honours is not a subject that has attracted much attention from historians' (p. 168). The complexities of the subject of locality and mobility are surveyed in David Crouch, *The Birth of Nobility: Constructing Aristocracy in England and France, 900–1300* (Harlow, 2005), 279–302, although with a different analytical framework from mine.

[66] C. P. Lewis, 'The Domesday Jurors', *HSJ*, v (1993), 17–45, and see esp. 20–1, 23–5.

[67] Henry's self-identity is discussed further later in this chapter.

[68] Of fundamental importance here is J. C. Holt, *What's in a Name? Family Nomenclature and the Norman Conquest*, Stenton Lecture, University of Reading (1981), 6–9, 12–16, 20–3 (*Colonial England*, 179–96, at 180–3, 186–8, 193–6).

favour enabled him not only to regain status, but to recover more land than he was strictly speaking entitled to; yet at the same time, other records show him in his local role as a functioning tenant of the abbey at the shire court.[69] His story shows that it is entirely justifiable to think that local and regional communities formed the framework within which many lives were lived in the new society of post-Conquest England. But it also indicates that we cannot exclude the wider world of empire from such individuals' lives. It has also shown that identity can rarely be reduced to something as simple as Norman or English, a point encapsulated in Katharine Keats-Rohan's comments that 'in general, it seems that the use of a literary descriptor is an invitation to consider the personal history of its bearer' and that 'there are insuperable difficulties in trying to establish what lies behind such labels'.[70] To this, I would add that the same can be said of a toponym, but that the examples in this paragraph indicate how the construction of multiple life-stories can sometimes overcome the 'apparently insuperable difficulties'.

By the same token, the fact that the vast majority of the population of Normandy did not obtain lands in the British Isles does not mean that they could not become active participants in empire. It was, as we shall see, quite possible to live in Rouen and make a fortune from business in England.[71] And the labourer who worked the stone in the quarries in Caen was an unquestioned participant in empire alongside the entrepreneurs who organized the carrying of the stone to England. The only survivor of the wreck of the White Ship, Beroul of Rouen, was a butcher who was crossing the Channel to collect debts accruing from selling meat on credit, a tradesman with an investment in empire.[72] There is enough material in these life-stories to set in train the arguments that the cross-Channel dynamic was a constant in the decades after 1066 for many more people than the members of the well-known aristocratic elites.

The same point about a continuing dynamic and the existence of a structural framework to sustain it can be made about the relationship between the northern and southern lands ruled by the Normans. Thus, in the case of the family of Ralph the Red de Pont-Echanfray, who was effectively one of the commanders of Henry I's military household and who died in the wreck of the White Ship, and about whose life we are well-informed by Orderic, there is both involvement in the affairs of the south across generations and evidence of the way in which resources were deployed to support the participation of individuals across the diaspora.[73] A participant in Bohemond's disastrous 1107 Durazzo campaign,

---

[69] *Historia Ecclesie Abbendonensis*, lxii–lxiii, 52–5; David Crouch, 'Robert of Gloucester's Mother and Sexual Politics in Norman Oxfordshire', *HR*, lxxii (1999), 323–33, at 329–31.
[70] *DP*, 41.
[71] Several sections of Chap. 5 illustrate this point.
[72] *Roman de Rou*, 314–15, ll. 10197–200.
[73] For Ralph's career, Chibnall, 'Mercenaries and the *Familia Regis* under Henry I', *History*, lxii (1977), 15–23, at 16–17 (reprinted in Strickland (ed.), *Anglo-Norman Warfare*, 85–6).

Ralph subsequently went on to Constantinople and Jerusalem, in all probability entering the service of the Byzantine emperor for a while; it was presumably Bohemond who put up the money that enabled him to take part in the Durazzo campaign. That his wife travelled with him indicates the possibility that they were contemplating making a new life in the south. And, in all likelihood, his father at some point had fought for Robert Guiscard, before returning home to Normandy.[74]

Among other stories that illustrate the same theme is Orderic's scathing denunciation of Robert de Montfort, who also joined the Durazzo campaign, and who, for Orderic, was a man of whom no good could be said, because he believed that he had betrayed both Henry I and Bohemond. What is, however, striking is that Bohemond immediately gave Robert a prominent military position in his army because of his standing in the north.[75] Another notable phenomenon is the way in which relatively impoverished individuals could recruit sizeable military retinues to fight in the wars in southern Europe. Thus, the last survivor of the Old English line, Edgar the Ætheling, a man of great prestige but little landed wealth, could recruit a force of two hundred knights to travel with him to Apulia in 1086 and Robert Bordet, a minor Norman landowner, was able in the 1120s to recruit forces in Normandy to build up and defend a small principality at Tarragona in Catalonia.[76] The remainder of the twelfth century has many stories of individuals from the north who made careers in the south.[77] The south indeed was over decades a source of wealth on which the north drew directly, with, for example, in the eleventh century, two bishops, Geoffrey of Coutances (1048–93) and Ivo of Sées ($c.$1035–$c.$1070), obtaining funds there to finance the re-building of their cathedrals, and Duke Robert Curthose, through his marriage to Sybil of Conversano, acquiring sufficient money to pay off the loan he had taken from his brother King William Rufus to fund his participation in the First Crusade. And the number of northern European churchmen, from Saint-Evroult's turbulent abbot Robert de Grandmesnil (1059–61), who became abbot of the monastery of St Eufemia in Calabria, to Richard 'Palmer' and Herbert of Middlesex appointed to the bishoprics of Syracuse and Conza in 1157 and 1169, respectively, who made successful careers in the south is considerable. The historian Geoffrey Malaterra was even recruited from the north in the late eleventh century to write a history to describe and justify the life of Roger the Great Count and, specifically, his conquest of Sicily.[78] All this, like the story of Payn Peverel mentioned earlier, shows both the enduring dynamic

---

[74] OV, vi, 102–5. For Ralph, son of Walchelin, OV, ii, 30–1; for the suggestion that he was Ralph the Red's father, OV, vi, 71 n. 7.

[75] OV, vi, 100–1.

[76] JW, iii, 44–5. For Robert and others, OV, vi, 402–5; L. J. McCrank, 'Norman crusaders in the Catalan Reconquest', *JMH*, vii (1981), 67–82; Kathleen Thompson, *Power and Border Lordship in Medieval France: the County of Perche, 1000–1226*, Royal Historical Society Studies in History (Woodbridge, 2002), 73–4.

[77] For general surveys, Ralph V. Turner, 'Les contacts entre l'Angleterre normanno-angevine et la Sicile normande', *Etudes normandes*, no. 3 (1986), 39–55; G. A. Loud, 'The Kingdom of Sicily and the Kingdom of England, 1066–1266', *History*, lxxxviii (2003), 540–67, at 545–63.

[78] Most recently, Marie-Agnès Lucas-Avenel, 'Le récit de Geoffroi Malaterra ou la légitimation de Roger, Grand Comte de Sicile', *ANS*, xxxiv (2012), 169–92, at 170–6.

of activity across the Norman worlds and the existence of a mental infrastructure that facilitated movement and migration, a factor of absolutely central importance to the histories of power and identity.

A multiplicity of social and cultural forces other than ethnicity constituted the predominant influences in many situations. The *Life* of Christina of Markyate shows its heroine's English aunt's role as the concubine of the Norman Bishop Rannulf of Durham and how it benefitted the family. Christina's resistance to Rannulf's sexual advances immediately and entirely reasonably suggest imperial exploitation that was both gendered and sexual, but class and masculinity are every bit as persuasive a framework of interpretation.[79] Liaisons between men of higher social status and women of lower status were commonplace throughout the eleventh- and twelfth-century West, and not just a feature of the conquest of England.[80] The *Vita* also shows that Christina, who became the spiritual counsellor of Abbot Geoffrey of St Albans, was bilingual in English and French by her mid-teens and that, taking account of the suggestion that she might join one of the two great French religious houses of Marcigni-sur-Loire or Fontevrault, she was well integrated into the Franco-Norman world that the Conquest had brought to England.[81] Another religious life about which we are well informed, that of the nun of Wilton and anchoress Eva, to whom Goscelin of Saint-Bertin addressed his *Liber Confortatorius*, also epitomizes many aspects of the new world. In the first place, it is important that Goscelin describes her as 'the well-born daughter of a Danish father and a Lotharingian mother who turned out English', because it shows how, in this author's mind, it was place, rather than descent, that determined identity. And secondly, it is notable that Eva eventually left Wilton to live for many years a strict religious life near Angers. Again, therefore, apparent identity is no guide to how this particular cross-Channel life would actually be lived; mobility and movement are aspects of this life-story that make it notably diverse.[82]

The remarkable life of the Welsh princess Nest makes many points about relations between men and women in the context of the Welsh marches and about the creation of trans-ethnic networks across the core and peripheries of

---

[79] *The Life of Christina of Markyate: A Twelfth Century Recluse*, ed. and trans. C. H. Talbot (Oxford, 1959; reprinted, OMT, 1987), 40–7; *Vie de Christina de Markyate*, ed. and trans. Paulette L'Hermite-Leclercq and Anne-Marie Legras, 2 vols, Sources d'histoire médiévale, 35 (Paris, 2007), 80–5.

[80] William the Conqueror's mother's family and Henry I's many mistresses supply obvious examples of this. For the latter, see Kathleen Thompson, 'Affairs of State: The Illegitimate Children of Henry I', *JMH*, xxix (2003), 129–51; Green, *Henry I*, 27.

[81] *The Life of Christina*, 126–7; *Vie de Christina*, 150–1; cf, R. I. Moore, 'Ranulf Flambard and Christina of Markyate', in Samuel Fanous and Henrietta Leyser (eds), *Christina of Markyate: A Twelfth-Century Holy Woman* (London and New York, 2005), 138–42.

[82] *The Liber Confortatorius of Goscelin of Saint Bertin*, ed. C. H. Talbot, in *Analecta Monastica: textes et études sur la vie des moines au moyen âge*, ed. M. M. Lebreton et al. (Rome, 1955), 41 (Goscelin of St Bertin, *The Book of Encouragement and Consolation (Liber confortatorius)*, trans. Monika Otter (Cambridge, 2004), 42).

empire.[83] Daughter of Rhys ap Tewdwr, king of Deheubarth (d.1093), she in all probability spent her adolescence and early adulthood in the households of nobles who had defeated and killed her father and overrun his kingdom. That she became one of Henry I's mistresses and bore a child by him ensured that she had a supporter at the highest possible level. In due course she married the Norman castellan of Pembroke Gerald of Windsor and, after him, Stephen, constable of Ceredigion, and Hait, sheriff of Pembroke, in all probability producing a further nine children. She was, on one standard of values, the ultimate peace-weaver in that volatile part of the world and a key figure in the creation of a new society and new relationships there; one of her grandchildren, the historian and polemicist Gerald of Wales, noted that as a result of her life almost all the major families of west Wales were related to one another. The pressures and possibilities of the world she inhabited were multiple; once more we see the interaction of the local, the regional, and the imperial, except this time at the periphery. Nest's story is also the first mention in this book of a social norm of the greatest importance to the history of the Normans and empire, the marriage alliance across political boundaries, organized to consolidate friendship, but usually with unforeseeable consequences.

Treated as a set of monastic norms and rules, the Rule of St Benedict constituted a significant qualification to the hegemonic power of empire. Thus, the recalcitrant English monk Osbern was despatched from Canterbury to Le Bec by Lanfranc to mend his ways under Anselm's tutelage, and seemingly earning the future archbishop's friendship and respect, with Jay Rubinstein concluding that:

> instead of a rebel, we see only a monk with wide-ranging interests and with an inflated sense of his own importance.... We do not see a monk intent on preserving within his community a peculiarly Anglo-Saxon identity. In fact, based on his almost complete silence on the subject of the Norman Conquest, Osbern seems not to have realised that the Anglo-Saxon world had ended.[84]

The life-history of Herman of Bury St Edmunds is that of a pre-1066 immigrant from France to England, who saw service for the Norman bishop of Thetford Herfast (1070–84), before becoming a monk of Bury St Edmunds and undertaking in the 1090s the task of updating the record of the miracles of St Edmund. Yet for all his association with some of the greater figures of the new empire, Herman's sympathies manifestly lay with the defeated; for him, King Harold was a devout and

---

[83] For Nest's life, Kari Maund, *Princess Nest of Wales: Seductress of the English* (Stroud, 2007), esp. 83–118, 119–54; Susan M. Johns, 'Nest of Deheubarth: Reading Female Power in the Historiography of Wales', in Janet L. Nelson, Susan Reynolds, and Susan M. Johns (eds), *Gender and Historiography: Studies in the History of the Earlier Middle Ages in Honour of Pauline Stafford* (London, 2012), 91–100, at 91–4, 100. See, also, David Crouch, 'Nest (*b*. before 1092, *d.c.*1130)', *ODNB*; I. W. Rowlands, 'The Making of the March: Aspects of the Norman Settlement in Dyfed', *ANS*, iii (1981), 142–57.

[84] Jay Rubinstein, 'The Life and Writings of Osbern of Canterbury', in Richard Eales and Richard Sharpe (eds), *Canterbury and the Norman Conquest: Churches, Saints and Scholars, 1066–1109* (London, 1995), 27–40, with the quotation at p. 40.

honourable man and the Normans were greedy.[85] He also became a participant in the process that made the last king of the East Angles into a cross-Channel saint.[86]

The ultimate narrative of this kind is the celebrated case of Eadmer of Canterbury, an English fellow monk of Osbern's, and the source, in his description of the appointments to abbacies made by Henry I in 1114, of one of the best known of all statements that the English were being treated as an inferior people.[87] Yet Eadmer was also the devoted disciple and biographer of Archbishop Anselm (1093–1109) and an admirer, with some qualifications, of his predecessor Lanfranc. Here was an Englishman whose devoted service to his archbishop took him to many of the distant points of the Norman diaspora, to the extent that he witnessed the employment of Moslem troops by the conqueror of Sicily, Roger the Great Count, and, in old age, spent a short, unhappy period as bishop-elect of St Andrews. The dominant loyalties discernible in Eadmer's life are surely the personal one to Anselm and the institutional one to the traditions of Canterbury. However his life is interpreted, we see in it the complexity of one individual's personal identity, as well as a profound integration into the new world that transcended national boundaries.[88]

The English monks of Glastonbury murdered for failing to chant as their Norman abbot wished and the subsequent banishment of the delinquent abbot to Normandy are manifest signs that ethnic tensions were transferred into the cloister. Yet Abbot Thurstan's exile to Normandy is also a demonstration that extreme behaviour of this kind would not be tolerated by the new regime. And even here, at least according to William of Malmesbury, the situation was not entirely straightforward, since the zealot Abbot Thurstan was not only able to make his way back into his abbatial office by exploiting William Rufus's need for money, but is finally described by Malmesbury in terms of glowing personal virtue. Furthermore, when the general implications of the situation are explored, it turns out that, for all Thurstan's attempt at innovation, in many other places the history of chant is one of English survival and therefore of accommodations between newcomers and an existing community.[89] The history of script and book production also produces a story of changed communities working out new, mostly harmonious lives, even if disrupted at times over several decades by the transfer of precious books across the Channel to France; Teresa Webber, for example, in a study of the Canterbury *scriptorium* has observed that 'there was no politics of script', and Richard Gameson that 'it is debateable to what extent the changes that started to overtake English

---

[85] Tom Licence, 'History and Hagiography in the Late Eleventh Century: The Life and Work of Herman the Archdeacon, Monk of Bury St Edmunds', *EHR*, cxxiv (2009), 516–44, at 518–27, 532–3.

[86] This theme is discussed further later in this chapter and in Chap. 4 .

[87] Eadmer, *Historia Nouorum in Anglia*, ed. Martin Rule, Rolls Series (London, 1884), 224.

[88] The large literature is summed up in R. W. Southern, *Saint Anselm and his Biographer* (Cambridge, 1963), 229–40, 309–13; J. C. Rubinstein, 'Eadmer (Edmer) of Canterbury', *ODNB*.

[89] *The Early History of Glastonbury: An Edition, Translation and Study of William of Malmesbury's 'De Antiquitate Glastonie Ecclesie'*, ed. John Scott (Woodbridge, 1981), 156–9 (*Emulemur in eo feruorem religionis, non nullam pietatem in Deo, multam prudenciam in seculo*); see further, David Hiley, 'Thurstan of Caen and Plainchant at Glastonbury: Musicological Reflections on the Norman Conquest', *PBA*, lxxii (1986), 57–90.

book collections represented "normanisation" as opposed to simply moving with the times'.[90] St Anselm's advice to a new Norman abbot of an English monastery that he need not learn English, but could get by in French with the accompaniment of appropriate displays of holiness, is surely a barely veiled suggestion that the man would be better off learning English; that the advice was sought certainly demonstrates the pressures that the migrant monk was feeling.[91]

On a very different tack, we have a story that indicates how descendants of the newcomers took on a political identity that placed them firmly within the ideological framework of their adopted land. Thus, when the citizens of London—many of whom must have been immigrants from northern France, or descended from immigrants—found themselves negotiating with the Empress Matilda during the brief period in 1141 when her cause appeared to have triumphed, they announced they had no wish to live under the oppressive laws of the time of her father, King Henry I, but wished to have restored the excellent laws of King Edward's time.[92] There can be few better explicit examples of participants in a diaspora and an empire becoming totally absorbed into the legal culture of the land in which they had settled. All points to a multilayered world in which multiple factors played their part in determining how individual lives were lived, and to one in which the cross-Channel world of empire was a constant presence.

Networks were also developed southwards from Normandy. The story of the Dastin family, a kin group who scarcely appear in the sources at all, except that one of their number was made abbot of the abbey of Saint-Pierre de la Couture at Le Mans by William the Conqueror in 1075, following which his family made grants of land in the Avranchin to the abbey, is indicative of attempts to consolidate further networks of interests linking Maine and south-western Normandy, something that already existed within the patronage networks of the abbey of Le Mont Saint-Michel.[93] Orderic's story of how Samson, royal chaplain, treasurer, and archdeacon of Bayeux, and later bishop of Worcester, successfully refused the offer of the bishopric of Le Mans in 1081 provides evidence of an attempt to create networks at a higher social level. Since Samson has a reputation as a worldly man, Orderic's comments about his humility may be misplaced; his actions look like those of someone who knew a hot spot and decided not to go there. It is

---

[90] Teresa Webber, 'Script and Manuscript Production at Christ Church, Canterbury, after the Norman Conquest', in Eales and Sharpe (eds), *Canterbury and the Norman Conquest*, 145–58 at 156; Richard Gameson, *The Manuscripts of Early Norman England (c.1066–1130)*, British Academy Postdoctoral Fellowship Monograph (Oxford, 1999), 6.

[91] *Sancti Anselmi Opera Omnia*, iii, *ep.* 80 (trans. Fröhlich. *Letters*, i, 211–13); cit., Richard Sharpe, 'Peoples and Languages in Eleventh- and Twelfth-Century Britain and Ireland: Reading the Charter Evidence', in Dauvit Broun et al., *The Reality behind Charter Diplomatic in Anglo-Norman Britain* (Glasgow, 2011), 1–119, at 2–3.

[92] JW, iii, 296–7.

[93] Jean-Michel Bouvris, 'Pour une étude prosopographique des familles nobles d'importance moyenne en Normandie au XIe siècle: l'exemple du lignage des Dastin', *Revue de l'Avranchin et du Pays de Granville*, lxi (1984), 65–101, at 68–75. On networks linking Le Mont Saint-Michel with Maine and Brittany that evolved during the tenth and eleventh centuries, see esp. *The Cartulary of the Abbey of Mont-Saint-Michel*, ed. K. S. B. Keats-Rohan (Donnington, 2006), *passim*.

notable how Samson's refusal was followed by a reversion to a traditional pattern of appointing a member of the cathedral chapter of Le Mans, Bishop Hoel.[94] Many links and networks did exist between Normandy (especially southern Normandy) and Maine and the Loire valley, but they tend to be regional and were often less than fully integrated into those that bound Normandy and England together. That this conclusion is confirmed by architectural and literary evidence makes it all the stronger.[95]

Orderic's story, later narrated in somewhat different form by Wace, about the citizens of Caen in 1105 expelling Robert Curthose's castellan and surrendering without any resistance to the advancing army of King Henry I, is a most precious insight into values and opinions within Normandy. Since Henry had just burnt and sacked Bayeux, the act of pragmatic submission made undoubted sense. Henry then followed up with an acknowledgement of its usefulness by the grant of a valuable English manor, an act that, within the arguments being developed in this book, must surely be thought of as akin to a preconditioned reflex.[96] Yet Orderic, writing in the 1130s, noted that the manor had ever since been known as the 'Traitors' Manor' (*uilla traditorum*) and that it was no longer in the citizens' possession.[97] Wace's version is even more dramatic. Not only does he name the four citizens who had made the deal, he tells us that the place near the church of St Martin (destroyed in 1796) where the decision to surrender was taken had become barren ground; nothing had ever grown there thereafter, something that he regarded as a miracle, a display of God's displeasure at covetousness and treachery.[98] What is being denounced here is, on one standard of values, the ultimate and unforgiveable act of betrayal, the abandonment of one's lord, namely Duke Robert Curthose. Pragmatism had won out—and on humanitarian grounds we might think justifiably so—but cowardice and disloyalty were what were remembered.

In its two versions, this story brings to the surface the powerful undercurrents that flowed in twelfth-century Normandy. An expression of their strength can surely be found in the support given at various times against Henry I to Duke Robert Curthose's son William Clito until his death in 1128. Thus, Orderic, while being committed to justifying Henry I's invasion of Normandy on the grounds that it brought peace, describes them as being so powerful that Henry could not trust even those who were supposedly fighting for him, throwing in the standard

---

[94] OV, ii, xxxviii, 300–3; Yannick Hillion, 'Arnaud et Hoël, deux évêques du Mans au service de Guillaume le Conquérant', *Annales de Bretagne et des pays de l'Ouest*, cx (2003), 49–77, at 61–8.

[95] Lindy Grant, 'Les relations culturelles et artistiques entre le sud-ouest de la Normandie et le Maine autour de 1106', in *Tinchebray*, 235–47. This theme is discussed further in Chaps. 3 and 4.

[96] For Henry rewarding supporters with English lands after Tinchebray, Judith Green, 'La bataille de Tinchebray: un tournant dans l'histoire de la Normandie et de l'Angleterre', in *Tinchebray*, 47–60, at 48–9.

[97] OV, vi, 78–9; Charity Urbanski, 'Apology, Protest and Suppression: Interpreting the Surrender of Caen (1105)', *HSJ*, xix (2008, for 2007), 137–53.

[98] *Roman de Rou*, 336–7, ll. 11285–308. For barren ground, Jean-Claude Schmitt, *The Holy Greyhound: Guinefort, Healer of Children since the Thirteenth Century* (Cambridge, 1983), 64–5. For the site at which the surrender took place, Laurence Jean-Marie, *Caen aux XIe et XIIe siècles: espace urbain, pouvoirs et société* (Cormeilles-le-Royal, 2000), 23, 52–3, 214.

expressions about war between kinsmen being more than civil war. And in the mid-twelfth century, the author of the Warenne Chronicle commented that this opposition resembled a fire that could never be put out, with John of Salisbury doing the same by drawing attention to the depth of memory of these events among the inhabitants of Normandy.[99] It is notable, too, that the text known as the *Brevis Relatio*, of which the first version dates from between 1114 and 1120, described by its recent editor as 'written from a Norman perspective' and in general notably favourable to Henry I, clearly departs from its theme to say that Henry besieged Bayeux and destroyed most of it (*fere omnem destruxit*).[100] A contemporary and a resident of Bayeux, the poet Serlo described the sack in movingly graphic terms and opined that, in failing to fight against Henry's multi-ethnic army, the Normans who had once honourably subdued England, Apulia, Calabria, and Le Mans had become trash, unworthy of the great achievements of their ancestors.[101]

That there was a sense of a shared corporate identity among those living exclusively or primarily in Normandy that could run against any notion of a monolithic empire is also demonstrated by the decision to invite Theobald, count of Blois-Chartres, to become duke after Henry I's death at the meeting held at Le Neubourg, and Robert of Torigni's statement, written before 1139 and therefore in context a very precocious partisan declaration, that the Empress Matilda's sons were the true heirs of Henry I, an argument that he in part constructed in imperial terms by mentioning their descent from the Old English kings.[102] An anecdote that feels as if it expresses a regional Norman patriotic solidarity is Orderic's comment that there was support for Eustace de Breteuil in the disputed succession to the honour after William de Breteuil's death on 12 January 1103 on the grounds that the Normans preferred one of their own who was illegitimate to a legitimate Burgundian or Breton.[103] Local and regional identity on both sides of the Channel can thus be shown to have been significant forces in the life of the cross-Channel empire from the very beginning. But they could not exist in complete autonomy from the hard and soft power of the imperial elite who could at times intervene both violently and persuasively.

The story with which this section of this chapter must move towards its conclusion is the tale of personal commitment of Matilda of Wallingford, crossing

---

[99] OV, vi, 200–3; *The Warenne (Hyde) Chronicle*, ed. Elisabeth M. C. van Houts and Rosalind C. Love, OMT (Oxford, 2013), 54–5; *Ioannis Saresberiensis episcopi Carnotensis Policratici sive de Nugis Curialium et Uestigiis Philosophorum Libri VIII*, ed. C. C. I. Webb, 2 vols (Oxford, 1909), ii, 614; Judith A. Green, 'King Henry I and the Aristocracy of Normandy', in *La 'France Anglaise' au Moyen Age: actes du 111ᵉ congrès national des sociétés savantes* (Paris, 1988), 161–73, at 162–5.
[100] 'The *Brevis Relatio de Guillelmo nobilissimo comite Normannorum* written by a Monk of Battle Abbey', ed. Elisabeth M. C. van Houts, *Camden Miscellany*, 5th. ser., x (Cambridge, 1997) (*History and Family Traditions*, Chap. 7), 23, 38.
[101] 'Versus Serlonis de capta Bajocensium', in *Anglo-Latin Satirical Poets*, ed. Wright, ii, 244, 245. I have made use of a translation of the poem prepared by Moreed Arbabzadah for Elisabeth van Houts.
[102] *GND*, ii, 240–3.   [103] OV, vi, 40–1.

the Channel from England to the abbey of Le Bec in either 1150 or 1151 and confirming the grant of Ogbourne St. Andrew and Ogbourne St. George in Berkshire to the abbey in the presence of the Empress Matilda and her son Henry, already duke of Normandy, but otherwise uncertain of his future. Like the Montebourg charter used as a case study in the first chapter, this history confirms, but does so much more explicitly, the deep-seated expectation in its subjects' minds that the cross-Channel empire would continue once the civil war had been resolved. This is because she must have made her journey after the death of her husband, Brian fitz Count, and shortly before she herself retired to a nunnery, in all probability to die; it has a sequel in that soon afterwards, but still in 1151, presumably after her death, a Master Benedict again travelled to Normandy and met with the Empress and Henry at Notre-Dame-du-Pré, a priory of Le Bec near Rouen, and asked them to confirm the foundation of a house of regular canons authorized by Brian and Matilda at Wallingford.[104]

A Breton who had benefited from Henry I's patronage, Brian's unwavering commitment to the Empress's cause throughout the civil war is well known; the actions of what were surely his and his wife's last days must show the outcome that they had always been committed to and which they hoped would be fulfilled in the person of the young Henry; that the Empress and her son were always present to greet the family and their representatives shows the personal side of political alliances. Out of such commitment are empires made and continued, it might be remarked. But Brian's Breton origins and his promotion in Henry I's reign also show the empire's continuing dynamism after 1100 and its continuing magnetic pull—readily definable as soft power—on people based far beyond the territorial limits of Normandy and England. This history also shows the power over minds that could be exerted by a great Norman abbey such as Le Bec, closely associated with Matilda's first husband, Miles Crispin, who had died in 1107, and the place where the Empress had long before announced that she wished to be buried.[105] And it indicates again the importance of women as agents and consolidators of networks and family memory.[106] It is finally impossible not to suggest that the then prior of Le Bec, one Robert of Torigni, ought to have lurked somewhere in the background of these transactions, even if nowhere is he mentioned in the sources.[107]

One last story is of a capable and, arguably, less scrupulous man, Earl Robert of Leicester, one of the most celebrated and politically skilful of the great twelfth-century cross-Channel magnates, who in 1155 founded a priory of Fontevrauldine nuns at Nuneaton in Warwickshire, thereby patronizing liberally a famous religious

---

[104] For the story, K. S. B. Keats-Rohan, 'The Devolution of the Honour of Wallingford, 1066–1148', *Oxoniensia*, liv (1989), 311–18, at 315–16. For the charters, *RRAN*, iii, nos. 80 (*Select Documents of the English Lands of the Abbey of Bec*, ed. Marjorie Chibnall, Camden, 3rd ser., lxxiii (1951), no. XLVIII), 88. See, also, Edmund King, 'Brian fitz Count (*c*.1090–*c*.1149)', *ODNB*.

[105] *GND*, ii, 246–7.

[106] See the discussion of the Reviers family and the abbey of Montebourg in Chap. 1 for this theme.

[107] For Robert, see later in this chapter.

order whose greatest patrons were the counts of Anjou. Although no document connected with the foundation says as much, it is hard not to see the foundation as motivated by the politics of the moment. It also expanded an interest in Fontevrault on Earl Robert's part that already existed in Normandy. On these terms, it was yet another manifestation in a new context of the continuing dynamic creation of networks across imperial space that had started in the immediate aftermath of 1066.[108] What the future would hold was, of course, an open question.

THE HISTORIANS OF EMPIRE

The great eleventh- and twelfth-century historians of the cross-Channel empire rightly have been, and rightly remain, profoundly influential on the way we interpret its history. Yet, as has already been illustrated in the case of Orderic Vitalis, their testimony embodies personal and inherited ethical and literary values that, to a greater or lesser extent, determined what they wrote. To say that they were not objective is to state the obvious; to recognize how deeply embedded they were in conventions that go back centuries is less often acknowledged. The scale of their activity is of course in European terms both exceptional and quite extraordinary.[109] Together, they constitute our most articulate witnesses to the world of the cross-Channel empire, but—to be provocative—they may not necessarily be our best ones. At the least, they are not voices to be heard in isolation; what they wrote must be treated as being among the many life-stories of empire that are set out in this chapter, and not as being detached from them.

Out of the many passages from these historians that might be taken as the starting point for this discussion, the battle speech that Henry of Huntingdon composed for Ralph, bishop of the Orkneys, addressing the army assembled from northern England before the Battle of the Standard (22 August 1138), is a much studied one that opens up many vistas. It has the bishop harangue 'the noblemen of England, renowned sons of Normandy' (*Proceres Anglie, clarissimi Normannigene*), thereby combining much of the audience's territorial identity with their biological descent. He then credited those whom he was addressing with victories in Apulia, Jerusalem, and Antioch, after which, 'every *Englishman* answered and the hills and mountains echoed, Amen! Amen!'.[110] That a similar formulation appears in Ailred of Rievaulx's version of another speech given before the same battle must surely confirm that what we are dealing with is the partial fusion of the group ethnicity of

---

[108] Crouch, *The Beaumont Twins*, 199, 203–4; Marjorie Chibnall, 'L'ordre de Fontevrault en Angleterre au XIIe siècle', *Cahiers de civilisation médiévale*, xxix (1986), 41–7, at 43; Berenice Kerr, *Religious Life for Women c.1100–c.1350: Fontevraud in England* (Oxford, 1999), 10, 69–70.

[109] That I mostly concentrate on Henry of Huntingdon, William of Malmesbury, Orderic, Robert of Torigni, Wace, Ailred of Rievaulx, the Anglo-Saxon Chronicle, Geffrei Gaimar, and, in an oblique way, Geoffrey of Monmouth is mostly for convenience; the contributions of the likes of Simeon of Durham, John of Worcester, Eadmer, and Goscelin of Saint-Bertin will be mentioned, but usually to illustrate the general points made.

[110] HH, 712–15, 716–17.

the conquerors with that of the land they had occupied and—we might think more surprisingly—of the conquered into the achievements of the conquerors. Although Ailred's account of the battle did use Henry's *Historia* as a source and might be derivative, it is notable that John of Worcester overrides all considerations of ethnicity by describing the victors as 'our men' (*nostri*).[111]

Henry's version of the speech is usually seen as indicating the assimilation of Normans and French in England into a new type of English identity, an acceptable interpretation as long as it is also recognized that the wider issues of empire are also present. The passage indeed makes even more sense if we think of it as portraying both the Norman and English *gentes* as participants in empire and in a wider diaspora that had taken many of its inhabitants to some of the farther corners of the then known world, but then also recognizes that, as peoples, Normans and English were ultimately still clearly distinguishable. The warriors who went out to defeat King David's army may not have thought the speeches either an objective or a universally applicable statement of personal and ethnic identity, but they would, presumably, have found them acceptable representations of some sort of perceived actuality; in short, it is appropriate to think of them as a situational construct with some sort of relationship to the multiple identities in play in the middle of the twelfth century and to the changes that were continuing to take place.[112]

Like Eadmer, Osbern, and Herman, historians who have already been mentioned, and like William of Malmesbury, to whom I will turn later in this chapter, Henry was a historian both profoundly sensitive to the defeats and degradation of the English and an engaged participant in the imperial present who heaped praise on William the Conqueror and Henry I.[113] The son of a Norman named Nicholas, who was appointed to the archdeaconry of Huntingdon by Remigius (1067–92), the first Norman bishop of the huge diocese of Lincoln, and of an English wife whose name is unknown, Henry at first sight seems to have considered himself to be English. This appears to be made clear by his statement of his purpose in writing his *Historia Anglorum* ('The History of the English') as being 'to narrate the history of this kingdom and the origins of *our* people'.[114] Like Orderic, he almost certainly grew up speaking English as his first language; his love of his home went so far as to cause him to wax lyrical on the splendours of Huntingdon and the Fens.[115] What he meant by his Englishness is, however, eminently discussable. He surely epitomizes the point that the malleability of personal identity and the nature of diasporas can make it possible that he was

---

[111] Ailred of Rievaulx, 'Relatio de Standardo', in *Chronicles*, iii, 185–9, 192–3 (for a modern translation, *Aelred of Rievaulx: The Historical Works*, trans. Jane Patricia Freeland and Marsha L. Dutton, Cistercian Fathers Series, no. 56 (Kalamazoo, 2005), 252–7, 261–2); JW, iii, 252–5.

[112] A point well made by D. M. Hadley, 'Ethnicity and Acculturation', in Crick and van Houts (eds), *A Social History of England*, 235–46, at 237–41.

[113] See Chap. 1.

[114] HH, 6–7. For Henry's date of birth and background, HH, xxiii–xxviii. See further, John Gillingham, 'Henry of Huntingdon and the Twelfth-Century Revival of the English Nation', in *The English*, 123–44, and see esp. 126–31; Thomas, *English and Normans*, 63–5, 75, 245–6; Webber, *Norman Identity*, 154–64.

[115] HH, 320–1, 348–9.

expressing a sense of solidarity with the people of the nation he inhabited, that is, of his *patria*, rather than a straightforward statement that he considered himself to be a member of the English *gens*. It is both a statement that integration and assimilation were taking place and one that they most definitely were not. He also provided an unqualified expression of where power actually lay by entitling Book VII of the *Historia*, which covers the period from 1087 to 1135, 'On the Kingdom of the Normans' (*De Regno Normannorum*).[116]

Henry's visit to the abbey of Le Bec in 1139 and his conversation there with the younger historian Robert of Torigni is a pivotal moment in my argument for the continued twelfth-century dynamic of the cross-Channel empire. The visit is well known because, while Henry was at Le Bec, Robert showed him a copy of the recently completed *Historia Regum Britanniae* (or *De Gestis Britonum* as we must now call it) of Geoffrey of Monmouth, one of the most notorious and influential works of 'history' ever written.[117] That Geoffrey's work turned up in Normandy so soon after 'publication' is very important to my argument. Although Orderic knew some of it, specifically some of the prophecies of Merlin, Henry's visit to Le Bec could be the first reference we have to Geoffrey's full work in circulation. While in England, the use made of it by Geffrei Gaimar in perhaps 1136–7 and by Alfred of Beverley in his *Annales*, begun in 1143, does show an effectively contemporary dissemination, its rapid and simultaneous cross-Channel transmission is remarkable, and all the more so because Henry of Huntingdon first encountered it at Le Bec rather than anywhere in England.[118]

As a historian, Robert of Torigni does not arouse the same excitement as most of the others we read; this is probably because he seems to be a simple chronicler who does not include reflective passages of the kind that appear in Huntingdon, Orderic, and William of Malmesbury, and whose Latinity did not compare with theirs.[119] For all his limitations, however, Robert was undoubtedly a consummate man of business, a prior, and an abbot, who, among other things, knew the royal court, turned round a failing abbey, and was a friend of the Empress Matilda.[120] The extensive twelfth-century dissemination of Robert's work shows that it was

---

[116] HH, 412–13. See further, Chaps. 4 and 6.

[117] Henry's visit is mentioned in the letter to Warin; Neil Wright, 'The Place of Henry of Huntingdon's *Epistola ad Warinum* in the Text History of Geoffrey of Monmouth's *Historia regum Britannie*: A Preliminary Investigation', in G. Jondorf and D. N. Dumville (eds), *France and the British Isles in the Middle Ages and the Renaissance: Essays by Members of Girton College, Cambridge, in Memory of Ruth Morgan* (Woodbridge, 1991), 71–113, with the meeting between Henry and Robert discussed at 71–7; HH, 558–9. For the new edition of Geoffrey's history, see Geoffrey of Monmouth, *The History of the Kings of Britain*, ed. Michael D. Reeve and trans. Neil Wright (Woodbridge, 2007), with the discussion of the title at p. lix.

[118] For Geoffrey Gaimar's use of *De Gestis Britonum*, Geffrei Gaimar, *Estoire des Engleis (History of the English)*, ed. and trans. Ian Short (Oxford, 2009), xxxii; for Alfred, R.William Leckie, Jr., *The Passage of Dominion: Geoffrey of Monmouth and the Periodization of Insular History in the Twelfth Century* (Toronto, 1981), 45–6.

[119] For verdicts on Robert's limited literary skills, *GND*, i, xci; Chibnall, *World of Orderic*, 33–4. For Robert's writings in the context of power and identity, Shopkow, *History and Community*, 110–13, 124, 165–7, 235–8, a discussion influenced by opinions that I am now revising: cf. David Bates, 'The Rise and Fall of Normandy, *c.*911–1204', in *England and Normandy*, 19–35, at 31–3.

[120] *GND*, i, xci; Chibnall, *World of Orderic*, 33–4.

widely read and copied. Furthermore, while the surviving manuscripts of Robert's work are mostly from Normandy, both the *Gesta Normannorum Ducum* and the Chronicle were also copied at the abbey of Reading, founded by Henry I as his burial church and therefore one of the great centres of the cross-Channel empire; if the Reading manuscript, whose text ends in 1157, was actually copied at around that time, then we have a case for the active cross-Channel distribution of imperial histories being undertaken in the immediate aftermath of Henry II's reunification of Normandy and England.[121]

In 1139, at the time of Henry's visit, having already completed his interpolations and additions into the *Gesta Normannorum Ducum*, Robert was setting out to write a universal chronicle, with, as he put it in the prologue to what the great Léopold Delisle identified as 'the first edition' of his Chronicle, the declared aim of covering 'such incidents as have occurred in different provinces, but chiefly in Normandy and England up until the year 1150' (*ea quae in diversis provinciis, et maxime in Normannia et Anglia, evenerunt, et ad meam notitiam pervenerunt*).[122] We cannot be quite certain exactly when in the late 1140s or early 1150s this passage was written, but, whatever the case, it articulates an aim to write cross-Channel history which the acquisition of Geoffrey's book shows to have been already firmly established by 1139 at the latest, and which he continued from then on by slavishly inserting large chunks of Henry's *Historia* into his chronicle until the year 1147, as well as making additions to a manuscript thereof that had passed into the library of Le Bec. In practice, he found it impossible to integrate the *De Gestis Britonum* into his chronicle, perhaps because its information would have overwhelmed the materials from Eusebius and Jerome that were the basis of his account.[123] But Le Bec maintained its interest in the *De Gestis Britonum* since a version was copied there soon afterwards; that it and what is thought to be the manuscript of the *Gesta Normannorum Ducum* prepared under Robert's supervision had been bound together at Le Bec by 1164 at the latest is surely convincing evidence of an orchestrated campaign to assemble there the histories of empire.[124] And Robert continued his mission until his death, with the text in the celebrated Avranches manuscript of his Chronicle merely amending the prologue by changing the date of 1150 to 1182. He was also an active propagandist for the Norman diaspora,

---

[121] *GND*, i, cix–cxiii, cxxvi–cxxviii; Shopkow, *History and Community*, 232–9. For Reading's collection of the histories of empire, Richard Sharpe et al., *English Benedictine Libraries: The Shorter Catalogues*, Corpus of British Medieval Library Catalogues, 4 (London, 1996), 432; Alan Coates, *English Medieval Books: The Reading Abbey Collections from Foundation to Dispersal* (Oxford, 1999), 149.

[122] RT (D), i, 96; (H), 64. For Robert's life, Gazeau, *Normannia Monastica: Prosopographie*, 220–5. For the issues discussed, David Bates, 'Robert of Torigni and the *Historia Anglorum*', in Roffe (ed.), *The English and Their Legacy*, 175–84; HH, lxxii–lxxiii, lxxv, cl–clii.

[123] For this suggestion, see Leckie, *Passage of Dominion*, 46–9.

[124] Leiden, Bibliotheek der Rijksuniversiteit, ms. B.P.L. 20; *GND*, i, cix–cx; David N. Dumville, 'An Early Text of Geoffrey of Monmouth's *Historia Regum Britanniae* and the Circulation of Some Latin Histories in Twelfth-Century Normandy', *Arthurian Literature*, iv (1985), 1–36, at 2–6 (reprinted in David N. Dumville, *Histories and Pseudo-histories of the Insular Middle Ages*, Chap. 14); Julia Crick, *The Historia Regum Britannie of Geoffrey of Monmouth*, iii: *A Summary Catalogue of Manuscripts* (Cambridge, 1989), 124–6.

acquiring a now lost manuscript of William of Apulia's *Gesta Roberti Guiscardi* for Le Bec and subsequently having it copied at Le Mont Saint-Michel.[125]

Robert was not the only historian in Normandy who was writing what was believed to be English and British history in Normandy during the time of the civil war. Wace, whose *Roman de Brut*, an adaptation in 14,866 lines in Old French verse of Geoffrey's *De Gestis Britonum*, was completed in 1155, was also hard at work. Although the date at which he is thought to have started writing is controversial, around 1150, well before the date at which the future Henry II's victory in the civil war could be foreseen, is possible.[126] His and Robert of Torigni's work place Normandy, every bit as much as England and other parts of Britain, in the forefront of the reception and integration of the *De Gestis Britonum* and of the Arthurian 'histories' into the collective European historical consciousness.[127] As such, they represent the appropriation of a new imperial theme for the benefit of the imperial core, one that has even been interpreted as having as its unspoken message the notion that 'the history of the dukes of Normandy is the true continuation of the history of the kings of Britain'.[128]

That Wace's treatment of the so-called prophecies of Merlin and his decision to omit them on the grounds that he found them difficult to interpret are normally seen as part of a search for patronage underlines the point that he, and others, thought that favour could be gained in mid-twelfth-century Normandy and northern France by emphasizing a Norman future and transferring insular history to Normandy.[129] That some of the prophecies were predictive of the end of Norman domination over Britain means that their omission is usually seen in terms of the suppression of sensitive political material.[130] The already-mentioned anonymous poem written for the relatively new duke of Normandy, Count Geoffrey of Anjou, some time before 1150, identifying Rouen as the new Rome and writing of Rouen's rule over English, Welsh, and Scots, is an essay on a similar

---

[125] Marguerite Mathieu, 'Le manuscrit 162 d'Avranches et l'édition princeps des *Gesta Roberti Wiscardi* de Guillaume d'Apulie', *Byzantion*, xxiv (1954), 111–30, at 124–30; *Guglielmo di Puglia, Le Gesta di Roberto il Guiscardo*, ed. Francesco de Rosa (Cassino, 2003), 68–9.

[126] See *Wace's Roman de Brut: A History of the British*, trans. Judith Weiss, Exeter Medieval English Texts and Studies (Exeter, 1999), xii.

[127] For these issues, Dauvit Broun, *Scottish Independence and the Idea of Britain from the Picts to Alexander III* (Woodbridge, 2007), 40–6.

[128] Françoise H. M. Le Saux, *A Companion to Wace* (Cambridge, 2005), 185–8.

[129] For the key passage in which Wace declares that 'I do not wish to translate this book, since I do not know how to interpret it; I would not like to say anything, in case what I say does not happen', see *Wace's Roman de Brut*, trans. Weiss, 190–1. For prophecy's influence on Robert of Torigni and others at this time, Elisabeth van Houts, 'Gender, Memories and Prophecies in Medieval Europe', in *Medieval Narrative Sources: A Gateway into the Medieval Mind*, ed. Werner Verbeke, Ludo Milis, and Jean Goossens (Louvain, 2005), 21–36.

[130] For the most obvious prediction of the end of Norman rule, see Geoffrey of Monmouth, *History of the Kings of Britain*, 148–9. See further, Jean Blacker, '"Ne vuil sun livre translater": Wace's Omission of Merlin's Prophecies from the *Roman de Brut*', in *Anglo-Norman Anniversary Essays*, ed. Ian Short, Anglo-Norman Text Society, Occasional Publications Series, no. 2 (London, 1993), 49–59; Jean Blacker, 'Where Wace Feared to Tread: Latin Commentaries on Merlin's Prophecies in the Reign of Henry II', *Arthuriana*, vi (1995), 36–52; Aurell, *The Plantagenet Empire*, 146–7.

theme.[131] That it then proceeds to shower praise on King Roger of Sicily shows not only a continuing awareness of Normandy's place at the core of an empire and a diaspora, but also a capacity to distinguish between the two phenomena, since, after writing about directly exercised power over the English, Welsh, and Scots, it then describes Roger as being of Norman blood (*Ex te progenitus, Normanno sanguine clarus*). A further strand was Robert of Torigni's invitation to Gervase, prior of Saint-Céneri-le-Gérei, to continue the *Gesta Normannorum Ducum* by adding the reign of Count Geoffrey to that of his predecessors, thereby simply suggesting that all that is needed is to join material from Anjou and Maine to the Norman core.[132] Typically utilitarian, and typically Robert of Torigni, we might think; but it does show him thinking of Normandy as still at the core of a wider imperial world and of a diaspora. And, by adding that such a work would in all likelihood be pleasing to the future Henry II, he shows very clearly what he, Wace, and others were thinking. Treated as situational constructs, we can see that they were not straightforward guides to Norman identity. Although they were indeed extolling what they believed to be a great past and a relevant past, they, like the aforementioned Earl Robert of Leicester, had their eyes very much on the future that they hoped was coming.

The enthusiasm with which the *Roman de Brut* was copied on both sides of the Channel demonstrates that it struck an important chord in contemporary consciousness. Within Normandy, the subject was subsequently given elaborate treatment in the later twelfth century by another monk of Le Bec, Stephen of Rouen, in his *Draco Normannicus* and by Andrew of Coutances.[133] Within England, the same themes were taken up by Geffrei Gaimar in the first historical work to be written anywhere in the French vernacular. Given that its intended audience must have been the descendants of the conquerors, with, so it has been suggested, some very powerful people being among them, some of its contents are, at first sight, surprising.[134] Thus, so we are told, with the influence of Geoffrey of Monmouth to the fore:

> Had he (ie, William Rufus) been able to reign a little longer, he would have marched on Rome to reclaim his ancient rights to the country, which Belinus and Brennus before him had enjoyed there.[135]

And later it is stated that the county of Boulogne recognizes William as its king and the prospect is raised of the Burgundians and the French becoming subjects of the English crown.[136] That Hereward the Wake is given more space than William the Conqueror and that the treatment of the latter is far from being consistently

---

[131] Richard, 'Notice sur l'ancienne bibliothèque', 163; van Houts, 'Rouen as Another Rome', in Hicks and Brenner (eds.), *Society and Culture in Medieval Rouen*, 119. See Chap. 1.

[132] Note *et quod his omnibus maius est, noui ducis fauorem non modicum forsitan adquiret*. The letter is printed in RT (D), ii, 338–40. For an interpretation similar to mine, Elisabeth van Houts, 'The *Gesta Normannorum Ducum*: A History without an End', *ANS*, iii (1981), 106–18, 215–20, at 115.

[133] On dissemination, Le Saux, *A Companion to Wace*, 85–6. See further, Chap. 6.

[134] On Gaimar's likely audience, Gaimar, *Estoire des Engleis*, xxvii.

[135] Gaimar, *Estoire des Engleis*, 322–5 (ll. 5971–4).

[136] Gaimar, *Estoire des Engleis*, 340–1 (ll. 6284, 6302–4).

favourable might at first sight seem to make the *Estoire des Engleis* a patriotic work for the English, yet, as Ian Short has commented, the Norman Conquest is actually presented more as a union than a conquest.[137] For John Gillingham, what Gaimar wrote was part of 'the process by which people recovered their English past'.[138] Better, I would have thought, is to say that it was part of the process by which historians of the cross-Channel empire sought to integrate the several strands of their collective and individual pasts into an imperial present. For all the sentiments it expresses, that the *Estoire* was written in French for an audience that understood that language makes it a work for an imperial elite.

Given his background, it might initially seem perverse to suggest that Ailred of Rievaulx, who was pretty much of the same generation as Henry of Huntingdon and Robert of Torigni, was also writing in terms of empire and its continuation. While the apparent crucial difference between Ailred and Robert is that the latter was in Normandy at the core of empire and the former mostly at the periphery of it, their essential similarities are, however, in fact a magnificent demonstration of the impact of hegemonic power at the periphery. As the entirely English son of a priest of the church of Durham, who had made his way at the court of David, king of Scots (1124–53), before the spiritual crisis that took him into the newly founded Cistercian abbey of Rievaulx, Ailred had apparently grown up within a very different milieu from Robert. He was, however, as thoroughly engaged politically. As a result, when, because of the enduring alliance between King David and the Angevins, he set about the task of constructing a genealogy of the kings of the English for the incoming Henry II, his focus was almost exclusively English and Scottish, with Henry's descent from the Wessex line through St Margaret and Henry I's wife Edith/Matilda foregrounded. For the period after 1066 he actually wrote more about the kings of the Scots than about the new rulers of England.[139] The temptation to think of him as pulling the young Henry into an English and British identity, rather than a Norman one, should, however, be resisted; the illusory contrast is actually a demonstration of the multipolarity of empire and its inclusion of rule over multiple *regna*, rather than of disruptive centrifugal pulls. In his 'Epistle' to the future King Henry, Ailred addresses him as 'Duke of the Normans and Aquitanians and Count of the Angevins' and refers to him as 'the hope of the English'.[140] The future for him, too, was imperial.

William of Malmesbury, yet another product of a mixed marriage in England, was a self-proclaimed historian of the English and a man with contacts at the highest level, since his patrons included Henry I's first wife, Queen Matilda, King David I of Scotland, and Henry's favourite illegitimate son, Earl Robert of Gloucester. The Norman Conquest was for him a disaster for the English with

---

[137] Gaimar, *Estoire des Engleis*, xliv.
[138] John Gillingham, 'Gaimar, the Prose *Brut* and the making of English History', in *The English*, 113–22, at 120.
[139] Ailred, *De Genealogia Regum Anglorum*, in *PL*, cxcv, cols. 711–38, at cols. 734–8 (*Aelred of Rievaulx: The Historical Works*, 115–22).
[140] Ailred, *De Genealogia Regum Anglorum*, *PL*, cxcv, cols. 711–12 (*Aelred of Rievaulx: The Historical Works*, 41–2).

apparently unending consequences which were unquestionably an expression of God's judgement on a sinful people. The Normans and French were beyond question a civilizing and redemptive influence, even if sometimes inexplicably so. As Sigbjørn Olsen Sønnesyn has recently put it, the Conquest represented 'a correction of a basically solid entity in the process of losing its way' and William I and Henry I had to be seen as 'embodying the same virtues in the same way as the great kings of the Anglo-Saxon age'.[141] However, in a passage in the *Gesta Pontificum* that he eventually deleted, Malmesbury expressed what may well be his personal thoughts by remarking that, although he personally might be able to forgive what William the Conqueror had done because of the scale of his responsibilities, God might not.[142] In describing the wreck of the White Ship on 25 November 1120, he says that 'no ship that ever sailed brought such disaster to England' and wrote that the Normans were a kind and tolerant people, who were predisposed to live contentedly among other peoples. Yet he was in no doubt that the prophecy of the green tree had not been fulfilled by the time he was writing and that there had been no genuine assimilation of Normans and English; the former indeed continued to inflict innumerable miseries on the latter.[143]

In his narrative of the pre-1066 period, Malmesbury included the truly appalling prodigy of the conjoined twins whose single set of legs carried two torsos, of which one died and whose decomposing remains were then carried around for some years by the healthy body. He then interpreted the prodigy as representing England carrying around the defunct Normandy whose constant demands for money eventually exhausted her. This insertion is surely indicative of many things, the most obvious of them being the exploitative nature of empire. It does, however, also make clear his awareness that empires rise and fall and that human power was transitory. He knew that in the future there would be change, but he could not see when it would be.[144]

Malmesbury's place in the historical canon has arguably been excessively influenced by Sir Richard Southern's reference to the 'outrage, resentment and nostalgia' of men who had known the pre-Conquest world.[145] Far more persuasive in the context of the range of Malmesbury's writings are comments made almost thirty years ago by Rodney Thomson, and subsequently reinforced by James Campbell, that Malmesbury was essentially and by temperament a universal historian. Thus, in the *Gesta Regum*, completed in *c.*1125, he included material on the histories of the Franks and the empire; the effort he made on this topic is in fact truly remarkable, given how very little Carolingian historical writing was actually

---

[141] Sigbjørn Olsen Sønnesyn, *William of Malmesbury and the Ethics of History* (Woodbridge, 2012), 148–258, with the quotations at pp. 193 and 238. On Malmesbury and kingship, see also Bjørn Weiler, 'William of Malmesbury on Kingship', *History*, xc (2005), 3–22, at 10, 13.

[142] *GP*, i, 94–5. The same theme occurs in *GR*, i, 508–9.

[143] *GR*, i, 414–17, 460–1, 470–1, 760–1; Michael Winterbottom, 'William of Malmesbury and the Normans', *Journal of Medieval Latin*, xx (2010), 70–7.

[144] *GR*, i, 384–7; cf. Albu, *The Normans in their Histories*, 218. On the conjoined twins, Ian Short, 'Literary Culture at the Court of Henry II', in Harper-Bill and Vincent (eds), *Henry II: New Interpretations*, 335–61, at 336–9.

[145] Southern, 'Sense of the Past', 249–50 (Bartlett (ed.), *History and the Historians*, 69).

available to him.[146] In also writing about the First Crusade and other great contemporary matters, his aim was to put the history of conquest and empire into the universal history of the Christian peoples. He, therefore, took great care to incorporate the Norman Conquest into a broader historical scheme at an appropriate point; he even inserted a brief eulogy of one of the great figures of the duchy's history, Duke Richard II (996–1026), into his account of another of the disasters that had afflicted the English, namely, the contemporary reign of King Æthelred the Unready.[147] The writing of universal history has, in general, an underestimated place within the Anglo-Norman twelfth-century renaissance in historical writing, with, at an early stage in the process, John of Worcester, in the well-nigh unique circumstances of late eleventh-century Worcester under the English bishop Wulfstan, drawing on Marianus Scotus to provide England's history with its previously absent wider context.[148] The general picture for Durham—where the surviving collections are, of course, truly remarkable—is broadly speaking the same; the *Libellus de exordio* of Symeon of Durham dealt with the local and regional in the context of the new empire at the same time that books were written and collected that engaged with universal history as it was then understood.[149]

It is striking just how much other historical writing took an integrative view of the cross-Channel empire and its peoples. The fullest account of the 1091 agreement between Robert Curthose and William Rufus, conventionally known as the Treaty of Rouen, for example, appears in the 'E' version of the Anglo-Saxon Chronicle, with arguments for there being a court-produced text behind the Chronicle making this less surprising than it might once have been.[150] Arguably even more notable is the Chronicle's statement, which is usually not given the prominence it deserves, given that it is actually the only truly contemporary source for opinion about Henry I's arrangement of the marriage of his daughter, the Empress Matilda, and Count Geoffrey of Anjou (that is, written by a contemporary, but without hindsight based on events after 1135), that says that Henry organized the marriage 'despite the fact that it offended all the French *and* English' in order to have peace with the count of Anjou and obtain help against his nephew

---

[146] R. M. Thomson, 'William of Malmesbury's Carolingian Sources', *JMH*, vii (1981), 321–37, at 333–4 (reprinted in idem, *William of Malmesbury* (revised edn., Woodbridge, 2003), 137–53, at 152–3); James Campbell, 'Some Twelfth-Century Views of the Anglo-Saxon Past', in James Campbell, *Essays in Anglo-Saxon History* (London and Ronceverte, 1986), 209–28, at 211–12.

[147] *GR*, i, 304–7; Kirsten A. Fenton, *Gender, Nation and Conquest in the Works of William of Malmesbury* (Woodbridge, 2008), 25.

[148] Martin Brett, 'John of Worcester and His Contemporaries', in Davis and Wallace-Hadrill (eds), *The Writing of History*, 101–26, at 117–18, 124; Martin Brett, 'The Use of Universal Chronicle at Worcester', in Jean-Philippe Genet (ed.), *L'historiographie médiévale en Europe* (Paris, 1992), 277–85.

[149] The general themes are set out in David Rollason, 'Symeon's Contribution to Historical Writing in Northern England' and Richard Gameson, 'English Book Collections in the Late Eleventh and Early Twelfth Centuries: Symeon's Durham and its Context', in David Rollason (ed.), *Symeon of Durham: Historian of Durham and the North* (Stamford, 1998), 1–13, 230–5, at 248–51; Simon MacLean, 'Recycling the Franks in Twelfth-Century England: Regino of Prüm, the Monks of Durham and the Alexandrine Schism', *Speculum*, lxxxvii (2012), 649–81.

[150] ASC, 'E', 1091; Nicholas Brooks, 'Why is the Anglo-Saxon Chronicle about Kings?', *ASE*, xxxix (2011), 43–70, and esp. 52–62.

William Clito.[151] This passage becomes all the more remarkable in the light of the independent-mindedness of the writer who wrote the section of the Chronicle from 1122 to 1131; the likelihood that the writer was departing from the source he was using is made probable by the argument that John of Worcester and Henry of Huntingdon were drawing on the same source, but did not include this opinion.[152] It is, however, clear that the multi-authored versions of the Anglo-Saxon Chronicle can speak with many tongues. Thus, both 'D' and 'E' state that when William the Conqueror travelled north of the Forth in 1072, 'he found nothing there that he was anything the better for', a passage redolent of the theme of English cultural superiority over its British neighbours written long before William of Malmesbury's infamous exposition of the same theme. It demonstrates authors of undoubted English ethnicity associating their new king with an existing England-based opinion, and, as such, another hint that the empire I am writing about was to an extent made in England.[153] Yet, when we come to the year 1100, another of the anonymous authors of the Chronicle apparently articulated opposition to power exercised without consent in the most devastating way, Henry I's new wife, Edith/Matilda, being described as 'of the rightful kingly line of England'.[154]

That Herman's account of the miracles of St Edmund is an informative source for the eleventh-century history of Barfleur is another illustration of how historical writing in England takes in the cross-Channel world of empire; Edmund's renown and curative powers were soon felt across the Channel, showing that it was not only the living who might become participants in empire.[155] Abbot Baldwin, the monk of Saint-Denis and doctor appointed abbot of Bury in 1065 by Edward the Confessor and the only abbot of French origin in England in 1066, lost no time in disseminating Edmund's cult in France; there was, for example, among several manifestations, an altar dedicated to him in a tower at Saint-Denis financed by William the Conqueror that collapsed.[156] The abbey also played a small, but significant part in cross-Channel historical writing; it was there, for example, in the early twelfth century, that the so-called 'Annals of St Neots' were composed that contain borrowings from annals written in Normandy, with the deliberate purpose of creating a chronicle that contained both English and Norman

---

[151] ASC, 'E', 1127 (*The Peterborough Chronicle*, ed. Dorothy Whitelock, Early English Manuscripts in Facsimile, iv (Copenhagen, 1954)). For its composition, *The Peterborough Chronicle 1070–1154*, ed. Cecily Clark, 2nd edn. (Oxford, 1970), xvi, xxiv–xxv, lxxix–lxxxiii; *The Anglo-Saxon Chronicles*, trans. and ed. Michael Swanton (London, 2000), xxvi.

[152] Susan Irvine, 'The Production of the Peterborough Chronicle', in Alice Jorgensen (ed.), *Reading the Anglo-Saxon Chronicle: Language, Literature and History* (Turnhout, 2010), 49–66, at 56–66; on the independence of the writer, see also Malasree Home, 'Déjà Vu: The Complexity of the Peterborough Chronicle', in Jorgensen (ed.), *Reading the Anglo-Saxon Chronicle*, 67–90.

[153] ASC, 'D', 'E' 1072.

[154] ASC, 'E', 1100.

[155] *Memorials of Saint Edmund's Abbey*, ed. Thomas Arnold, Rolls Series, 3 vols (London, 1890–6), i, 73; Musset, 'Barfleur', 52.

[156] *Guibert de Nogent, Autobiographie*, ed. E.-R. Labande (Paris, 1981), 466–9.

history.[157] As such they are a landmark in the much larger process whereby versions of the Norman annals were transferred to England and adapted there, a part of what has been recently described as a 'significant unity in Anglo-Norman monastic culture'.[158]

As is well known, Wace's contribution after the *Roman de Brut* was much more ambivalent about the Normans than he had previously been. His other great work, the *Roman de Rou*, written between 1160 and the mid-1170s, is known for its apparent lukewarm treatment of aspects of the imperial history of the Normans and, in particular, for its sympathetic treatment of Robert Curthose and the associated critical one of Wace's patron, Henry II's grandfather, Henry I. His failure to complete the history and the transfer of the commission to Benoît de Sainte-Maure have been variously explained, with slow writing and his attitude to the Norman past being the main ones on offer; his treatment of the latter has even led to the *Roman de Rou* being supplied with an apocalyptic role at 'the end of *Normanitas*'.[159] Yet when what he wrote is set alongside other evidence of the deep-seated attitudes towards empire within some sections of Norman society already referred to and the general moral purpose of twelfth-century historical writing, all surely becomes comprehensible.[160] It is as if there were two main themes within historical writing in the twelfth-century duchy, one that in simple terms might be described as pro-imperial and one as anti-imperial. In this respect, Wace's choice of sources is also interesting, since he used Orderic's interpolations into the *Gesta Normannorum Ducum* and the *Historia Ecclesiastica* a great deal, and took trouble to master English material. Robert of Torigni, in contrast, although he knew them, used neither of Orderic's works, was content to reproduce large sections of Henry of Huntingdon's *Historia Anglorum* when writing about English history, and scarcely crossed the Channel.[161] The illegitimacy of empire is a regular theme in historical writing in Normandy in, for example, Orderic's treatment of William the Conqueror's last days and funeral; a nice barely coded message is included through his insertion of the word 'false' into the famous passage from the Psalms, 'Put not your trust in princes'.[162] Some of Orderic's and Wace's themes are

---

[157] *The Anglo-Saxon Chronicle: A Collaborative Edition*, 17: *The Annals of St Neots with 'Vita Primi Sancti Neoti'*, ed. David N. Dumville and Michael Lapidge (Cambridge, 1984), xiii–xiv, xliv–xlvii. I am grateful to Tom Licence for a discussion of the manuscript of the so-called Annals of St Neots.

[158] Alison Alexander, 'Annalistic Writing in Normandy, c.1050–c.1225', PhD Thesis, University of Cambridge (2011), 241–9, with the quotation at 248.

[159] Le Saux, *A Companion to Wace*, 156, summarizes the issues. On Wace and 'the end of *Normanitas*', Ashe, *Fiction and History*, 49–80, with Wace being lead 'into conflict with his culture's central truths' (p. 78) and *Normanitas* (which is of course a modern invention) being presented as 'an historical value...already located in the past' (p. 80). See further, Chap. 6.

[160] The matter is treated in detail in Le Saux, *A Companion to Wace*, 209–78.

[161] Elisabeth van Houts, 'The Adaptation of the *Gesta Normannorum Ducum* by Wace and Benoît', in M. Gosman and J. Van Os (eds), *Non Nova, sed Nove: Mélanges de civilisation médiévale dédiées à Willem Noomen* (Groningen, 1984), 115–24, at 117, 119 (*History and Family Traditions*, Chap. 11); Bates, 'Robert of Torigni and the *Historia Anglorum*', 178–81.

[162] OV, iv, 106–9; Kempshall, *Rhetoric and the Writing of History*, 404; David Bates, 'The Conqueror's Earliest Historians and the Writing of his Biography', in Bates, Crick, and Hamilton (eds), *Writing Medieval Biography*, 129–41, at 139.

treated even more negatively in the *Roman du Mont Saint-Michel*, written by William de Saint-Pair at Le Mont Saint-Michel, during the time that Robert of Torigni was abbot.[163] But at almost the same time within Normandy, Stephen of Rouen wrote of Henry II and Frederick Barbarossa as the only true successors of Charlemagne.[164]

Manifestly, all these writers were setting out to place the great events that had profoundly affected all their lives in terms of the history of the world, as they understood it. Therefore, while England's and Normandy's past and present mattered to many of them in the most profound way, they were not men writing sentimentally about a vanished past, but rather they were historians writing about a cross-Channel imperial present whose future they could not predict. They saw within past and present times many moral messages that they knew they must transmit. They make the point very clearly that, while it may be possible to write a history of the Normans and empire, there were in fact many histories of the Normans. One of its surprising features perhaps is that, when Orderic, Wace, Malmesbury, and Huntingdon are set alongside one another, the result is to create a good case to argue for William the Conqueror being the subject of a more positive presentation in twelfth-century histories written in England than in those written in Normandy.[165]

To put all this in another way, while modern historians can with justification write about ongoing processes of cultural and social assimilation and integration into English society—and *mutatis mutandis* into Scottish as well—such a narrowing of the focus on to national history is only a part of the story. Alongside them is an enduring articulation of the continuation of a dynamic cross-Channel world that was imperial. Thus, while a mid-twelfth-century writer might insist that a true Norman was someone brought up in Normandy with both parents being Normans and, much later, Robert de Chesney, bishop of Lincoln (1148–66), could be described by Gerald of Wales as 'English by birth, but Norman by ancestry', both were showing that, when it came to issues of identity, the cross-Channel world of empire still mattered.[166] That most prosaic of sources—and for that reason, one of the most revealing and also difficult to interpret—the address clauses of writs makes the same point. Whether the prime meaning is considered to be linguistic or ethnic, in continuing to deploy the phrase *francis et anglis* they continue to demonstrate the dynamism of empire. The usage might reduce significantly after 1154, but it actually continues into the thirteenth century. On my arguments indeed, the search for a distinction between an ethnic and a linguistic meaning is a chimera, since the fundamental explanation of

---

[163] Catherine Bougy, 'L'Image des ducs de Normandie dans le *Roman de Rou* de Wace et dans le *Roman du Mont Saint-Michel* de Guillaume de Saint-Pair', in Glyn S. Burgess and Judith Weiss (eds), *Maistre Wace: A Celebration: Proceedings of the International Colloquium held in Jersey, 10–12 September 2004*, Société Jersiaise (2006), 73–90, at 77–82.

[164] Stephen of Rouen, *Draco Normannicus*, in *Chronicles*, ii, 670–3, 720.

[165] See further Chaps. 3 and 6.

[166] *Liber Eliensis*, ed. E. O. Blake, Camden, 3rd ser., xcii (1962), 171, Bk. 2, *c*.101 (*utroque parente Normanni et in Normannia sunt educati*) (translated, *Liber Eliensis: A History of the Isle of Ely from the Seventh Century to the Twelfth*, trans. Janet Fairweather (Woodbridge, 2005), 203); 'Vita S. Remigii', in *Giraldus Cambrensis: Opera Omnia*, vii, 34 (*natione quidem Anglicus, sed cognatione Normannus*).

the usage must be an awareness of multilingualism and the historic multi-ethnicity associated with a diaspora.[167]

A final point is that, when class is brought into the analysis, the picture that emerges is that of an elite whose upper reaches remained even by the late twelfth century well-nigh impenetrable by those of English birth and descent, and for whom French and Latin were the languages of choice. While historians of earlier societies have brought the word 'apartheid' into discussions of situations of this kind, a cross-reference to an ideology that practised and preached separate racial development is not appropriate to the twelfth-century empire I am writing about. To mention it does, however, throw the subject into stark and possibly helpful relief.[168] The telling of life-stories shows that cross-Channel empire remained dynamic well on into the twelfth century and that many people continued to invest in its continuation. But it also shows the continuing dominance of an elite whose interests were from the start cross-Channel, and which remained so. This domination was ultimately based on the exploitation of a defeated people.

---

[167] Sharpe, 'Peoples and Languages', 16–25, 109–12.

[168] Cf. Alex Woolf, 'Apartheid and Economics in Anglo-Saxon England', in Nick Higham (ed.), *Britons in Anglo-Saxon England* (Woodbridge, 2007), 115–29; Mark G. Thomas, Michael P. H. Stumpf, and Heinrich Härke, 'Evidence for an Apartheid-Like Social Structure in Early Anglo-Saxon England', *Proceedings of the Royal Society B*, no. 273 (2006), 2651–7.

3
William the Conqueror as Maker of Empire

That medieval rule was fundamentally based on the channelling of political power through one man (and occasionally one woman) means that we can, broadly speaking, assume that, even though a dominant figure like William would exercise an important influence on events, and often in all likelihood a decisive one, he would also mediate through his actions the policies, expectations, and attitudes of others. To concentrate on the one man is therefore a legitimate way to approach the subject of the making of empire. But the multiple dialogues, interactions, and, where it is possible to construct them, the life-stories that swirl around William the Conqueror and shape his actions are every bit as much a central theme as his personality and decisions; they initiate and perpetuate patterns that have fundamental long-term importance.

This concentration on William and those associated with him is also justified by treating identity as a construct, the product of context, beliefs, and values that may not all be rational or conscious. It means that the supposed values that have sometimes been thought to be described by the word *Normanitas* are in no way a causative or creative factor in the making of empire. Instead, the process must be seen in terms of multiple acts of human agency that were founded in a contemporary range of norms, scripts, and rules that were much more concrete than that nebulous word implies. In the end, one basic question to be answered is what it was that persuaded those who joined William to cross the Channel in 1066 to participate in what was from a military point of view an exceptionally hazardous operation and, some might have thought a morally dubious one as well. And a second question is what they all expected to get out of the enterprise. This approach does not rule out the possibility that a sense of group identity and associated expectations played a part, but it does mean that John Le Patourel's famous statement that 'the spread of Norman domination in northern France and Britain was a continuous and consistent process' that began 'with the first settlements of the Vikings in the lower Seine Valley' must be set aside.[1] The tenth and early eleventh centuries must be seen as creating context rather than impetus.

---

[1] Le Patourel, *The Norman Empire*, 319. See Chap. 6 for the tenth and early eleventh centuries as context.

WILLIAM AND HIS HISTORIANS

That William the Conqueror was a difficult man to write about for writers in the eleventh and twelfth centuries is arguably not as often recognized as it ought to be.[2] As a man of violence responsible directly and indirectly for thousands of deaths, his life and actions inevitably evoked then—just as they can still evoke now—passion and disagreement. Also, because he was on several standards of values so successful, moral uncertainty as to why such terrible things were allowed to happen, and how they might be explained, was for contemporaries and the subsequent generations an issue to be pondered. All who thought and wrote about William's life had, and have, ultimately to confront the eternal dilemma at the heart of the history of all empires, namely, the morality and moralities, both absolute and relative, of the use of extreme violence to achieve what was claimed to be a legitimate goal. As a result, the history of the conquest of England was being written from several different moral perspectives almost from the day after the Battle of Hastings, a process that is observable across western Europe as well. The removal by violence of a crowned king hit some very raw nerves, and in some places produced outrage.[3]

Eleventh-century changes in attitudes to violence, the conduct of war, and personal deportment, as well as deep-rooted concepts of kingship and the responsibilities conferred by coronation, are all part of the conceptual framework involved in the making of empire.[4] While both the exact nature of the changes taking place and their impact on William remain very much under discussion, the model of early medieval warrior kingship in large measure made explicit in the work of the late Timothy Reuter, and more recently set out by Guy Halsall, covers most bases. Above all, there is the emphasis not just on military leadership, but on the capacity to distribute rewards and to create an ambience of legitimacy and confidence.[5] In addition, the voluminous literature on the tensions and dynamics of the imperial

---

[2] The main arguments of this chapter are developed in detail in my forthcoming *William the Conqueror*, which I am writing for the Yale University Press English Monarchs series. On some aspects of this chapter, see David Bates, 'Anger, Emotion and a Biography of William the Conqueror', in Nelson et al. (eds), *Gender and Historiography*, 21–33. Mark Hagger, *William: King and Conqueror* (London, 2012), came to my notice too late to be given serious consideration.

[3] Van Houts, 'The Norman Conquest through European Eyes', 835–43, 851–3; also David Bates, 'William the Conqueror and His Wider Western World', *HSJ*, xv (2006, for 2004), 73–87, at 86–7, for some suggestions on political context.

[4] For differing perspectives on eleventh-century change, John Gillingham, '1066 and the Introduction of Chivalry into England', in George Garnett and John Hudson (eds), *Law and Government in Medieval England and Normandy: Essays in Honour of Sir James Holt* (Cambridge, 1994), 31–55 (reprinted, *The English*, 209–31); Crouch, *The Birth of Nobility*, 7–86; David Crouch, 'Chivalry and Courtliness: Colliding Constructs', in Peter Coss and Christopher Tyerman (eds), *Soldiers, Nobles and Gentlemen: Essays in Honour of Maurice Keen* (Woodbridge, 2009), 32–48, and esp. 41–7; Dominique Barthélemy, 'The Chivalric Transformation and the Origins of Tournament as seen through Norman Chroniclers', *HSJ*, xx (2009, for 2008), 141–60.

[5] Timothy Reuter, 'Plunder and Tribute in the Carolingian Empire', *TRHS*, 5th. ser., xxxv (1985), 75–94 (reprinted in *Medieval Polities and Modern Mentalities*, ed. Janet L. Nelson (Cambridge, 2006), Chap. 13); cf, Janet L. Nelson, *Charlemagne and the Paradoxes of Power*, The Reuter Lecture 2005 (Southampton, 2006), 4–11; Guy Halsall, *Warfare and Society in the Barbarian West, 450–900* (London, 2003), 1–39.

aristocracy of the Carolingian Empire provides a template against which the similar forces operating in a later and equally turbulent world can be viewed.[6]

There must have been many in the army that crossed the Channel who recognized William as capable both of an appropriate distribution of rewards and of conducting the whole operation in a way that would not jeopardize the ultimate fate of the souls of those who were undoubtedly going to have to commit many acts of violence. At the most basic level, most would want to emerge physically safe, a lot richer than they had been before, and spiritually and politically reassured. In the aftermath of the victory at Hastings, the principal requirements expected of William of prowess in war, to reward his supporters, to keep the peace, to act justly, to respect the teachings of Christianity, and to protect the vulnerable, intermingled bewilderingly; they must have become not just infinitely more complex than usual, but, in the immediately following years, mind-bogglingly so.[7]

It is a feature of the modern historiography of the Conquest and of the Normans that the intensive engagement elsewhere over more than two decades with anthropology, sociology, *Spielregeln* ('the rules of the game'), and cultural biography has scarcely been brought to bear on William the Conqueror's life and career until now. Distinguished as they are, the books by David Douglas, Frank Barlow, and Michel de Boüard were all published long before what is conventionally referred to as 'the cultural turn'.[8] Symptomatic of this state-of-affairs is the fact that the story in the early-twelfth-century *Historia* of the church of York that has William throw himself at the feet in full view of the entire court of Archbishop Ealdred of York to beg forgiveness for the conduct of officials acting in his name was, to my knowledge, last mentioned in relation to William in the fourth volume of Freeman's encyclopaedic *History of the Norman Conquest*, which was published in 1871.[9] That the story is nowadays instantly identifiable as the sort of demonstrative behaviour by which rulers theatrically communicated their will surely means that we should accept its essential veracity.[10] It also means that we can analyse William's actions within the framework of what has often too loosely been called ritual; and in this specific instance, we can examine them in a case of cardinal importance, his public

---

[6] Stuart Airlie, *Power and Its Problems in Carolingian Europe* (Farnham, 2012), contains many excellent essays on this theme. For the management of change on a massive scale, see, in particular, 'Towards a Carolingian Aristocracy' (Chap. 2).

[7] For a survey of these complexities that covers the period from the eighth century until the mid-eleventh, Paul J. E. Kershaw, *Peaceful Kings: Peace, Power and the Early Medieval Political Imagination* (Oxford, 2011), and see esp. 1–28.

[8] David C. Douglas, *William the Conqueror: The Norman Impact upon England* (London, 1964); Frank Barlow, *William I and the Norman Conquest* (London, 1965); Michel de Boüard, *Guillaume le Conquérant* (Paris, 1984). For Frank Barlow's unpublished comments on his book, David Bates, 'Preface', in Bates, Crick, and Hamilton (eds), *Writing Medieval Biography*, viii, n. 2.

[9] *The Historians of the Church of York and its Archbishops*, ed. J. Raine, 2 vols, Rolls Series (London, 1879–94), ii, 351–3 (R. C. van Caenegem (ed.), *English Lawsuits from William I to Richard I*, 2 vols, Selden Society, vols cvi–cvii (London, 1990–1), i, 1–2, n. 1); E. A Freeman, *The History of the Norman Conquest of England: Its Causes and Its Results*, 6 vols (Oxford, 1867–79), iv, 262–5. For the story cited in relation to Ealdred, Frank Barlow, *The English Church, 1000–1066*, 2nd edn. (London, 1979), 89, who announced that he did not believe it. See, however, Hyams, *Rancor and Reconciliation*, 151.

[10] See, for example, Sarah Hamilton, *The Practice of Penance, 900–1050*, Royal Historical Society Studies in History (Woodbridge, 2001), 174–82.

personal interaction with the Englishman who had crowned him king of the English, and who had thereby taken responsibility before God and the English people for William's kingship. In the face of a story of this kind, my approach to the subject of ritual is one which argues that conventionalized theatre cannot be used as a reason to ignore agency and biography.[11] It has a lot in common with Christina Pössel's statement that: 'If ritual doesn't do anything... then the question arises why these actors made these choices'.[12] Rituals are on the surface. It is the underlying narratives that are crucial.

That William possessed personal attributes relevant to the model of warrior kingship is most evident from the writings of William of Malmesbury, of the major twelfth-century historians, the one most interested in biography. He described William as a large powerful man with exceptional skills on horseback, who dressed magnificently, entertained lavishly, and at court, terrified all around him with oaths and a loud voice. Yet he also presented him as a man who lived as religious a life as was possible for a layman and who, one story to the contrary notwithstanding, he thought to have been devoted to his wife.[13] As a demonstration of the theatrical physicality described by Malmesbury, there is no story better than the narrative in a charter of 1069 granting an estate in England to the abbey of La Trinité-du-Mont of Rouen and, when the abbot queried how secure the grant was likely to be, William in jest making as if to pin the abbot's hand to a flat surface with a knife.[14] Having crossed the Channel to receive the grant, the abbot's expression of anxiety was, in the context of the England of 1069, not unreasonable. That the abbot and monks of La Trinité thought it worth inserting the story into a charter shows that the abbot, no doubt once he had recovered from the shock, had decided that William's display of confidence should be told to all and sundry; William would surely have been playing to the gallery with precisely this outcome in mind. A less tangible factor in William's behaviour, again supplied by Malmesbury, is his statement that William felt that he must not be outdone by a social inferior like Robert Guiscard, the great Norman conqueror of southern Italy and his near contemporary. If true, this suggests not only that William measured his achievements against those of other members of the Norman *gens* and therefore that ethnic identity contributed seriously to his thinking, but also that his sense of reputation and achievement was fuelled by drawing comparisons with the most successful individuals of his time.[15] That rivalry communicated across the Europe-wide diaspora was a significant factor in motivating the maker of empire introduces a theme that will be developed later.[16]

---

[11] For valuable reflections, Pauline Stafford, 'Writing the Biography of Eleventh-Century Queens', in Bates, Crick, and Hamilton (eds), *Writing Medieval Biography*, 99–109.

[12] Christina Pössel, 'The Magic of Early Medieval Ritual', *EME*, xvii (2009), 111–25, with the quotation at 117. The classic modern discussions of the subject are Philippe Buc, *The Dangers of Ritual: Between Early Medieval Texts and Social Scientific Theory* (Princeton, NJ, 2001); Geoffrey Koziol, 'The Dangers of Polemic: Is Ritual Still an Interesting Topic for Historical Study?', *EME*, xi (2002), 367–88.

[13] *GR*, i, 492–3, 508–11; see further, Weiler, 'William of Malmesbury on Kingship', and esp. 13–14.

[14] *Regesta*, no. 232.   [15] *GR*, i, 482–3; Johnson, 'Origin Myth', 164.   [16] See Chap. 6.

A scenario that encapsulates many of the problems of understanding William the Conqueror as a maker of empire is provided by Orderic's description of the court William held in London at Christmas 1067. This is both because of the nature of the sources for the event and because of the context in which the assembly occurred. William, so Orderic tells us, after returning to his kingdom from a triumphal progress around Normandy to confront a situation that was becoming increasingly unstable, welcomed the English very warmly and sought to instruct his followers to behave similarly, since kindness was often the best way to persuade waverers.[17] If he actually said this, it represents a highly idealistic pronouncement on his part. It might even be interpreted as a straightforward proof that he was setting out to abide by the supplementary oath he had sworn at his coronation to treat his English subjects equally with the newcomers who had accompanied him to England.[18] But, if so, it sits most oddly with the behaviour of a man who was in the end to resolve many conflicts by the use of an extreme form of hard power.

The question of sources is crucial to the interpretation of this passage. Orderic's narrative was undoubtedly copied from lost sections of the *Gesta Guillelmi* of William of Poitiers, the panegyric written in the 1070s with the specific purpose of praising and justifying William. The *Gesta*'s mix of history, extravagant eulogy, and apparently tendentious rhetoric has led to it being described as propaganda, as dishonest, as sycophantic, and as much worse besides.[19] Yet, since Orderic is known to have used Poitiers critically, and this being a passage he retained in all probability unaltered, we have to assume that we must take it seriously as a comment on William, even if we then recognize that, as a historian, Orderic shared with most others the traditional ideological opinions on the role of kings, and that for him the behaviour he portrayed might just be a *topos*.[20] In the end, all that can be safely said is that Orderic, like others, regarded William as a king who knew and followed the basic conventions of kingly rule, a conclusion that is important because, if he did actually behave like this, it highlights his capacity to portray himself as an embodiment of an illustrious kingly tradition of ritualised detachment and also of the ethnic plurality that was present from the beginning of the cross-Channel empire. If he did not, then we have a problem that all sources available to us cannot be believed. But whatever the case, it is certainly self-evident that a multitude of destabilising forces were at work at this time that involved ambition, expectation,

---

[17] OV, ii, 210–11 (*Desertores huiusmodi arte aliquoties reducuntur. Pari sedulitate et sollertia Gallos nunc instruebat*...).

[18] On William's coronation oath, see later in this chapter.

[19] For 'nauseatingly sycophantic', John Gillingham, 'William the Bastard at War', in Chistopher Harper-Bill, Christopher Holdsworth, and Janet L. Nelson (eds), *Studies in Medieval History Presented to R. Allen Brown* (Woodbridge, 1989), 141–58, at 141 (reprinted in Strickland (ed.), *Anglo-Norman Warfare*, 143–60); for 'a rare moment of honesty', George Garnett, 'Coronation and Propaganda: Some Implications of the Norman Claim to the Throne of England in 1066', *TRHS*, 5th ser., xxxvi (1986), 91–116, at 95.

[20] *GG*, xxxv–xxxix; Pierre Bouet, 'Orderic Vital, lecteur critique de Guillaume de Poitiers', *Medievalia Christiana xie–xiiie siècles. Hommage à Raymonde Foreville de ses amis, ses collègues et ses anciens élèves*, ed. C. E. Viola (Paris, 1989), 25–50, and esp. 27–9, 36–7. A full-scale study of the *Gesta Guillelmi* that builds on work such as this is urgently needed.

anxiety, trauma, and fear; the implications of this volatile and unpredictable mix will resurface regularly during this chapter, as will William's response to them.

In terms of using the *Gesta Guillelmi* to understand William the Conqueror, it is at least clear that it belongs within a long-established kind of medieval historical writing that used history as 'a theatre of example'.[21] Its treatment of William runs along the well-established lines whereby a king was seen as having a moral duty to make war in order to secure peace; it, therefore, responds well to Paul Kershaw's implied argument that the study of peace and rule as a kingly responsibility could be profitably extended into the Anglo-Norman period, and indeed beyond it. There are, for example, clear generic parallels between the *Gesta Guillelmi* and Wipo's *Gesta Chuonradi*, a biography of the Emperor Conrad II (1024–39) written to tutor his son Henry III (1039–56).[22] Geoffrey Malaterra's *De rebus gestis Rogerii Calabriae et Siciliae comitis et Roberti Guiscardi ducis fratris ejus*, written between 1098 and 1101 to legitimate and justify the acts of Roger the Great Count, also obviously drew from the same well.[23] It is therefore a mistake to describe it as either 'official history' or 'the exposition of a legal case'; it may incorporate something of both, but literary genre and an intellectual range that brings in rhetoric and ethics makes it into much more.[24] That Poitiers was for a long time William's chaplain and would therefore have had regular access to him—indeed might well have heard his confession—must mean that William knew that the *Gesta* was being written.[25] Hence, its deployment of Roman themes such as flattery becomes a reflection of William's personal identity, of the place of Latin learning at his court, and of a belief on his part that he should be portrayed as an exceptional king, another significant element in terms of understanding William the Conqueror as the maker of an empire.[26]

Among the many problematic passages in the *Gesta Guillelmi* is the statement that, even though extensive grants of land were made immediately after William's coronation to his followers, nothing was given to a Frenchman that had been taken unjustly from an Englishman. Others are the praise and justification of Bishop Odo of Bayeux's conduct in 1067 and the comment that William made compensation to English churches for the gifts he made to French ones. It is notable that Orderic not only omitted them all, he went further and specifically condemned Odo's activities.[27] But the most telling commentary on William's rule over an ethnically plural empire and his personal application of the norms, scripts and rules of kingly governance is to juxtapose the *Gesta Guillelmi* and the 'D' version of the Anglo-Saxon Chronicle.

---

[21] Thus, Nicholas Vincent, 'The Strange Case of the Missing Biographies: The Lives of the Plantagenet Kings of England 1154–1272', in Bates, Crick, and Hamilton (eds), *Writing Medieval Biography*, 237–57, at 237–8.
[22] Kershaw, *Peaceful Kings*, 264–8; Sverre Bagge, *Kings, Politics and the Right Order of the World in German Historiography, c.950–1150* (Leiden, 2002), 189–220.
[23] Lucas-Avenel, 'Le récit de Geoffroi Malaterra', 176–92.
[24] Cf. George Garnett, *Conquered England: Kingship, Succession, and Tenure, 1066–1166* (Oxford, 2007), 40.
[25] OV, ii, 184–5.   [26] *GG*, 114–15, 154–5, 168–75. For Poitiers' Latin, *GG*, xvii–xxii.
[27] *GG*, 164–5, 166–7, 178–9, 180–3; OV, ii, 194–7, 266–7.

Some recent reservations notwithstanding, the revival of the argument that the 'D' version of the Chronicle was produced within the entourage of the man who crowned William on 25 December 1066, Archbishop Ealdred of York, makes compelling the suggestion that the two histories should be read as a dialogue—albeit almost certainly an indirect one—on the morality of William's conduct.[28] At the core of this dialogue would have been the preliminary oath that William agreed to take before he was crowned: 'that he would hold this nation as well as the best of any kings before him, if they would be loyal to him', an oath that John of Worcester and William of Malmesbury subsequently rendered somewhat differently, making it explicit in their versions that William swore to treat French and English equally.[29] So approached, wherever and however it was produced, the text of 'D' up until 1069 reads like a sad commentary on any assumption that might have been made by Ealdred and others that, by following the processes by which Ealdred's illustrious predecessor at York, Archbishop Wulfstan, had managed a previous conqueror, Cnut, they might guide William and protect the English.[30] It is worth observing too that Poitiers actually compared William's conduct to that of Cnut, arguing that, if only the English would allow it, William would turn out to be a mild and merciful ruler unlike the cruel Cnut who had slaughtered the noblest of the English. If he is here deliberately focusing on the model that Ealdred and his associates were trying to apply, he is somewhat incoherently bringing into the open the unbridgeable chasm of expectations that was inherent in the processes initiated in Normandy before the invasion and the oath William swore on 25 December 1066.[31]

A narrative in 'D' that begins with a justification of the claims of Edgar the Ætheling to be king—something that was entirely logical in terms of a search for the solution that would be pleasing to God, and therefore an indication of the right-mindedness of those involved—then proceeds to William's coronation, and subsequently to a series of condemnations of heavy taxation, the oppressive behaviour of William's regents, Bishop Odo and William fitz Osbern, and to a litany of promises fulfilled badly. What sets out at the start as a presentation of a search for a legitimate solution that would allow resistance to continue after the defeat at Hastings therefore evolved into a mixture of acceptance of defeat and scarcely veiled statements that William was failing to fulfil the promise made at his coronation.

---

[28] *The Anglo-Saxon Chronicle: A Collaborative Edition*, vol. 6: *ms. D*, ed. G. P. Cubbin (Cambridge, 1996), lxxviii–lxxix; Patrick Wormald, *How Do We Know So Much about Anglo-Saxon Deerhurst*, Deerhurst Lecture, 1991 (Deerhurst: Friends of Deerhurst Church, 1991), 9–17 (reprinted in Patrick Wormald, *The Times of Bede: Studies in Early English Christian Society and its Historian*, ed. Stephen Baxter (Oxford, 2006), 229–48, at 236–9). For reservations, Pauline Stafford, 'Archbishop Ealdred and the D Chronicle', in *Normandy and Neighbours*, 135–56. Note especially, 'It may be as much commentary, critique, retrospect, and apologia as simple record of events and actions' (p. 156). See also Brooks, 'Why is the *Anglo-Saxon Chronicle* about Kings?', 55–6.

[29] ASC, 'D', 1066; JW, ii, 606–7; GP, i, 384–5.

[30] GR, i: 470–1; for Ealdred as modeling his actions on Wulfstan, Patrick Wormald, *The Making of English Law: King Alfred to the Twelfth Century*, vol. 1: *Legislation and Its Limits* (Oxford, 1999), 130–4, 223–4.

[31] GG, 156–7.

The text also makes it clear that those for whom it was written believed that divine displeasure was at the root of all, by quoting Matthew 10:29 to the effect that a sparrow cannot fall into a trap unless God has ordained it, and making frequent reference to the English being punished for sin. The defeated must recognize their failings and repent and atone, but the victors were proving unworthy of their new responsibilities. The totemic moment in the story of these years must surely be William's crown-wearing in the cathedral at York at Christmas 1069 in the midst of a city blackened by fire, by which date Archbishop Ealdred was dead. In 'D''s words in the annal for the previous year, William had made St Peter's Minster an object of scorn.[32] In William of Malmesbury's portrait of him, Ealdred was a man who had tried to love William as a son, but who subsequently lost patience with him and formally cursed him, a vigorous and energetic man who died broken in body and spirit.[33] William of Poitiers singles him out as having been especially helpful to William.[34]

That William of Poitiers did not finish the *Gesta Guillelmi* raises the possibility that he came to find his subject morally repugnant: Orderic's comment that he was prevented from finishing by unfavourable circumstances, and that he then gave himself up to silence and prayer, does not quite fit this suggestion, but it does not rule it out; that the *Gesta Guillelmi* must have come to an incomplete end after the fall of Ely and the death of Earl Edwin is certainly suggestive that the subject was becoming difficult. The parallel with Stephen of Rouen's similarly unexplained abandonment of his eulogy of the rulers of Normandy, the *Draco Normannicus*, in 1169, after forecasting that it was safe for Archbishop Thomas Becket to return to England, is at least striking.[35] It may also be significant that, in his appeal to the English to put aside prejudice and learn to appreciate William's worth, Poitiers acknowledged that his arguments on William's behalf were not, at the time of writing, proving convincing.[36] To pile on another hypothesis, it is also irresistible to raise the possibility that Poitiers was not the only historian to abandon the task of writing about William, since—admittedly without supplying a reason—William of Jumièges in the mid-1050s also appears to have given up on the section of the *Gesta Normannorum Ducum* devoted to William, resuming his task again in rather cursory fashion after the triumph of 1066.[37] If there is anything in these arguments, they suggest that aspects of William's conduct were thought extreme even by those trying to write favourably on his behalf. When it comes to William as the maker of empire, however, even if they point to a ruthlessness that shocked and disquieted and to a man who could push convention to its limits and, in all probability, beyond them, they can also be read as suggesting a mixture of political and military effectiveness that would reassure most who joined the invasion of 1066, a skilful and resourceful practitioner of the norms and scripts of early medieval warrior kingship.

---

[32] ASC, 'D', 1068.   [33] *GP*, i, 384–5.   [34] *GG*, 186–7.
[35] OV, ii, 184–5, 258–9; Stephen of Rouen, *Draco Normannicus*, in *Chronicles*, ii, 677.
[36] *GG*, 156–7.   [37] *GND*, i, xxxii–xxxv.

THE MAKER OF EMPIRE

In the conduct of warfare, so William of Poitiers tells us, it was one of William's praiseworthy characteristics that he avoided unnecessary slaughter.[38] The theatrical preliminaries with which he prefaced his account of the Battle of Hastings are the best known illustration of the theme.[39] Notably specific on what was meant by the avoidance of excessive violence, however, is Poitiers's account of the so-called Battle of Varaville (1057). In an elaboration of a passage that is also in the *Gesta Normannorum Ducum* of William of Jumièges, he has, on William's orders, a small troop of enemy warriors waiting to cross the marshes of the Dives killed almost to the last man. The justification he provides, which is within the notion of legitimate conduct in a just war set out by Isidore of Seville and others, is that to have spared the soldiers would actually have been a crime (*parcere flagitium credens*) because this act of calculated butchery was necessary to save Normandy from invasion.[40] Similar arguments are used to justify the way in which William brought about the surrender of the city of Le Mans and the aristocracy of the county of Maine in 1063; it was more humane to devastate vineyards and fields through frequent ravaging of the countryside than to have attacked the city directly because of the destruction that this would have caused.[41]

Instances from other sources of this type of behaviour are provided by the well-known passage in William of Jumièges, omitted by Poitiers, describing the mutilation of the defenders of Alençon, in all probability in either 1050 or 1051, and, from after 1066, the blinding of a hostage to communicate symbolically a message about treachery to the defenders of Exeter in 1068.[42] And Guibert of Nogent, whose father had been taken prisoner fighting in a war against William, commented that William had a reputation for treating prisoners of war more harshly than his contemporaries by holding them in prison for longer than the

---

[38] 'Monet equidem digna ratio et hoc memoriae prodere, quam pia continentia caedem semper uitauerit, nisi bellica ui alia graui necessitudine urgente' (*GG*, 38–9). For the general issues, Matthew Strickland, 'Killing or Clemency? Ransom, Chivalry and Changing Attitudes to Defeated Opponents in Britain and Northern France, 7th–12th Centuries', in *Krieg im Mittelalter*, ed. Hans-Hennin Kortüm (Berlin, 2001), 93–122. Also important is Gillingham, 'Holding to the Rules of War', 1–15.

[39] See Matthew Strickland, 'Provoking or Avoiding Battle? Challenge, Judicial Duel, and Single Combat in Eleventh- and Twelfth-Century Warfare', in *Armies, Chivalry and Warfare in Medieval Britain and France: Proceedings of the 1995 Harlaxton Symposium*, ed. Matthew Strickland (Stamford, 1998), 317–43, and esp. 317–20, 324.

[40] *GG*, 54–7; *GND*, ii, 152–3. For a recent discussion of the battle, Stéphane Lainé, 'La bataille de Varaville (1057): examen critique des récits médiévaux', *Bulletin de la Société des Antiquaires de Normandie*, lxvii (2009, for 2008), 257–88, and esp. 260–9. It is interesting that Poitiers, for once, increases the sense of slaughter, while reducing the numbers attacked and killed.

[41] *GG*, 60–1.

[42] *GND*, ii, 124–5; *GG*, 28–9. For 1068, *GND*, ii, 124–5; OV, ii, 212–13. For blinding, Geneviève Bührer-Thierry, '"Just Anger" or "Vengeful Anger"? The Punishment of Blinding in the Early Medieval West', in Barbara H. Rosenwein (ed.), *Anger's Past: The Social Uses of Emotion in the Middle Ages* (Ithaca, NY, 1998), 75–91.

norm. While Poitiers tried to deny this charge, his arguments are not convincing.[43] We can reasonably conclude that intimidatory violence, within which was included the destruction of the countryside and the killing of outnumbered opponents, was a central part of William's armoury as a general.[44] Guibert's story, with its implication that William used conventions about prisoner exchange as a negotiating device, suggests that he pushed these norms to the extreme, just as he in all likelihood consistently took a maximum view of what was legitimate violence.

Similar conclusions emerge from William's treatment of rebellion. Thus, the chief rebels defeated in 1047 at Val-ès-Dunes seem at a superficial level to have been mercifully treated. Whether the revolt's ringleader, Count Guy of Brionne, either chose or was forced into permanent exile, a point on which the narratives of William of Jumièges and William of Poitiers disagree, the discrepancy clarifies what an act of mercy on William's part actually meant, with Jumièges equating what Poitiers described as merciful treatment with house arrest; he thereby indicates that William could have been more severe than he actually was.[45] The reappearance among the *signa* of charters of other former rebels would appear to argue in favour of an ultimately merciful reintegration, but their later life histories clearly show that they were always at most on the margins of favour. While Grimoald du Plessis-Grimoult, who had tried to assassinate William, was a special case involving disloyalty at a level that led to total forfeiture, and therefore dying a prisoner, having been kept perpetually in chains throughout his imprisonment,[46] it is notable that, of the rebels' descendants, only the children of Haimo Dentatus received significant rewards in England after 1066, subsequently working their way there to considerable prominence.[47] The two *vicomtes* Nigel and Rannulf received almost no lands in England after 1066, although some of the former's subtenants did.[48] Ralph Taisson, who had changed sides at Val-ès-Dunes, remained prominent in Normandy in the 1050s, but his descendants were also excluded from major rewards after 1066.[49] Orderic's comment that certain Normans disinherited by William decided that it was safe to return to the duchy from Apulia and Calabria only after having heard of his death highlights the extent of both his reach and his reputation and reinforces the view that William's anger—using the word in the technical sense—was indeed terrifying and implacable.[50] While, as is nowadays often argued, the overall framework of revolt and exile was frequently one of

---

[43] 'Cuius comitis consuetude fuerat, ut nunquam captiuos suos ad redemptionem cogeret sed perpetua dum aduiuerent carceris relegatione damnauit'; *Guibert de Nogent, Autobiographie*, 88; cf. *GG*, 38–9, 50–1.

[44] Fundamental for the moral dimension of ravaging in eleventh-century warfare is Strickland, *War and Chivalry*, 258–90, 335–6.

[45] *GG*, 12–13; *GND*, ii, 122–7 ('cum domesticis eum in sua manere domo iussit').

[46] On the whole subject, Emily Zack Tabuteau, 'Punishments in Eleventh-Century Normandy', in Warren C. Brown and Piotr Górecki (eds), *Conflict in Medieval Europe: Changing Perspectives on Society and Culture* (Aldershot, 2003), 131–49, and see esp. 137, 143–7; Strickland, *War and Chivalry*, 231–57.

[47] *The Domesday Monachorum of Christ Church, Canterbury*, ed. D. C. Douglas (London, 1944), 55–6; *DP*, 242.

[48] For Nigel, *DP*, 7.   [49] For Ralph, *RADN*, nos. 115, 122, 140, 141.

[50] OV, iv, 98–101, 102–3.

dialogue, the route to reconciliation in William's Normandy was certainly not a predictable one, was frequently a long one, and was sometimes fruitless.[51] There could be a long afterlife of qualified favour after apparent reconciliation.

The formation around William of a small group of politically dominant individuals, with his two half-brothers, Bishop Odo of Bayeux and Count Robert of Mortain, William fitz Osbern, Roger de Montgommery, Roger de Beaumont, William de Warenne, and Richard fitz Gilbert being the most cited names, is one of the great and incontestable themes of all historical writing on William the Conqueror. The creation for almost all of them of vast cross-Channel estates was to become the central pillar in the edifice of empire. Inevitably too, it was around this core that orbited the lives of a mass of expectant individuals whose destinies were constantly being determined by their massive power. It is further notable that by 1087, some forty ecclesiastical institutions in Normandy and northern France already possessed property in England valued at over £1,000 in Domesday Book values.[52] The creation of multiple cross-Channel networks was a feature of the making of empire that was present from the very beginning. And, as was noted in Chapter 1, the scale and sheer intensity of the takeover of the sources and sinews of wealth and power in England was truly remarkable.

While it is of course right to highlight the cohesion of the renowned group that carried out the conquest of England, it is also wrong to overstate its stability. That many conflicts were superficially quiescent during William's adult years is an obvious testimony to his capacity to unite strong personalities around him through a mixture of example, persuasion, and sheer force of will. But this does not mean that we are dealing with a powerful sense of unified Norman endeavour. Rather it makes the conquest of England the product of a moment. Feud, defined as a mindset that motivated individuals and families to seek the righting of wrongs through whatever means were expedient, was a constant in political society.[53] In this context, it should be noted that William's Norman legislation of the year 1075 did not ban the seeking of violent revenge; it merely restricted it to the son or father of the victim.[54] Orderic's narratives of relations between what we can call the Beaumont and Tosny families show that interfamilial conflict could run across generations and erupt when ducal authority was not sufficiently well entrenched to act as an effective umpire.[55] Further issues are regional differences within Normandy, the impact of horizontal bonds of generational friendship that created the

---

[51] Most recently, Ewan Johnson, 'The Process of Norman Exile into Southern Italy', in Laura Napran and Elisabeth van Houts (eds), *Exile in the Middle Ages: Selected Proceedings from the International Medieval Congress, University of Leeds, 8–11 July 2002* (Turnhout, 2004), 29–38, and esp. 34–7. The extensive case study of Robert de Grandmesnil, abbot of Saint-Evroult, illustrates very well these arguments; OV, ii: 90–1; Bates, 'Anger, Emotion and a Biography', 26–8.

[52] Donald Matthew, *The Norman Monasteries and Their English Possessions* (Oxford, 1962), 13–14.

[53] These arguments are cogently made in Hyams, *Rancor and Reconciliation*, 3–14, 111–94.

[54] For the legislation, Haskins, *Norman Institutions*, 278 n. 9.

[55] Hyams, *Rancor and Reconciliation*, 125–31, 281; Thomas Roche, 'The Way Vengeance Comes: Rancorous Deeds and Words in the World of Orderic Vitalis', in Susanna A. Throop and Paul R. Hyams (eds), *Vengeance in the Middle Ages: Emotion, Religion and Feud* (Farnham, 2010), 115–36, at 134.

party that supported Robert Curthose's revolt against his father in the late 1070s, the differing gender roles demonstrated by Queen Matilda's covert support for her eldest son, and the rapid breakdown of cohesion after William's death. All these fault-lines within the aristocratic society of pre- and post-1066 Normandy were in varying forms transferred into the new cross-Channel society.[56] However, when the argument is expressed in systemic terms, instability can become one of the constituents of stability. Competition and rivalry were elements in the impetus towards homeostasis, just as they were also disruptive.[57]

In the same way, although the invasion of 1066 drew in warriors and an aristocratic elite from many regions of northern and western France, the alliances involved were often recent creations, products of the extraordinary circumstances of the time. Thus, the collaboration between William and Eustace, count of Boulogne, Edward the Confessor's brother-in-law, was so much a matter of immediate personal interest to Eustace that he attempted an invasion of England before the year 1067 was out. The subsequent reconciliation between William and Eustace, probably dateable to 1071–2, not only recreated a cross-Channel estate for Eustace, but was in all likelihood caused by the breakdown of another alliance that had been beneficial in 1066, namely that with one of the truly great powers of the northern French littoral, the counts of Flanders, William's wife's family.[58] The surprisingly obscure episode of Harold Godwineson's capture by Guy, count of Ponthieu, in 1064, may well be another manifestation of the tensions and rivalries that ran through northern French political society. Theoretically obligated to William, the fact that William had to send ambassadors to secure Harold's release must surely indicate that Guy was trying to exploit the situation to some personal advantage.[59]

Taken as a whole, one of the most significant aspects of William's career before 1066 is its disruption of long-standing alliances across northern France, with the ending in 1052 of a long-standing collaborative relationship with the Capetian kings of France being an event of the greatest importance. William's generally aggressive demeanour involving warfare around Normandy's frontiers and an interest in the English succession must be a central factor in this process. The invasions of Normandy by King Henry I and Count Geoffrey Martel in 1054 and 1057 must have been intended to bring William to heel. Their deaths in 1060 cleared the decks for William to emerge as the strong man in this volatile world. The conquest of Maine in 1062–3 was the apparent great gain that he made out of this new balance of power.[60] But nothing fundamental had changed as a result. In this milieu of multiple entrenched networks and of well-resourced and unassailable territorial princes

---

[56] *DP*, 73–5; OV, iii, 100–5, 110–13; iv, 102–7, 112–15.
[57] See further, Chaps. 4 and 6.
[58] Heather J. Tanner, *Families, Friends and Allies: Boulogne and Politics in Northern France and England, c.879–1160* (Leiden, 2004), 100–3; Elijas Oksanen, *Flanders and the Anglo-Norman World, 1066–1216* (Cambridge, 2012), 13, 17.
[59] Most recently, Alban Gautier, 'Comment Harold prêta serment: circonstances et interprétations d'un rituel politique', *Cahiers de civilisation médiévale*, lv (2012), 33–56, at 44, 47–8.
[60] For this approach to William's rule in the 1050s, David Bates, 'The Conqueror's Adolescence', *ANS*, xxv (2003), 1–18, at 15–18.

based at a considerable distance beyond Normandy's frontiers, a decisive military victory was never possible.

William's attention to religious detail, very evident in the pre-1066 evidence, must surely have supplied considerable reassurance to those who joined him. From a charter written outside the duchy, we learn of the case of Richard de Reviers, who died excommunicate in *c*.1060 while defending the castle of Thimert beyond Normandy's southern frontier to the south of Dreux on William's behalf. All hostilities were brought to a temporary end and Richard's suitable burial in the abbey of Saint-Père of Chartres was arranged.[61] Along with the long-term cultivation of good relations with a series of popes, the procurement of a banner from Pope Alexander II in 1066 itself, and, subsequently, papal approval of penances for those who had taken part in the warfare, the dedication on 18 June 1066 of the new abbey church of La Trinité of Caen, located a few miles away from the assembled army and fleet, fit within a long-established framework that sought to reassure through religious demonstrations.[62] At the same time, the enclosure as a child oblate at La Trinité of one of William's and Matilda's daughters, Cecilia, demonstrated in the most profound way possible the couple's dedication to the cause, with the personal sacrifice later being described by a poet—with quite a few inaccuracies—as equivalent to that made by the biblical king Jephthah who had had sacrificially to kill a daughter in return for a military victory.[63]

If, as the *cause célèbre* of William and Matilda's marriage within the prohibited degrees of kinship surely makes clear, William might be slow to react to religious advice, that he usually did so is equally obvious; the same point is demonstrated by his eventual punishment of the blasphemous jester who had compared him to God and made explicit by William of Malmesbury.[64] There may well have been personal crises along the way that were a significant formative influence; the charter establishing a house of canons at Cherbourg refers to a near-death illness in the years immediately before 1066, for example.[65] However, in the modern discourse of empire, this performance of the religious role required of William by the model of warrior kingship is easily identified as soft power, the creation of an enabling environment aimed to make the underlying hard power seem more acceptable. It is a combination that must have made William a persuasive leader of the invasion of England. And it was also one that imposed a powerful imprint on the cross-Channel empire that was created.

---

[61] *RADN*, no. 147 (version *a*).
[62] In general, David S. Bachrach, *Religion and the Conduct of War, c.300–1215* (Woodbridge, 2003), 84–5, 98–103, 152–64.
[63] *Les actes de Guillaume le Conquérant et de la reine Mathilde pour les abbayes caennaises*, ed. L. Musset (Caen, 1967), no. 2; M. Colker, 'Fulcoii Belvacensis epistolae', *Traditio*, x (1954), 191–273, at 245–6 (*Normans in Europe*, 132–3).
[64] *GP*, i, 90–1; *Vita Lanfranci*, ed. Margaret Gibson, in G. D'Onofrio (ed.), *Lanfranco di Pavia e l'Europa del secolo XI nel IX centenario della morte* (Rome, 1993), 661–715, at 708–9. On the incident with the jester, Margaret Gibson, 'The Image of Lanfranc', in *Lanfranco di Pavia*, 21–8, at 25–6; H. E. J. Cowdrey, *Lanfranc: Scholar, Monk and Archbishop* (Oxford, 2003), 187.
[65] *RADN*, no. 224; *Le cartulaire du chapitre cathedral de Coutances*, ed. Julie Fontanel (Saint-Lô, 2003), no. 339 (*cum ab ipsa infirmitate in qua fuit, pene omnino de uita desperatus*).

AN EMPIRE MADE

The origins of William's aggressive attitude towards the count of Anjou's hegemonic hold on the county of Maine and his conquest of the county in 1062–3 lie in the 1040s, with the issue of rule over the large strategically placed county being a central factor in many of the wars between northern French territorial rulers in that decade and the following one. The subjugation of Maine is presented by William of Poitiers in ways that appear to make it almost a test-bed for 1066, involving a promise of the succession by Count Herbert II and a military intervention against those who sought to oppose its implementation.[66] The takeover was almost immediately legitimized by William's eldest son, Robert, doing homage and fealty to the then count of Anjou, Geoffrey III the Bearded (1060–7), a recognition of lordship that instantly created a framework of legitimacy within which relationships would henceforth have to be negotiated.[67] It is, however, there that similarities between the two conquests end.

The combination of the apparent rapid establishment of the *modus vivendi* with the count of Anjou and the existence of extensive networks linking the Manceau aristocracy to the Loire valley probably explain why the exercise of hegemonic power over the county after 1062–3 was so dramatically different from England after 1066. The most striking expression of this difference is that there was no dispossession of Manceau castellans at any point between the successful invasion of 1062–3 and William's death in 1087, and this despite the fact that a man such as Geoffrey de Mayenne had a record of rebellion every bit as long as anyone in England.[68] Orderic's account of the two-year siege of the rebel *vicomte* Hubert in Sainte-Suzanne from 1083/4 onwards typifies a world that was politically and militarily very different from England between 1066 and 1072; the besiegers and the garrison were approximately equal in numbers, skirmishes, when they took place, involved the ransoming of prisoners, and William's strategy was ultimately based on containment through the construction of the magnificent earthwork 'Le Camp de Beugy'.[69] William's power in Maine was therefore fundamentally sustained by alliances with the bishops of Le Mans and the major abbeys, by a garrison in Le Mans, and by the encouragement of regional networks linking western Normandy and Maine.[70] His and his son Robert's rule was overthrown between 1069 and 1073 and frequently threatened. The networks linking the main churches and castellans of Maine to the Loire valley,

---

[66] *GG*, 60–3; most recently, Garnett, *Conquered England*, 9.

[67] For the main details of William's relationship with the county of Maine, OV, ii, 304–11; William M. Aird, *Robert Curthose, Duke of Normandy (c.1050–1134)* (Woodbridge, 2008), 45 n. 22, suggests 1063 for the act of homage.

[68] Richard E. Barton, *Lordship in the County of Maine, c.890–1160* (Woodbridge, 2004), 166–7.

[69] OV, iv, 46–53. For the likely length of the siege, see 48 n. 3.

[70] See, for example, Yannick Hillion, 'Arnaud et Hoël, deux évêques du Mans au service de Guillaume le Conquérant', *Annales de Bretagne et des pays de l'Ouest*, cx (2003), 49–77, at 61–8. Difficulties in Maine that involved papal intervention were usually resolved in William's favour, H. E. J. Cowdrey, 'Pope Gregory VII and the Anglo-Norman Church and Kingdom', *Studi Gregoriani*, ix (1972), 79–114, at 98–100 (reprinted in H. E. J. Cowdrey, *Popes, Monks and Crusaders* (London, 1984), Chap. 9).

and, most importantly in terms of the politics of the situation, to the counts of Anjou, continued to develop over the whole period.[71]

At the same time, no attempt was made to integrate the aristocracy of Maine into the new cross-Channel empire through grants of land in England. As Katharine Keats-Rohan has succinctly pointed out, there is 'no indisputable documentary evidence of any landholding by a Manceau layman (in England) before 1087', even though men from Maine were certainly present at Hastings and took part in the campaign in northern England of 1069–70.[72] This failure to reward the aristocracy of Maine in England must in all likelihood be associated with William's severe attitude to rebellion; actions on his part that might appear to reward disloyalty were evidently not possible, even if, on a different standard of values, they might have been thought politically expedient. That the revolts could appear to be timed to exploit his difficulties in England must have further fuelled these attitudes. The evidence for any effort at all being made to create power structures that integrated Maine into the cross-Channel Anglo-Norman complex in William's time is very thin.[73]

Two further possible contributing factors to this situation were the severely limited customary powers of the counts of Maine that arguably put drastic disciplinary action off limits, and concern that too heavy-handed an intervention would provoke military action from the counts of Anjou and the king of France. It is also notable that, despite his theoretical lordship, Count Geoffrey the Bearded's supplanter, Count Fulk IV Rechin (1067–1109), did not intervene much in Maine; the big powers kept their distance and avoided the dangers of confrontation.[74] The one occasion when battle might have been joined was speedily defused by a papal legate, and was followed by the so-called treaty of 'Blanchelande' and a renewal of Robert's homage and fealty to Count Fulk. It nonetheless remains a paradox that the conquest of England up until 1087 absorbed men and women from across the whole of northern France into a complex of networks and relationships, but that individuals from a territory over which William usually exercised direct rule gained little out of it. English warriors were deployed in Maine by William from as early as 1073, whereas Manceaux seem to have been kept out of England.[75]

The campaigns in England after 1066 exhibit on an extreme scale the calculated use of intimidation and violence that had characterized William's conduct in northern France before 1066. Thus, as Frank Barlow and John Gillingham have

---

[71] For a clear statement of this point, Daniel Pichot, *Le Bas-Maine du Xe au XIIIe siècle: étude d'une société* (Laval, 1995), 132–3.

[72] *DP*, 33. For Manceaux at Hastings, *GG*, 130–1; *Actus Pontificum Cenomannis in urbe degentium*, ed. G. Busson and A. Ledru (Le Mans, 1902), 376. For northern England, OV, ii, 234–5.

[73] Note, in particular, *Regesta*, no. 170. Only two of the abbeys of Maine, Saint-Calais and Saint-Pierre de la Couture, are recorded in Domesday Book (*DP*, 522–3) as holding English lands, but neither apparently as the result of a grant by William (*DB*, i, fos 147^v (as a tenant of Walter Giffard), 340^v (as a tenant of the bishop of Durham)).

[74] For this interpretation, Bruno Lemesle, *La société aristocratique dans le Haut-Maine (XIe–XIIe siècles)* (Rennes, 1999), 32–8.

[75] ASC, 'D', 'E', 1073; OV, ii, 306–7.

pointed out in relation to Hastings, both William of Jumièges and, most especially, the *Carmen de Hastingae Proelio* put much more emphasis on the scale of the slaughter of the English than does Poitiers; the later stages of the battle should, in fact, probably be seen as having been a massacre.[76] The punishment at Romney, soon after the start of the march around the Sussex and Kent coasts that began after the battle, of those English who had killed a group from the invasion force that had sailed off course and landed there, was presumably done to sustain the morale of William's troops and crush identifiable opposition to the rear as his army set off inland.[77] Poitiers's subsequent attempt to explain why William did not punish his troops' indiscipline at Dover on the grounds that the culprits were so numerous that they could not be identified may strain credulity, but it did indicate to William's troops that their welfare was the uppermost consideration and, as such, represents an important illustration of the conflicting interests that he needed to take account of.[78] Not only was the subsequent march around the south of London an unqualified display of hard power, the campaigns conducted by William and others in the north and west of England between 1068 and 1070 all involved the killing of defeated opponents.[79] Later, at the conclusion of the 1075 revolt, some of the Bretons who had participated were blinded on William's orders, while his generals mutilated all the prisoners taken after the battle at Fawdon in Whaddon (Cambridgeshire).[80]

To seek explanations for this course of events is to move into the domain of biography. The statistics recorded in the 'D' version of the Anglo-Saxon Chronicle to the effect that, after Harold's victory at the Battle of Stamford Bridge, the survivors of an army which had arrived in three hundred ships left in twenty-four must be a factor; William, it can be surmised, knew the sort of enemy he was up against and acted accordingly.[81] However, if William might have been expected to change the way he conducted war after he had been crowned king and because of his coronation oath, it did not happen. An influential factor—and one of the likely explanations for what happened—must surely be supplied by the words that Poitiers claims were addressed directly by William to Harold before the Battle of Hastings, namely, that the one of them who would eventually triumph was the one who had the confidence to distribute his enemy's possessions no less than his own, an allusion surely to William's having agreed well before his victory at Hastings—albeit probably in most cases in general terms—to distribute the lands of those who had opposed him to his own supporters.[82] Of similar import is Poitiers's statement

---

[76] *The Carmen de Hastingae Proelio of Guy Bishop of Amiens*, ed. F. Barlow, OMT (Oxford, 1999), lxxxii–lxxxviii; Gillingham, 'Holding to the Rules of War', 12–13; M. K. Lawson, *The Battle of Hastings, 1066* (Stroud, 2002), 213–14.

[77] *GG*, 142–3.   [78] *GG*, 144–5.

[79] J. J. N. Palmer, 'The Conqueror's Footprints in Domesday Book', in *The Medieval Military Revolution: State, Society and Military Change in Medieval and Early Modern Europe*, ed. Andrew Ayton and J. L. Price (London, 1995), 23–44, at 36–8; *GND*, ii, 180–1; OV, ii, 222–3, 228–31, 230–3; ASC, 'D', 1066, 1067, 1068.

[80] ASC, 'D', 'E', 1075; OV, ii, 316–17.   [81] ASC, 'D', 1066.

[82] 'Hostem haud dubie superabit qui non minus quae hostis possidet quampropria largiri ualet'; *GG*, 108–9. The statement in the so-called Ship List that William had granted the earldom of Kent to

that many individuals from outside Normandy were attracted to William's cause, not simply, or only, because it was a just one, but because of his reputation for being generous.[83] Like the other passage, it again foregrounds in the most fundamental way the tension between the requirement of the supplementary oath to treat his English subjects equitably and the convention that an early medieval war leader would distribute rewards. Given that the army that sailed across the Channel was substantially drawn from the entourages of the aristocratic elites of northern and western France, most notably from the lands of the counts of Flanders and the family of the dukes of Brittany, and from the lands close to Normandy's eastern frontier, such people are not likely to have come cheaply.[84] In company of this kind the price of either failure or of a lack of appropriate generosity on William's part was surely beyond contemplation. These norms and expectations drove on a comprehensive takeover and destroyed the prospects of ethnic equilibrium in the uppermost levels of aristocratic society.

The complexities created by the irreconcilability of these promises and the ideological ethnic plurality of the cross-Channel empire is illuminated by the transfer to Normandy in 1067 in William's entourage of the chief English nobles who had submitted in 1066. While attendance at court would have been the expectation of aristocrats of the highest birth, what happened was also, as Poitiers actually said, a consequence of their loyalty being suspect; although treated generously while in Normandy, they were effectively under house arrest.[85] While rearranging Poitiers's material, Orderic kept most of it in, presenting William's conduct as calculated kindness, with his choice of words surely putting the emphasis on calculation (*Benigna calliditate est usus*).[86] And another manifestation of the volatility of these times is illuminated by major figures who had participated in the campaigns of 1066, such as Geoffrey de Chaumont and Aimeri de Thouars, returning to France, and by others who stayed or were recruited later, such as the Breton Count Brian and the Fleming brothers Frederick and Gerbod, briefly the second earl of Chester, either abandoning their charges or being killed.[87] In addition, William would certainly have been aware that a revolt had taken place in Maine in the spring of 1069, just as he was also facing up to a coordinated campaign by his enemies in

---

his wife, Matilda, in return for her gift of a ship both demonstrates that grants were made in advance of the victory at Hastings and that, since Matilda did not receive the earldom, such grants were reconsidered after the victory; Elisabeth van Houts, 'The Ship List of William the Conqueror', *ANS*, x (1988), 159–83, at 176 (van Houts, *History and Family Traditions*, Chap. 6).

[83] *GG*, 102–3. On this theme, note *GR*, i, 446–7 ('largis sumptibus milites suos continebat, alienos inuitabat'), 448–9 ('omnes eius uoluntatem plausibus excipientes magnificis promissis animasset').

[84] This point is made very effectively in Keats-Rohan, *DP*, 30–75. See further, Jane Martindale, 'Aimeri of Thouars and the Poitevin Connection', *ANS*, vii (1985), 224–45; Katharine Keats-Rohan, 'William I and the Breton Contingent in the Non-Norman Conquest, 1066–1087', *ANS*, xiii (1991), 157–72; Jean Dunbabin, 'Geoffrey of Chaumont, Thibaud of Blois and William the Conqueror', *ANS*, xvi (1994), 101–16, at 110–12; Renée Nip, 'The Political Relations between England and Flanders (1066–1128)', *ANS*, xxi (1999), 145–67, at 151–3; Oksanen, *Flanders and the Anglo-Norman World*, 180–4.

[85] *GG*, 166–9, 178–81.   [86] OV, ii, 196–7.   [87] For unrest, OV, ii, 236–7.

northern and eastern England. At that point, if not before, what they had taken on would have become starkly apparent to him and his closest associates.

Orderic interpreted the disruption of William's coronation as evidence of a direct intervention of the Devil in human affairs.[88] In other words, for him, men and women might play out their lives according to the conventions that normally sustained them, but they were at the mercy of forces beyond their control. So might these terrible times be interpreted, but, if human agency is foregrounded, the most illuminating and evocative of the great set-pieces of this period is surely William's display of tears when he learnt of the betrayal and murder of Earl Edwin of Mercia in 1071, a theatrical performance followed by a display of severity against the killers, who had brought Edwin's severed head into William's presence, and who had hoped for a reward.[89] A reconstruction of the narrative beneath the theatre ought probably to go along the lines of interpreting William's tears as showing appropriate disapproval for the killing of a noble and of a man to whom he had at one point promised a daughter in marriage, while at the same time extricating himself from any direct responsibility for Edwin's death and doing nothing to stop processes already under way gathering even greater momentum, which had since 1066 included the undermining of Edwin's status within his huge earldom.[90] The contradictory values that determined these events and William's conduct are exemplified by the differences between Orderic's and William of Malmesbury's treatments of what still feels like a truly terrible scene. It was Orderic's view—presumably again departing from William of Poitiers—that William had treated Edwin badly by reneging on the promise of the marriage and giving way to the pressures exerted by newcomers greedy for his lands. Malmesbury, however, while also recording the tears, says that Edwin could have enjoyed William's favour but for his frequent disloyalty; ultimately therefore, he was a rebel rightly punished.[91]

As a maker of empire therefore, we might reasonably from this episode think William either skilful at riding the waves of unstoppable change, or alternatively, as shamelessly and hypocritically washing his hands of responsibility for a human and political disaster. The morality of his treatment of Edwin, and much else besides, can still be discussed with every bit as much passion as it was in the early twelfth century and, in all probability, in 1071. We might also see Edwin's killers as examples of English seeking to make their way in the new world created by the conquest and to benefit therefrom. The case for believing that William of Poitiers abandoned the *Gesta Guillelmi* as an impossible task at about this point in compiling the narrative seems to me to be growing ever stronger as material of this kind is presented.

The argument for the creation of an enabling environment of soft power in England from even before William's coronation can be developed in many ways,

---

[88] OV, ii, 184–5. I am grateful to Leonie Hicks for help with this point.
[89] OV, ii, 258–9.
[90] OV, ii, 214–17, 258–61; Stephen Baxter, *The Earls of Mercia: Lordship and Power in Late Anglo-Saxon England* (Oxford, 2007), 270–97, and esp. 281–97.
[91] *GR*, i, 468–9. On this scene, see further, Bates, 'Anger, Emotion and a Biography', 25–6.

with reference, for example, to correspondence with Pope Alexander II, to the Penitential Ordinance, and to the early English writs and charters issued in William's name. All contributed to the creation of a religious and legal framework to legitimate victory and rule and to supply penitential reassurance for the many who had committed acts of violence. They also set out to create a framework for the legal integration of victors and vanquished that was elaborated over time, as, for example, with the procedure of the *murdrum* fine, and—fancifully—by a mid-twelfth-century writer who created a great council held in 1070 at which twelve men from every shire declared on oath the customs of the land.[92] It is striking that in the *Laudes* sung at Queen Matilda's coronation in Westminster Abbey on 11 May 1068, the whole assembled aristocratic laity were referred to as the *principes Anglorum*, without a trace of *Normanni, Franci*, or any other continental peoples in sight.[93] It was as if the author of the *Laudes* wanted to portray a new English nation as having been created within two years of the conquest. Within the conceptual framework of an empire, such idealism was hopelessly optimistic.

What is ultimately striking about this ideological and legal paraphernalia is not the depth or originality of thought involved in what was done, but rather the speed and political energy with which it was put in place, a speed exemplified by the so-called Penitential Ordinance and its use of the canon law term *publicum bellum*, and by William's famous writ for the citizens of London that must date from the first weeks of 1067.[94] The former drew on a centuries-old framework of canon law, and the latter granted to the citizens all the laws that they were worthy of in King Edward's day and that every child should be his father's heir after the father's death, thereby immediately associating the regime with the conventional linking of *lex* and *gens*.[95] This range of legitimizing reference drew on the conventional assumptions of centuries past and on a small number of the basic textbooks of contemporary religious thought and ethnology, namely, the *Etymologies* of Isidore of Seville and from the Pseudo-Isidorean Decretals and its derivative, the *Collectio Lanfranci*, with the two base texts both being well known in Normandy long before 1066.[96]

---

[92] George Garnett, '*Franci et Angli*: The Legal Distinctions between Peoples after the Conquest', *ANS*, viii (1985), 109–37, at 116–28; Bruce R. O'Brien, 'From *Morðor* to *Murdrum*: The Preconquest Origin and Norman Revival of the Murder Fine', *Speculum*, lxxi (1996), 321–5; Bruce R. O'Brien, *God's Peace and King's Peace: The Laws of Edward the Confessor* (Philadelphia, 1999), 31–6, 158–9; John Hudson, *The Oxford History of the Laws of England*, vol. II: *871–1216* (Oxford, 2012), 405–9.

[93] H. E. J. Cowdrey, 'The Anglo-Norman *Laudes Regiae*', *Viator*, xii (1981), 37–78, at 71, with commentary at 60–1 (reprinted in Cowdrey, *Popes, Monks and Crusaders*, Chap. 8).

[94] Cf. Garnett, *Conquered England*, 33–40.

[95] *Councils and Synods*, i, pt. ii, 581–4. I accept a 1067 date for the Penitential Ordinance; see further, H. E. J. Cowdrey, 'Bishop Ermenfrid of Sion and the Penitential Ordinance Following the Battle of Hastings', *Journal of Ecclesiastical History*, xx (1969), 225–42, at 233–40. For a facsimile of the famous London writ, T. A. M. Bishop and P. Chaplais (eds), *Facsimiles of English Royal Writs to A.D. 1100 presented to V. H. Galbraith* (Oxford, 1957), Plate XIV (*Regesta*, no. 180).

[96] For reference to Pseudo-Isidore in Archbishop Malger of Rouen's synodal letter, see Richard Allen, 'Avant Lanfranc. Un réexamen de la carrière de Mauger, archevêque de Rouen (1037–1054/55)', in Julia Barrow and Véronique Gazeau (eds), *Autour de Lanfranc (1010–2010: réforme et réformateurs dans l'Europe du Nord-Ouest (XIe-XIIe siècles))*, forthcoming. I am grateful to Richard Allen for allowing me to consult his article in advance of publication. For the *Etymologiae* of Isidore of

The consequence was that, from even before William the Conqueror's coronation, it was predetermined that his empire would conform to the classic plural imperial formula of *imperium* over multiple *gentes* and *regna*; in terms of the comparative history of medieval empires, therefore, it would be just like the Carolingian Empire.[97] But, chillingly, in relation to those who had fought for Harold at Hastings and those who continued to remain in rebellion, the decision taken was the one already exemplified in the London writ, namely that Harold had not been king and that all who had stood by him were guilty of treason and therefore could be deprived of their lands if they were still alive and could not acquire protectors. It was a decision that articulated William's responsibility to protect his new subjects, yet it explicitly excluded many of them from that protection and had massive consequences for the families of those so excluded. The confrontation between Archbishop Ealdred and William referred to at the start of this chapter is just one illustration of the problems that occurred in a kingdom, large sections of which were scarcely under control and in which the newcomers employed the characteristic methods of intimidation and ravaging to impose themselves.[98] And soft power was also not without other complications. Pope Alexander II's letters indicate a stricter attitude on his part towards the leading English clergy than, for example, William's treatment of Archbishop Stigand between 1066 and 1070 might suggest he wished to take.[99] And later, once Lanfranc was installed at Canterbury, the assertion of Canterbury's primacy and over all the churches of the British Isles involved recourse to Rome that set many precedents for the future. While the final decision to proceed on the basis of what Lanfranc and others believed to be English precedent was imposed by a characteristically ferocious display of William's anger, it opened the floodgates for appeals to the papal court for clarification and exemption.[100]

After 1072 William's itinerary saw him spend most of his time in Normandy, where his main preoccupation was undoubtedly the resumed ongoing round of campaigns against other northern French rulers, a situation that was made more difficult by the quarrel with his eldest son, Robert, that first broke out in either 1077 or 1078.[101] It is notable that military interventions beyond the duchy's borders were unsuccessful, with William's great associate and friend William fitz Osbern being killed at the Battle of Cassel in 1071 when leading a campaign

Seville and *lex* and *gens* in Normandy, see most recently, Hagger, 'Secular Law and Custom', 831–2. On *gens* and *lex* in general, Reynolds, *Kingdoms and Communities*, 18–21, 256–67.

[97] The argument for analysing the takeover of England in comparative terms is also set out in Nicholas Vincent, 'More Tales of the Conquest', in *Normandy and Neighbours*, 271–301, at 295.

[98] Garnett, *Conquered England*, 9–43.

[99] H. E. J. Cowdrey, 'Lanfranc, the Papacy and Canterbury', in D'Onofrio (ed.), *Lanfranco di Pavia*, 439–500, at 449–56 (*Popes and Church Reform in the 11th Century* (Aldershot, 2000), Chap. 10).

[100] Hugh the Chanter, *The History of the Church of York 1066–1127*, ed. Martin Brett, C. N. L. Brooke, and Michael Winterbottom (Oxford, 1990), 6–7. For my comments here, see further, Cowdrey, *Lanfranc*, 87–103; Bates, 'Anger, Emotion and a Biography', 30–1.

[101] For William's post-1072 itinerary, *Regesta*, 75–84. For a suggested revised chronology of the quarrels between William and Robert, Katherine Lack, 'Robert Curthose: Ineffectual Duke or Victim of Spin?', *HSJ*, xx (2009, for 2008), 110–40, at 126–9.

into Flanders ultimately motivated by the family connections of Queen Matilda, and William himself in 1076 suffering what appears to have been the first significant military setback of his life when his forces were taken by surprise while besieging Dol in Brittany by an army led by the French king Philip I. It was in 1087 at Mantes in the French Vexin, when leading yet another campaign into the lands of the French king, that William suffered the intestinal injuries that were to lead eventually to his death.

Most of the marriages arranged for William's and Matilda's daughters involved alliances across northern France; indeed, only one of the proposed marriages we know about involved a distant prince. Thus, three of the failed attempts to marry the unfortunate Adelida were to either Manceau or English aristocrats, and two other daughters, Constance and Adela, were married, respectively, to the counts of Brittany and of Blois-Chartres.[102] They therefore continued a policy already established in the three marriages arranged before 1066 for the Conqueror's sister Adelaide.[103] Rather than demonstrating an aggressive grandeur beyond the territorial core of empire, they suggest defensiveness. And they also perpetuated the social and linguistic exclusiveness of the empire's elite by reinforcing networks into a French-speaking elite, especially since several members of the greatest cross-Channel families, such as William I de Warenne, Roger de Montgommery, and Count Robert of Mortain, also organized marriages with other great aristocratic families across northern and western France.

William's and his wife Matilda's religious patronage expanded hugely in range and scope after 1066; this was not confined to Normandy and England, but took in some very prestigious institutions across France and even further afield.[104] It surely betokens a man who had come to see himself as a European figure and a special king; we should note in this respect the comment of William's son-in-law, Stephen, count of Blois-Chartres, writing to his wife as he travelled with the First Crusade, that he had encountered nothing as magnificent as the couple's largesse until he reached Constantinople.[105] Also of great interest are the insistent, if rather incoherent, references to the possibility that William might intervene in the 1070s in the civil war in Germany and subsequently in the 1080s in the war in Italy between King Henry IV and Pope Gregory VII. In the midst of this, the pro-Gregorian Bishop Hugh of Langres went as far as to prophesy that William would become emperor, while for Pope Gregory VII, William was the only king he would address in Gelasian terms, and, thus, as a worthy partner with the pope in Christian rule.[106]

---

[102] Elisabeth van Houts, 'The Echo of the Conquest in the Latin Sources: Duchess Matilda, Her Daughters, and the Enigma of the Golden Child', in Pierre Bouet, Brian Levy, and François Neveux (eds), *The Bayeux Tapestry: Embroidering the Facts of History* (Caen, 2004), 135–53, at 141–9.

[103] Kathleen Thompson, 'Being the Ducal Sister: The Role of Adelaide of Aumale', in *Normandy and Neighbours*, 61–76, and esp. 65–73.

[104] For details, Lucien Musset, 'Le mécenat des princes normands au XIe siècle', in X. Barret I. Altet (ed.), *Artistes, artisans et production artistique au Moyen Age*, 3 vols (Paris, 1986–90), ii: 121–33, at 125–30; Bates, 'William the Conqueror and His Wider Western World', 74–6.

[105] *Die Krezzugsbriefe aus dem Jahren 1088–1100*, ed. H. Hagenmeyer (Innsbruck, 1901), 139.

[106] 'Chronicon Sancti Huberti Andaginensis', ed. L. Bethmann and W. Wattenbach, MGH, *Scriptores*, viii: 577; for discussion, van Houts, 'Latin Poetry', 42. For Gregory's ways of addressing

In the *De Bello Saxonico*, the author actually says that William failed to intervene in Germany only because he feared to lose England.[107] Other mooted distant projects did not come off, the saddest of which is undoubtedly that of William's daughter Adelida, who was involved in four failed marriage projects, one of which was with a Spanish king, before retiring from the world to become a nun at Saint-Léger de Préaux.[108] A bishop of Santiago, Diego Paláez, was said to have been trying to secure William's intervention there with the offer of the kingdom of Galicia.[109] The extensive networks of the new empire and its ostentation are surely also reasons why we should accept that William's brother Bishop Odo of Bayeux was seeking to become pope in 1082, although the fact that William disapproved of the plan and imprisoned him for setting out to desert his responsibilities in England brings us back to the practicalities of the exercise of actual power. The suggestion that Berengar of Tours wrote to Odo as if writing to a pope fuels further this argument; on a minimum interpretation it suggests that an experienced churchman could think of Odo in quite extraordinary terms.[110]

The self-conscious presentation of William as a special king through architectural language is another aspect of the establishment of empire. The recent book on the White Tower of London contains arguments that show that it was planned in its entirety in the Conqueror's time and that its size and functioning were specifically designed both to overawe London and demonstrate symbolically extraordinary power.[111] It was, of course, located on a Roman site. The same point about symbolic display is also made by the architectural contrast between the two Caen abbeys: La Trinité, pre-1066 in conception, rather small and archaic in style, but significantly elaborated after 1066; Saint-Etienne, post-1066, much larger and innovative.[112] Although William's sons tended to build on a grander scale than their father, as at Westminster, Norwich, Caen, and Falaise, he established a

---

William, H. E. J. Cowdrey, 'The Gregorian Reform in the Anglo-Norman Lands and Scandinavia', *Studi Gregoriani*, xiii (1989), 321–52, at 336–7 (*Popes and Church Reform in the 11th Century*, Chap. 7).

[107] Bruno, 'De Bello Saxonico', ed. F. Schmale, in *Quellen zur Geschichte Kaiser Heinrich IV* (Darmstadt, 1963), 242.

[108] For Adelida, Elisabeth van Houts, 'The Echo of the Conquest in the Latin Sources', 141–4. See also F. R. Cordero Carrete, 'Los esponsales de una hija de Guillermo el Conquistador con un "Rey de Galicia"', *Cuaderno de Estudios Gallegos*, xxi (1952), 57–8.

[109] Emma Falque Rey, *Historia Compostellana* (Turnhout, 1988), 15; Manuel Castiñeiras, '*Didacus Gelmiras*, Patron of the Arts. Compostela's Long Journey: from the Periphery to the Center of Romanesque Art', in Manuel Castiñeiras (ed.), *Compostela and Europe: The Story of Diego Gelmirez* (Santiago de Compostela, 2010), 32–97, at 38; Fernie, 'Three Romanesque Great Churches', 16–17, 22 n. 17. I am grateful to Eric Fernie for drawing my attention to this reference.

[110] OV, iv, 38–45; *GR*, i, 506–7; David Bates, 'The Character and Career of Odo, Bishop of Bayeux (1049/50–1097)', *Speculum*, l (1975), 1–20, at 15–16; H. E. J. Cowdrey 'The Papacy and the Berengarian Controversy', in R. B. C. Huygens and F. Niewöhner (eds), *Auctoritas und Ratio. Studien zu Berengar von Tours* (Wiesbaden, 1990), 109–38, at 137–8 (reprinted in *Popes and Church Reform in the 11th Century*, Chap. 6).

[111] Edward Impey (ed.), *The White Tower* (New Haven, CT, 2008); see esp. the chapters by Roland B. Harris (29–93), Jeremy Ashbee (125–39), Edward Impey (227–41), and Philip Dixon (243–75).

[112] Baylé (ed.), *L'architecture normande au Moyen Age*, ii: 50–61; Fernie, *Architecture of Norman England*, 98–102.

fashion for grandeur that they followed.[113] A more fanciful take on the same theme is to visualize William and his half-brother Bishop Odo of Bayeux staring at what has come to be known as the Bayeux Tapestry, recognizing—although perhaps requiring some help to do so—the references to the origin legends of imperial Rome and nodding with approval.[114] However, the fables in the borders might have had them reflecting ironically on the ultimate follies of worldly power.[115] If they did see the Tapestry—the matter, of course, much debated—they cannot but have reflected on its ambiguities; on the moral uncertainties and the responsibilities that come with empire.[116]

The intention in 1066, it would appear, was originally to create a north-western European cross-Channel political space in which the elites of the whole northern French littoral featured more prominently than was eventually to be the case; the withdrawals from England, either voluntarily or because of exile following rebellion, of the Breton Count Brian, the Anglo-Breton Earl Ralph, the Fleming Gerbod, and the French Aubrey de Coucy-le-Château-Auffrique, and the transfer of the majority of their lands in England to Normans, with the most generously rewarded replacements being William's brother Count Robert of Mortain, William de Warenne, and Earl Hugh of Chester, created a much more concentrated Anglo-Norman core than originally envisaged. The result was also the creation within England of a territorial configuration of aristocratic power that linked core and periphery in ways that were conceptually as good as identical to those existing in both Normandy and England before 1066, but which now emphatically became cross-Channel.[117] This was the framework that created opportunity for many of the strong-minded among the victors and, within limits, for the vanquished; the foundations for the life-histories surveyed in the previous chapter and the structures within which the dynamic of empire flourished. The aftermath of the 1075 revolt in England, for example, was a reorganization of land tenure in East Anglia in which both English and Bretons prospered from the misfortunes of others.[118]

The mixing of hard and soft power is very evident in William's visits to the extreme parts of the lands of empire. The 1072 expedition to Scotland not only saw him become the first English king to cross the Forth for two centuries, it was also the occasion on the return journey for a visit to St Cuthbert in Durham, a visit

---

[113] Philip Dixon, 'The Influence of the White Tower on the Great Towers of the Twelfth Century', in Impey (ed.), *The White Tower*, 243–75.

[114] T. A. Heslop, 'Regarding the Spectators of the Bayeux Tapestry: Bishop Odo and His Circle', *Art History*, xxxiii (2009), 223–49, at 237–40.

[115] Stephen D. White, 'The Beasts Who Talk on the Bayeux Embroidery: The Fables Revisited', *ANS*, xxxiv (2012), 209–36, at 228–30.

[116] Most recently, Howard B. Clarke, 'The Identity of the Designer of the Bayeux Tapestry', *ANS*, xxxv (2013), 119–39, at 136–9.

[117] Fleming, *Kings and Lords*, 215–31. Most recently, Max Lieberman, 'The Medieval "Marches" of Normandy and Wales', *EHR*, cxxv (2010), 1357–81, at 1370–9; Charles Insley, 'The Family of Wulfric Spott: An Anglo-Saxon Mercian Marcher Dynasty?', in Roffe (ed.), *The English and Their Legacy*, 115–28.

[118] Lucy Marten, 'The Rebellion of 1075 and Its Impact in East Anglia', in *Medieval East Anglia*, ed. C. Harper-Bill (Woodbridge, 2005), 168–82.

during which he may at first have encountered hostility from the formidable saint, but in due course became a generous benefactor of the church.[119] The slightly different versions of the same opinion in the two versions of the Anglo-Saxon Chronicle that William found nothing worth bothering with beyond the Forth is presumably a reference to a perceived absence of appropriately venerable religious sites; like the comment on the boisterous behaviour of English warriors in Maine, it is also a sign of English writers climbing into the saddle of empire and the Chronicler writing in terms of a new collective identity.[120] The campaign into Wales in 1081, while undoubtedly being a military expedition, also involved an appropriate visit to St David's, as well as the establishment of a new framework for the relationship with the king of Deheubarth, Rhys ap Tewdwr.[121] And on the other side of the Channel, the cathedral church of Le Mans was compensated for war damage after the 1073 campaign.[122]

The links of St Margaret, sister of Edgar the Ætheling, and wife of the king of Scots Mael Coluim III, with William's family and within the heartlands of Wessex demonstrate how soft power was being deployed in relation to the kings of Scots and their kin from an early date. Thus, for example, the future King Donnchad (Duncan) II is argued to have been placed within the household of Count Robert of Mortain, Robert Curthose was certainly godfather to Margaret's daughter Edith/Matilda, the future wife of Robert's brother, King Henry I, and Queen Matilda was her godmother. In all this are the foundations of the better known relationships of the twelfth century.[123] Mael Coluim (Malcolm) III's submission to William at Abernethy in 1072 in the face of an invasion that, given William's recent record, must have been truly terrifying, set personal relationships on a new and defined footing.[124] And lurking in the wings of all these events was Margaret's brother Edgar the Ætheling, the great rebel whom William never punished, the symbolical pensioner at the court of William and his sons, always treated with honour, often prominent in a range of events, and even described as virtually the foster-brother of Robert Curthose, yet utterly without influence. Edgar's career, the honorary Englishman at the courts of the kings of the English and the Scots and the duke

---

[119] Symeon of Durham, *Libellus de Exordio atque Procursu istius, hoc est Dunhelmensis Ecclesie*, ed. and trans. David Rollason (Oxford, 2000), 196–7, with commentary on the different Durham versions of the story at 197 n. 72.

[120] ASC, 'D', 'E', 1072. If the base text on which both versions of the Chronicle were drawing was written at court, then the narratives might become a direct record of William's opinion, Brooks, 'Why is the *Anglo-Saxon Chronicle* about Kings?', 55–62; nb, 'then we might begin to see why the *Chronicle* should have been so quick to accept new rulers' (p. 62).

[121] ASC, 'E', 1081; *Brut y Tywysogyon (Red Book of Hergest Version)*, 30–1; *Brut y Tywysogyon (Peniarth ms. 20 Version)*, 17; Robert S. Babcock, 'Rhys ap Tewdwr, King of Deheubarth', *ANS*, xvi (1994), 21–35, at 26; John Reuben Davies, 'Cathedrals and Cults of Saints in Eleventh- and Twelfth-Century Wales', in. Paul Dalton, Charles Insley, and Louise J. Wilkinson (eds), *Cathedrals, Communities and Conflict in the Anglo-Norman World* (Woodbridge, 2011), 99–115, at 100.

[122] *Regesta*, no. 169.

[123] Stephen Marritt, 'Coincidences of Names, Anglo-Scottish Connections and Anglo-Saxon Society in the Late Eleventh Century', *SHR*, lxxxiii (2004), 150–70.

[124] On the submission of Abernethy, see now, Broun, *Scottish Independence and the Idea of Britain*, 101–3.

of the Normans, whose last years were being lived out in obscurity some sixty years after his brief 'kingship' and rather cruelly assessed by William of Malmesbury, illuminates many facets of the new world of empire.[125] Symbolically and practically all of this represents a concerted and deliberate policy of integration by the new regime into the elites that had survived the cataclysm of 1066 and the years that followed. It was also both a continuation of and a variant version of the empire created in the tenth century by King Æthelstan and continued by his successors.[126]

The Anglo-Saxon Chronicle's statement that, had he lived, William would have imposed himself in Ireland without having to fight to do so, is another facet of the multiple networks created by empire. Beyond doubt incredible as it stands, it may just be believable if it is thought of in terms of the kind of regal overlordship that characterized William's relations with the kings of Scots and several kings and princes in Wales. It was also another expression of the Chronicle's pride at English participation in a new empire and a variant on the long history of early medieval relationship across the Irish Sea.[127] However events are interpreted, the ways in which Toirrdelbach Ua Briain, king of Munster (1063–86), and others responded positively to the new regime in England and encouraged recourse to Lanfranc and the associated potential to be gained from Canterbury's primacy illuminate how those beyond direct rule thought that William's power and prestige could be turned to their advantage.[128]

The making of Domesday Book should also be seen as an imperial project. While any such argument must go back to V. H. Galbraith's famous 1942 article, Ralph Davis's and Sir James Holt's addresses to the 1986 novocentenary conference remain, for me, of central importance.[129] Sir James's two final sentences ('As such it was not intended to "do" anything. It simply "was"') are crucial because they seem to me above all to free discussion from the notion that Domesday Book belongs exclusively in any of the domains of so-called administrative, financial, or legal history.[130] Or as David Roffe would put it, but for different reasons: 'It was, then, no bureaucratic process'. Of equally great importance are the arguments for placing Domesday Book within a tradition of *descriptiones* going back to Caesar Augustus,

---

[125] *GR*, i: 416–17, 466–7; Nicholas Hooper, 'Edgar the Ætheling: Anglo-Saxon Prince, Rebel and Crusader', *ASE*, xiv (1985), 197–214; Simon Keynes, 'The Crowland Psalter and the Sons of Edmund Ironside', *Bodleian Library Record*, xi (1985), 359–70. For Edgar and Robert as brothers, OV, v: 272–3 ('quasi collactaneum fratrem').

[126] See further, Chaps. 1 and 6.

[127] ASC, 'E', 1087; see further, Benjamin Hudson, 'William the Conqueror and Ireland', *Irish Historical Studies*, xxix (1994), 145–58, and esp. 149–58; Clare Downham, 'England and the Irish-Sea Zone in the Eleventh Century', *ANS*, xxvi (2004), 55–73, at 68–71.

[128] *Letters of Lanfranc*, nos. 9, 10; see most recently, Mark Philpott, 'Some Interactions between the English and Irish Churches', *ANS*, xx (1998), 187–204; Martin Holland, 'Dublin and the Reform of the Irish Church in the Eleventh and Twelfth Centuries', *Peritia*, xiv (2000), 111–60, at 111–25; Martin Holland, 'The Synod of Dublin in 1080', in Seán Duffy (ed.), *Medieval Dublin III* (Dublin, 2002), 81–94; Downham, 'England and the Irish-Sea Zone', 69–70.

[129] V. H. Galbraith, 'The Making of Domesday Book', *EHR*, lvii (1942), 160–77.

[130] J. C. Holt, '1086', in J. C. Holt (ed.), *Domesday Studies: Papers Read at the Novocentenary Conference of the Royal Historical Society and the Institute of British Geographers, Winchester, 1986* (Woodbridge, 1987), 41–64, at 64; David Roffe, *Domesday: The Inquest and the Book* (Oxford, 2000), 251.

and the recent arguments of Janet Nelson, who draws particular attention to the survey associated with the Treaty of Verdun (843) and also offers further suggestions as to how we can bridge the tenth-century 'gap'; points to which can be added the fact that we know that Charlemagne had commissioned a survey of conquered lands in Istria which included reference to conditions under the previous rule of the Byzantine emperors.[131] Of course there was 'deep speech' at Gloucester and it may well have involved hard bargaining, although my reconstruction would involve less confrontation than Holt's because all the main players were in the exercise together. It represented an ultimate confirmation of conquest and possession and the basis from which discussion of title could proceed.[132]

An extraordinarily detailed record of people and resources, Domesday Book is a remarkable testimony to the capacities of the local communities of conquered England and the new empire's capacity to mobilize them. But to comprehend its making, it is not necessary to search for direct textual models in the past or to think that a search for precursors must be confined to Normandy and England, a mistake that is sometimes made, and which ignores the culturally wide-ranging influences that typify the development of both the kingdom and the duchy.[133] The project's mastermind need not even have seen a polyptych, although there was one still in use as a working document at Saint-Germain-des-Prés, which is not very far from Normandy.[134] Detailed records of a monastery's properties were a commonplace in both England and the Normandy of the 1070s and 1080s, which was also a time when many of them were formally confirmed by William; there is even the well-known case from the records of the abbey of Fontenay where the local community swore to some of the document's accuracy on oath; their textual fluidity and readiness to draw on existing documentation is also a feature present within Domesday Book.[135] The scribe who wrote Great Domesday Book was innovating as he went along, another sign that he and his associates were responding to new conditions.[136] It is, however, finally irresistible to speculate that what might have weighed most with

---

[131] R. H. C. Davis, 'Domesday Book: Continental Parallels', in Holt (ed.), *Domesday Studies*, 15–39; John Percival, 'The Precursors of Domesday: Roman and Carolingian Land Registers', in P. H. Sawyer (ed.), *Domesday Book: A Reassessment* (London, 1985), 5–27; Janet L. Nelson, 'Henry Loyn and the Context of Anglo-Saxon England', Henry Loyn Memorial Lecture for 2006, *HSJ*, xix (2007), 154–70, at 164–9; Stefan Esders, 'Regionale Selbstbehauptung zwischen Byzanz und dem Frankenreich: Die *inquisitio* der Rechtsgewohnheiten Istriens durch die Sendboten Karls der Großen und Pippins von Italien', in Stefan Esders and Thomas Scharff (eds), *Eid und Wahrheitssuche. Studien zu rechtlichen Befragungspraktiken im Mittelalter und früher Neuzeit*, Gesellschaft, Kultur und Schrift Mediävistische Beiträge, vii (1999), 49–112, at 7–8.

[132] P. R. Hyams, '"No Register of Title": The Domesday Inquest and Land Adjudication', *ANS*, ix (1987), 127–41, at 139.

[133] Cf. Roffe, *Domesday: The Inquest and the Book*, 54–5.

[134] Robert F. Berkhofer III, *Day of Reckoning: Power and Accountability in Medieval France* (Philadelphia, 2004), 112–13.

[135] David Bates, 'Les chartes de confirmation et les pancartes normandes du règne de Guillaume le Conquérant', in M. Parisse, P. Pégeot, and B.-M. Tock (eds), *Pancartes monstiques des XIe et XIIe siècles* (Turnhout, 1998), 95–109, at 105; *Regesta*, no. 149.

[136] David Roffe, 'Domesday Book and Northern Society: A Reassessment', *EHR*, cv (1990), 310–36; C. P. Lewis, 'The Invention of the Manor in Norman England', *ANS*, xxxiv (2012), 123–50; Baxter, 'The Making of Domesday Book and the Languages of Lordship', 292–308.

William was that great emperors had done these things in the past; there were plenty of people around to remind him of Luke 2:1 (*ut describeretur universis orbis*). And even if this were not the case, the general approach fits the conception and implementation of the Domesday Book project into one of the central themes of this chapter and this book, namely, the deployment of the resources of the past that created, often in unforeseen ways, a new present.

As William lay dying in the precincts of the church of Saint-Gervais outside the city of Rouen in the summer of 1087, he divided Normandy and England between his two oldest sons, Robert and William. A few qualifications notwithstanding, George Garnett's basic point that incompatible Norman and English practices were being brought to bear seems to me to be spot on.[137] However, taking a broader perspective, what we are dealing with parallels the transfer to a ruler's sons of ninth- and tenth-century *regna* that were seen as constituting an imperial whole, done on the assumption that all members of the ruler's closest kin retained an interest in the future. The fact that what mattered first of all was the ruler's wishes expressed on the deathbed epitomizes a moment where biography, individual agency, and norms come together; it is clear from the much discussed surviving accounts that William's animosity towards his rebellious first son could not overturn pre-existing arrangements in relation to Normandy and Maine, but did allow England to be granted to the second son, William Rufus.[138] It may also be significant that one anonymous writer thought that the best way to record the events was to use the templates of Einhard's 'Life of Charlemagne' (the *Vita Karoli*) and the Astronomer's *Life* of Charlemagne's son, the emperor Louis the Pious. The notion that these were texts suitable for the death of a special king may be convincing in the case of the *Vita Karoli*, but is much less so in relation to the *Vita Hludouuici*. It may well be important, however, that the author chose as a base text one that described especially well the transmission of multiple *regna* to sons.[139]

A kind interpretation of William the Conqueror's conduct after his victory at the Battle of Hastings would be that he was called upon to reconcile the irreconcilable, the demands of his many followers with his oath to protect his new subjects. It would add that he did make use of the conventions available to him, but was so overwhelmed by the impossibility of drawing the lines between the requirement to reward and the requirement to be just that conquest stretched the available norms, scripts, and rules beyond breaking point. A more realistic one is probably that William did indeed reconcile the irreconcilable, but only through the use of sustained and extreme violence and the infliction of immense human suffering; in this case, the respect for norms and scripts was real, but, in terms of underlying ethical considerations, only superficial. His rule in England has the appearance of

---

[137] Garnett, *Conquered England*, 152–85.

[138] On William's deathbed and the assumption that kings could change their minds at that point, John Gillingham, 'At the Deathbeds of the Kings of England, 1066–1216', in *Herrscher- und Fürstentestamente im Westeuropäischen Mittelalter*, ed. Brigitte Kasten (Cologne, 2008), 509–30, at 512–13, 515–16.

[139] See, most recently, Katherine Lack, 'The *De Obitu Willelmi*: Propaganda for the Anglo-Norman Succession, 1087–88', *EHR*, cxxiii (2008), 1417–56, at 1419–22.

being ideologically and actively integrative; and in terms of laying the foundations for the long term, it actually was. He is said to have tried to learn English and the narratives of his encounters with formidable English saints such as St Æthelfrith and St Cuthbert show that he tried to placate them.[140] His treatment of Earl Edwin undoubtedly appears to be an attempt to try to represent himself as being above ethnic conflict.

Yet ultimately the evidence for the continuation of Englishness is of a highly abstract kind. It was essentially an ideology designed to support legitimacy rather than the politics of actual power. It ensured the short- and long-term survival of English ethnicity, law, language, saints' cults, and much else besides. Indeed, it was based on predetermined principles that it would do exactly this. But in the short term, it was executed at huge cost to William's new subjects. And there is enough evidence from before and after 1066 to show that, as a maker of empire, William the Conqueror drew on a set of norms that he frequently pushed towards and beyond acceptable boundaries. The *locus classicus* of all debate is the so-called 'Harrying of the North', a strategic decision to reduce the north of England to a state that could not support further rebellions. It also ended the possibility of further disruptive invasions by the king of Scots Mael Coluim (Malcolm) III, since his troops could no longer live off the land in the north of England; in the history of such ravaging, however, the deliberate deprivation of the peasantry's long-term livelihoods and the starving of non-combatants was arguably more extreme than the normal practice.[141] In addition, the recent demonstration that the execution on William's orders in 1076 of the last English earl, Waltheof, had nothing to do with specifically English law, but rather was William's personal application of arbitrary power that he would have recognized as vested in him in both Normandy and England, again demonstrates that he was a man prepared to go to the limits of what was accepted; he was after all advised to be merciful after Waltheof had confessed to involvement in the revolt, did then take his time before deciding, and then chose, as he often did, an extreme course of action.[142]

There are, in fact, occasions when William did compensate individuals and institutions for loss, but overall almost everything in England, including the takeover of land to construct castles in towns, was done without compensation; in other words, on the basis of the arbitrary power that the treatment of rebellion and the maintenance of peace and order allowed, and therefore outside law, but within the long-established framework of what might be thought of as necessary for the defence of the *res publica*.[143] What emerged out of all this was an overwhelmingly powerful imperial elite exercising domination without the consent of many of its subjects. In England and the British Isles, it was a situation that would inevitably

---

[140] *Liber Eliensis*, 194 (trans. Fairweather, 229). For Cuthbert, see earlier in this chapter.

[141] Palmer, 'War and Domesday Waste', 273–4. Note the comment by John Gillingham, 'Women, Children and the Profits of War', in Nelson et al., *Gender and Historiography*, 61–74, at 61 n. 4.

[142] John Hudson, 'The Fate of Earl Waltheof and the Idea of Personal Law in England after 1066', in *Normandy and Neighbours*, 223–35.

[143] Susan Reynolds, *Before Eminent Domain: Towards a History of the Expropriation of Land for the Common Good* (Chapel Hill, 2010), 22–32.

be creative simultaneously of both ethnic hostility and energetic and innovative collaboration. In northern France, as many problems had been created as had been solved. But, for good or ill, Normandy and England were henceforth inseparably linked, with networks having been created that stretched across much of the British Isles and of northern and western France. An empire had been founded in which many from the south side of the Channel had invested very heavily. This simple fact must be placed at the heart of the empire's subsequent history.

Of William Rufus, we are told by William of Malmesbury that he was 'a prince unquestionably without peer in his own time, had he not been overshadowed by his father', an indication surely of the way in which William's reputation controlled the behaviour of the next generation.[144] Then of William's two long-lived daughters, one, Cecilia, handed over to become a nun in 1066 and living on until 1127, becoming the second abbess of her parents' foundation of La Trinité of Caen, and in charters being described not only as a nun and subsequently abbess, but also often as 'the king's daughter' (*filia regis*).[145] And whether we accept as factually accurate Baudri of Bourgueil's statement that the other long-lived daughter, the formidable Adela, countess of Blois-Chartres (died 1137), someone who would have met a high proportion of the topmost elite of the contemporary medieval West, had an embroidery of her father's achievements close to her bed in her private chamber, that a poet seeking to flatter her considered this an appropriate thing to write is crucial to my argument. That she was thought, in such private moments that she had, to have contemplated her father's achievements once more says pretty well all that needs to be said. As Baudri, surely again in the midst of imperial language writing what he believed she wanted to read, put it, in and comparisons:

> In the end his power was so great that his name alone
> Made the entire earth tremble and bow to his rule.[146]

It is no surprise that William's children and many others were committed to continuing what he had founded. Yet in focusing on one man and on kingship and on the elite culture of imperial society, it has also foregrounded the structure's dependence on a single individual's capacity to sustain power amidst a maelstrom of contradictory expectations and entrenched interests. Through good times and bad, the empire thus created was to last for almost 140 years.

---

[144] *GR*, i, 542–3.
[145] *Les actes pour les abbayes caennaises*, ed. Musset, nos. 25, 27 (pp. 138, 139); *Charters and Custumals of the Abbey of Holy Trinity Caen, Part 2: The French Estates*, ed. John Walmsley, Records of Social and Economic History, new series, no. 22 (Oxford, 1994), 131–2 (Cartulary Documents, no. 20).
[146] For a convenient translation of Baudri's famous poem, Monika Otter (trans.), 'Baudri of Bourgueil, "To Countess Adela"', *Journal of Medieval Latin*, xi (2001), 60–141, with the key passages for my argument at 66 (ll. 17–18) and 80 (ll. 581–2).

4

Hegemony

This chapter is about the power structure, the continuing dynamic, and the changing character of the cross-Channel empire after the death of William the Conqueror. The word hegemony is the title chosen because it allows for multiple shades of power and it confers agency on individuals and institutions in a way that other possible titles do not. It operates as a means to analyse difference and diversity across space where direct rule was exercised, but it also works in relation to the empire's many peripheries across northern France and the British Isles. In fact, given the combination of just how strategically limited the objectives of the rulers of the cross-Channel empire actually were and the extent of the autonomy displayed around the periphery, it can often seem that cultural transfer, mutuality, and reciprocity are in many situations more appropriate terms to use than hegemony. Hegemony has, however, ultimately been chosen because it encompasses the hard power of empire in ways that the other terms do not. The result is that the study of empire becomes an analysis of interacting power structures, agencies, networks, and cultures, and not of a homogenous monolith; ideas and practices are permitted to flow in multiple directions.[1]

A corollary is that across the British Isles state structures are permitted to develop in relative independence at the periphery, while doing so in a symbiotic relationship with the hegemonic core. In consequence, the word domination often employed by Rees Davies to describe relationships across the British Isles be set aside; it is at most only a part of the story. Analysis must focus on both the nation and the state and on other collective and individual identities that interact with them.[2] Thus, for example, the European-wide developments associated with the so-called Gregorian Reform provide important mechanisms through which the periphery could bite

---

[1] The subjects of networks and cultural transfer will be tackled in Chap. 5.
[2] For broader issues involved here, R. R. Davies, 'The Medieval State: The Tyranny of a Concept?', *Journal of Historical Sociology*, xvi (2003), 280–300, and esp. 293–7. See also Patrick Wormald, 'Germanic Power Structures: the early English Experience', and Sarah Foot, 'The Historiography of the Anglo-Saxon "Nation-State"', in Len Scales and Oliver Zimmer (eds), *Power and Nation in European History* (Cambridge, 2005), 105–24 and 125–42; Huw Pryce, 'The Normans in Welsh History', *ANS*, xxx (2008), 1–18; Matthew H. Hammond, 'Ethnicity and the Writing of Medieval Scottish History', *SHR*, lxxxv (2006), 1–27, and esp. 6–11, 14–15, 20–7. For an excellent study of core and periphery for an earlier period, Julia M. H. Smith, *Province and Empire: Brittany and the Carolingians* (Cambridge, 1992), 206. See further, Julia M. H. Smith, '*Fines Imperii*: The Marches', in Rosamond McKitterick (ed.), *The New Cambridge Medieval History*, vol. ii: *c.700–c.900* (Cambridge, 1995), 169–89.

back.[3] But no analysis of the Normans and empire and can ever be undertaken without keeping the northern French dimensions of the subject in the forefront of the discussion. Furthermore, cultural transfer is also a valuable tool with which to analyse change across the lands of the diaspora of the Normans in northern and southern Europe.[4]

After 1087 the succession to Normandy and England was only clear and/or undisputed for approximately two years during the whole of the period up until 1154. The situation was also far from straightforward after that date.[5] The resultant tensions and the search for legitimacy produced some remarkable moments, the most dramatic of which are surely Orderic's set-piece account of Henry I prostrating himself and justifying the imprisonment of Robert Curthose before Pope Calixtus II in November 1119 and the rival claimants after 1135, not only resorting to the papacy for confirmation of their right to rule, but presenting their arguments before the pope and assembled cardinals at the Second Lateran Council.[6] Looking at the situation from the perspective of the early thirteenth century, Gerald of Wales commented that there had not been a straightforward lineal succession and that the Norman tyrants (as he called them) had decided every succession by war and by princes slaughtering their own.[7] He was, of course, a man with quite a few axes to grind. And he wrote this after the succession crisis of 1199–1204 had been followed by the end of empire. The situation is indeed once more one in which so-called literary sources should not be taken at face value.

In a systemic model, the times of transition are always the time of vulnerability, the time when the fault-lines come to the surface. And in this case, given the personal basis of rule, it was not just the disputed successions that represent a fault-line, but also the rupture of personal relationships across the whole spectrum of the imperial elite that accompanied the arrival of a new ruler (or rulers). What George Garnett has called 'the resolutely un-abstract conception of royal authority', followed by a quotation from Maitland about 'a certain thoughtlessness or poverty of ideas' is an important observation to which I will return in the final chapter.[8] Yet

---

[3] Cf. Pryce, 'Welsh Rulers and European Change' and Alexander Grant, 'Lordship and Society in Twelfth-Century Clydesdale', in Pryce and Watts (eds), *Power and Identity in the Middle Ages*, 37–51, and 98–124, and esp. 37–9, 50–1, 98–9, and 112–14. On the papacy and religious issues beyond the imperial core, Brendan Smith, 'The Frontiers of Church Reform in the British Isles, 1170–1230', in David Abulafia and Nora Berend (eds), *Medieval Frontiers: Concepts and Practices*, (Aldershot/Burlington VT, 2002), 239–53, at 244–53; Broun, *Scottish Independence and the Idea of Britain*, 101–57.

[4] See further, Chap. 6.

[5] The succession was undisputed between the deaths of Robert Curthose at Cardiff on 10 February 1134 and Henry I at Lyons-la-Forêt on 1 December 1135 and between the settlement reached between Stephen and the future Henry II on 6 November 1153 at Winchester and Stephen's death on 25 October 1154. For 1154–1204, see Chap. 6.

[6] OV, vi, 282–9. For the Second Lateran Council, see most recently, Chibnall, *Empress Matilda*, 75–7; King, *King Stephen*, 101–5.

[7] 'De principis instructione', in *Giraldus Cambrensis, Opera Omnia*, ed. J. S. Brewer, J. F. Dimock, and G. F. Warner, 8 vols, Rolls Series (London, 1861–91), viii, 320 (*qui non lineali propagine sibi invicem succedentes, sed per hysteron proteron potius, perque caedes suorum et strages propinquorum violentam adepti dominationem*). See further, Gillingham, 'At the Deathbeds of the Kings', 528.

[8] Garnett, *Conquered England, passim*, with the quotations at 353.

for all this the empire possessed an inherent resilience that carried it through all crises until its final and sudden collapse. When all is placed in context, even if the building above ground often appears to have been in a precarious state, the foundations were until 1204 deep enough to withstand the shocks that rocked it; it is with the values and norms that underpinned the building that this chapter will often be concerned.

When it comes to the periphery, William of Malmesbury's comments to the effect that David I, king of Scots, because he had been brought up among the English, had through a good education shaken off barbarous Scottish manners has echoes in other histories of the time. Thus, the author of the *Gesta Stephani* commented that the Welsh had been civilized through the construction of castles and the imposition of taxes. Malmesbury's piece of cultural snobbery does, however, pose the simple question of what David was doing among 'the English' in the first place?[9] On one standard of values, David and many others can be seen as living out their lives in the menacing shadow of the empire's hard power. On another, however, they can be seen as feeding off it to their personal benefit.

The so-called *murdrum* fine might appear to be a potential litmus test of relations between those who can be placed—or would place themselves—on one side or another of the French/Norman and English ethnic divide in the twelfth-century English kingdom. However, the absence of narratives to reveal the motives for the killings described by the term in the surviving records makes this a blind alley.[10] An at-first-sight potentially more profitable line of enquiry is provided by the notable phenomenon of the first half of the twelfth century whereby apparently 'anti-Norman' material like the *Gesta* devoted to the deeds of Hereward the Wake, the cult of the beheaded Earl Waltheof at Crowland, and the incipient cult that developed around King Harold II at Waltham appear, all created in communities whose personnel must have included either newcomers to England or, more probably, the descendants of newcomers. That all of them articulate an enduring resentment on the part of the conquered English is very probable. However, they and Geffrei Gaimar's *Estoire des Engleis* must also be viewed as convincing evidence of a new multiculturalism and of changing identities created within the communities and relationships brought into being by the cross-Channel empire.[11]

In addition to an identification with a new homeland on the part of many of such newcomers to England, it is likely that both the multiculturalism and the changing identities associated with new communities and relationships also embraced a widespread resentment against an empire that was exploiting its peoples to finance war in

---

[9] *GR*, i, 726–7; *Gesta Stephani*, ed. and trans. K. R. Potter and R. H. C. Davis, OMT (Oxford, 1976), 15–18. On these and other passages, see Gillingham, 'Beginnings of English Imperialism', in *The English*, 7–9.

[10] Garnett, 'Franci et Angli', 116–35; O'Brien, 'From Morðor to Murdrum', 354–5; Hudson, *The Oxford History of the Laws of England*, 405–9.

[11] Williams, *The English and the Norman Conquest*, 146–7, 181–2; Gillingham, *The English, passim*; Ian Short, 'Patrons and Polyglots: French Literature in Twelfth-Century England', *ANS*, xiv (1992), 229–49, at 243–5; *Gaimar*, xlvii–xlix. For the evidence for continuing hostility, Thomas, *English and Normans*, 62–9. For Gaimar, see Chap. 2.

France, and that this was channelled into a superficially ethnic discourse. Thus, in Book VI of the *Historia Anglorum*, completed before *c.*1130, Henry of Huntingdon observed that the Normans, having crushed their enemies, then proceeded to do the same thing to their own people. He then went on to observe that this was not just happening in England, but in Normandy, Apulia, Calabria, Sicily, and Antioch as well.[12] Henry's breadth of vision is indicative of communication and cultural transfer across the diaspora of the Normans in ways to which I will return in the final chapter. For my present purpose, however, what is exceptionally interesting is his inclusion of Normandy in his critique, a perspective that parallels what Orderic was writing at the same time and which was in due course to feed into the writings of others. Thus, in the famous passage in Book VIII of the *Historia Ecclesiastica*, which was probably written between 1133 and 1135, offering a commentary on conditions in Normandy during the period when Robert Curthose had been duke:

> What disasters now overwhelmed proud Normandy, which once had boasted of the conquest of England, and now that the native English were slain or put to flight, usurped their goods and authority! See how Normandy now uses the great wealth which she plundered from others and proudly flaunted as she triumphed over them to her own destruction, not for her own delight, but only to cause grief and torment. Now, like Babylon, she drinks from the same cup of sorrows that she used unrighteously to force on others.[13]

Yet if the price of empire was becoming clear to all, at the same time, Henry could write of Henry I's victory over the French king Louis VI at the Battle of Brémule in 1119 that 'laurels and eternal praise crown the Normans'.[14] For all that Henry, William of Malmesbury, and Gaimar were describing a form of ethnic integration within England, all had no doubt that it was the cross-Channel elite that continued to rule. The word 'Normans' is often used by them to describe a politicized imperial identity, to articulate through ethnic language the hard power of the cross-Channel elite. Not only was the title of Henry's Book VII 'On the Kingdom of the Normans' (*De Regno Normannorum*), but Geffrei's *Histoire* was consistently favourable in its treatment of the massively powerful imperial elite.[15] And, while Malmesbury could explode into anger in his later years in his commentary on the Lamentations of Jeremiah against the continuing dominant and exploitative role of what he referred to as the Normans, accompanied by the unending degradation of the English, he, like the other two historians, was also aware of the glories and creativity of the imperial present, of which he, again like the others, was of course a notable beneficiary.[16]

The absence of narrative sources from early twelfth-century Scotland comparable to those available for England and, to a lesser extent Wales, means that analogous

---

[12] HH, 402–3, 404–5, 410–11.
[13] OV, iv, 226–7. For the date of Book VIII, OV, iv, p. xix.   [14] HH, 464–5.
[15] HH, 412–13; *Gaimar*, 292–3, ll. 5376–404.
[16] Winterbottom, 'William of Malmesbury and the Normans', 70–7. See this book's Chap. 2 for this theme.

material is not so much on offer there. A short poem referring to the future David I as plundering the kingdom of Scots, and in all likelihood basing this opinion on his installation of warriors from the cross-Channel empire into the massive earldom he had received between Solway and Forth under the terms of his brother King Edgar's will, must at the least be an expression of resentment of change.[17] A later perspective is supplied by the Verse Chronicle inserted into the margins of the Chronicle of Melrose in the mid-thirteenth century to the effect that David 'wisely taking thought for the future, furnished his kingdom with castles and weaponry'; that is, with the capacity to make war and organize for war, or in other words, with hard power.[18] The purpose, namely to secure for himself a military advantage within the kingdom of Scots, is a classic example of the periphery drawing on the resources of empire for its own purposes.

From Wales, Rhygyfarch ap Sulien's statement that 'the people and the priest are despised by the word, the heart, and the work of the Normans', with more following on the crimes of 'this evil people' (*scelerum cumulus gentis iniquae*), articulates the feelings of peoples who saw the imperial power, not in terms of the civilizing mission set out by Malmesbury and others, but as a threat to a treasured civilization.[19] Welsh sources, in fact, frequently express criticism verging on contempt; the *Brut y Tywysogyon*, for example, works its way through themes that highlight untrustworthiness and cowardice as the chief characteristics of 'the French'.[20] Interestingly, the theme of untrustworthiness also appears in northern France in, for example, the comments attributed by John of Salisbury to Ulger, bishop of Angers, after he had been cynically outmanoeuvred when presenting the Empress's case to Pope Innocent II and the assembled cardinals at the Second Lateran Council in 1139.[21]

The *Brut y Tywysogyon*, in what purports to be a record of Henry I's direct speech, provides a superb statement of the effects that the hard and soft power of empire frequently have on those around the periphery in setting out the benefits to be enjoyed by Owain ap Cadwgan ab Bleddyn, king of Powys (d.1116), from enjoying Henry's favour:

'Since you have come to me of your free will and since you have believed the message brought by my messengers, I will exalt you and raise you up to be the most elevated

---

[17] Thomas O. Clancy, 'A Gaelic Polemic Quatrain from the Reign of Alexander I, ca.1113', *Scottish Gaelic Studies*, xx (2000), 88–96, at 91–4.

[18] On the 'Verse Chronicle', see now, Dauvit Broun and Julian Harrison, *The Chronicle of Melrose Abbey: A Stratigraphic Edition. I. Introduction and Facsimile*, Scottish History Society (Woodbridge, 2007), 149–51; *The Chronicle of Melrose*, ed. Alan Orr Anderson and Marjorie Ogilvie Anderson (London, 1936), 32.

[19] M. T. Lapidge, 'The Welsh-Latin Poetry of Sulien's Family', *Studia Celtica*, viii/ix (1973–4), 68–106, at 88–91.

[20] *Brut y Tywysogyon (Red Book of Hergest Version)*, 84–5 (s.a. 1115) ('And as it is the way of the French to deceive people with promises'), 94–5 (s.a. 1116) ('And then, as it is the way of the French to do everything by guile'), 114–15 (s.a. 1136) ('the Flemings and the Normans took to flight as was their custom').

[21] John of Salisbury, *Historia Pontificalis: Memoirs of the Papal Court*, ed. Marjorie Chibnall, OMT (Oxford, 1986), 84.

and prominent of your kin. And I will reward you to such an extent that all of your kin will be envious of you. And I will give you all of your territory to hold freely'.[22]

It would be hard to find a blunter or more effective statement from any historical period of one of the basic components of hegemony, namely the magnetism of raw power and its capacity to draw the aspiring into a reciprocal, yet dependant, relationship. Similar themes run through the relationships of the second half of the twelfth century and the way in which they are presented in many writings of those times.[23] If Geoffrey of Monmouth's *De Gestis Britonum* can be regarded as a Welsh/British fight-back to set a glorious British past against the claims being made at the same time for the English and Norman pasts, as well as, of course, an expression of a wider movement of historical writing animated by the changes of the twelfth century, in terms of the history of power and the phenomenon of empire, the process set in train by the efforts of the likes of Robert of Torigni and Wace by which it was integrated into imperial, and indeed European, culture is every bit as important, perhaps indeed even more so. It shows how hegemonic power stimulated responses, then absorbed and re-cycled them.[24]

CROSS-CHANNEL RULE

Along with the political behaviour of the most powerful of the cross-Channel magnates, the unifying political and social roles of the rulers' court and household were central to John Le Patourel's arguments. In the later eleventh and early twelfth centuries, the royal chapel at times played a similar role for aspiring clerics.[25] Since the publication of *The Norman Empire*, we have become much more aware of the tentacular nature of the operations of court and household and the cultures that shaped conduct and participation; they were places where the mightiest were expected to play their part and honey-pots that attracted the opportunist.[26] They were the ultimate stabilizing core of empire and the motor that drove its continuing dynamic, the epicentre of hierarchy and of multiple interacting interests; they were also places where fortunes could be made and broken.[27]

---

[22] *Brut y Tywysogyon (Red Book of Hergest Version)*, 80–1 (s.a. 1114); cit., Rowlands, 'The making of the March', 151. See further, K. L. Maund, 'Owain ap Cadwgan: a Rebel Revisited', *HSJ*, xiii (2004, for 1999), 65–74, at 73–4.

[23] Thus, Seán Duffy, 'Henry II and England's Insular Neighbours', in Harper-Bill and Vincent (eds), *Henry II: New Interpretations*, 129–53, at 137–51.

[24] John Gillingham, 'The Context and Purposes of Geoffrey of Monmouth's *History of the Kings of Britain*', *ANS*, xiii (1992), 99–118 (*The English*, 19–39). For the re-cycling, see Chap. 2.

[25] Le Patourel, *The Norman Empire*, 132–48, 191–201; David Spear, 'The Norman Empire and the Secular Clergy, 1066–1204', *Journal of British Studies*, xxi (1982), 1–10.

[26] Marjorie Chibnall, 'Mercenaries and the *Familia Regis* under Henry I', 15–23; J. O. Prestwich, 'The Military Household of the Norman Kings', *EHR*, xcvi (1981), 1–37 (both reprinted in Strickland (ed.), *Anglo-Norman Warfare*, 84–92, 93–127); S. D. Church, *The Household Knights of King John* (Cambridge, 1999). The phenomenon's ultimate expression is, of course, the remarkable career of William Marshal: Crouch, *William Marshal*, 29–56.

[27] Above all, Barlow, *William Rufus*, 99–119; Green, *Government*, 19–37; Judith A. Green, 'The Piety and Patronage of Henry I', *HSJ*, x (2001), 1–16; Judith A. Green, 'Networks and Solidarities at

On this basis, they become the places around which an infinite number of life-stories can be constructed, something that will be done later in this chapter. But, at the same time, analysis of their social and political roles must take into account modern approaches to the aristocratic family, with their political role needing to be located within the cultural world of the aristocracy and a set of phenomena that can be conveniently defined by the word lordship.[28] Aristocratic courts and households, cathedral chapters, and monastic communities, all linked into the imperial networks of the rulers' court, forming a constellation across which the personal power of the empire's rulers flowed, and across which patronage was exercised. When Normandy and England were under a single ruler, the range of the operations of court and household was always cross-Channel. This was also the case during the long periods of divided rule, except that the game was differently played.

The health-warning already attached to the contemporary sources' treatments of the military prowess of the Normans is crucial to the way in which we interpret the rulers' supposed military ambitions.[29] There is always the danger that what was written down records boastfulness and disingenuous responses to less than realistic propositions, rather than actual aims. This must surely be the case, for example, with the story recorded in different forms by Orderic and William of Malmesbury and, briefly, by Geffrei Gaimar, that, but for his death, William Rufus was going to take control of the duchy of Aquitaine while its duke went on crusade.[30] Like the invitations apparently made to the Conqueror to intervene in the Empire or the Anglo-Saxon Chronicle's statement that he might have conquered Ireland, an offer of this kind would have been treated as flattering and prestigious, and a man like Rufus would have bragged loudly about it. But, if he had lived, he might well have ultimately turned down whatever proposition had been made, as his father had done.

Of the Conqueror's offspring, William Rufus was beyond doubt the most thorough-going practitioner of hard power. The differences between him and Henry I can, however, be overstated.[31] For all Rufus's apparently continuous military activity on both sides of the Channel, his campaigns all had specific strategic objectives. He was also manifestly capable of subtlety as well as of full frontal attack. Thus, alongside his two campaigns to Le Mans in 1098 and 1099

---

the Court of Henry I Beauclerc', in David Bates, Véronique Gazeau et al. (eds), *Liens personnels, réseaux, solidarités en France et dans les îles Britanniques (XIe–XXe siècle)* (Paris, 2006), 113–26; Green, *Henry I*, 289–98. For patronage, C. Warren Hollister, 'The Rise of Administrative Kingship', *American Historical Review*, lxxx (1978), 868–91, and 'Henry I and the Anglo-Norman Magnates', *ANS*, ii (1980), 93–107, 184–8 (*Monarchy and Magnates*, 171–89, 223–45); Hollister, *Henry I*, 327–48; Stephanie L. Mooers, 'Patronage in the Pipe Roll of 1130', *Speculum*, lix (1984), 282–307.

[28] For the family, Crouch, *The Birth of Nobility*, 99–155.
[29] See Chap. 1 ('Hard Power').
[30] OV, v, 280–1; *GR*, i, 576–7; *Gaimar*, 322–3, ll. 5967–8; Barlow, *Rufus*, 416–19. The practicalities of the expedition are assessed by Bernard S. Bachrach, 'William Rufus' Plan for the Invasion of Aquitaine', in Richard P. Abels and Bernard S. Bachrach (eds), *The Normans and Their Adversaries at War: Essays in Memory of C. Warren Hollister* (Woodbridge, 2001), 31–63, at 37–62.
[31] Cf. *GR*, i, 742–3.

while he was guardian of Normandy during his brother Robert Curthose's absence on the First Crusade, his recruitment of the major nobles Winebald and Hamelin de Ballon and Patrick of Chaworth (from Sources) from Maine and his grant to them of lands in England and Wales, and in Patrick's case of a profitable marriage, can be seen as attempts at bridge-building to make up for his father's omissions. He also oversaw the first stages of the establishment of bishoprics into Wales, with, again, the consequent expansion of imperial networks that followed.[32]

With all this in mind, although William of Malmesbury's statement that William Rufus's attitude towards the kingdom of Scots was conciliatory at first sight appears extremely eccentric, given that he conquered Cumbria and added it to the kingdom of the English, it may make some sense in terms of his basic achievement otherwise being to have restored the status quo of his father's time after an especially turbulent period.[33] And, after 1093, in the persons of King Máel Coluim (Malcolm) III's and Queen Margaret's sons Donchadd (Duncan) and Edgar, he had installed kings who were likely to cooperate with the rulers of Normandy and England. While the language of clientage does appear in King Edgar's charter of 1095 for Durham (*totam terram de Lodeneio et regnum Scotie dono domini mei Willelmi Anglorum regis et paterna hereditate possidens*), it was never repeated.[34] Furthermore, Rufus's action in giving Edgar the Ætheling command of the army that in 1097 installed the Ætheling's nephew Edgar as king continued the special relationship with the descendants of the Old English kings established under William the Conqueror. As a result, it might even be thought that Ailred's later and highly idealized concept of the 'holy family' linking the rulers of both kingdoms to their English and British pasts was taking shape, except that before 1100 it was being enforced by the hard power of the cross-Channel empire.[35] Peace-weaving was consolidated by the marriage of Edith/Matilda, the Ætheling's niece and Margaret and Mael Coluim (Malcolm) III's daughter, to Henry I in 1100, at the conclusion of many fraught discussions about a possible marriage for her into the new imperial elite.[36] One of its most significant outcomes, the remarkable collaboration between Henry I and his queen's brother, the later David I, was nonetheless in many respects the fortuitous product of circumstances; his succession to kingship after the reigns of two childless older brothers was certainly against the odds.

Taken as a whole, the period of the reigns of the Conqueror's three sons cumulatively mark the effective end of the empire's period of expansion. In

---

[32] For further details, Green, *Aristocracy*, 278; Keats-Rohan, *DD*, 19–21.

[33] *GR*, i, 554–5, 724–5. For modern accounts of these campaigns, Barlow, *William Rufus*, 288–98, 353–4, 371; Richard Oram, *David I: The King who Made Scotland* (Stroud, 2004), 41–8.

[34] A. A. M. Duncan, 'Yes, the Earliest Scottish Charters', *SHR*, lxxviii (1999), 1–38, at 16. In general, A. A. M. Duncan, *The Kingship of the Scots, 842–1292: Succession and Independence* (Edinburgh, 2002), 56–7; Broun, *Scottish Independence and the Idea of Britain*, 19–20, 101–5.

[35] ASC, 'E', 1097. For Ailred and the 'holy family', see later in this chapter.

[36] For the events and the issues, Lois L. Huneycutt, *Matilda of Scotland: A Study in Medieval Queenship* (Woodbridge, 2003), 21–30; Green, *Henry I*, 53–5.

northern France, it was actually a time of retreat; although the process was not straightforward, hegemonic power over the county of Maine coming to an end in 1100. The takeover of Cumbria and of south and south-west Wales as far north as Ceredigion does represent further expansion, but losses of territory in both zones occurred when the civil war started after 1135. And as a result of the political changes that had taken place over the whole period since 1066, King Stephen, when facing a situation that was strategically similar to that which had confronted William the Conqueror in 1069–70, could not respond, as his grandfather had done, by devastating a substantial part of the territory theoretically under his rule. Whatever is made of his conduct between the start of his reign and the second Treaty of Durham (9 April 1139), most of the landholders whose lands would be ruined by such action showed themselves ready at this point to fight for him.[37] From *c.*1100 the evolution of frontier societies in the British Isles put the conduct of war there on a footing closer to that which had existed in northern France throughout the eleventh century, even if the potential enemies might be deemed less militarily threatening.[38] There is indeed something of a delightful irony in that a classic display of soft power, Henry I's alliance and collaboration with David I, and one of hard power, his cool treatment of William Talvas, count of Ponthieu, the son of the former great cross-Channel magnate Robert de Bellême, meant that, for different reasons, the two were instantly on the same side when Stephen seized Normandy and England in 1135.[39] Their actions—presumably taken spontaneously and independently—in invading northern England and handing over castles around Sées and Argentan to the Empress and her husband before the end of the year 1135, had a decisive strategic impact on the whole course of the civil war. After 1087, the descendants of the generation that had made an empire now consistently had to work to keep it going. The politics of empire had, however, become a tangled web of complex, multiple interests.

While we cannot know what would have happened if, on his deathbed, William the Conqueror had made arrangements for the succession other than those that he did, such as deciding in favour of a unified succession for either Robert Curthose or William Rufus, the basic point that all close kin had an interest in ruling the inherited territories would still have applied. Intra-family conflicts of previous centuries—and indeed of the eleventh-century present—indicate that in all likelihood there would have been tension and conflict whatever he had done. The huge support for Robert's projected invasion of England in 1087 and 1088 that did not happen suggests that a single inheritance for William Rufus would have been forcefully contested. And however much attempts are made to rehabilitate Robert Curthose as a man and as a ruler of Normandy, his actual performance suggests that there must always be doubts about his competence to rule so vast an

---

[37] In general, Judith Green, 'King Henry I and Northern England', *TRHS*, 6th. ser., xvii (2007), 35–55.
[38] For this thesis, Lieberman, 'The Medieval "Marches" of Normandy and Wales', 1372–9.
[39] For Count William, Kathleen Thompson, 'William Talvas, Count of Ponthieu, and the Politics of the Anglo-Norman Realm', in *England and Normandy*, 169–84, at 171–6.

assemblage of territories; a single inheritance for him would have arguably have been contested too.

Writing about what was the effective end of the Carolingian Empire in the later ninth century, Regino of Prüm, in a famous passage, stated that:

> After his death [i.e., the Emperor Charles III the Fat in 888] the kingdoms which had obeyed his authority, just as though a legitimate king were lacking, dissolved into separate parts and, without waiting for their natural lord, each decided to elect a king from its own guts. . . . For *Francia* would have produced many leaders capable of controlling the government of the kingdom, had not Fortune equipped them to destroy each other in the competition for power.[40]

In the case of the cross-Channel empire, there was no absence of 'natural lords' after the death of each ruler and there were always powerful forces working for the empire's continued unity. There was always a son of William the Conqueror ready to take over and the civil war of 1135 to 1154 was fought for control of the whole. The politics might be complicated, but the question ultimately was who would take over, when they would do it, and how.[41]

For these reasons, the basic themes observable in the so-called Treaties of Rouen (1091) and Alton (1101) were either reunification or one of defining the terms of a continuing short-term separation; and, from the perspective of the many individual and family interests involved, establishing their place within a fast-moving political world. There is plentiful evidence from these times that draws attention to the importance of brotherly collaboration; the 1091 document known as the *Consuetudines et Iusticie*, for example, describes Robert and William as 'the sons and heirs of the King William who acquired the kingdom of England' and Orderic in particular puts a special emphasis on the three brothers' collective responsibility to preserve the paternal inheritance intact.[42] Robert Curthose and William Rufus collaborated on campaigns in Maine and Scotland to each other's benefit and also against their disruptive brother Henry.[43] There are also charters in which the brothers confirm each others' grants. Although the surviving ones are mostly for the abbey of Saint-Etienne of Caen founded by their father, and therefore may be an expression of filial devotion rather than cross-Channel political cooperation, the focus on a place that arguably more than any other symbolized the new world of

---

[40] *History and Politics in Late Carolingian and Ottonian Europe: The 'Chronicle' of Regino of Prüm and Adalbert of Magdeburg*, trans. and annotated Simon MacLean (Manchester, 2009), 199.

[41] J. C. Holt, 'Feudal Society and the Family: Notions of Patrimony', *TRHS*, 5th. ser., xxxiii (1983), 193–220, at 211–13 (reprinted in Holt, *Colonial England*, 197–221, at 213–15); Kathleen Thompson, 'L'héritier et le remplaçant: le rôle du frère puîné dans la politique anglo-normande (1066–1204)', in *Tinchebray*, 93–101.

[42] Haskins, *Norman Institutions*, 281 (*filii eius et heredes predicti regis*); OV, iv, 180–1, 196–9, 268–71.

[43] For the main recent discussions of these treaties, C. W. Hollister, 'The Anglo-Norman Civil War: 1101', *EHR*, lxxxviii (1973), 315–34, at 328–31 (*Monarchy and Magnates*, 77–96, at 90–3); Hollister, *Henry I*, 140–5; Barlow, *William Rufus*, 281–4; Neil Strevett, 'The Anglo-Norman Civil War of 1101 Reconsidered', *ANS*, xxvi (2004), 159–75; Green, *Henry I*, 64–5; Garnett, *Conquered England*, 183–4, 272–3, 285–7; Katherine Lack, *Conqueror's Son: Duke Robert Curthose, Thwarted King* (Stroud, 2007), 148–52; Aird, *Robert Curthose*, 140–1, 208–11.

empire must be significant.[44] Furthermore, Henry I's dealings with cross-Channel magnates in the years between 1100 and 1106 which, many would now with justification argue constituted an unscrupulous subversion of his older brother, can also be seen as being directed towards reunification.[45] Analogies with earlier times that show how apparently subversive behaviour could in due course be sanitized into constructive politics are also very evident in Henry I's self-justifying arguments to the effect that he had made war on his brother in order to create a better peace. After 1106 they were justified by him on the grounds that they brought peace to a troubled land. All is so reminiscent of the host of Carolingian intellectuals who praised the virtues of the Emperor Charlemagne and of his father, Pippin, for the latter's removal of, in their eyes, the ineffectual last Merovingian Childeric III.[46]

The networks across northern France created by William the Conqueror also continued through the period of the conflicts between his sons; the political culture remained one that stretched beyond the political frontiers of the cross-Channel empire. Thus, the 1101 agreement between Henry I (then only king of the English) and Robert II, count of Flanders, included in its provisions military support for Henry in Normandy and Maine.[47] Since there is no compelling reason, and no evidence in the text of the agreement to think that the treaty was directed against Robert Curthose, then it was simply another aspect of the continuation of hegemonic power that stretched beyond the frontiers of the lands directly controlled by the empire's rulers; this is all the more so if, as is usually thought, the prime purpose was to renew old agreements. Likewise, Helias de La Flèche, the apparent nemesis of Norman power in Maine, fought with Henry I against his brother to capture Bayeux and Caen in 1105 and at the Battle of Tinchebrai in 1106. Like the count of Flanders, he was continuing to participate in a way that he would have judged served his best interests.

After 1106 Henry I spent around 62% of his time in Normandy, in comparison to his father's approximate 75% after 1072.[48] In contrast, over the whole of his reign in England, he visited Wales twice, in 1114 and 1121, and the north of England possibly four times, in 1105, 1109, and 1122, with a visit in 1113 being a

---

[44] For joint-confirmations, David Bates, 'A Neglected English Charter of Robert Curthose, Duke of Normandy', *(BI)HR*, lix (1986), 121–4.

[45] This point is developed further later in this chapter.

[46] For Henry's arguments, Gilduin Davy, 'Autour de la restauration de l'ordre: les justifications juridiques de la bataille de Tinchebrai dans "l'Histoire ecclésiastique" d'Orderic Vital', in Gazeau and Green (eds), *Tinchebray*, 21–34. See further, Kershaw, *Peaceful Kings*, 133–4, with references there cited.

[47] *Diplomatic Documents Preserved in the Public Record Office*, ed. Pierre Chaplais, i (1101–1272) (London, 1964), 1–4, no. 1; *Actes des comtes de Flandre, 1071–1128*, ed. F. Vercauteren (Brussels, 1938), 88–95, no. 30; translated, by Elisabeth van Houts, 'The Anglo-Flemish Treaty of 1101', *ANS*, xxi (1999), 169–74. The sections relating to Normandy and Maine are clauses 10–15 in the Vercauteren edition and Elisabeth van Houts's translation. For William Rufus's negotiation of the treaty in 1093, Barlow, *William Rufus*, 325–6. On the treaties as a whole, Oksanen, *Flanders and the Anglo-Norman World*, 59–72.

[48] This statistic is based on W. Farrer, 'An Outline Itinerary of Henry I', *EHR*, xxxiii (1919), 303–82, 507–79; *RRAN*, ii, pp. xxix–xxi.

possibility; in writing that Normandy was the principal cause of Henry's wars William of Malmesbury was stating the obvious.[49] So great apparently were Henry's difficulties within the duchy that Malmesbury also chose to interpret what he believed to be a prodigy, the conjoined twins mentioned previously, as indicating a state-of-affairs that he believed could not last; the union of Normandy and England was against nature, with England, the still living twin carrying around a rotting corpse that symbolized Normandy into which England was pouring vast amounts of money.[50] A perspective from Normandy is, however, arguably provided by Robert of Torigni in his *Gesta Normannorum Ducum*, written at a time when he had not even visited England, when he describes England's wealth as 'inexhaustible' in an interlinear insertion that smacks of a widely held perception.[51] It is notable too that Robert was the only one of the major twelfth-century historians to mention the discovery of the silver mines near Carlisle in 1133, writing in some detail about the amount of money the king received from them.[52]

Having suffered a military defeat in southern Normandy against Count Fulk V of Anjou at Alençon in 1118, Henry's subsequent victory at Brémule over King Louis VI (20 August 1119) looks to have concentrated loyalty in Normandy around his rule, an antidote to the deep discontents running through the duchy's society that by this time were also feeding on the claims of Robert Curthose's son William Clito.[53] However, Henry's general approach to defending Normandy was to consolidate the duchy's defences through castle-building at the frontier and to construct a zone of spatial influence that was as large as possible.[54] The Capetian kings, and in particular King Louis VI, were acknowledged as having superior status within the *regnum Francorum*, at the same time that everything was done to emphasize the personal equality of the two kings. When homage was performed, it was a means to demonstrate friendship or, from the rulers of the cross-Channel empire's perspective, to reinforce the legitimacy of succession arrangements or of a takeover.[55] At the same time, collaboration with his sister, Adela, countess of Blois, until she retired from the world and became a nun at Marcigni in 1120 and the recruitment to his cause of Adela's sons, Stephen, the future king, and Henry, the future bishop of Winchester and abbot of Glastonbury, was a crucial element in

---

[49] *GR*, i, 744–5. For visits to northern England, Green, 'King Henry I and Northern England', 37.
[50] *GR*, i, 384–7. For commentary, Ian Short, 'Literary Culture at the Court of Henry II', in Harper-Bill and Vincent (eds), *Henry II: New Interpretations*, 335–61, at 336–9.
[51] *GND*, ii, 244–5 (*de inexhaustis Anglorum thesauris*).
[52] RT (D), i, 192; (H), 123.
[53] OV, vi, 240–1. On all matters, see now, Matthew Strickland, 'Henry I and the Battle of the Two Kings: Brémule, 1119', in *Normandy and Neighbours*, 77–116, with the issue of loyalty discussed at 94–102. For the discontent, see Chaps. 2 and 6.
[54] RT (D), i, 164–5; (H), 106–7.
[55] See the survey by John Gillingham, 'The Meetings of the Kings of France and England, 1066–1204', in *Normandy and Neighbours*, 17–42, at 19–21, 30–2. See also Klaus van Eickels, '*Homagium* and *Amicitia*: Rituals of Peace and Their Significance in the Anglo-French Negotiations of the Twelfth Century', *Francia*, xxiv (1997), 133–40; Klaus van Eickels, *Vom inszenierten Konsens zum systematisierten Konflikt: Die englische-französischen Beziechengen und ihre Wahrnehmung an der Wende vom Hoch- zum Spätmittelalter* (Stuttgart, 2002), 47–131; J. E. M. Benham, 'Anglo-French Peace Conferences in the Twelfth Century', *ANS*, xxvii (2005), 52–67, at 57–9, 61–3.

his policies in northern France.⁵⁶ Stephen's subsequent marriage to the heiress to the county of Boulogne consolidated further these networks. With a preference for rewarding individuals from Maine and Anjou also noted as part of his modus operandi, a cross-Channel estate created for the powerful lord of a territorial lordship to the south of Normandy Rotrou, count of the Perche, and advancement given to men from Brittany such as Brian fitz Count, Henry would appear to have been trying to create an expanded version of the pan-north-western European networks that had not fully materialized under William the Conqueror.⁵⁷

Before the disaster of Barfleur on 25 November 1120, Henry's son William had already been named as his successor in both Normandy and England and the cross-Channel dimension remained central to all subsequent succession planning. Whatever is made of the arrangements made, or not made, from 1 January 1127 onwards in favour of the widowed Empress Matilda, and subsequently of her husband, Count Geoffrey Plantagenet, the oath taken to the Empress in January 1127 certainly encompassed Normandy and England.⁵⁸ At the same time, the aforementioned statement in the Anglo-Saxon Chronicle that the marriage of the Empress Matilda and Count Geoffrey of Anjou 'offended all the French and English', while being a direct criticism of how Henry was going about things, reveals on the part of an author writing in Old English an assumption that the continuation of empire was at the heart of the everyone's thinking. Furthermore, when proposing peace terms to William Clito at some point before 1120, Henry is said to have offered him three English counties and a place at court; this was, of course, intended to buy Clito off, but the mechanism of his insertion into the dynamic of the cross-Channel empire highlights yet again the norms thought appropriate at the highest level.⁵⁹ It is further notable that Clito, during his brief time as Count of Flanders in 1127–8, thought in terms of strengthening cross-Channel links by promising privileges in England, should he and his uncle make peace, implying that Clito, after more than a decade of fomenting opposition to his uncle Henry, was now thinking in terms of turning the power of empire to his advantage in the succession dispute in Flanders.⁶⁰ In other words, those who aspired to rule thought every bit as much in cross-Channel terms as those

---

⁵⁶ For a full narrative, Kimberly A. LoPrete, *Adela of Blois: Countess and Lord (c.1067–1137)* (Dublin, 2007), Chaps. 6 and 7. On the illegitimate daughters' marriages, Thompson, 'Affairs of State', 139–41.

⁵⁷ Hollister, *Henry I*, 228–9; Thompson, *Power and Border Lordship*, 55–6, 71–8.

⁵⁸ For the main modern treatments, Judith Green, 'Henry I and the Origins of the Civil War', in Dalton and White (eds.), *King Stephen's Reign*, 11–26; Chibnall, *The Empress Matilda*, 51–4; Garnett, *Conquered England*, 209–13; Crouch, *Reign of Stephen*, 25–7; Hollister, *Henry I*, 309–25; Green, *Henry I*, 134–7, 162–3, 193–5, 320. For the broader context of female succession, Jane Martindale, 'Succession and Politics in the Romance-speaking World, c.1000–1140', in Michael Jones and Malcolm Vale (ed.), *England and Her Neighbours, 1066–1453: Essays in Honour of Pierre Chaplais* (London and Ronceverte, 1989), 19–41, and especially, 22–3, 27–8, 32–40.

⁵⁹ OV, vi, 288–9.

⁶⁰ *Si contigerit mihi aliquo tempore preter terram Flandrie aliam conquirere, aut si concordia pacis inter me et avunculum meum H(enrici) regem Anglie facta fuerit, in conquisita terra illa aut in toto regno Anglorm eos liberos ab omni teloneo et ab omni consuetudine in concordia illa recepi faciam*, Actes des comtes de Flandre, 296, no. 127.

who actually did rule. The Empress and her husband, in their quarrel with Henry at the very end of his reign, also put their demands in cross-Channel terms, with the personally involved Robert of Torigni saying that they asked Henry to do homage to them for all the fortresses of Normandy and England on behalf of their sons.[61]

The theme of cross-Channel union remains at the heart of politics after Stephen's 1135 coup. Thus, the magnates gathered in Normandy went back on their offer of the duchy to Stephen's brother Count Theobald of Blois-Chartres when they learned what had happened in England. And, in the desperate times of 1141, magnates in Normandy offered Normandy and England to Count Theobald, an offer he refused, but on terms, which were not accepted, that transferred both to Count Geoffrey of Anjou.[62] When Stephen reached the point of thinking in terms of a possible victory in the civil war, he immediately organized a military intervention in northern France which took place in 1151–2 that must have been intended as a step towards the recreation of rule over Normandy and England. And finally, although the treaties that ended the civil war were actually concerned with England only, the theme of reunification of Normandy and England is always present.[63] It is notable too that the address-clauses of the future Henry II's charters dating from before the Treaty of Winchester make mention of the two lands (*fidelibus suis Normannie et Anglie salutem*) even when the document concerned dealt with only either English or Norman matters.[64]

THE CROSS-CHANNEL ELITE

Over the past twenty or so years, much of the emphasis in the analysis of aristocratic behaviour has broadened out from a focus on politics and property to encompass a combination of military and courtly prowess and what can, for the sake of convenience, be called lordship. David Crouch's formulation in terms of 'loyalty, endeavour and hardiness' and Thomas Bisson's in terms of 'honour, fidelity, generosity, prowess' both make the basic points about what was expected of a great magnate, albeit in slightly different ways; in the end, it is a phenomenon that was organically both protective and acquisitive.[65] It has many of the same characteristics as kingship, with an emphasis on leadership, generosity, supportiveness, and virtue. It incorporates the responsibility of serving the ruler of the cross-Channel empire, of sustaining the fortunes of followers who were often

---

[61] RT (D), i, 200; (H), 128. For a translation, Edmund King, *King Stephen* (New Haven, CT/London, 2010), 39.

[62] OV, vi, 548–9; Chibnall, *The Empress Matilda*, 95. Crouch, 'King Stephen and Northern France', 51 n. 23, suggests that Normandy alone was on offer. In view of the prevalent emphases on maintaining the union of Normandy and England, this strikes me as unlikely.

[63] *Regesta*, iii, no. 272.

[64] Note, for example, *Regesta*, iii, nos. 180, 321, the former for Earl Rannulf of Chester and the latter, entirely English document for Flaxley abbey. On this point, Edmund King, 'The Accession of Henry II', in Harper-Bill and Vincent (eds), *Henry II: New Interpretations*, 24–46, at 29.

[65] For the quotations, David Crouch, *The English Aristocracy, 1070–1272: A Social Transformation* (New Haven, CT/London, 2011), 31; Bisson, *Crisis of the Twelfth Century*, 82.

themselves cross-Channel landholders, and of safeguarding local and regional interests, usually though deputies.

The outcome of this shift towards a cultural history of the cross-Channel aristocracy does not contradict Le Patourel's basic point about cross-Channel interests being paramount; it does, however, re-orchestrate motivations and their expression. His predominantly expansionist colonizing and cross-Channel unity-seeking great families have been replaced with a more consistently turbulent and self-seeking set of individuals, who had to know how to play the political game at court, had to reward their tenants and followers, and had to serve their rulers as long as certain norms were followed; his aggressive colonizers and his conservative unifiers have been combined into a single sociological phenomenon. Wives and daughters were also fully paid up members of this apparatus of rule and power.[66]

The empire made by William the Conqueror had created an imperial elite that was responsible for its continuation. Not only did court and household bind them in a tight embrace, their whole cultural ethos made it impossible for them to abandon their imperial responsibilities. On these terms, it is, of course, misleading—and indeed truly feeble—to describe them as 'Anglo-Norman'. Not only were some of them, such as the descendants of Count Alan Rufus and his brother Count Alan Niger (d.1098), not from Normandy at all, all had an identity that cannot be reduced to a mere combination of two ethnicities; their identity was imperial. Furthermore, when their collective behaviour is analysed in context and through multiple life-stories, the multifaceted nature of their performance of their inherited responsibility becomes dependent on an array of factors, such as decisions about which claimant to imperial rule they should support, how they might display and increase their power further, whether they felt themselves undervalued, and so on. Yet tortuous as the road taken by each individual may sometimes seem, the ultimate objective, while sometimes hidden by the exigencies of the moment, was the continuation of the cross-Channel empire on the most favourable terms achievable to each one of them.

In two well-known passages, Orderic articulates effectively many of the issues.[67] Thus, in 1088, there is Bishop Odo of Bayeux voicing concerns about the impossibility of serving two lords as a prelude to the failed campaign to replace William Rufus as king of the English in favour of Robert Curthose. Reunification was what he was aiming for, but the circumstances made it essential that he take sides between the two brothers to secure it on the basis of a mixture of principle and self-interest. Then secondly, there is Orderic's description of the immediate cross-Channel disruption following Earl Robert of Gloucester's renunciation of homage to King Stephen on 22 May 1138, with his English and south Welsh tenants rising in his support at the same time that Earl Robert joined forces in Normandy with the armies of his sister and her husband.[68] Because William of Malmesbury wrote

---

[66] For many issues, Susan M. Johns, *Noblewomen, Aristocracy and Power in the Twelfth-Century Anglo-Norman Realm* (Manchester/New York, 2003), 53–121; Crouch, *The Birth of Nobility*, 303–22.
[67] OV, iv, 122–3; vi, 514–19. Green, *Aristocracy*, 270–1, makes the same point as in this paragraph.
[68] David Crouch, 'Robert, first earl of Gloucester (*b.* before 1100, *d.*1147)', *ODNB*.

so much about them, Earl Robert's dilemmas about the ethics of the renunciation and the change of loyalty it involved are a subject that we know a lot about; in the end, his half-sister's cause became his own, with reunification under her and her sons' rule, a non-negotiable objective.[69] But in addition to signalling the complexities of decision-making, the story also illustrates the scale of the disruption that someone wielding such immense power could cause.

For all this, a sociological continuity prevails throughout the whole period. Some great cross-Channel estates actually have a continuous history from 1066 until 1204. Before 1154, the casualties of failed rebellion notwithstanding, most notably Bishop Odo in 1088, Count William of Mortain in 1106, and the family of Montgommery-Bellême over the period from 1101 to 1112, the consistent objective of the cross-Channel rulers was to install others in their places. Thus, for example, there is the advancement under Rufus and Henry I of the sons and grandsons of the great magnate of the Conquest generation who had supposedly refused land in England, Roger de Beaumont, to the status of great magnates. In all cases, their landholdings were distributed across the full geographical range of the empire. Likewise, the advancement by Henry I of his nephew Stephen and of his illegitimate son Robert represents essentially a continuation of the principles that had underpinned the cross-Channel empire from its beginning. Most of Stephen's estate was created in one go. And the wife chosen for Henry's favourite illegitimate son Robert instantly provided him with lands in western England, south Wales, and the Bessin around Creully.[70] The biographies of both Stephen and Robert show just how much such individuals were required to act in the ruler's name, and from a narrative such as the well-known one of Henry I taking the oath in favour of his daughter the Empress, we can see just how crucial they were when big decisions were taken.[71] Yet what is also striking is how the lands of the empire were treated as being entirely at the disposal of its rulers and the imperial elite, with no apparent respect for local interests. This is obviously the case when Henry installed the future King Stephen, a man with at that stage no landed interest in Normandy at all, at Alençon and neighbouring places in c.1118, an act that provoked discontent, and eventually revolt, among the sitting tenants subjected to him.[72] In all likelihood born in England, Earl Robert of Gloucester was also elevated to the highest status within the imperial aristocracy because of kinship to the ruler. In his case, there is no Orderic to tell us about the values and concerns that shaped the political behaviour of lesser people. It is, however, difficult not to think that some mixed feelings were involved; the cultivation of tenant loyalty was a necessary task at which some became notably adept.

---

[69] William of Malmesbury, *Historia Novella: The Contemporary History*, ed. Edmund King and trans. K. R. Potter, OMT (Oxford, 1998), xliv–xlix, 30–42; Strevett, 'Anglo-Norman Civil War', 171–4, tackles some of the moral dimensions for the period between 1087 and 1106.

[70] For the creation of Stephen's cross-Channel estate as 'a package deal', King, *King Stephen*, 11–12. For Robert, most recently, Crouch, 'Robert, first earl of Gloucester'.

[71] Edmund King, 'Stephen, Count of Mortain and Boulogne', *EHR*, cxv (2000), 271–96, at 275–86; King, *King Stephen*, 11–28.

[72] OV, vi, 204–9; King, *King Stephen*, 14–15.

There is much in all this that has the character of cross-Channel social engineering. So much so indeed that it is important to observe now that the principle of the cross-Channel estate as the foundation of the wealth and power of a small imperial elite was not fundamentally infringed by the divisions among sons that were a feature of the first post-Conquest generation; estates might be divided, but some were reunited, and new ones were being constantly created.[73] Thus when, for example, Henry, the younger son of Roger de Beaumont, was made earl of Warwick by William Rufus in 1088, a cross-Channel estate was deliberately created for him, involving among other things his brother Count Robert of Meulan giving up lands to him in Warwickshire and Leicestershire, and his receiving estates out of the family patrimony in Normandy, mainly at Le Neubourg. In due course he received the lordship of Gower in *c*.1107, thereby expanding his range of responsibilities even more widely across the empire and atypically giving him spatial interests that were imperial in their extent.[74] In the next generation of the same family, Count Robert famously made provision for his twin sons Waleran and Robert in a way that took into account all the major eventualities that might befall them in the future, a complete reunification of the cross-Channel estate being envisaged if either one or both of them should die.[75] A variant on the theme was Henry I's patronage of his wife's brother, the future King David I, who, after an early career in Henry's household accumulated extensive property and interests in and beyond Normandy, in England, and across the whole of southern Scotland. This created a similar, but also different, kind of a landed estate that was not only cross-Channel, but emphatically trans-regnal.[76]

The same continuities were maintained after 1154. Although Henry II's ideological commitment to restoring and maintaining the conditions of his grandfather's time might be infringed by the pragmatic needs of present politics, as, for example, with the partial dismantling of the huge estates left by King Stephen to his son William IV de Warenne, vast new cross-Channel complexes were in due course created for Henry's youngest sons Geoffrey and John.[77] And Henry's oldest son, the Young King Henry, took exactly the same approach when in revolt against his father in 1173–4, promising the restoration of King Stephen's former estate to William IV's heir Matthew, count of Boulogne, and the whole of Kent to Matthew's father, Count Philip of Flanders.[78] A symbolic feature of the imperial role of these great cross-Channel estates may well be the way in which monastic foundations were made at their territorial extremities, as could apply in the case of Count Alan Rufus's foundation of St Mary's, York, and certainly does apply in Arnulf de Montgommery's establishment in *c*.1098 of a priory of Saint-Martin of

---

[73] See further, Chap. 5; cf. Tabuteau, 'The Role of Law', 155–67.
[74] David Crouch, 'Beaumont, Henry de, first earl of Warwick (*d*.1119)', *ODNB*.
[75] *RRAN*, ii, no. 843 (no. LI); Crouch, *Beaumont Twins*, 8–10.
[76] For the details of this process, Duncan, *Kingship of the Scots*, 59–64; Oram, *David I*, 62–5; Green, *Henry I*, 128–9.
[77] In general, Graeme J. White, *Restoration and Reform, 1153–1165: Recovery from Civil War in England* (Cambridge, 2000), 77–122. See further, Chap. 6.
[78] Oksanen, *Flanders and the Anglo-Norman World*, 39–41.

Sées at Pembroke on his short-lived cross-Channel estate, in the future King Stephen's establishment of a Savignac house at Furness (Cumbria), in David I's of a Tironensian house at Selkirk/Kelso, and in Earl Robert of Gloucester's of a Cistercian house at Margam. The requirement to display a presence in the distant parts of empire may also a factor in the story told in the *Brut y Twysygion* about Gilbert fitz Richard, the second generation holder of the massive Clare family lands in England and a man with a distinctly dubious record of loyalty to William Rufus and Henry I, regularly pestering Henry until provided with the opportunity to take over the risky outpost of Ceredigion.[79]

With the benefit of hindsight we can see that over the years some individuals played the politics of the cross-Channel empire better than others, something that is hardly surprising. Apparently dramatically different biographies are provided by the lives of Robert de Bellême (spectacularly unsuccessful) and Robert II, earl of Leicester (spectacularly successful). One might suggest that the brutal and outrageous Robert de Bellême stored up trouble for himself, whereas the careful and judicious Robert made himself trusted by all, yet when the biographies are set out in detail, as they have been by Kathleen Thompson and David Crouch, it is possible to suggest that the eventual outcome of their respective careers was far from as predictable as their fates might suggest; both after all set out to make themselves useful to rulers on both sides of the Channel and both were notably ambitious, but the first ultimately threw in his lot with the wrong potential ruler (Robert Curthose) and the latter ingratiated himself splendidly with the future Henry II. But Robert had collaborated well with William Rufus and had re-created a huge cross-Channel estate as a result; it was this relationship with Henry I that was his undoing.[80]

Another case study is provided by William II de Warenne, earl of Surrey from 1088 to 1138, the son of William I de Warenne, a man who had been raised from middling status in Normandy before 1066 to immense cross-Channel wealth by William the Conqueror. Generally seen by most historians from Oderic onwards as a constructive supporter of kings and dukes and, in particular, after a difficult period after 1100, when he had chosen to support Robert Curthose against Henry I, as one of Henry's most loyal adherents, his life was not in fact quite so straightforward. Having favoured William Rufus against Robert Curthose, and with his English estates dwarfing his Norman ones, the decision to support Robert in 1101 is likely to reflect either a personal animosity to Henry or a belief that Robert's claim was the better one; the two possibilities are of course not mutually exclusive.[81] Yet by 1103, he had persuaded Robert that the losses he had suffered in his cause, namely of all the lands that his father and he had acquired in England, required that the duke cross the Channel uninvited by Henry I to make representations on his behalf, with the outcome being that Robert's unannounced arrival in England was treated

---

[79] *Brut y Tywysogyon (Peniarth ms. 20 Version)*, 34.
[80] Kathleen Thompson, 'Robert of Bellême reconsidered', *ANS*, xiii (1991), 263–86; Kathleen Thompson, 'Bellême, Robert de, earl of Shrewsbury and count of Ponthieu', *ODNB*; Crouch, *Beaumont Twins*, 79–98; David Crouch, 'Robert, second earl of Leicester (1104–1168)', *ODNB*.
[81] For William making jokes at Henry's expense, *Roman de Rou*, 320–1, ll. 10,513–54.

as a hostile act. William therefore secured his objective and at the same time seriously weakened Robert's position; he soon afterwards changed sides to join Henry.[82] The virtues of the loyal magnate are then presented to us in the Warenne Chronicle, written in the late 1150s for his granddaughter's husband, William IV de Warenne, the aforementioned son of King Stephen, where William II is portrayed as prominent in rallying the troops for Henry I before the Battle of Brémule.[83]

To suggest that there are close parallels between William's behaviour and that of Earl Rannulf II of Chester, in the historiography one of the darker figures of the civil war of 1135–53, might at first sight seem perverse.[84] Yet the systemic parallels are actually very striking, with, for example, Rannulf securing in 1140 the grant of Lincoln from King Stephen until the king should regain his Norman estates for him, and later, having changed sides and done homage to the future Henry II in 1149, securing from Henry not only a promise of the restoration of his Norman lands, but also of their augmentation, a deal, secured from the politically desperate young Henry, described by David Crouch as 'a charter of confirmation of breathtaking generosity'.[85] That Wace could present William II de Warenne's dealings with Robert Curthose and Henry as a case of entrapment, by which Henry I and William cooked up a plan to humiliate Curthose in order to deprive him of the annual payment from England promised by Henry, shows just how similar to Rannulf's his behaviour actually was in some twelfth-century eyes.[86]

Since both were in fact playing off the conflicting interests of rivals for cross-Channel rule to secure their own and their followers' fortunes, it is arguably the eventual outcome that makes their behaviour seem different, rather than their conduct. In either astutely or fortunately choosing the winning side and then spending a lifetime serving a successful ruler, William ensured his good reputation for posterity; Rannulf, in contrast, although he might have gone to his grave on 17 December 1153 believing that he had secured the future, was to become after the event one of the villains of the 'nineteen long winters' as Henry II stripped his heir of his father's gains and made him appear to be one of the anarchic spirits of extraordinary times. Yet two historians saw them in similar terms; the anonymous author of the *Gesta Stephani*

---

[82] OV, vi, 12–15; C. Warren Hollister, 'The Taming of a Turbulent Earl: Henry I and William of Warenne', *Réflexions historiques*, iii (1976), 83–91 (*Monarchy and Magnates*), 137–44; Green, *Henry I*, 76; Aird, *Robert Curthose*, 215–18.

[83] *The Warenne (Hyde) Chronicle*, 74–7.

[84] For Rannulf, Paul Dalton, '*In neutro latere*: The Armed Neutrality of Rannulf II, earl of Chester in King Stephen's Reign', *ANS*, xiv (1992), 39–59; Graeme White, 'Ranulf (II), fourth earl of Chester (d.1153)', *ODNB*.

[85] *RRAN*, iii, nos. 178 (*donec idem rex fecerit ei terram suam Norm(annie) et omnia castella sua habere*), 180. David Crouch's revival of A. L. Poole's dating of late 1140 for the agreement between Earl Rannulf and King Stephen, as against 1146 that has been preferred since the publication of the third volume of the *Regesta Regum Anglo-Normannorum*, must be justified because it was only in 1140 that Stephen had any realistic expectation of helping him in Normandy; Crouch, *Reign of Stephen*, 143–4. Also in favour of 1140 is Edmund King, 'The Foundation of Pipewell Abbey, Northamptonshire', *HSJ*, ii (1990), 167–77, at 171 n. 23, although what he says there about the Norman lands must be incorrect.

[86] *Roman de Rou*, 320–3, ll. 10,555–62.

described Rannulf as congenitally disloyal and Wace could comment that many thought Earl William 'very skilled at plotting to do harm'.[87]

However they are interpreted, the basic point that is central to both of the stories of these two earls is that not only did rulers consistently behave in an imperial way even when they did not control Normandy and England together, but that the great cross-Channel magnates of their kind reinforced this imperial behaviour by consistently stressing the cross-Channel factor in their dealings with them. An illustration of the near-universality of the phenomenon is provided by Wace's statement that many complained to Robert Curthose about the losses that they were suffering in England as a result of supporting him in Normandy, while Orderic has the great cross-Channel magnate Ralph de Tosny and others with difficulties in Normandy turn to Rufus when Robert could not assist them; it is indeed extraordinarily ironic that Orderic also has the Norman Church seek a patron and protector in Rufus, given that he had set out stinging criticisms of Rufus's conduct in ecclesiastical matters in England in the passage that immediately preceded this statement.[88] John of Worcester tells us how the loyalty of another great cross-Channel magnate, Count William of Eu, was secured by Rufus by bribery.[89] It is striking too how the cross-Channel empire at this time remained the political focus for someone who had in theory been excluded from it. Thus, Eustace III, count of Boulogne, who had been deprived of all of his English lands by William Rufus for supporting Robert Curthose in 1088, turns up frequently in Normandy in the 1090s, despite holding no land there; the outcome of this attentiveness was that, after his return from the First Crusade and even after supporting Robert against Henry in 1101, he was restored in 1101 to his English lands by Henry I and, like William II de Warenne, became for some years notably assiduous in his attendance at Henry's court.[90]

These case studies make me doubt that, whatever we make of Robert Curthose's character, his rule in Normandy could possibly have survived the pressures imposed by the superior financial resources that William Rufus and Henry I could deploy against him; evocatively describing the barrels and carts in which Henry transported the money that enabled him to recruit mercenaries, Wace once more arguably supplies an acute analysis of the balance of forces of the time.[91] Also, as count of the Cotentin from 1088, Henry already had a huge stake in Normandy when he became king, and this contributed to a rivalry with William, count of Mortain, that was of fundamental importance in the politics of western Normandy. In addition, his readiness to stir up the business of the succession to the southern Norman lordship of Breteuil furthered the destabilization of his brother's hold on the duchy.[92] Henry I from 1100 remained a cross-Channel political figure, just as

---

[87] *Gesta Stephani*, 184–5, 192–3; *Roman de Rou*, 320–1, ll. 10,557–62.
[88] *Roman de Rou*, 320–1, ll. 10,495–504; OV, iv, 178–81, 214–15, 236–7.
[89] JW, iii, 68–9.   [90] Tanner, *Families, Friends and Allies*, 132–3, 145–7.
[91] *Roman de Rou*, 326–9, ll. 10851–68. For Henry's wealth as a decisive factor, see also JW, iii, 106–7.
[92] Kerrith Davies, 'The Count of the Cotentin: Western Normandy, William of Mortain, and the Career of Henry I', *HSJ*, xxii (2012, for 2010), 123–40, at 130–7; Crouch, *Beaumont Twins*, 108; Aird, *Robert Curthose*, 215–18, 221–3.

he had been from birth; his main objective after 1100 was arguably to enhance further that status.

Although the fact that conditions during the civil war of 1135–53 were different from those that had existed between 1087 and 1106 because the two sides were more evenly balanced, with each of them having bases on both sides of the Channel, there are, alongside Earl Rannulf of Chester's activities, plenty of other examples of cross-Channel wheeling-and-dealing. The Empress's famous 1141 charters for Geoffrey de Mandeville, for example, can be interpreted as effectively a piece of cross-Channel bribery to secure his support, because they increased his holdings in Normandy, over which she and her husband had at that point no legal right, as well as confirming property in England, sometimes in regions she did not control.[93] The settlement between Roger, earl of Hereford, and William de Briouze, which is usually treated primarily as regulating differences in the marches of Wales, in fact also dealt with mutual interests in Normandy.[94] This case is an especially important one because Earl Roger was effectively the leader of the Angevin cause in England after the death of Earl Robert of Gloucester in 1147; in other words, here was a man operating near to the highest levels of power, the surviving evidence for whose career appears to be exclusively English, making arrangements for the new cross-Channel *imperium* that he hoped was going to come about.

One further example is supplied by a much better known imperial figure, Robert, earl of Leicester, who had Stephen confirm to him the borough, castle, and county of Hereford on the same terms that they had been held by the great Conquest period magnate William fitz Osbern and subsequently had Duke Henry confirm to him the stewardship of Normandy and England, an office once held by William fitz Osbern. Robert may not have been consciously aiming to recreate the cross-Channel estate of William fitz Osbern, but the fact that by 1153 he had as good as achieved precisely this, taken alongside the reference back to the Conqueror's great friend in two charters relevant to this process, on a minimum case suggest yet again the potency of memory imbued within the values and practice of empire. It certainly shows once again the depth of commitment to the preservation and continuation of the cross-Channel empire, on—of course—the best terms that could be achieved.[95]

Another group with a commitment to the continuation of empire was the bishops of Normandy, many of whom appear in England in the early years of Stephen's reign, and in particular through the special role played by Archbishop Hugh of Rouen in the aftermath of the arrest of the bishops in 1139.[96] And

---

[93] *RRAN*, iii, no. 275; Chibnall, *Empress Matilda*, 109–12; Crouch, *Reign of Stephen*, 181–2.

[94] Z. N. Brooke and C. N. L. Brooke, 'Hereford Cathedral Dignitaries in the Twelfth Century: Supplement (*Conventio* between Roger, Earl of Hereford, and William de Braose, his Brother-in-Law (1148–1154))', *Cambridge Historical Journal*, viii (1944–6), 179–85, at 185 (*Castellum uero de Breuse et terram suam de Normandie* (sic in ms.) *aut per me aut per nuncios meos infra annum a proxima festa* (sic in ms.) *sancti Iohannis in pace habere faciam*); calendared, David Walker, 'Charters of the Earldom of Hereford, 1095–1201', *Camden Miscellany*, xxii, Camden, 4th ser., i (1964), 20 no. 15.

[95] *Regesta*, iii, nos. 437, 438; Crouch, *Beaumont Twins*, 87.

[96] David Luscombe, 'Hugh (*d.*1164), Abbot of Reading and Archbishop of Rouen', *ODNB*.

furthermore, four, and probably five, out of the seven Norman bishops were present at Henry II's coronation as king of the English at Westminster on 19 December 1154, with one of the absentees, Gerard, bishop of Sées, having reputedly been savagely mutilated by officials acting for Henry's father, Count Geoffrey, and the other certain absentee, Bishop Richard of Coutances, seemingly heavily preoccupied with the affairs of his see.[97]

The subject of cross-Channel networks during the civil war is a neglected one. Although it has already appeared prominently in my two case studies of the Reviers family and of the grants by Adeliza Peverel and of Matilda of Wallingford, it is worth dwelling on it a little more here as a prelude to further treatment in the next chapter.[98] Thus, Roger de Montbrai (Mowbray), a man who, after his return from the Second Crusade, manoeuvred to regain lands lost in Normandy and in the territories controlled by David I, is known to have crossed to Normandy as part of this process to answer a plea concerning the castle of Bazouches-en-Houlme, a story that is particularly interesting because King Stephen warranted Roger's possession long after he had lost control of Normandy.[99] And in 1143, Rotrou, bishop of Evreux, accused his brother, the rather ineffectual Roger, earl of Warwick, of breaking an agreement to allow him personal patronage of the church of St Mary's, Warwick, that eventually led to Rotrou crossing to England in the company of a papal legate.[100] That a crucial preparatory element to the settlement between King Stephen and Duke Henry was the collective refusal of the great magnates to take part in a decisive fight between the two claimants is well known. It was famously placed within the framework of 'The Magnates' Peace' by R. H. C. Davis as the title to Chapter 10 of his *King Stephen*, a phrase whose exact interpretation has subsequently been much discussed and variously interpreted.[101] Whatever view is taken, however, its analytical basis in an imposed pacification and local English treaties between great men must now be extended to include a positive drive towards the reunification of Normandy and England. All were bricks in the wall of what Frank Barlow called *renovatio imperii* (a nice phrase since it avoids the contentious issues of my arguments for empire, even if in this case he did actually interpret *imperium* as meaning empire).[102]

It has been remarked that one of the fundamental reasons for the success of the settlement between Stephen and Duke Henry in late 1153 is that it did not look to

---

[97] Jörg Peltzer, 'Henry II and the Norman Bishops', *EHR*, cxix (2004), 1202–29, at 1208–11.
[98] For the case studies, see Chaps. 1 and 2.
[99] *The Foundation History of the Abbeys of Byland and Jervaulx*, ed. Janet Burton, Borthwick Texts and Studies, no. 35 (York, 2006), 19–20 (Van Caenegem, *Lawsuits*, i, no. 323, where the unlikely identification of the castle as that of Bayeux is accepted). For Roger's manipulation of alliances to reconstruct the family's cross-Channel estate, *Charters of the Honour of Mowbray, 1107–1191*, ed. Diana E. Greenway, British Academy Records of Social and Economic History, new series, vol. 1 (Oxford, 1972), xxvi–xxvii.
[100] *Papsturkunden in England*, ed. W. Holtzmann, 3 vols (Berlin, 1930–52), i, 256; Crouch, *Beaumont Twins*, 55–6.
[101] R. H. C. Davis, *King Stephen*, 3rd edn. (London, 1990), 108–24.
[102] Frank Barlow, *The English Church, 1066–1154* (London, 1979), 317.

the future.[103] Yet those many individuals who secured charters of confirmation from Henry were surely doing so, as also were those citizens of Rouen who had invested money in his cause, and as of course was Robert of Torigni, recently installed as abbot of Mont Saint-Michel.[104] And so too, as already mentioned, was Robert, earl of Leicester, with his Fontevrauldine priory at Nuneaton. That the long-reigned Thierry, count of Flanders (1128–68), was also present at Henry's coronation as an evident prelude to the restoration of good personal relations points to the way in which the process of stabilization of empire took in the wider networks of the northern French and western European world of the post-1066 empire.[105] The cross-Channel elite were ready for the next stage in their history. The past would have taught them that it would not be a straightforward one.

UNIFORMITY AND DIVERSITY

That a monk from Fécamp, who visited his abbey's priory of Cogges in Oxfordshire in the 1150s, expressed confusion at the complexities of local jurisdictions in England is a good way to draw attention to the continuation of the plurality that had characterized the cross-Channel empire since its beginning.[106] Although others seem to have worked out how to deal with the continuing differences in the customary traditions of distinct *regna* of the empire, the poor man's difficulties are certainly comprehensible when the same word can mean different things in the two places.[107] Thus, while *uicecomes* was used to describe both a Norman *vicomte* and an English sheriff as a means to indicate responsibilities in local government that were subordinate to those of an earl or count, there were in practice significant differences of meaning, above all because Normandy had no equivalent of the shire court.[108] Likewise, a Norman 'count' and an English 'earl' (to use the later terminology) might well be described by the same word in the twelfth century (*comes*), but anyone who tried then to describe what it meant to be a *comes* in

---

[103] J. C. Holt, 'The Treaty of Winchester, 1153', in Edmund King (ed.), *The Anarchy of King Stephen's Reign* (Oxford, 1994), 291–316, at 315–16 (reprinted in Holt, *Colonial England*, 271–90, at 290).

[104] For comment on confirmation charters, Holt, 'Treaty of Winchester', 297–316 (*Colonial England*, 276–90); Lucien Musset, 'Y eut-il une aristocratie d'affaires commune aux grandes villes de Normandie et d'Angleterre entre 1066 et 1204?', *Etudes normandes*, xxxv, no. 3 (1986), 7–19, at 10–11.

[105] Oksanen, *Flanders and the Anglo-Norman World*, 32–3.

[106] '*Epistulae Fiscannenses*: lettres d'amitié, de gouvernement et d'affaires', ed. J. Laporte, *Revue Mabillon*, xliii (1953), 5–31, at 30. For differences between the powers of lords in Normandy and England, Crouch, *Beaumont Twins*, 101–95; Daniel Power, 'Le régime seigneurial en Normandie (XIIe–XIIIe s.)', in Martin Aurell and Frédéric Boutoulle (eds), *Les seigneuries dans l'espace Plantagenêt (c.1150–c.1250)* (Bordeaux, 2009), 117–36, esp. at 120–3, 130–1.

[107] For cross-Channel management, see Chap. 5.

[108] Mark Hagger, 'The Norman *Vicomte*, c.1035–1135: What Did He Do?', *ANS*, xxix (2007), 65–83, and see esp. 81; David Crouch, 'Between Three Realms: The Acts of Waleran II, Count of Meulan and Worcester', in Nicholas Vincent (ed.), *Records, Administration and Aristocratic Society in the Anglo-Norman Realm: Papers Commemorating the 800th Anniversary of King John's Loss of Normandy* (Woodbridge, 2009), 75–90, at 82–4.

England—and also Scotland—would come up with a definition that would be a bit different from the word's Norman equivalent.[109] This point about similarity and difference becomes even clearer when, with surviving late twelfth-century rolls of the Norman Exchequer for guidance, we can effectively read as parallel texts the structures from which account was rendered.[110] A different kind of diversity is demonstrated by the already-mentioned case of ecclesiastical architecture, with England after 1066 supplying a much more dynamic picture than the rather conservative Normandy of the first half of the twelfth century. But the overall situation was also one that produced some notable examples of linguistic creativity to deal with unfamiliar phenomena.[111] And around the peripheries, the same processes both encouraged uniformity and entrenched diversity within significantly different contexts; language might be transferred to describe what were deemed to be analogous phenomena, but society and culture were shaped by a host of factors that ensured continuing difference.[112]

The pragmatic use of existing cultural forms is evident in the well-nigh immediate development after 1066 of a formalized partnership in cross-Channel rule by William and Matilda that owed much to the exploitation in a different context of existing matrices that conferred exceptional power on a woman when she was either a regent or an heiress. However, in terms of Matilda's participation in the doing of justice, it was certainly an innovative response to the new situation created by the cross-Channel empire, the product of exceptional circumstances that, diplomatic differences between the types of document produced in England and Normandy notwithstanding, operated identically on both sides of the Channel. The arrangement was continued by Henry I and his first wife, Matilda, with the qualification that, with the exception of a visit to Normandy shortly after the Battle of Tinchebrai, Matilda's role was performed exclusively in England.[113] Had conditions been normal, a similar partnership would probably have been operated by Stephen and his wife, Matilda.[114] The arrangements should not, however, be seen as institutionalizing cross-gender collaboration or as a formal scheme of imperial government. They were rather the consequence of three exceptional marriages and of the characters of three strong-minded women; that the same role was not given to Henry I's second queen, Adeliza of Louvain, demonstrates that they operated *ad*

---

[109] Crouch, *Image of Aristocracy*, 46–50; Crouch, *The Birth of Nobility*, 202–4.

[110] Vincent Moss, 'Normandy and England in 1180: The Pipe Roll Evidence', in *England and Normandy*, 185–95, at 188–95.

[111] Lewis, 'The Invention of the Manor', *passim*.

[112] For an excellent statement of this line of argument, Susan Reynolds, 'Fiefs and Vassals in Scotland: A View from the Outside', *SHR*, lxxxii (2003), 176–93, at 180–9.

[113] David Bates, 'The Representation of Queens and Queenship in Anglo-Norman Royal Charters', in Paul Fouracre and David Ganz (eds), *Frankland: Essays in Honour of Dame Jinty Nelson* (Manchester, 2008), 285–303; Judith A. Green, 'Duchesses of Normandy in the Eleventh and Twelfth Centuries', *Normandy and Neighbours*, 43–59.

[114] Heather J. Tanner, 'Queenship: Office, Custom or Ad Hoc? The Case of Queen Matilda III of England (1135–1152)', in Bonnie Wheeler and John Carmi Parsons (eds), *Eleanor of Aquitaine: Lord and Lady* (New York, 2002), 133–58; Marjorie Chibnall, 'Matilda [Matilda of Boulogne] (*c.*1103–1152), queen of England', in *ODNB*.

personam. When there were neither wives nor suitable close kindred available after 1120, association in rule did involve trusted administrators, but not before.[115]

As a demonstration of evolving uniformity, Mark Hagger's reconsideration of the introduction of the routine use of the writ and writ-charter into Normandy by Henry I after Tinchebrai shows that the essential functionality of both was as good as identical on the two sides of the Channel, while at the same time reinforcing once more the point about organizational difference between Normandy and England.[116] It also shows again the hegemonic power of empire drawing on English, rather than Continental, precedent and draws attention to cultural dissemination beyond the cross-Channel territorial core, since writ-form had before the middle of the twelfth century become a regular style of communication for aristocratic management in northern France beyond the duchy of Normandy, as well as also spreading extensively within the kingdom of Scots and, to a lesser extent, into the Welsh principalities.[117]

The *Laudes Regiae*, liturgical acclamations of the ruler's dignity sung at religious festivals, but chanted differently in Normandy and England after 1066, are another manifestation of this same combination of cross-Channel distinctiveness and cultural unity.[118] The crucial point once more is that the one generic form was adapted to local circumstance. The argument that an inauguration ceremony for the Norman duke was introduced into the duchy by Henry I in or soon after 1106, rather than much later under Richard I as previously thought, on the basis that the surviving text *Officium ad ducem Normannie consuetudinum* draws on the second English coronation *ordo*, and not the third, lends further weight to an argument for a general cultural uniformity within an ideology of empire that stressed plurality.[119]

A host of phenomena draws attention to other manifestations of similar evolutionary processes. Thus, there is, firstly, the development of those two precocious financial organizations, the two Exchequers in Normandy and England, and, secondly, of a common style of magnate domestic architecture on both sides of the Channel, with the free-standing hall seen as evolving from the residences of the pre-1066 English aristocracy. Both are especially important for the cultural history of empire because there are no contemporary equivalents outside the lands of the cross-Channel empire.[120] The export to Normandy of veneration for certain

---

[115] David Bates, 'The Origins of the Justiciarship', *ANS*, iv (1982), 1–12, 167–71, at 11–12; Green, *Henry I*, 182.

[116] Mark Hagger, 'The earliest Norman writs revisited', *Historical Research*, lxxxii (2009), 181–206; cf, David Bates, 'The earliest Norman writs', *EHR*, c (1985), 266–84.

[117] Hagger, 'Writs', 186–7; Crouch, 'Between Three Realms', 81–2. For Scotland, see further, Chap. 5. For Wales, Charles Insley, 'Kings, Lords, Charters, and the Political Culture of Twelfth-Century Wales', *ANS*, xxx (2008), 133–53, at 142–50.

[118] Cowdrey, 'The Anglo-Norman *Laudes Regiae*', 48–55, 67.

[119] Guilhelm Pépin, 'Les couronnements et les investitures des ducs d'Aquitaine (XIe–XIIe siècle)', *Francia*, xxxvi (2009), 35–65, at 53–4. This argument gains support from the suggestion that the third *ordo* dates from 'early in the reign of Henry I at the latest'; George Garnett, 'The Third Recension of the English Coronation *Ordo*: The Manuscripts', *HSJ*, xi (2003, for 1998), 43–71, with the quotation at 67.

[120] For the exchequers, Green, *Henry I*, 236–8, and *The Great Roll of the Pipe for the Thirty-First Year of King Henry I, Michaelmas 1130*, ed. Judith Green, Pipe Roll Society, new series, vol. LVII,

English saints, most notably St Edmund, is further evidence of a new post-1066 cross-Channel participation in particularly prestigious cults in which the influence did not come from Normandy and France to England, but travelled in the reverse direction.[121] And, even in a case where the initial inspiration was undoubtedly Continental, namely, the design and construction of great *donjons*, the similarities between the *donjon* of Norwich castle and the chronologically later one of Falaise provide another example of cultural transfer that was flowing in both directions across the Channel.[122] Cross-Channel exchange and interaction is also important in the development of script.[123] The trap for the unwary, however, lies in those apparent examples of cross-Channel development that are actually examples of European change. It is crucial not to give the cultural label 'Norman' to developments that were shared with the wider world beyond the empire's borders.[124]

The differences in the style and weight of Norman and English coinages is an area where there was apparently not assimilation, with the light-weight and aesthetically inferior Norman money sometimes being described in derogatory terms.[125] However, work around the complex subject of the weight of English coin suggests that a system of cross-Channel monetary transfer was put in place quite soon after 1066. While an exact dating of this process might ultimately depend on issues such as the dating of the PAX issue and whether it should be assigned to William the Conqueror or William Rufus, once more, we are looking at hegemonic structures rapidly created.[126] More generally—and, in terms of the apparent contradiction between documentary references to payments to Norman religious institutions in pounds sterling and the absence of archaeological finds of English pennies in Normandy, this is the obvious explanation—it looks as if the English money that was transported across the Channel was melted down and put back into circulation as Rouen money. In economic terms, this must be what

ix–xiv, summarize a great deal of scholarship. On residences, see Edward Impey, 'La demeure seigneuriale en Normandie entre 1125 et 1225 et la tradition anglo-normande', in Baylé (ed.), *L'architecture normande*, i, 219–41, and esp. at 236–41; and Edward Impey, 'The Seigneurial Residence in Normandy, 1125–1225: An Anglo-Norman Tradition?', *Medieval Archaeology*, xliii, (1999), 45–73, at 68–73. See further, Impey and McNeill, 'La grande salle des ducs de Normandie', 95–131.

[121] Marjorie Chibnall, 'Les Normands et les saints anglo-saxons', in Pierre Bouet and François Neveux (eds), *Les Saints dans la Normandie médiévale: Colloque de Cerisy-la-Salle (26–29 septembre 1996)* (Caen, 2000), 259–68, at 263–8.

[122] Heslop, *Norwich Castle Keep*, 57–63; Joseph Decaëns, 'Le château de Falaise', in Baylé (ed.), *L'architecture normande*, ii, 305–9, at 307.

[123] Marc H. Smith, 'Aux origines incertaine de l'écriture gothique, entre Angleterre et Normandie', in Jean-Paulle Hervieu, Emmanuel Poulle and Philippe Manneville (eds), *La place de la Normandie dans la diffusion des savoirs: Du livre manuscript à la bibliothèque virtuelle* (Rouen, 2006), 79–94, and esp. at 87–94.

[124] See further, Chap. 5.

[125] Françoise Dumas, 'Les monnaies normandes des Xe–XIIe siècles avec un répertoire', *Revue numismatique*, xxi (1979), 84–140, and esp. 92–102, remains fundamental.

[126] Pamela Nightingale, 'The Evolution of Weight-Standards and the Creation of New Monetary and Commercial Links in Northern Europe from the Tenth to the Twelfth Century', *Economic History Review*, 2nd ser., xxxviii (1985), 192–209, at 200–1 (reprinted in Pamela Nightingale, *Trade, Money, and Power in Medieval England* (Aldershot/Burlington VT, 2007), Chap. 4); Martin Allen, *Mints and Money in Medieval England* (Cambridge, 2012), 25–6.

happened given the extent to which the circulation of Rouen money was integrated into that of other northern French coinages, and to which Normandy had a money economy long before 1066. To have gone for uniformity in this area across the cross-Channel empire would have produced an economic disaster; it would also have infringed the custom that operated in both *regna* of excluding as far as possible coinage other than the officially minted one.[127] Coinage exchanges of this kind had been managed long before the twelfth century and Norman money was readily exchanged with Arabic and Byzantine money on the First Crusade; Raymond of Aguilers' description of the pragmatic creation of rates of exchange between Frankish and Arabic coinages during the First Crusade and the short-lived circulation of Rouen money at Latakia described by Guibert of Nogent make the point very well.[128]

This manifestation of apparently feeble cross-Channel integration was, in fact, therefore, the exact opposite. Everyone knew very well how the process worked and that to try to buck the system was a route to the most savage of punishments, as moneyers in England discovered in 1124 when Henry I's soldiers in Normandy complained that the money they received was so debased as to be virtually valueless.[129] The Anglo-Saxon Chronicle throughout Henry I's reign provides a repetitious and undoubtedly, to an extent, formulaic litany of associating crossings to Normandy during Henry I's time with mentions of war with the king of France or count of Anjou, or with both of them, and of the levying of tax on England, the detail that goes with William of Malmesbury's story of the conjoined twins.[130] It is a moot point as to whether the empire could have afforded William Rufus for much longer, but it looks as if the more prudent and politic Henry I may ultimately have been equally rapacious, even if his methods were generally less outrageous.[131] Even if the specific

---

[127] For this argument, Arnoux, 'L'événement et la conjuncture', in *1204*, 229, 234–5; Gareth Williams, 'Monetary Contacts between England and Normandy, c.973–1180: A Numismatic Perspective', in Jérémie Chameroy and Pierre-Marie Guihard (eds), *Circulations monétaires en Normandie et dans le Nord-Ouest européen (Antiquité-Moyen-Âge)* (Caen, 2012), 173–84, at 182–3. The classic article on monetary circulation in Normandy is Lucien Musset, 'Réflexions sur les moyens de paiement en Normandie au XIe et XIIe siècle', in Lucien Musset, Jean-Michel Bouvris, and Véronique Gazeau (eds), *Aspects de la société et de l'économie dans la Normandie médiévale (X^e–XIIIe siècles)*, Cahiers des Annales de Normandie, no. 22 (Caen, 1989), 65–89. For a survey of the evidence for English coin finds in Normandy, Jens Christian Moesgaard, 'Two Finds from Normandy of English Coins of the Norman Kings (1066–1154)', *Numismatic Chronicle*, cliv (1994), 209–13.

[128] For some comment on coinage exchange among late-ninth-century Anglo-Saxon kingdoms, Barrie Cook, 'Foreign Coins in Medieval England', in *Moneta Locale, Moneta Straniera: Italia ed Europa XI–XV secolo*, ed. Lucia Traviaini (Milan, 1999), 231–84, at 233; *Guibertus abbas S. Mariae Nogenti, Gesta Dei per Francos*, ed. R. B. C. Huygens, Corpus Christianorum Continuatio Medievalis, no.127A (Turnhout, 1996), 336 (*The Deeds of God through the Franks: A Translation of Guibert of Nogent's 'Gesta Dei per Francos'*, trans. R. Levine (Woodbridge, 1997), 159). See further, A. V. Murray, 'Money and Logistics in the Forces of the First Crusade: Coinage, Bullion, Service and Supply, 1096–99', in J. H. Pryor (ed.), *Logistics of Warfare in the Age of the Crusades* (London, 2006), 229–49, at 234–7.

[129] *GND*, ii, 236–9.

[130] Henry's visits to Normandy are almost always specifically associated with war and often with severe taxation, ASC, 'E', 1111, 1112, 1116, 1117, 1118, 1119, 1123, 1124, 1128.

[131] For Rufus and taxation, Barlow, *William Rufus*, 214–62.

detail required to construct an economic and financial history of the cross-Channel empire is at this point lacking, when all the networks of exploitation that joined lands in England to monasteries in Normandy and elsewhere in France are added in, there can be no doubt that the relationship of Normandy and England was financially and economically beneficial to many in the duchy and very important to the maintenance of rule there.[132] It is arguable that we might still use John Le Patourel's concept of assimilation as part of the analysis of empire, but evolving within a focus on uniformity, plurality, diversity, and systematic exploitation.

HEGEMONY AND MUTUALITY BEYOND THE CORE

Gruffudd ap Cynan, prince of Gwynedd (1095–1137), David I, king of Scots (1124–53), and Helias de La Flèche, count of Maine (1092–1110) were three individuals who prospered by skilfully participating in the hegemonic power of the cross-Channel empire and, at times, by successfully opposing it. There are obvious differences of context and achievement, but the common factor of personal ability justifies using their lives as mirror-images of the hegemonic strengths and weaknesses of the empire.

Helias de La Flèche took over the county of Maine in 1092 by emerging as a victor in a succession dispute that took place when the ruler of Normandy, Robert Curthose, was ill-placed to intervene in it. He then proceeded to negotiate his way around William Rufus's dramatic interventions in Maine in 1098 and 1099 and to flit in and out of the courts of the rulers of the cross-Channel empire, experiencing, for example, a spectacular putdown from William Rufus when he proposed to go on the First Crusade; it is, of course, a significant comment on Helias's capacity to assess the balance of forces that he first of all thought to ask Robert Curthose and Rufus for their agreement and that, having failed to obtain it, took the politically prudent course of staying at home.[133] Orderic, in one of his fund of relevant stories about these times, also describes how William Rufus's idea that Helias could be recruited to his military household was talked down by Count Robert of Meulan on the grounds that Helias was a capable man who would constitute a personal rival to Robert; in the context of later events, this was surely a significant error of judgement on Rufus's part, but a comprehensible decision within the here-and-now of late-eleventh-century politics. It illustrates again the seductive and hegemonic power of the rulers' court and household and how they might have provided a route to safeguard power over the county of Maine.[134]

After 1100 Helias remained a prominent participant in the affairs of the cross-Channel empire, collaborating with Henry I's conquest of the duchy and taking part on his side in the sieges of Bayeux and Caen and the Battle of Tinchebrai. Seemingly at first sight illogical because the re-establishment of the cross-Channel

---

[132] This theme will be developed further in Chaps. 5 and 6.
[133] For this episode, OV, v, 228–33. The main modern accounts are Barlow, *William Rufus*, 367–8, 382–8, 390–2, 402–5; Richard E. Barton, 'Henry I, Count Helias of Maine and the Battle of Tinchebray', in Fleming and Pope (eds), *Henry I and the Anglo-Norman World*, 63–90.
[134] OV, v, 246–9.

realm under a single ruler might be reasonably thought likely to enhance the threat to his power in Maine, his actions were probably based on the calculation that Henry, with his personal base close to Maine at Domfront, was likely to prove a much better ally than the disorderly efforts of Robert Curthose against the two men's common enemy around the southern regions of Normandy and the northern parts of Maine, namely Robert de Bellême.[135] At the same time, however, Helias's strategy for survival was also southward looking, most obviously expressed by the successive marriages of his only offspring, his daughter Eremberge, to two sons of Count Fulk IV Rechin of Anjou, Geoffrey Martel and the future Count Fulk V. That the second marriage led in due course to Eremberge and her husband Fulk taking over Maine at Helias's death in 1110, and to their son Geoffrey becoming both count of Anjou and Maine after Fulk departed from western Europe in 1128 to take over the kingdom of Jerusalem, was certainly not in the script written for the future by Henry I, and probably not by Helias either.

For all that the eventual outcome was the creation of the massive territorial complex ruled by Henry II, in terms of the rational decision-making of the moment, what needs to be stressed is the conventionality of it all. Not for the first or last time in the history of the Normans and empire, the unpredictability of the human reproductive process then played a decisive part. After 1110 Henry's attempts to retrieve the situation included Maine being the dowry of Fulk and Eremburge's daughter Matilda when she married Henry's son William in 1120 and subsequently, of course, the marriage of his daughter the Empress Matilda to Count Geoffrey in 1128. Arguably 1110 must with hindsight be seen as one of the great turning-points in the history of the cross-Channel empire. But if Henry I's second marriage had produced a male heir, or if Henry had become sympathetic to the claims of his nephew William Clito, then all would have been very different.

David I's career resembles Helias's in that the kingdom of Scots provided him with a power base beyond the empire's hegemonic core and with extensive autonomy, and therefore with a multiplicity of options. Although his rise to kingship was distinctly fortuitous, the combination of friendship and kinship with Henry I and the latter's preoccupations in Normandy effectively gave him a free hand in the kingdom of Scots.[136] In addition, as a direct descendant of the Old English kings through his mother and, from 1113, the holder of an earldom in England, David was not just a participant in empire, but an integral player within it; in 1127, for example, he was the first to swear the fateful oath in support of his niece, the Empress Matilda. He was a regular visitor to southern England, and also a man with cross-Channel responsibilities and a place in the wider northern French world that extended beyond Normandy, since, although his own lands in Normandy were small, those whom he recruited to the Scottish kingdom almost all had landed interests in western Normandy or Brittany that they would wish to

---

[135] For the argument that friendship was central to the relationship, Barton, 'Henry I, Count Helias of Maine and the Battle of Tinchebray', 79–90.
[136] On David's designation and related issues, Duncan, *The Kingship of the Scots*, 65.

preserve.[137] He was also a participant in the religious world of western France. The monks he acquired from Tiron to install at Selkirk in 1113, before subsequently moving them to Kelso, were among the first representatives of the new monasticism of western France to obtain an institutional foothold in the British Isles.[138]

After 1135, the seriousness with which David took the oath made to his niece, the Empress, was a factor of significant importance in the civil war. His commitment to her cause fits with his reputation as a principled, religious king that is a regular theme in the literary sources. There is no need, as has frequently been done, to see his support for Matilda and his takeover of northern England and creation of a Scoto-Northumbrian kingdom as separate or irreconcilable ambitions.[139] In particular, to see him as cutting himself adrift from his niece in the 1140s seems to me to be mistaken; the fact that the young future Henry II was sent to Carlisle to be knighted by David in 1149 is testimony to the endurance of personal links, and of the networks and ideologies that sustained both the cross-Channel empire and David's power in the kingdom of Scots. For Matilda, Duke Geoffrey, and Henry, the ceremony surely had to be performed by their one supporter of sufficient status to make it convincing. For David, his views on the subject mirrored by Ailred of Rievaulx, he was fulfilling his role within what the latter, writing in the last weeks of 1153 or in early 1154, idealistically portrayed as the 'holy family' whose members were the sons of the Empress Matilda, of 'the pious King Stephen', and of Henry, son of the, at the time of writing, recently deceased David. Ailred's focus might well have been primarily on the descent of the kings of the English and the Scots from the Old English kings through St Margaret, yet he was most certainly looking forward to a prosperous future under (when he wrote) the future King Henry II and, by implication, in the kingdom of Scots, under Mael Coluim (Malcolm) IV.[140]

On this analysis, as A. A. M. Duncan has surely correctly emphasized, the story that he made use of the meeting at Carlisle to have Henry agree that he would keep his acquisitions in northern England was a creation of the post-Treaty of Falaise (1174) period. In 1149 he must have believed that his place in the 'holy family' meant all that he had acquired was safe.[141] The follow-up to the knighting at

---

[137] See further, Chap. 5.
[138] See Kathleen Thompson, 'The Arrival of the Tironensians: Twelfth-Century Monastic Foundations in the British Isles', *Nottingham Medieval Studies*, lv (2011), 79–103, at 84–6.
[139] For David and northern England, see above all, Keith J. Stringer, 'State-Building in Twelfth-Century Britain: David I, King of Scots, and Northern England', in J. C. Appleby and Paul Dalton (eds), *Government, Religion and Society in Northern England, 1000–1700* (Stroud, 1997), 40–62.
[140] Ailred of Rievaulx, *De Genealogia Regum Anglorum*, in *PL*, cxcv, cols. 711–38, at col. 737. For a translation and a commentary, Edmund King, 'The Accession of Henry II', in Harper-Bill and Vincent (eds), *Henry II: New Interpretations*, 24–46, at 41–2, with discussion of the date at 41 n. 7. On the wider issues raised by the *De Genealogia*, see, Joanna Huntington, 'David of Scotland: "Vir tam necessarius mundo"', in Steve Boardman, John Reuben Davies, and Eila Williamson (eds), *Saints' Cults in the Celtic World* (Woodbridge, 2009), 130–45, and esp. 138–45; Alice Taylor, 'Historical Writing in Twelfth- and Thirteenth-Century Scotland: the Dunfermline Compilation', *HR*, lxxxiii (2010), 1–25, and esp. 10–17; Elizabeth Freeman, *Narratives of a New Order: Cistercian Historical Writing in England, 1150–1220* (Turnhout, 2002), 55–87. On the kings of Scots as the true heirs of the English kings, Broun, *Scottish Independence and the Idea of Britain*, 51.
[141] Note that William of Newburgh inserted those telling words *ut dicitur*: Duncan, *The Kingship of the Scots*, 68; *William of Newburgh, The History of English Affairs, Book I*, ed. P. G. Walsh and

Carlisle was the logical one, namely an invasion of England, an enterprise that stalled at Lancaster. However, unlike Earl Rannulf of Chester, with whom he did a great deal of business, David did not need a charter to consolidate his place under the conditions emerging as the civil war seemed to be moving into a new phase. But like Rannulf, David must have gone to his grave in 1153 thinking that he had done well.

David's installation in the kingdom of Scots of individuals recruited mostly from the earldom of Huntingdon followed the conventions that had determined events in England after 1066, namely that a lord should reward his followers. The themes of hard power, soft power, and core and periphery are in fact every bit as relevant to David I's kingship as they are to the history of the cross-Channel empire. The suggestion that his itinerary rarely took him north of the Tay into Gaelic Alba before 1139 or 1140 may well be a replication of Henry I's, rather than a demonstration of a lack of control further north.[142] That the rebellion of 1130, defeated at the Battle of Strathcathro, occurred while David was in the south of England was a situation that had many parallels in the history of the cross-Channel empire. Its defeat shows how, within the kingdom of Scots, power concentrated at the core can increase dominance over the periphery; as already noted, David's achievement was later seen as increasing the military power of the kings of Scots.

David I's and Henry I's collaboration was in several key respects a continuation of the relationship established in the time of William the Conqueror and Mael Coluim (Malcolm) III. Yet it was also a unique and exceptional period because of the depth of the ties that bound the two men, a mixture of friendship, kinship, and mutual self-interest laying the basis for the establishment of trans-regnal networks that, within the British Isles, was to have profound long-term consequences. It is certainly a time for which hegemony might seem an inappropriate term to use and for which cultural transfer and mutuality might be better suited. But at the same time, hegemony is also justified because of the multiple kinds and varying intensities of power that the rulers of the cross-Channel empire exercised and, in William Rufus's time, had shown that they could use. That David's successor Mael Coluim (Malcolm) IV chose to take part in Henry II's campaign to Toulouse in 1159 and William the Lion joined the 1173–4 revolt against Henry, while in his case being at the same time every bit as much a successful state-builder as the rulers of the cross-Channel empire, are both indications of a continuing psychological inability to detach themselves from participation in an empire to which they were also tied by the extensive cross-border landholdings of many of their chief subjects.[143]

M. J. Kennedy (Warminster, 1988), 100–1; *Chronica Rogeri de Houedene*, ed. W. Stubbs, 4 vols, Rolls Series (London, 1868–71), i, 211.

[142] Oram, *David I*, 77–8, who argues for David's personal aversion to these northern regions.

[143] Judith Green, 'Aristocratic Loyalties on the Northern Frontier of England, *c.*1100–1174', in Daniel Williams (ed.), *England in the Twelfth Century: Proceedings of the 1988 Harlaxton Symposium* (Woodbridge, 1990), 83–100.

Gruffudd ap Cynan's installation within Gwynedd, although couched in the remarkable *Historia* devoted to his life within the framework of legitimacy, was arguably either ultimately dependent on Henry I's support or, at the least, consolidated with that support.[144] One especially striking aspect of this legitimacy is that it was constructed, not just in a Welsh context, but within that of the new world of empire as well; the unknown author of the *Historia* goes to the trouble of establishing—somewhat tortuously—the common ancestry of Gruffudd and the contemporary Norman rulers of England.[145] A second is that Gruffudd's conduct within the politics of Wales was conducted with an awareness of the hegemonic power of empire, to the extent that, in 1121, for example, he refused to support the beleaguered rulers of Powys on the grounds of a peace treaty with Henry I.[146] And a third manifestation of this is his dealings with the bishopric of Bangor, where his conduct was initially to side with local opinion against the importation of a new kind of bishop from the lands of the cross-Channel empire, only, in the end, in 1120, for him to light on the distinguished scholar David (the Scot), an Irish clerk so familiar with Henry I's court that he had earlier been among those who accompanied the king's daughter Matilda to Germany for her marriage to the Emperor Henry V.[147]

The degrees of both autonomy and agency exercised throughout the twelfth century by those who ruled within *pura Wallia* and the extent of their interdependence and interaction with the hegemonic cross-Channel empire are very striking.[148] While events by and large confirmed that a conquest of Wales was impossible without the deployment of massive resources that just were not available, many lives were lived out within a hegemonic structure that involved active participation in empire, with, for example, Owain ap Cadwgan of Powys travelling at Henry I's invitation to Normandy in 1114–15 and participating in his military household, and even later being commissioned by Henry to lead troops.[149] The *Brut* indeed, up until the apparent change of authorship in 1126–7, has characteristics which can make it seem to be a chronicle both of the Welsh princes and of the cross-Channel empire. Not only does it treat Owain's experiences as that of an honoured guest, it also makes regular reference to events such as Henry I's Channel crossings and

---

[144] For legitimacy, see K. L. Maund, 'Gruffudd, Grandson of Iago: *Historia Gruffud vab Kenan* and the Construction of Legitimacy', in K. L. Maund (ed.), *Gruffudd ap Cynan: A Collaborative Biography* (Woodbridge, 1996), 109–16. For Gruffudd's relationship with the newcomers, C. P. Lewis, 'Gruffudd ap Cynan and the Normans', in Maund (ed.), *Gruffudd ap Cynan*, 61–77, and esp. 73–5.

[145] *Vita Griffini filii Conani*, 54–7.

[146] *Brut y Tywysogyon (Red Book of Hergest Version)*, 104–5; *Brut y Tywysogyon (Peniarth ms. 20 Version)*, 48.

[147] See most recently, John Reuben Davies, 'Aspects of Church Reform in Wales, *c.*1093–*c.*1223', *ANS*, xxx (2008), 85–99, at 87, 89; Martin Brett, 'David (*d.*1137×9), bishop of Bangor', *ODNB*.

[148] Above all, Huw Pryce, 'Welsh Rulers and European Change'; Insley, 'Kings, Lords and the Political Culture'.

[149] On the subject of conquest, see the judicious remarks in R. R. Davies, *Conquest, Coexistence, and Change, Wales, 1063–1415* (Oxford, 1987), 89–93 ('a complex, precarious, and shifting patchwork, ranging from firm control in the environs of castles to barely noticeable overlordship in upland regions', 93).

describes in detail the wreck of the White Ship.[150] Similar arguments about territorial and dynastic consolidation as can be developed for Gwynedd can be made for the kingdom of Powys.[151]

In the initial period of relative confusion after Stephen's coup, Welsh rulers did gain military victories in 1135, 1136, and 1137, castles were captured, and territory was regained in several regions. However, in 1139 and 1141, large numbers of auxiliary troops from Wales appear in the armies of Robert, earl of Gloucester, Rannulf, earl of Chester, and Miles, earl of Hereford, with them in particular playing a crucial role in 1141 at the Battle of Lincoln.[152] Evidently not only the three earls, but also the Welsh leaders of the contingents, Morgan ab Owain, king of Morgannwg, Cadwaladr ap Gruffudd, brother of Owain Gwynedd, the ruler of Gwynedd, and Madog ap Maredudd of Powys, had made rational and business-like calculations based on likely military advantage and profit. The calculations involved were ultimately surely those of individuals from a relatively poor place (economically speaking) seeking financial advantage from the internal conflicts of an empire to whose continuation they were paradoxically contributing, and in whose continuation they were, for the most part undoubtedly unconsciously, investing.

The use made of Welsh auxiliary troops during the civil war between Stephen and the Empress Matilda was just one aspect of a phenomenon that runs through the whole history of the cross-Channel empire. Not only had William the Conqueror's victories between 1066 and 1072 drawn on troops from across much of northern France and his successors made a formal arrangement with the counts of Flanders to continue to draw on paid troops from that part of the world, troops from outside the core territories of Normandy and England regularly participate in warfare during periods of political disorder.[153] Thus, Orderic has Bretons, Flemings, and other French peoples flock to join William Rufus's invasion of Normandy in 1091 and William of Malmesbury, with characteristic acerbity, remarked on the attractions of the civil war of the period after 1135 to Bretons and Flemings.[154] The poet Serlo has the army that sacked Bayeux in 1105 consist of English, Bretons, and Manceaux.[155] The extensive use of troops from Wales in the civil war prefaces their deployment by Henry II and his sons across the whole Angevin/Plantagenet Empire. But they also have antecedents that go back to the alliance of Ælfgar, earl of Mercia, and Gruffudd ap Llywelyn in the 1050s and Robert de Bellême's use

---

[150] Stephenson, 'The "Resurgence" of Powys', 185–9, with the point about references to the cross-Channel empire at 185.
[151] David Stephenson, 'Madog ap Maredudd: *Rex Powissensium*', *WHR*, xxiv (2008), 1–28, at 11–17.
[152] OV, vi, 542–3; HH, 726–7, 734–5; *Gesta Stephani*, 110–11; *Liber Eliensis*, 321 (trans. Fairweather, 395). In general, David Crouch, 'The March and the Welsh Kings', in King (ed.), *The Anarchy of King Stephen's Reign*, 255–89, at 275–8; Crouch, *The Reign of King Stephen*, 141–2.
[153] The subject of Flemish participation is fully discussed in Oksanen, *Flanders and the Anglo-Norman World*, 54–81.
[154] OV, iv, 236–7; William of Malmesbury, *Historia Novella*, 32–3, 72–3.
[155] 'Versus Serlonis de capta Baiocensium ciuitate', in *Anglo-Latin Satirical Poets*, ed. Wright, ii, 242.

of Welsh auxiliaries during his rebellion in 1101–2.[156] What is ultimately striking is that the arrangements underpinning these arrangements were almost always formal agreements with rulers and aristocrats around the periphery of the empire.

Thus, a host of tangible and intangible factors sustained the cross-Channel empire. One of these was unquestionably the way in which its power and wealth could be turned to profit by those around the periphery. David I was far from alone in choosing to feed off the military dynamic of empire to strengthen his own position. Several Welsh princes, for example, recruited 'Norman' warriors to assist in their wars, although their capacity to retain them for long was limited.[157] And while David by and large got away with this tactic, others were not to be so fortunate, with Diarmait mac Murchada's invitation in the 1160s to 'Strongbow' to intervene in the politics of Ireland being the classic example of how it could all go wrong. Yet none of this is unique to the history of the empire of the Normans. The history of empires through the ages is littered with examples of those who, successfully or unsuccessfully, chose to collaborate with an empire for hoped-for advantage.

CONCLUSION

William of Malmesbury—somewhat perplexingly—noted that at the Battle of Tinchebrai Normandy submitted to England on the fortieth anniversary of William the Conqueror's landing in England.[158] As a commentary on a civil war between rulers who undoubtedly considered themselves to be Normans, it smacks of sophistry. But it does pinpoint a disequilibrium between the imperial homeland and a conquered kingdom where much more ruthless financial exploitation was possible. As already noted, the impact on collective memory of Henry I's campaigns in 1105 and 1106 in the duchy seems to have been a profound one.[159] Yet for all that there were deep discontents and some who chose to swim against the tide, the great majority of the dominant imperial elite was wholeheartedly committed to the empire's continuation. And not only this. While interpretation of Orderic's famous statement that Henry I 'raised men from the dust' is an obvious manifestation of individuals' exploitation of the multifaceted framework of cross-Channel patronage and power to rise socially,[160] Emma Cownie has concluded that while gift-giving to, and foundation of, religious houses in England by the newcomers expanded vastly from the 1090s, what is equally striking is the continuing support for Norman and Continental houses not just by the great cross-Channel elite, but also by the very group once conventionally referred to as Henry I's 'new men'.[161] In other words, they become testimony to the self-perpetuating dynamism of the

---

[156] ASC, 'C', 'D', 1055; OV, vi, 24–5. On the subject as a whole, I. W. Rowlands, ' "Warriors Fit for a Prince": Welsh Troops in Angevin Service, 1154–1216', in John France (ed.), *Mercenaries and Paid Men: The Mercenary Identity in the Middle Ages* (Leiden/Boston, 2008), 207–30.
[157] Davies, *Welsh Military Institutions*, 75, 124–5.   [158] *GR*, i, 722–5.
[159] See Chap. 2.   [160] Green, *Aristocracy*, 126–40; Hollister, *Henry I*, 327–48.
[161] Emma Cownie, *Religious Patronage in Anglo-Norman England, 1066–1135*, Royal Historical Society Studies in History (Woodbridge, 1998), 193–200, with the specific point at 196.

empire, with the 'new men' becoming a fresh set of individuals committed to the active life of the cross-Channel world.

An argument can easily be constructed for Henry I's reign as the Golden Age of empire. With equal facility one can be constructed that sees it as a time of profound crisis and a time of misjudgements that led to chaos after his death and a shift in the centre of gravity that was ultimately disastrous. This chapter has deliberately fed both perspectives, because both were present. It has tried to convey complexity and awareness of multiple uncertainties, while at the same time arguing that the cross-Channel empire should ultimately be seen as an inherently stable and continually dynamic one. The particular subject of comment must nonetheless be that Normandy was twice conquered in the period between 1100 and 1154. It is no wonder that the life histories set out in Chapter 2 tell a diverse and sometimes seemingly contradictory story.

5
Core, Periphery, and Networks

Orderic's use of Jeremiah Chapter 51, Verses 7–8 ('Babylon has been the golden cup in the Lord's hand that made all the Earth drunk; the nations have drunk of her wine; therefore the nations are mad. Babylon is suddenly fallen and destroyed') to describe conditions in Normandy during Robert Curthose's reign clearly identifies Normandy as the core of empire ('What disasters now overwhelmed proud Normandy, which once had boasted of the conquest of England, and now that the native English were slain or put to flight, usurped their goods and authority!').[1] The passage as a whole contains a host of imperial and hegemonic themes, most obviously the references to the exercise of power without the consent of the English and the despoliation and exploitation of the English for the benefit of Normandy. But present too is the theme of empire as the bringer of corruption and ruin to the imperialists and, by implication, that it was the fruits of empire that brought disorder to Normandy ('See how Normandy now uses the great wealth which she plundered from others and proudly flaunted as she triumphed over them to her own destruction, not for her own delight, but only to cause grief and torment.')

William of Malmesbury's interpretation of the prodigy of the conjoined twins, mentioned earlier, also identifies Normandy as the core of empire, while drawing attention additionally to a long-term exploitative relationship in which wealth travelled from conquered England to Normandy. Like Orderic, he was writing about Normandy's problems and about a portent that he believed presaged the eventual collapse of the cross-Channel empire; the living twin could not long continue to carry the rotting corpse.[2] Yet, alongside pessimistic prognostications of this kind must be placed the anonymous poem of the late 1140s that described Rouen as the new Rome, and, in doing so, looked forward to the empire's continuation.[3] Such apparently conflicting and confusing messages are yet another warning against giving too much prominence to any particular narrative and literary source, and indeed to narrative and literary sources in general. They demonstrate the truism that written history is inevitably a product of the contemporary present and, in these cases, very obviously illustrate the utterly different agendas of their writers. And, taken with a pinch of salt, they might also be thought to epitomize the near-ubiquity in various forms in the discourse on the rise and fall of empires, past,

---

[1] OV, iv, 226–7. For more discussion of this passage, see Chap. 4.
[2] GR, i, 384–7. See also Chaps. 2 and 4.
[3] Richard, 'Notice sur l'ancienne bibliothèque', 163; van Houts, 'Rouen as another Rome', forthcoming. See also Chaps. 1 and 2.

contemporary, and future, of the Götterdamerung theme of the Nibelungen saga and of the prophecies in the Book of Revelations that the end of everything is inevitable.[4]

In all these passages, Normandy is clearly identified as the imperial core; it was both the ancestral homeland and the beneficiary of the exploitation of conquered peoples. Yet, core and periphery actually defy a simple definition in the case of the empire I am writing about.[5] Thus, if core is defined as the centre of hegemonic power, it must be the itinerant rulers' court and household. In territorial terms, this would identify Normandy and southern England as the core on the basis of the rulers' regular itinerary. It also fits with William of Malmesbury's version of the English North–South divide in the *Gesta Pontificum*, where he referred to the incomprehensibility of northern dialect to the southern English and that the kings could only visit those parts accompanied by a strong military presence.[6] However, if core is defined as place of ancestral origin, it must for the majority be located in Normandy or, for a significant proportion of participants in the cross-Channel world, somewhere else in northern and western France. Alternatively, thinking once more in terms of hegemonic core, it is the ruling family that can be identified as core. In the idealistic portrayal in the last weeks of 1153 or early 1154 by Ailred of Rievaulx the core was the 'holy family', whose members were the sons of the Empress Matilda, of 'the pious King Stephen', and of Henry, son of David I.[7] That this version includes the kings of Scots within the core may at first sight seem surprising, but, in terms of a definition based around dynastic, rather than 'national' considerations, it is an entirely logical statement; at least in terms of how the situation stood when Ailred was writing the passage. And finally, for everyone involved in the life of empire, from the greatest to the least, there would be a personal version of core and periphery to be set alongside the imperial, a point well illustrated by the gathering of the Reviers family at Montebourg, used in Chapter 1 to set up my argument. This in turn underlines the point that core and periphery are as much internal psychological phenomena as physical and geographical ones.[8]

Branding these various versions of core and periphery as hegemonic, exploitative, political, familial, and personal creates a framework to make sense of the infinite diversity of networks that sustained—and sometimes disrupted—empire. From this basis an approach founded on social network analysis that posits that actors are interdependent becomes possible; that is, that there exist relational ties between the actors that are channels for the transfer of resources of all kinds, that networks are aspects of a structural environment that provides both opportunities and

---

[4] Ferguson, *Civilization: The West and the Rest*, 293.
[5] On the complexities of core and periphery for my subject, Robert Bartlett, 'Heartland and Border: The Mental and Physical Geography of Medieval Europe', in Pryce and Watts (eds), *Power and Identity in the Middle Ages*, 23–36.
[6] *GP*, i, 326–7. For the rulers' itineraries, see Chap. 4.
[7] Ailred, *De Genealogia Regum Anglorum*, PL, cxcv, col. 737; King, 'The Accession of Henry II', in Harper-Bill and Vincent (eds), *Henry II: New Interpretations*, 41–2. See also Chaps. 2 and 4.
[8] For core and periphery as psychological, Peter Burke, *History and Social Theory*, 2nd edn. (Cambridge, UK, and Malden MA, 2005), 82–91, and esp. 85.

constraints on individual actions, and that network models conceptualize structures of all kinds as lasting patterns of relations among the actors.[9] With this in mind, it can be seen that the interplay of the imperial, national, regional, and local networks with the various cores and peripheries makes it possible to tackle the tangible and intangible forces that held communities together and which could also be the basis of competition between them. Many individuals would be members of a multiplicity of networks. These could, and often did, overlap, with factors of circumstances, political turbulence, status, gender, life-cycle, and personal agency all playing a role in the processes associated with them. The strength and resilience of particular types of network is, of course, the absolutely fundamental foundation of empire.

THE NETWORKS OF EMPIRE

An obscure document, printed in local publications in Normandy from two cartularies, both of which were destroyed in 1944, namely, the grant in 1144 by Adam I de Brix of several churches to the abbey of Saint-Sauveur-le-Vicomte in the Cotentin is of central importance for what it tells us about the Norman landholdings of the Bruce family.[10] However, in the contexts of 1144 and of the networks of the cross-Channel empire, it takes on a different significance. It draws attention to networks that stretched across Lowland Scotland, northern England, and western Normandy, and provides a basis for understanding their operation in times of peace and of strife. It illuminates both deep structures and a coping strategy at a time of crisis. The extended microanalysis to which I am going to subject it is absolutely crucial to my theme. It shows how one piece of apparently stray evidence is actually extremely important. It represents an invitation to do the same thing with thousands of other transactions.

Like the Montebourg charter used as a case study in Chapter 1, it is a charter of the civil war, one that dates from a particularly difficult time for the Bruce family, since not only had Adam's father fought at the Battle of the Standard in 1138 on the side of the barons of northern England supporting King Stephen against his chief patron, King David I, but because, on account of the subsequent course of the civil war, by 1144 the family's lands were mostly in territories controlled by David and by Geoffrey, count of Anjou, two men with whom their relations are likely to have been tense. That the grants to Saint-Sauveur-le-Vicomte were of churches, and that the witnesses included Adam's younger brother Robert II and two men demonstrably associated with the family in both Yorkshire and Normandy, is indicative of great seriousness of purpose; proprietary churches were important business, requiring attention to fabric and personnel, and, even if the confirmation

---

[9] For these definitions, Stanley Wassermann and Katherine Faust, *Social Network Analysis: Methods and Applications* (Cambridge, 1994), 4–5.
[10] For the charter, J.-L. Adam, 'Le prieuré de Saint-Pierre de la Luthumière à Brix', *Revue catholique de Normandie*, ii (1892), 174–92, at 185–6; Claude Pithois, *Brix, berceau des rois d'Ecosse* (Condé-sur-Noireau, 1980), 503–4. For modern discussion, Ruth M. Blakely, *The Brus Family in England and Scotland, 1100–1295* (Woodbridge, 2005), 6–7, 32–3.

was actually made in England, the presence of the family's senior followers shows that the transaction was regarded by all involved as an important one. In other words, even if, as is likely, Robert I de Brus (d.1142) and David I were rapidly reconciled, the document appears to indicate that in profoundly troubled times, the family engaged with its Cotentin home and sought divine favour by a grant to a local abbey there. It is also possible that Adam (d.1144) was close to death, something that strengthens the argument.

Although, in relation to the overwhelming preponderance of the Scottish and northern English evidence for our knowledge of the Bruce family, this document might appear peripheral, this is not the case. It is actually of central importance because it brings into the light of day a reality that had long been in existence. While we know nothing of the narrative that led up to the grant, it is surely clear from it that, even though their greatest wealth lay in Scotland and northern England, the family had remained physically in contact with their Norman lands, had continued to administer them effectively, and in all likelihood had accorded to them a special significance in terms of memory and emotional attachment, a point reinforced by the family member's continued use of their Norman toponym as it established itself across the Channel. Their behaviour in fact accords exactly with the framework of 'mobilities' set out in John Urry.[11] That the family ultimately opted for regional rather than cross-Channel hegemony through their subsequent concentration on Scotland and northern England, with the Norman lands passing to a daughter married to a Cotentin neighbour, William du Hommet, constable of Normandy, only reinforces the basic point further, while at the same time drawing attention to a significant landmark for this one family in the evolving history of empire.[12] It is notable too that in the 1140s the family turned to the most stable source of authority available in the difficult circumstances of the civil war through a second charter in which the grant is confirmed by a man generally seen as being morally above the short-term immediacies of divided loyalty in the civil war, Archbishop Hugh of Rouen.[13]

For the aristocratic laity, the main types of network were associated with participation in the rulers' courts and households, in seigneurial courts and households, in shire, hundred, and vicecomital courts, and in religious patronage. They frequently involved membership of an affinity and the often associated obligations

---

[11] See Chap. 2. The presence of Richard, abbot of Montebourg (the only Norman abbot to be present) at the making of the Treaty of Falaise between Kings Henry II and William the Lion in 1174 supplies another excellent example of the enduring strength of ties between the kingdom of Scots and the northern Cotentin; Christophe Mauduit, 'Les pouvoirs anglais et l'abbaye de Montebourg (XIe-XIIIe siècles)', in Bernard Bodinier (ed.), *Les Anglais en Normandie: Actes du 45e congrès organisé par la fédération des sociétés historiques et archéologiques de Normandie* (Louviers, 2011), 127–33, at 129–31.

[12] Blakely, *The Brus Family*, 7, for the family's later history.

[13] Bibliothèque Nationale de France, ms. lat. fos. 137^{rv}; printed, Thomas G. Waldman, 'Hugh "of Amiens", Archbishop of Rouen (1130–64)', DPhil Thesis, University of Oxford (1970), 461–2, no. 147. Note that Adam is not named as the grantor in the charter, but his name does appear in a confirmation of Henry II, dateable to 1156 × 1161, *Recueil des actes de Henri II, roi d'Angleterre et duc de Normandie*, ed. L. Delisle and E. Berger, 4 vols (Paris, 1909–27), no. CXCVII (*sicut Adam de Bruis dedit illis*).

of landholding that can for sake of convenience be termed lordship and vassalage, kinship, friendship, and a status as neighbours.[14] Marriages were especially important in the creation of new networks or the reinforcement of old ones. Within the Church, networks involved membership of cathedral chapters and the links defined by friendship and membership of particular religious groupings. In both lay and ecclesiastical society networks would be associated with very strong infrastructures which, at the same time, were rarely static; they therefore fit perfectly into the analytical framework of social network analysis.

One consequence of the core social role of the rulers' court and households was that it was possible to have a cross-Channel career and to be influential politically with the cross-Channel rulers without holding property on both sides of the Channel. Multiple examples can be cited in support of this statement, but striking ones are that Roger de Beaumont's already-mentioned refusal of land in England after 1066 in no way impaired his place at the very heart of the Conqueror's regime.[15] From the same period, Count William of Evreux, who also held little land in England, was notably prominent in the *familia* of William the Conqueror and, some ups-and-downs notwithstanding, in that of Henry I too.[16] Exceedingly interesting is the presence in England, at the time of William Rufus's accidental death, of William de Breteuil, eldest son of William fitz Osbern, and therefore a man who belonged in the highest echelons of the aristocracy, yet someone with no land at all in England because his father's cross-Channel estate had been divided as long ago as 1071.[17] What was he doing in England? In the circumstances, it is arguably unsurprising that he should have spoken up for the claims of Robert Curthose against Henry I's coup, but that he was present in England at all is the crucial point for my argument. In the reverse direction is the career of another great magnate, Hugh Bigod, massively wealthy in eastern England, but with little land in Normandy, yet frequently with Henry I in Normandy when a search for favour apparently required it.[18] The general point that inheritance and property were only one part of the framework of power, opportunity, and social networks that fuelled imperial dynamism must—once more—be emphasized.[19]

Much studied in recent times, with David Crouch's work on the so-called 'Beaumonts', that is the descendants of the aforementioned Roger de Beaumont, representing a case study of outstanding importance, the histories of the great cross-Channel families demonstrate how, in varying ways, power was sustained and adjusted over time. In particular, they show how the Beaumonts maintained communications across large distances even during the civil war in ways that

---

[14] Crouch, *The English Aristocracy*, 133–59, is especially important for the multiple forms of association involved in aristocratic power.

[15] For Roger, see Chap. 2; Bates, 'Origins of the Justiciarship', 7.

[16] For Count William, OV, iv, 50–1; *DB*, i, 60^{rv}, 156^{v}–57^{r}; *DP*, 469.

[17] OV, v, 290–1.

[18] For this case, Andrew Wareham, 'The Motives and Politics of the Bigod Family, *c*.1066–177', *ANS*, xvii (1995), 223–42, at 232.

[19] For a treatment of specific cases that reaches similar conclusions, Stephanie Mooers Christelow, 'The Division of Inheritance and the Provision of Non-Inheriting Offspring among the Anglo-Norman Elite', *Medieval Prosopography*, xvii (1994), 3–43, at 25–41.

involved many individuals who lived cross-Channel lives, how they developed interests that stretched well beyond the Anglo-Norman lands, and how sophisticated in contemporary organizational terms the infrastructure that sustained this operation became.[20] A crucial aspect of their thought-world is illustrated by Orderic's comments on the devotion of the several branches of the descendants of Roger de Beaumont to the abbey of Saint-Pierre of Préaux, founded in the 1030s by Roger's father Humphrey de Vieilles.[21] Like the Reviers/Montebourg case study, it pinpoints a sustained and dynamic association with a place of origin maintained over generations, a distinguished past referenced in a place where several members of the family, including Count Robert (d.1118), his son Count Waleran (d.1166), and his brother Henry, earl of Warwick (d.1119), were buried.

At the same time the family members' activities demonstrate a constant concern that is apparent across the whole of imperial space to innovate to sustain the loyalty of their followers and to ground their power in multiple legitimacies; the adoption in the mid-twelfth century of the toponymic surname 'de Breteuil' by the descendants of Robert, earl of Leicester, for example, was blatantly intended to establish a history that linked them directly to another of the greats of the Conquest generation, William fitz Osbern.[22] A demonstration of how networks were reinforced and developed is Earl Robert II's skilful persuasion of the barons of the potentially troublesome southern Norman honour of Breteuil that he had acquired by marriage in 1121 to support him, by giving their chief members extensive grants of land in the Midlands of England. Another is the way in which Count Waleran of Meulan in the 1140s used a marriage alliance and his brother's influence to uphold his interests in Worcestershire, even though he was permanently in Normandy and, at least nominally, a supporter of the Empress.[23] And, if this was not enough, Count Robert of Meulan had married Isabel, daughter of Count Hugh of Vermandois, an alliance outside Normandy that reinforced networks across northern France, and, most importantly of all, was with a woman who was known to be a descendant of the Emperor Charlemagne. In ethos, performance, and power, this truly was an imperial family. And—to ram home the point—Isabel's second husband was a member of the imperial elite whom we have already encountered, William II de Warenne.[24]

The conquest of 1066 had raised William I de Warenne almost instantly to a far more elevated social level than he and his ancestors had occupied in Normandy before 1066. His Domesday estates, conventionally valued at well over £1,000, make him by 1086 the fourth wealthiest magnate in England.[25] He and his

---

[20] Crouch, *Beaumont Twins*, 1–98, 196–212, and 'Between Three Realms', *passim*, supply a wealth of evidence in support of this argument.

[21] OV, iv, 304–5. The abbey's exceptionally full cartulary demonstrates how this support went on long beyond Orderic's lifetime. For comment, *Le Cartulaire de l'abbaye bénédictine de Saint-Pierre-de-Préaux*, xxi–xxii.

[22] Crouch, *Beaumont Twins*, 112–13.

[23] Crouch, *Beaumont Twins*, 110–13; Crouch, 'Between Three Realms', 80, 89.

[24] For Elizabeth, Crouch, *Beaumont Twins*, 10–12.

[25] In particular, C. P. Lewis, 'Warenne, William (I) de, first earl of Surrey', *ODNB*. For several aspects of what follows, see Elisabeth van Houts, 'The Warenne View of the Past, 1066–1203', *ANS*,

descendants consciously expressed awareness of their rise in multiple ways, including a series of marriages into princely and royal families whose power bases were beyond the limits of Normandy and England. William I, for example, married Gundrada, daughter of Gerbod, hereditary advocate of the monastery of Saint-Bertin at Saint-Omer in Flanders, and a distant relative of Queen Matilda; a brother was briefly earl of Chester. As already noted, William II married Isabel of Vermandois, the widow of Robert, count of Meulan, and one of their daughters, Ada, married Henry, the son of David I, king of Scots. Religious patronage of the most spectacular kind also featured. William I and Gundrada founded Cluniac houses at Lewes and Castle Acre at a time when there was no Cluniac house in Normandy and when the family had no monastic foundation of their own in Normandy; they were here leading a trend that was adopted at the very highest levels of the cross-Channel aristocracy. The scale of building in both these places is notable, as also is the prominent role accorded to William III de Warenne in the Second Crusade by the French king Louis VII—of whom he was a kinsman—and, after William III's death in 1148, the marriage of his heiress Isabel in the same year to William, King Stephen's younger son, followed in 1164 by a second marriage to Hamelin, an illegitimate half-brother of King Henry II.[26] The concentration of the families' main estates in Upper Normandy, East Anglia, and the south of Yorkshire, with the links into Flanders created by William I's marriage to Gundrada, made him and his descendants crucial to hegemonic power across the whole of the eastern lands of the cross-Channel empire and the lands beyond.

Although William I's cross-Channel lands were divided between his two sons William II and Reginald, with the former taking those in England and, in all probability, Normandy, and the latter those in Flanders, it looks as if a single family interest usually took precedence over the potential division of loyalty that William the Conqueror's division of Normandy and England between his two sons might have been expected to initiate.[27] In 1090, for example, Reginald intervened dramatically at Rouen on William Rufus's behalf, with his brother also supporting the king; William II also appears in Flanders at this time. After William's rapprochement with Henry I in 1103 the brothers do go their separate ways for a while, with Reginald taking a prominent part on Duke Robert's side in the campaigns of 1105–6, before apparently being reconciled with his brother and with King Henry.[28] The period of calm associated with William II and his friendship with Henry I was followed after William's death in 1138 by a fraught

---

xxvi (2004), 103–21. For Lewes in context, Brian Golding, 'The Coming of the Cluniacs', *ANS*, iii (1981), 65–77, 208–12, at 65, 71–2.

[26] For details, C. W. Hollister, 'Warenne, William (II) de, second earl of Surrey (*d*.1138)', *ODNB*; Victoria Chandler, 'Warenne, William (III) de, third earl of Surrey (*d*.1148)', *ODNB*.

[27] OV, iv, 222–3. On the division of the inheritance, *The Warenne (Hyde) Chronicle*, 17–18, which is unclear on which son was the older and does not specifically mention which brother took the Norman estates (*Willelmum uidelicet in Anglia et Reginaldum in Flandria*).

[28] OV, iv, 222–3, for Reginald de Warenne at Rouen; for William and Henry I in 1103, see Chap. 4; and for the campaigns of 1105–6, OV, vi, 60–1, 80–3, 88–9; *The Warenne (Hyde) Chronicle*, 52–5.

time, made more complex after 1148 by the close links to King Stephen's family by the marriage of Isabel, the sole heiress to the family lands, to his son William. It is notable nonetheless that all the negotiations involving the lands to be held by Isabel and William in the Treaty of Winchester of 1153 and afterwards were always conducted on a cross-Channel basis.[29] And that Henry II's brother Hamelin and Isabel emphasized a cross-Channel identity by symbolically constructing castles at Conisbrough and Mortemer that not only had considerable architectural similarities but, so it is now argued, made conscious allusions to a Roman imperial past, and that, in the 1180s, they successfully regained some of the Flemish lands that had once been held by Gundrada's family, even though the family had apparently ceased to hold land in Flanders after the generation of William II and Reginald.[30] This re-acquisition of estates lost two generations earlier shows how awareness of descent and past interests fuelled present strategy throughout this family's history. It is also very likely that the motive for Isabel and her first husband William's patronage of historical writing in the later 1150s was to make these very points about the family's distinction, their transimperial networks, and their loyalty to previous rulers; in other words, to articulate the strength of the multiple networks that linked them to the imperial core.[31]

Another much studied family, the Clares, differ from the Warennes in having more than one branch of the family endowed in England after 1066, in already having a Norman religious house—the great abbey of Le Bec—to patronize from the beginning, and in sailing close to the political wind in England in 1088 and 1095 when the most powerful English representative of the family, Gilbert fitz Richard, flirted with revolts against William Rufus and had to regain favour with Henry I by campaigning in Wales and establishing the lordship of Ceredigion. We are therefore dealing with a family whose history and relationship to the multiple cores of empire must be constructed through examining the lives of many individuals, rather than through those of the one dominant line.[32] The same basic points nonetheless apply; it is notable, for example, that, despite the division of the cross-Channel estates that took place after the retirement/death of the great beneficiary of the post-Conquest share-out, Richard fitz Gilbert, his heir in Normandy Roger fitz Richard had a cross-Channel career, escorting the king's daughter Matilda to

---

[29] *Regesta*, iii, no. 272. By the agreement of 1157 William lost all his fortifications in both England and Normandy, RT (D), i, 305–6; (H), 192–3; Emilie Amt, *The Accession of Henry II in England: Royal Government Restored, 1149–1159* (Woodbridge, 1993), 27.

[30] On Mortemer and Conisbrough, H. Sands, H. Braun, and L. C. Loyd, 'Conisbrough and Mortemer', *Yorkshire Archaeological Journal*, xxxii (1936), 147–59; Steven Brindle, 'The Keep at Conisbrough Castle, Yorkshire', *Château Gaillard*, xxv (2012), 61–74, at 64–5. For the recovery of the Flemish lands, van Houts, 'Warenne View', 116–19; Oksanen, *Flanders and the Anglo-Norman World*, 206.

[31] Van Houts, 'Warenne View', 110–14; *The Warenne (Hyde) Chronicle*, xxix–xliii.

[32] For the main family lives, see the following *ODNB* articles: Richard Mortimer, 'Clare, Baldwin de (*fl.*1130–1154)'; Richard Mortimer, 'Clare, Gilbert de (*d.*1117)'; Richard Mortimer, 'Clare, Richard de (1030×35–1087×90)', David Crouch, 'Clare, Richard de (*d.*1136)'; M. T. Flanagan, 'Clare, Richard fitz Gilbert de [*called* Strongbow], second earl of Pembroke (*c.*1130–1176)'; Richard Mortimer, 'Clare, Roger de, second earl of Hertford (*d.*1173)'; J. H. Round, rev. C. Warren Hollister, 'Clare, Walter de (*d.*1137/8?)'.

Germany in 1109 to be betrothed to the Emperor Henry V, saving Henry I's life at the Battle of Brémule, and eventually receiving lands in England from the king to create a new cross-Channel estate.[33] The family's history over generations is in fact littered with the creation of new cross-Channel territorial complexes, with the most spectacular example being that of Gilbert 'Strongbow', second son of Gilbert fitz Richard, described in the *Gesta Stephani* as 'a poor knight' (*ex paupere milite*) raised to great wealth, who, between 1131 and *c*.1138, was granted the lands in Normandy, England, and Wales of his two uncles Roger and Walter, and who was made earl of Pembroke by King Stephen in 1138.[34]

Another example of cross-Channel renewal occurs in the career of Richard fitz Gilbert's younger son, Baldwin, sheriff of Devon under William the Conqueror, and his sons. Although Baldwin's cross-Channel estate was divided between two of his sons, one of them recreated it after his brother's death in 1096, at the time that Robert Curthose was preparing to depart on the First Crusade.[35] And, as an example of cross-Channel activity, Gilbert fitz Richard's son Walter, although seemingly based in England, turned up in Normandy in the autumn of 1136 defending the castle of Le Sap on King Stephen's behalf.[36] In addition, although Le Bec priories, such as Stoke-by-Clare, where some members of the family were buried, were founded in England and Wales by members of the family, their identity as priories of Le Bec was consistently emphasized throughout the twelfth century in, for example, phrases like *qui sunt apud Stokes monachi de Becco* in charters of Henry II and Richard I.[37] In practical and monastic terms, the cross-Channel links were continued by the appointment of the priors of Stoke-by-Clare by the abbots of Le Bec and the use there of Le Bec's liturgy.[38] In the fourth post-Conquest generation, networks were extended further within the British Isles when a daughter of Richard, son of Gilbert fitz Richard, married Cadwaladr, son of Gruffudd ap Cynan of Gwynedd. Finally, if a story told by Robert of Torigni is to be believed, the history of the family's claim to the castle of Brionne in Normandy, held before *c*.1040 by Richard fitz Gilbert's father, but then taken from the family, is an excellent example of how the division of cross-Channel lands could be both disruptive and integrative. With Richard, so Robert tells us, having been pacified after 1066 by the grant of Tonbridge and the feud therefore put into abeyance, it was his son Roger, when he succeeded only to his father's Norman estates, who revived the claim to Brionne during Robert Curthose's time as duke, seizing the castle from Robert, count of Meulan, to whom the duke had granted it, presumably on the grounds that the compensating grant was no longer benefitting him.[39]

---

[33] OV, v, 200–1, 208–9; for an account of Roger's career, Jennifer C. Ward, 'Royal Service and Reward: The Clare Family and the Crown, 1066–1154', *ANS*, xi (1989), 261–78, at 268–71.
[34] *Gesta Stephani*, 202–03; Crouch, *The Reign of King Stephen*, 129–30.
[35] OV, iv, 210–11.
[36] OV, vi, 470–1.
[37] *Stoke by Clare Cartulary: BL Cotton Appx. xxi*, ed. Christopher Harper-Bill and Richard Mortimer, 3 vols, Suffolk Records Society (Woodbridge, 1982–4), i, nos. 5, 6.
[38] *Stoke by Clare Cartulary*, 4–6.
[39] *GND*, ii, 228–9.

To conclude the section devoted to this particular 'family', it is important to point out that even its most famous member, the invader of Ireland, Richard fitz Gilbert, earl of Pembroke and, like his father, generally known as 'Strongbow', was also a participant in the cross-Channel world, since, at the very time when he first crossed the Irish Sea, he had to send messengers to Henry II in Normandy at Argentan. In general, all this shows that while it is possible to debate endlessly what might be meant by terms like 'kinship' and 'family', in the present context it is pointless to do this. Although the practical expression of these two abstract phenomena varies from one case to another, both existed throughout the period covered by this book as organisms of memory and shared aspirations that were cross-Channel; for all members of this family named in this section, the theatre of political space was the cross-Channel empire. Also, although England, Wales, and Ireland may be the zones of expansion—and occasionally of setbacks and disasters—for this extensive family cast list, the ancestral home of Normandy never, it would appear, ceased to be a part of the conscious world of all the players. The networks that dominated were local, regional, and—emphatically—imperial. Strongbow's intervention in Ireland, for example, followed on from a piece of politics that grew out of long-standing networks that linked powerful people on both sides of the Irish Sea, and included his marriage to the daughter of Diarmait mac Murchada, king of Leinster.[40] But, in his life, as in many others, the imperial networks that converged on the royal court and household constituted a dominant framework from which he could not escape. And, although networks linking him to the abbey of Le Bec are not evident as they are in other cases, for many family members, and for the monks involved, these links were also a powerful and enduring influence.

The networks and infrastructure that developed around the lives and the cross-Channel interests of the descendants of another of the first great cross-Channel magnates, Count Alan Rufus (d.1093), illuminate a world that stretched far beyond the core territories of Normandy and England; the *Early Yorkshire Charters* volumes devoted to the Honour of Richmond are—it must be said—a superb basis from which to construct this history of networks and infrastructure.[41] Marriages to women of the highest possible status feature in this family's history as in the others. In particular—and most remarkably—Alan Rufus had a lengthy relationship with King Harold's daughter Gunnhild that must in all likelihood have been a marriage, albeit probably an unconsecrated one.[42] His brother Count Alan Niger (d.1098) seemingly occurs as a possible husband for Edith/Matilda, the future wife of Henry I.[43] The complexities for the family of the politics of the period from

---

[40] For Irish Sea networks, see Chaps. 3 and 6. For Strongbow's invasion within an Irish Sea context, see especially, Marie Therese Flanagan, *Irish Society, Anglo-Norman Settlers, Angevin Kingship: Interactions in Ireland in the Late Twelfth Century* (Oxford, 1989), 56–111.

[41] *Early Yorkshire Charters*, vols iv and v: *The Honour of Richmond*, Yorkshire Archaeological Society Record Series, ed. C. T. Clay (Wakefield, 1935 and 1936). For Alan Rufus, K. S. B. Keats-Rohan, 'Alan Rufus (*d*.1093)', *ODNB*.

[42] On these much written about subjects, see above all now, Richard Sharpe, 'King Harold's Daughter', *HSJ*, xix (2008, for 2007), 1–27, at 19–27.

[43] Eadmer, *Historia Novorum*, 122.

1135 to 1156 when, after the death of Count Stephen in 1135, the younger brother of the two Count Alans, the cross-Channel complex was divided between three sons, can appear to be a time when the networks of empire appear to be severely compromised. Yet the marriage of Stephen's second son, Count Alan III (1135–46), who had received the English lands, to Bertha, daughter of Conan III, duke of Brittany (1112–48), led ultimately in 1156, after what was effectively a period of civil war within Brittany to parallel that in the cross-Channel empire, to both the reunification of the cross-Channel estate and the reunification of the duchy of Brittany in the hands of Conan IV, grandson of Count Stephen and Duke Conan III. This was followed by Henry II's intervention at Nantes in 1158 and Conan IV's daughter and sole heiress Constance being married to Henry's son Geoffrey.[44]

The surviving record of the family's activities contains straightforward examples of the cross-Channel lordship operating as an effective unity. Thus, for example, a grant consisting entirely of properties in Yorkshire to the abbey of St Mary's, York, was confirmed by Count Stephen at Rennes, in all probability between 1100 and 1107, with a formal confirmation by the archbishop of Dol.[45] The archbishop's confirmation might possibly be interpreted as an example of the perceived superior authority of the Breton core over the northern English periphery; alternatively, it may just reflect a pragmatic approach to the exercise of power. There is also the splendid case, dated 1123, of a cross-Channel family consultation about a grant to the abbey of Saint-Melaine of Rennes that was entirely Breton in content, with the third brother's consent being added after his return to Brittany from England.[46] The formation of new networks across this huge territorial complex goes back to the earliest period, with Count Alan Rufus founding a priory of the abbey of Saint-Serge and Saint-Bacchus of Angers at Swavesey (Cambs.), an action whose motivation must derive from his and his predecessors' pre-existing links to the Loire valley and, specifically, to the lands of the counts of Anjou.[47] A second foundation of this kind at Isleham (Cambs.) (later moved to Linton), made in the late eleventh century as a priory of the abbey of Saint-Jacut near Dinan, established a link to northern Brittany.[48]

At the same time, however, Alan was unique among his contemporary peers in stepping outside the available existing family religious foundations and being buried at the English abbey of Bury St Edmund's, an act that was presumably motivated by the strength of the East Anglian ties that stemmed from his

---

[44] For the politics of the marriage and the career of Conan IV, J. A. Everard, *Brittany and the Angevins: Province and Empire, 1158–1203* (Cambridge, 2000), 27–48; K. S. B. Keats-Rohan, 'Le rôle des Bretons dans la politique de colonisation norman de l'Angleterre (vers 1042–1135)', *Mémoires de la Société d'Histoire et d'Archéologie de Bretagne*, lxxiv (1996), 181–215, at 205. See also Michael Jones, 'Conan (IV), duke of Brittany (c.1135–1171)', *ODNB*.

[45] *Early Yorkshire Charters*, xxxxx, no. 4.

[46] *Early Yorkshire Charters*, iv, no. 7 (*Et hoc concesserunt et confirmaverunt duo filii eius Gaufridus videlicet et Henricus qui tunc Gencampi erant, Alanus vero qui in Anglia erat, ut cum reverteretur hoc idem concederet*).

[47] *Early Yorkshire Charters*, iv, no. 1.

[48] Judith A. Everard, 'The Foundation of an Alien Priory at Linton, Cambridgeshire', *Proceedings of the Cambridge Antiquarian Society*, lxxxvi (1997), 169–74.

relationship to Gunnhild, daughter of King Harold and Edith Swanneck, who had been a wealthy landowner in the region; the family foundation at St Mary's, York, although a recent one, would surely have been sufficiently advanced to receive him had that been his and the family's wishes. Whatever the explanation, this case surely shows that neither ethnicity nor loyalty to the homeland were the predominant factors in the choice that was made; what mattered was status and the symbolism of an association with an abbey whose pre- and post-1066 history made it an exceptionally prestigious institution and the emotional and regional factors associated with two remarkable life stories.[49]

Viewed superficially, the civil war after 1135 can be seen as a time that split the family, with Count Alan III (d.1146) supporting Stephen in England and his elder brother, Geoffrey Boterel II, who had succeeded to the Breton estates around Penthièvre, being an active supporter of the Empress and her husband in Normandy. Yet this was also the time when Count Alan, who had Breton interests through his marriage, chose to announce more emphatically than his predecessors had done his cross-Channel identity; while his father, Count Stephen, had put the accent on a Breton identity with titles such as *Dei gratia Britannorum comes* ('by the grace of God a count of the Bretons') and variants thereon, Alan's charters frequently have *comes Britannie et Anglie* ('a count of Brittany and England') and once, quite remarkably, in a charter for the abbey of Savigny which dealt with the affairs of the abbey of Jervaulx, 'a count of England and by birth a count of Brittany' (*comes Anglie et indigena comesque Britannie*).[50] While the period of the civil war does supply a story to illustrate the difficulties of cross-Channel management, with Count Alan's deathbed grant of Gayton-le-Wold (Lincs.) to the Breton abbey of Bégard being later transferred to the abbey of Kirkstead (Lincs.) on the grounds of its excessive distance from Bégard,[51] it also supplies one that demonstrates how these immensely powerful individuals could continue to weave new cross-Channel networks, with Alan acting in 1145 × 1146 as a cross-Channel ambassador for the monks of the fledgling monastic community that was to become the abbey of Jervaulx to facilitate its inclusion within the congregation of Savigny, despite the anxieties of the abbot of Savigny himself.[52] In the period after the agreement made at Winchester between King Stephen and the future King Henry II in November 1153, a charter that survives only in a late-fourteenth-century French translation specifically refers to the re-creation for Conan IV of the inheritance his parents had held, yet another explicit statement that an empire was being restored.[53]

---

[49] Sharpe, 'King Harold's Daughter', 9–10. The burial is noted in *Early Yorkshire Charters*, iv, no. 11. For Alan's family and Anjou, Keats-Rohan, 'Alan Rufus', 557.
[50] For Count Stephen, *Early Yorkshire Charters*, nos. 6, 8–11A. For the Savigny charter, *Early Yorkshire Charters*, no. 27. For *comes Britannie et Anglie*, *Early Yorkshire Charters*, nos. 12, 16–24, 26.
[51] *Early Yorkshire Charters*, no. 28.
[52] *Foundation History of the Abbeys of Byland and Jervaulx*, ed. Burton, 36–41, and esp. 40; *Early Yorkshire Charters*, no. 23.
[53] Michael Jones, 'The House of Brittany and the Honour of Richmond in the Late Eleventh and Twelfth Centuries: Some New Charter Evidence', in Karl Borchardt and Enno Bünz (eds),

There are many references to tenants moving with the counts between Brittany and northern and eastern England in a way that identifies them as members of the cross-Channel elite.[54] This particular group is, in fact, especially interesting because they can be shown over generations to have intermarried and to have perpetuated a sense of identity through the continued usage of Breton personal names. As Katharine Keats-Rohan has rightly pointed out, this undoubtedly has its roots in the repetitive naming practices of the period and not in any wish to emphasize an identity that is distinct from either the Normans or the English.[55] It does, however, identify them as a group with distinctive characteristics, characteristics that can surely be identified as those of an elite around the counts who saw their lives as imperial. Yet for all that the events of the 1150s seemed to represent a continuation and reunification, the turbulence around the northern French networks of the counts led to a gravitational shift, above all on account of the tensions around the southern Breton county of Nantes and, for Henry II in his role of count of Anjou, the necessity that it be kept under control. The marriage of Conan IV's daughter Constance to King Henry II's son Geoffrey on the face of it looked like a sound piece of consolidation of a kind that had become the norm; it did after all create an even larger cross-Channel estate in the hands of the son of the empire's ruler. Yet, as with the marriage of the Empress Matilda to Count Geoffrey, there were to be destabilising consequences after the death in 1199 of the childless Richard the Lionheart that cannot possibly have figured in King Henry's plans.[56]

The points made here about these cross-Channel imperial networks and power structures could be developed with many other examples; it was, for example, a feature of the cross-Channel estate of the counts of Boulogne that they also developed cross-Channel networks from an early date.[57] As in the case of the ruling family, the range of evidence, where it has been analysed, also demonstrates an increasing uniformity across distance and the existence of peripatetic cross-Channel households in each instance composed of major tenants with cross-Channel land-holdings. Associated with this phenomenon were regional cores of individuals and families who usually did not move around in the same way, but who represent the bedrock of local power.[58] In addition, the cross-Channel role of this aristocratic elite was paralleled by their ecclesiastical equivalents, namely, the bishops, with David Spear having pointed out with some impressive statistics almost thirty years ago that it was common for secular clergy to take up ecclesiastical positions on the other side of the Channel; and of course added that with the clergy, as with the

---

Forschungen zur Reichs-, Papst- und Landesgeschichte: Peter Herde zum 65. Geburstag von Freunden, Schülern und Kollegen, 2 vols (Stuttgart, 1998), i, 161–73, at 170.

[54] *Early Yorkshire Charters*, iv, pp. ix–x.
[55] Katharine S. B. Keats-Rohan, 'Les Bretons en Angleterre au XIIe siècle', in Joëlle Quaghebeur and Bernard Merdrignac (eds), *Bretons et Normands au Moyen Age: Rivalités, malentendus, convergences* (Rennes, 2008), 263–80, at 274–6.
[56] See Chap. 6.
[57] Tanner, *Families, Friends and Allies*, 166–7.
[58] King, 'Stephen, Count of Mortain and Boulogne', 286–8; Crouch, 'Between Three Realms', *passim*.

laity, each new appointee brought with him a group of kin, administrators, and protégés that both had a local and regional impact and created additional new imperial networks.[59]

If the focus so far has been on the most powerful and prominent of the cross-Channel elites, this is because their role is central to hegemonic power; in other words, to the maintenance, equilibrium, and development of the relationship of core and periphery. In terms of this book's overall argument, this factor is of absolutely fundamental importance. They were, however, merely the tip of an iceberg. The networks of empire involved a multitude of individuals below the highest elites often directly dependent for their fortunes on them. The development of this point is the theme of the rest of this chapter. But it can immediately be illustrated magnificently by the Flemish and Aquitanian networks associated with the refoundation of Bardney Abbey in Lincolnshire with monks from the Poitevin abbey of Charroux before the end of the eleventh century by a Fleming; Bardney's early history demonstrates both remarkable enterprise and the skilful establishment of networks linking south-western France, Flanders, and eastern England.[60]

It was not therefore just the likes of William the Conqueror, Henry I, and successive Williams de Warenne who inhabited a world of long-distance and robust networks. And from this particular example and from other material in this section, it can be suggested that networks of this kind stretching across northern and western France mean that there were many forces at work in addition to Henry I's controversial decision to marry his daughter the Empress to Count Geoffrey of Anjou that contributed to the making of the Angevin/Plantagenet Empire, albeit often unconsciously. At the least, it must be accepted that the thought-world of many people stretched far beyond the territorial limits of Normandy and England. The networks linking the core and the multiple peripheries that stretched across northern and western France and much of the British Isles were varied and resilient. For some, and most obviously for Henry I, the political problems of northern France combined with the cultural stimulus that came from that part of the world, most notably in terms of religious innovation and new fashions in aristocratic lifestyles, must have made the solution of the problems of Normandy's place within the French kingdom a political issue that eclipsed all others. Yet the impact of the local and the regional interests and networks on the situation must have made others think along lines that were much closer to home. In noting widespread opposition to the marriage of the Empress Matilda and Count Geoffrey of Anjou, the author of the Anglo-Saxon Chronicle gave expression to voices that articulated priorities that were different from those of the imperial elite.

---

[59] Spear, 'The Norman Empire and the Secular Clergy', *passim*.
[60] George Beech, 'Aquitanians and Flemings in the Refoundation of Bardney Abbey (Lincolnshire) in the Later Eleventh Century', *HSJ*, i (1989), 73–90.

LOCAL AND REGIONAL NETWORKS AND EMPIRE

The formation of networks around secular and spiritual centres of power is a feature of the creation of the new societies that formed and thrived in England and the British Isles that can be illustrated with what feels like an infinite number of examples. That, subject to differences of detail varying from one region to another, such regional networks were characteristic of most of the medieval West, makes the conclusion as unsurprising as it is important. The issue in relation to this book's argument is therefore to establish in general terms the relationship between imperial, local, and regional networks and, in particular, the extent to which cross-Channel networks remained dynamic.

Some significant, but mostly short-term, individual vicissitudes notwithstanding, the history of the cults of several major English saints is one of a basic continuity over 1066. New networks of devotion can be shown to have formed around several such saints that were, as a sociological type, a continuation of those that had existed before the Conquest. These same saints were indeed often the subject of grand ceremonial translations in the large new churches that were built in England; as already noted, the decades after 1066 brought especial prosperity to St Edmund.[61] On the other hand, and fully in keeping with the overall degradation of the English, lesser saints were often wiped out of the calendar or greatly reduced in status; the subject is a complicated one, but, in terms of the life histories of English saints, it is tempting to see them as being similar to those of the living English; the resourceful and the powerful might survive, but ultimately the imperialists picked and chose as it suited them, or at least sometimes as the principles of sanctity as they understood them dictated.[62]

At a micro-level, a local study of Cumbria published in the early 1980s produced the conclusion that local saints continued to prosper.[63] It is notable too that English saints remained stubbornly present in the dedications of monastic houses.[64] When the history of cathedral chapters at the periphery, such as Llandaf and Durham, is analysed, the results demonstrate considerable levels of continuity

---

[61] Susan J. Ridyard, '*Condigna Veneratio*: Post-Conquest Attitudes to the Saints of the Anglo-Saxons', *ANS*, ix (1987), 179–206; Susan J. Ridyard, *The Royal Saints of Anglo-Saxon England* (Cambridge, 1988), 121–9, 196–210, 228–33; Simon Yarrow, *Saints and their Communities: Miracle Stories in Twelfth-Century England* (Oxford, 2006), 3–7; Richard Sharpe, 'The Setting of St Augustine's Translation, 1091', in Eales and Sharpe (eds), *Canterbury and the Norman Conquest*, 1–13. For St Edmund, see Chap. 2.

[62] See in particular, Richard W. Pfaff, 'Lanfranc's Supposed Purge of the Anglo-Saxon Calendar', in Timothy Reuter (ed.), *Warriors and Churchmen in the High Middle Ages: Essays Presented to Karl Leyser* (London/Rio Grande, 1992), 95–108, at 103–8; T. A. Heslop, 'The Canterbury Calendars and the Norman Conquest', in Eales and Sharpe (eds), *Canterbury and the Norman Conquest*, 53–85, at 56–9, 63–6; P. A. Hayward, 'Translation-Narratives in Post-Conquest Hagiography and English Resistance to the Norman Conquest', *ANS*, xxi (2000), 67–93, at 79–81, 89–93.

[63] R. K. Rose, 'Cumbrian society and the Anglo-Norman Church', in Stuart Mews (ed.), *Religion and National Identity: Papers Read at the Nineteenth Summer Meeting of the Twentieth Winter Meeting of the Ecclesiastical History Society* (Oxford, 1982), 119–35.

[64] Alison Binns, *Dedications of Monastic Houses in England and Wales, 1066–1216* (Woodbridge, 1989), 18–58.

and local influence and personnel, just as is also the case in such communities across the core; it was above all the bishops who sought to bring in outsiders to sustain wider networks of influence.[65] And when an analysis of a regional aristocratic society has been undertaken, as, for example, in places as distant from one another as the so-called Welsh March and Roxburghshire, the results produce the conclusion that although relationships were primarily determined by geographical proximity, in both cases links to the wider world were a significant factor.[66] Thus, in line with this theme, in the Welsh March, after the fall of the family of Montgomery-Bellême in 1102, Henry I used the redistributive power of punitive rule to introduce new men to replace dispossessed followers of the exiled earl, Robert de Bellême.[67] For all that it was the local and the regional networks that shaped everyday lives, intervention from the imperial power—or in Roxburghshire from the king of Scots—could never be ruled out.

The same phenomena within eleventh- and twelfth-century Normandy have been splendidly illuminated by several major monographs published in recent years. Thus, Daniel Power's study of the Norman frontier has produced a portrait of a multilayered world where lordships and communities functioned often in near-autonomy from the dukes of Normandy/cross-Channel rulers and where networks were usually local, yet with intervention and integration into the broader structures of empire always a possibility. It also shows how influences that we would think of as cross-border were often the most powerful force in regional life, as, for example, is demonstrated by the exceptionally plentiful archive of the abbey of Savigny. Yet, at the same time, ducal authority could intrude itself decisively, as in Henry I's construction of frontier castles and, at the same time, purposefully to direct military service towards frontier zones, as well as—it can be assumed—to influence the near-disappearance of the earlier practice of cross-border aristocratic marriages that is a feature of the second half of the twelfth century.[68] The construction of such frontier castles, of course, involved major schemes of public works and rearrangement of the landscape, serious interventions by the imperial powers.[69]

Véronique Gazeau's magnum opus demonstrates that Norman Benedictine abbots were most often appointed from abbeys within Normandy, either from within the community or from other Norman abbeys, and that they were

---

[65] *Llandaff Episcopal Acta, 1140–1287*, ed. David Crouch, South Wales Record Society (Cardiff, 1988), xxviii–xxx; W. M. Aird, *St. Cuthbert and the Normans: the Church of Durham, 1071–1153* (Woodbridge, 1998), 6, 121–41; Julia Barrow, 'Origins and Careers of Cathedral Canons in Twelfth-Century England', *Medieval Prosopography*, xxi (2000), 23–40; Julia Barrow, 'Clergy in the Diocese of Hereford in the Eleventh and Twelfth Centuries', *ANS*, xxvi (2004), 37–53, at 48–53.

[66] Max Lieberman, *The Medieval March of Wales: The Creation and Perception of a Frontier, 1066–1283* (Cambridge, 2010), 56–102; Nigel M. Webb, 'Settlement and Integration: the Establishment of an Aristocracy in Scotland (1124–1214)', *ANS*, xxv (2003), 227–38.

[67] Liebermann, *Medieval March*, 68–75.

[68] Power, *Norman Frontier*, passim, with military service, the abbey of Savigny, and marriages treated at 30–4, 51–3, and 231–42, respectively.

[69] Thus, Astrid Lemoine Descourtieux, 'La ville fortifiée de Verneuil-sur-Avre et son complexe castral aux XIIe et XIIIe siècles', in Jean-Paul Hervieu, Gilles Désiré dit Gosset and Eric Barré (eds), *Construire, reconstruire, aménager le château en Normandie*, Congrès des societies historiques et archéologiques en Normandie, ix (Caen, 2004), 51–70, at 52–5.

frequently members of the duchy's minor aristocratic families; only five abbots came from England into Normandy over the course of the entire twelfth century, while, at the same time, the rulers would at times intervene to ensure the appointment of men they considered acceptable.[70] David Spear's massive prosopography of the cathedral chapters of Normandy shows that members of chapters were frequently drawn from members of the local aristocracy, but that bishops and rulers would significantly influence composition, a conclusion amplified with the statement that 'when ducal or episcopal leadership was weak, power tended to flow back to local level'.[71] And Lindy Grant's magisterial survey of Norman Gothic architecture shows firstly the force of regionality in that the cultural influences at work in the first half of the twelfth century were notably different from those operating in England. And secondly, that when influences from the mid-twelfth-century architectural powerhouse of the Ile-de-France started to be adopted in Normandy, their three most ambitious proponents were men with impeccable backgrounds within the elite of the cross-Channel empire, namely, Archbishop Rotrou of Rouen, Bishop Arnulf of Lisieux, and Henry de Sully, abbot of Fécamp.[72] As is often the case, non-literary sources can provide a more nuanced picture than literary ones. What emerges from all of them is an image of a self-contained and distinctive Norman society, displaying considerable confidence and able to assimilate outside influences to suit its requirements. When not disturbed by warfare, it was a solid imperial core that drew extensively on resources, financial and cultural, coming from many directions.

The interplay of the local, regional, and imperial in England can be illuminated in many ways. That gift-giving to, and foundation of, religious houses in England by the newcomers expanded vastly from the 1090s illustrates the theme of the formation of new local societies and communities. The two Norfolk priories of Binham and Wymondham, founded by Peter de Valognes and William d'Aubigny *pincerna* respectively, as dependencies of the abbey of St Albans, were both foundations by individuals whose fortunes had been made by the Conquest; however, before the significance of region and a new integration into the society of eastern England is too heavily emphasized, it is worth intruding the fact that stone from Caen was used extensively at Binham.[73] The formation of new relationships around a great new monastery in northern England such as the Cistercian abbey of Rievaulx, founded in 1132 by Walter Espec in North Yorkshire, exemplifies again the operation of networks that were not just local, regional, or imperial, but European. While Rievaulx's patrons were all prominent members of the regional aristocracy of northern England and the lands it accumulated were all

---

[70] Gazeau, *Normannia Monastica: Princes normands et abbés bénédictins (X^e–XIIe siècle)*, 167–267. See also the summary of conclusions in Gazeau, 'Les abbés bénédictins de la Normandie ducale', *ANS*, xxvi (2004), 75–86, at 79–83.

[71] Spear, *The Personnel of the Norman Cathedrals, passim*; for the quotation, David S. Spear, 'Power, Patronage and Personality in the Norman Cathedral Chapters, 911–1204', *ANS*, xx (1998), 205–21, at 220.

[72] Grant, *Architecture and Society*, 43–95. See Chap. 1 on the general significance of English and Norman difference.

[73] Cownie, *Religious Patronage*, 90–1.

located within Yorkshire, making the abbey, in other words, the focus of new regional networks and, at times, of the tensions that afflicted the society within which it was situated, its foundation was also inextricably associated with the burgeoning of the Cistercian order and European change.[74]

In a similar vein, a great lay figure in the life of mid-twelfth-century northern England, Eustace fitz John, illuminates the complexities of networks, core, and periphery in troubled times. A man with only a moderate amount of land in Normandy, he rose to great power in the North in the later years of Henry I's reign. His disenchantment with the new regime after 1135 was, however, so great that in 1138 he fought on the side of King David I at the Battle of the Standard. The rest of the story is one of remarkable personal agency, of a man who, while seeming to be on the periphery, always managed to interact with the core as he attached himself to the two men who mattered most in northern England after 1139, namely King David and Earl Rannulf of Chester, and, who, after 1154, managed to ingratiate himself with Henry II. His violent death, while accompanying the new king on his 1157 campaign into Wales, arguably epitomizes his career; even at a relatively advanced age he still knew that power and profit stemmed from working at the core while at the same time maintaining an effective local base; his life represents one of the most intelligent—or ruthless—exploitations of multiple social networks that we are ever likely to find to stay close to the centres of imperial power.[75] And his life-story, like that of many others, reveals a gravitation back into pre-1135 patterns once it became clear the 1153 settlement had rubber-stamped the succession of Henry II.[76]

The north of England is indeed almost an ideal test-bed for analysis of the interplay of local, regional, and imperial forces; far enough from the territorial core of southern England and Normandy and close enough to the emerging power of the kings of Scots to open up the possibility of developing networks to another core. Thus, for example, Henry I's insertion of Nigel d'Aubigny into the region did not exclude the possibility that others who had been deprived for his benefit could return to positions that they had previously held there, with a particularly remarkable case being the restoration in the later 1130s of Robert III d'Etoutteville ('Stuteville'), an event that Robert dramatically trumpeted by confirming his grandfather's grants to the abbey of St Mary's, York, 'after I have recovered my inheritance in England' (*postquam recuperaui hereditatem meam in Anglia*). The 'Stuteville' family also supplies another example of apparent division of estates between heirs not proving to be a barrier to cross-Channel activity, with Robert III's older brother Nicholas, the founder of the abbey of Valmont in Normandy, apparently receiving only the Norman family lands but then rapidly creating a new

---

[74] Emilia Jamroziak, *Rievaulx Abbey and its social context, 1132–1300: Memory, Locality, and Networks* (Turnhout, 2005), 57–110.
[75] For Eustace, Paul Dalton, 'Eustace fitz John and the Politics of Anglo-Norman England: The Rise and Survival of a Twelfth-Century Royal Servant', *Speculum*, lxxi (1996), 358–83. For his Norman lands, Green, *Government*, 287.
[76] Crouch, *The Reign of King Stephen*, 270–80.

cross-Channel estate.[77] At an earlier time, however, the division of a cross-Channel estate, involving a recently created fortune in the north of England, might be made to preserve the interests of all members. Thus, the Paynel family, with a background of connections to pretty well everyone whom Henry I was likely to dislike, made a division that seems to have been designed to conserve cross-Channel interest as well as Ralph Paynel's massive gains in northern England and elsewhere; awareness of the cross-Channel is nonetheless also evident in this case.[78] And as ideal as the north of England may be as a test-bed, East Anglia can demonstrate exactly the same species of interaction. The expedition that diverted in 1147 from the journey to the Holy Land and the Second Crusade in order to capture Lisbon was in all likelihood one whose core was built around the mutual understanding of participants from the towns of the East Anglian coast, Flanders, and the Rhineland. Here, with the main account, the *De Expugnatione Lyxbonensi*, plausibly identified as a work of Suffolk patriotism, what we know shows the newcomers to have slotted into the pre-existing North Sea networks. Yet at the same time, with the participants identified as *Normanni* and *Angli*, there is also an explicit recognition of the plurality of the cross-Channel empire, as well as of a much wider world.[79]

The creation of new cross-Channel land-holdings by grants of English land looks to be an almost conventional part of a political process that rewarded loyalty and sustained empire. For Henry I in particular, they constituted a way of consolidating loyalty that was deployed many times.[80] Grants of English lands were obviously integral to his management of the Norman frontier. Thus, when he seized the castles of Ambrières and Gorron in northern Maine from Hamelin de Mayenne in c.1120, he compensated him with lands in Devon.[81] And following the pattern established immediately after 1066, new religious foundations in and beyond Normandy continued to acquire cross-Channel possessions in the way that their predecessors had done, as happened in the cases of the abbey of Le Val Richer, founded in the 1120s, of the Augustinian re-foundation at Sainte-Barbe-en-Auge, and, following the marriage of Isabella de Montfort(-en-Yvelines) to Ralph II de Tosny, to the non-Norman Fontevrauldine priory of Hautes-Bruyères, founded by Queen Bertrada of France.[82] Cross-Channel involvement was also part of Henry I's

---

[77] *Early Yorkshire Charters*, ix, 1–67; *Charters of the Honour of Mowbray*, xxiv–xxix; Janet Burton, 'Fundator Noster: Roger de Mowbray as a Founder and Patron of Monasteries', in Emilia Jamroziak and Janet Burton (eds), *Religious and Laity in Western Europe, 1000–1400: Interaction, Negotiation and Power* (Turnhout, 2006), 23–39, at 31. For the confirmation for St. Mary's, *Early Yorkshire Charters*, no. 4, dated to c.1135 × 1140.

[78] Maxime Guilmin, 'Un exemple de réseau relationnel de l'aristocratie anglo-normande, les Paynel et leur entourage (milieu du XIe siècle-début du XIIe siècle)', in *Tinchebray*, 221–34, at 231–3.

[79] Charles West, 'All in the Same Boat? East Anglia, the North Sea World and the 1147 Expedition to Lisbon', in Bates and Liddiard (eds), *East Anglia and its North Sea World*, 287–300, at 296–300.

[80] For some examples, see Chap. 2 and, most recently, Judith Green, 'Henri Ier entre Angleterre et Normandie', in Véronique Gazeau and Jean-Philippe Genet (eds), *La France et les îles Britanniques: un couple impossible?* (Paris, 2012), 29–41, at 36–41.

[81] Power, *Norman Frontier*, 72.

[82] Mathieu Arnoux and Christophe Maneuvrier, 'Deux abbayes de la Basse-Normandie: Notre-Dame du Val et le Val Richer', *Le Pays Bas-Normand*, nos. 237–8 (2000), 9–13; 'Chronique de Sainte-Barbe-

repertoire for urban management, with two prominent citizens of Rouen, Baldwin son of Clarus and Anselm, who was *vicomte* of the city, appearing as successive sheriffs of Berkshire.[83] After 1135, Henry's second wife, Adeliza of Louvain, used the possibilities created by her second marriage to William d'Aubigny, earl of Arundel, to endow protégés from her native land.[84]

In all this there were also psychological forces at work that sometimes come very clearly to the surface. The proverbial loyalty of Henry's protégés to the Empress's cause is well known, with Brian fitz Count's unswerving devotion illuminated during his and his wife's last days by actions designed to strengthen cross-Channel networks.[85] Attitudes and values associated with an enduring attachment to lost landholdings were dramatically expressed in the murder of William Maltravers, pushed into the honour of Pontefract by Henry I, and in December 1135, immediately after the king's death, killed by the tenants of the son of the former lord Robert de Lacy. How far Robert's son, Ilbert II de Lacy, was complicit in the deed is not exactly known, but the sequel to the murder, which was Ilbert's reinstallation at Pontefract, was surely what Maltravers's killers were seeking. The subsequent tenurial complications that also created a cross-Channel holding within the honour of Pontefract for the descendants of another former lord, the Laval family from Maine, illuminate further these complex forces at work; superficially corrosive and in the short term disruptive, such episodes illustrate again assumptions that ultimately envisaged politics as continuing to be played out within a cross-Channel framework.[86] In another case, King Stephen's mercenary captain, the Fleming William d'Ypres, not only created a cross-Channel estate in Kent and Flanders during the civil war, but made a monastic foundation in Kent as well, an enterprise that failed when he was driven from England, but which does illustrate what was surely an expected norm.[87] And, although William might have been driven out of England, a new cross-Channel estate was created by a grant he made to the abbey of Saint-Bertin.[88] The stresses and strains of the civil war did lead occasionally to the termination of cross-Channel landholdings, as with Aubrey III de Vere who became count of Guines by marriage in 1137, but found it impossible to maintain the link and divorced his

---

en-Auge', in Mathieu Arnoux (ed.), *Des clercs au service de la réforme*, Bibliotheca Victorina, vol. xi (Turnhout, 2000), 277; Jean-Marc Bienvenu, 'L'ordre de Fontevraud et la Normandie au XIIe siècle', *AN*, xxv (1985), 3–15, at 7–8; Power, *Norman Frontier*, 295–6.

[83] *The Great Roll of the Pipe for the Thirty-First Year of King Henry I*, 96.

[84] Kathleen Thompson, 'Queen Adeliza and the Lotharingian Connection', *Sussex Archaeological Collections*, cxl (2002), 57–64, at 59–61.

[85] See Chap. 2.

[86] On this episode, W. E. Wightman, *The Lacy Family in England and Normandy, 1066–1194* (Oxford, 1966), 66–93.

[87] Richard Eales, 'Local Loyalties in Norman England: Kent in Stephen's Reign', *ANS*, viii (1986), 88–108, at 100–1.

[88] *English Episcopal Acta II: Canterbury, 1162–1190*, ed. C. R. Cheney and B. E. A. Jones (Oxford, 1986), no. 39 (*CDF*, no. 1337).

wife in c.1142 seemingly to concentrate his efforts in England, but this seems to have been an exceptional case.[89]

The networks that linked so-called 'alien priories' to their parent monasteries in Normandy and northern France and the English possessions of Norman and northern French monasteries supply evidence of cross-Channel management and sometimes of the difficulties it involved. Most monasteries were granted privileged exemption from tolls at the Channel ports, evidence that is also a guide to the identity of the main crossing routes.[90] The twelfth-century surveys conducted on behalf of the nuns of the first Queen Matilda's foundation of La Trinité of Caen provide well-nigh unique quantitative and qualitative evidence and demonstrate a system in place in the early twelfth century to transfer revenue from the abbey's scattered estates through Winchester to Normandy.[91] Taken alongside the abbey's surviving charters, they also show that the abbesses are likely to have made regular cross-Channel journeys, and the existence of a cross-Channel administration that was ultimately conducted from Caen; every single document from the eleventh and twelfth centuries that now survives comes from archives held at the abbey, with there being no sign at all of any record-keeping in England, even though Simon of Felsted for a long time operated as the nuns' manager in England. Contrary to what was previously thought, conservation of demesne and direct management thereof were the nuns' guiding principles on their English estates. As a result, the manors remained integrated into their local economies and at the same time provided additional income for La Trinité, rather than serving as crude milch cows for a Norman landlord; the economic data drawn from Domesday Book and the twelfth-century surveys reinforce this view because it demonstrates underlying economic continuity that goes back to before 1066.[92]

Taken as a whole, the evidence for the management of religious houses' cross-Channel estates indicates that there was a lot of similar direct management from Normandy and other regions of France of cross-Channel estates. So great indeed was the confidence that estates could be managed across great distances that, on the basis of King Stephen's charter for Cluny of 1136, which replaced a earlier grant by

---

[89] David Crouch, 'Vere, Aubrey (III), de, count of Guînes and earl of Oxford (d.1194)', *ODNB*; Oksanen, *Flanders and the Anglo-Norman World*, 205.

[90] The foundations of all modern scholarship are Marjorie Morgan, *The English Lands of the Abbey of Bec* (Oxford, 1946), 9–37; Matthew, *Norman Monasteries and Their English Possessions*, 27–70. For a survey of many issues, Marjorie Chibnall, 'Monastic Foundations in England and Normandy, 1066–1189', in *England and Normandy*, 37–49. For a succinct statement about the Channel ports, Musset, 'Barfleur', 51.

[91] *Charters and Custumals of the Abbey of Holy Trinity Caen*, ed. Marjorie Chibnall, British Academy Records of Social and Economic History, new series, v (Oxford, 1982), 34, 36. On the surveys and cross-Channel management, see now Catherine Letouzey-Réty, *Écrit et gestion du temporel dans une grande abbaye de femmes anglo-normande: la Sainte-Trinité de Caen (XIe–XIIIe siècle)*, Doctoral Thesis, Université de Paris I and University of London (2011), i, 202–332.

[92] Catherine Letouzey, 'L'organisation seigneuriale dans les possessions anglaises et normandes de l'abbaye de la Trinité de Caen au XIIe siècle', *AN*, lv (2005), 213–45, 291–332; for economic continuity, see esp. 237–40. See also Catherine Letouzey, 'Entre Angleterre et Normandie: la politique de conversion des redevances de l'abbaye de la Trinité de Caen (XIIe–XIIIe siècle)', in *Calculs et rationalités dans la seigneurie médiévale: les conversions de redevances entre XIe et XVe siècles*, ed. Laurent Feller (Paris, 2009), 73–108, and esp. 83–95.

Henry I of a fixed sum from the Exchequer with a manor in Berkshire that was presumably managed directly from Cluny, it would appear that the monks believed that they could do a better job from Burgundy than the supposed renowned efficiency of the officers of the English Exchequer.[93] Paul Le Cacheux long ago identified the foundation of Cluny's Norman priories, most of which were near the coast, as part of a communication system to England.[94] And the specific case of Longueville and its cell at Newington Longueville, from which a magnificent archive survives because the English materials were transferred to New College, Oxford, show that the one or two monks who lived in England were effectively agents of the Norman monastery.[95] So centralized indeed was this sort of cross-Channel management that, where miracles occurred at a priory, as they did at St Michael's Mount in Cornwall, the record of them was kept at the parent house of Le Mont Saint-Michel.[96]

There are also a significant number of examples of the difficulties of cross-Channel management. It was, for example, both a commentary on normal expectations and the problems of distance that a grant of exemption from tax that assumed that a ship would travel from Tiron to the Scottish borders eventually proved to be unworkable; the author of the *Life* of the founder of Tiron evocatively writes of the immense distance that separated the Scottish borders from Tiron.[97] And in a remarkable account of cross-Channel communication during the civil war of 1135 to 1154, Prior William of the Augustinian house of Sainte-Barbe-en-Auge made regular cross-Channel crossings to protect the priory of Beckford (Glos.) from its local persecutor, William de Beauchamp of Elmsley (*specialis persecutor noster*), seeking protection from the likes of Archbishop Theobald of Canterbury and the Empress Matilda; for all the difficulties that are described, however, the canons held on.[98] After 1154 Robert of Torigni crossed the Channel to organize the affairs of Mont Saint-Michel's English possessions, defeating by an appeal to Henry II an attempt to have tolls levied at the Channel port.[99] The early years of Henry II's reign witnessed a notable number of confirmations of the cross-Channel estates of Norman religious houses.[100] This is another facet of *renovatio imperii*, another sign of a cross-Channel world returning to normal. Even so, of course, not everyone could be happy. The monk of Fécamp, who has already be mentioned in Chapter 4

---

[93] *Regesta*, iii, no. 204.

[94] *Chartes du prieuré de Longueville*, ed. Paul Le Cacheux, Société de l'Histoire de Normandie (Rouen, 1934), ix–xi.

[95] *Chartes du prieuré de Longueville*, xvi–xvii; *Newington Longueville Charters*, ed. H. E. Salter, Oxfordshire Record Society, iii (1921), xv–xvi.

[96] D. J. A. Matthew, 'Mont Saint-Michel and England', in Dom. J. Laporte (ed.), *Millénaire monastique du Mont Saint-Michel*, tom i: *Histoire et vie monastique* (Paris, 1966), 677–702, at 687.

[97] *The Charters of King David I*, ed. G. W. S. Barrow (Woodbridge, 1999), nos. 97, 102; Geoffrey Grossus, 'Vita Beati Bernardi Tironiensis', *PL*, clxii, cols. 1426 (*The Life of the Blessed Bernard of Tiron/Geoffrey Grossus*. 107) (*Britannici maris emenso spatio, Northmanniaeque prouinciis transcursis*).

[98] For this remarkable narrative, 'Chronique de Sainte-Barbe-en-Auge', 279–90, with the description of William de Beauchamp at 287.

[99] RT (D), ii, 238–9, 245; Matthew, 'Mont Saint-Michel and England', 688.

[100] Note, for example, *Recueil des actes de Henri II*, nos. III, V, VI, XXXVI, XLIII, L, LXIII, LXIV, LXV, etc.

and who crossed the Channel soon after 1154 to visit the priory of Cogges, described his experience in terms of a journey from Jerusalem to Jericho; in England he fell among thieves.[101]

The wealthiest Norman monasteries did not found priories in England. Instead, they used English resources to supplement already substantial incomes; their religious mission was founded in the frequent grants to them of parish churches, although in the case of Le Mont Saint-Michel, where the documentation is remarkably extensive, it can be shown that these were sometimes used as livings to win friends at court.[102] The wealth that all this brought to Norman religious houses and to Normandy in general has recently been seen as the basis in favour of an argument for something amounting to a twelfth-century industrial revolution in Normandy.[103] One remarkable indication of growth that must have derived in considerable measure from the cross-Channel links is suggested by the huge twelfth-century expansion in the urban area at Caen and the scale of immigration into the town, not only from the countryside, but from other towns in Lower Normandy.[104] Even if archaeological work at the quarries around the outskirts of the town has produced little direct evidence of twelfth-century activity, the pattern of use suggests an industry on a massive scale.[105] Further progress can undoubtedly be made by precise local studies in England of where and how the stone was used; a survey of parish churches in Kent suggests the extraction and transportation of stone from Caen in vast quantities up until the mid-twelfth century, with a concentration on use for decorative purposes thereafter.[106] Another indication of robust cross-Channel commercial—and also intellectual—networks are supplied by the links between the Jewish communities based in Rouen and those in major English towns.[107]

While none of the above contradicts the well-established orthodoxy that England's main eleventh- and twelfth- century trading links were with Flanders and the Empire, the expansion of economic relations between Normandy and England is an undeniable phenomenon.[108] This was to an extent a process that built on

---

[101] '*Epistulae Fiscannenses*', ed. Laporte, 29.

[102] Matthew, *Norman Monasteries and their English Possessions*, 29, 43–4, 58–70; Matthew, 'Mont Saint-Michel and England', 681–2.

[103] Arnoux, 'L'événement et la conjuncture', 231–4.

[104] Laurence Jean-Marie, 'Anthroponymie caennaise et origine géographique des caennais (XIe-milieu au XIVe siècle)', *AN*, xlviii (1998), 33–65, at 40–9; Laurence Jean-Marie, 'La population de Caen XIe–XVe siècles', *AN*, xlix (1999), 115–37, at 120–5.

[105] Laurent Dujardin, *Carrières de Pierre en Normandie. Contribution à l'étude historique et archéologique des carriers de pierre à bâtir à Caen (Calvados) et en Normandie aux époques medieval et modern*, 3 vols, Thèse de Doctorat de l'Université de Caen (1998), i, 190–5.

[106] Mary Berg and Howard Jones, *Norman Churches in the Canterbury Diocese* (Stroud, 2009), 13, 15, 18, 26, and *passim*. See also Gardiner, 'Shipping and Trade', 81–2.

[107] For a survey, Joe Hillaby, 'Jewish Colonisation in the Twelfth Century', in Patricia Skinner (ed.), *The Jews in Medieval Britain: Historical, Literary and Archaeological Perspectives* (Woodbridge, 2003), 15–40, at 16–17. Note the suggestion of 'something . . . .much closer to a single Anglo-Norman community, dominated intellectually from Rouen', Paul R. Hyams, 'The Jews in Medieval England, 1066–1290', in Alfred Haverkamp and Hanna Vollrath (eds), *England and Germany in the High Middle Ages* (Oxford, 1996), 173–92, at 177.

[108] On England's commercial links to Flanders and the Empire, see in general, Gardiner, 'Shipping and Trade', 71–4, 86–8; Oksanen, *Flanders and the Anglo-Norman World*, 145–77.

pre-existing links, but it was also one that was structured by the networks of power. Normandy's precocity in the development of the technology of fulling and tanning mills, several decades in advance of what is indicated by the English evidence, can arguably be seen as a consequence of the injection of English money into an already-monetized economy and what is known of the organization of great cross-Channel landholdings.[109] Financial networks also operated to the benefit of the urban bourgeoisie, with the remarkable career in the second half of the twelfth century of Emma the *vicomtesse* of Rouen supplying evidence of an individual with networks that stretched across the Channel and also took in Paris. That a woman should have achieved such prominence remains unexplained. What she accomplished is, however, just one more example of how the cross-Channel empire was exploited to the benefit of institutions and individuals living in Normandy.[110] She and others in Rouen may indeed have been at the heart of the financial operations that channelled money from England into the Norman economy.[111]

The sheer dynamism and strength of cross-Channel networks ultimately confirms John Le Patourel's conclusion about the continuity of cross-Channel estates as a phenomenon through the civil war of 1135 to 1154. They do, however, bring into question his statement that it constituted a 'real break', an opinion that others have followed and developed, and which has also taken its place in Rees Davies's *First English Empire*.[112] With an almost bottomless pit of evidence to draw on, any argument against there having been a 'real break' must be a provisional one. What is, however, striking is just how much evidence there is of cross-Channel contact that was concerned with routine business during the two civil wars of 1087–1106 and 1135–54. To the examples already cited can be added the foundation at Folkestone of a priory of the abbey of Lonlay by Nigel de Monville in 1095, the continuation of cross-Channel religious patronage between 1135 and 1154, and all the business associated with the incorporation in 1147 of the monasteries on both sides of the Channel of the order of Savigny into the Cistercian order; there is indeed here a subject where a multitude of life-stories could be developed to

---

[109] Arnoux, 'L'événement et la conjuncture', 231–4; Crouch, *Beaumont Twins*, 178–89. It is worth noting that Mathieu Arnoux comments that the fulling mill recorded on the estates of the abbey of Saint-Wandrille in 1086 is the earliest record of this type of mill in the whole of Europe.

[110] Manon Six, 'De la Vicomtesse Emma et son entourage', *Tabularia 'Etudes'*, iv (2004), 79–103 (<http://www.unicaen.fr/mrsh/craham/revue/tabularia>).

[111] For this suggestion, Manon Six, 'The Burgesses of Rouen in the Late Twelfth and Early Thirteenth Centuries', in Hicks and Brenner (eds), *Society and Culture in Medieval Rouen*, 247–78, at 259–60.

[112] Le Patourel, *The Norman Empire*, 116–17. For Le Patourel's arguments in concise form, see his 'The Norman Conquest, 1066, 1106, 1154?', *ANS*, i (1979), 103–20, 216–20; and also, 'The Plantagenet Dominions', *History*, l (1965), 289–308 (reprinted in *Feudal Empires*, ed. Jones, Chap. 8) and 'Angevin Successions and the Angevin Empire', *Feudal Empires*, Chap. 9. Note in particular his comment that 'the fact that the two parties to the succession dispute belonged to two different dynasties seems less important than the continuing strength of the ties created by the Norman colonization of Britain'; 'What Did Not Happen in Stephen's Reign', *History*, lviii (1973), 1–17, at 16. For 'a real break', *The Norman Empire*, 116, with the idea developed in some detail in Davies, *The First English Empire*, 10–12; Crouch, *The Reign of King Stephen*, 324–5.

illustrate the theme.[113] There is surely enough here, however, to suggest that, to the ultimate determinants of reunification supplied by the aspirations of all who sought to rule Normandy and England and the massive power of the cross-Channel aristocracy that was pushing in the same direction, must be added the attitudes and values associated with a remarkable range of networks that were operated by a very large number of people.

As I have already observed several times, at the moment of the succession of Henry II, many were looking forward to a prosperous future and the ideological emphasis was on a return to the Golden Age of King Henry I. To say this is not to deny that change did not take place between 1135 and 1154; it must have done. But to understand it fully we need to abandon the practice that has determined too much of the shape of two important sets of essays on the civil war that have both included an essay on Normandy as if it can be examined as a discrete entity.[114] The framework for this analysis must be cross-Channel and conceptually it must focus on war as a solvent of beliefs, values, and opportunities, as well as territorial fortunes, but ultimately, and above all, on the resilience of those same values and beliefs. With Orderic, the poet Serlo, and Wace to guide us, we can have some idea how change was felt in Normandy after the period between 1087 and 1106. With Robert of Torigni and the young Wace, in a very different mood from his later self, for the late 1140s and early 1150s, we witness a remarkable investment of optimism in the future. The society of the cross-Channel empire was one where local, regional, and imperial networks interacted. In terms of strong and weak networks, it is the local and regional ones that are the most robust, if only because—in the end—life must go on. But it was the imperial ones that determined the fate of many. They reached to the far corners of the cross-Channel empire and far beyond, and were expected to continue to do so.

CORE, PERIPHERY, AND CULTURAL TRANSFER

On the basis of this book's argument that the rulers of the cross-Channel empire were—with the possible exception of a short period in William Rufus's reign—concerned to regulate relationships with other rulers across the British Isles from a position of superior status and much greater wealth, rather than to conquer or dominate them, cultural transfer becomes an appropriate term to describe interactions across core and periphery, with, as was observed in Chapter 4, hegemony needing also to be kept in place because an awareness of superior power undoubtedly influenced relationships. In addition, the Church needs to be viewed

---

[113] *English Episcopal Acta II: Canterbury 1162–1190*, no. 163. For a general indication of what could be done on this subject, Janet Burton, 'English Monasteries and the Continent in the Reign of King Stephen', in Dalton and White (eds), *King Stephen's Reign*, 98–114.

[114] Cf. King (ed.), *The Anarchy of King Stephen's Reign*; Dalton and White (eds), *King Stephen's Reign*. The importance of the cross-Channel most definitely informs Marjorie Chibnall's 'Introduction' to the second of these volumes, 1–9, and the essays by David Crouch and Janet Burton.

as one huge trans-ethnic network, even if, around the peripheries as well as at the core, its leaders were usually drawn from descendants of the conquerors. The history of the churches in Wales and Scotland nonetheless point to the importance of collaborative trans-ethnic networks that belie the apparently confrontational issues of Canterbury's claim to primacy over the British Isles and York's to metropolitan status over the bishoprics of the kingdom of Scots. Indeed the levels of interaction and autonomy at the periphery can suggest that several aspects of the supposed imperial civilizing mission and sense of cultural superiority that might be deduced from the likes of William of Malmesbury were in certain respects as much a literary construct as a reality. The many interactions that all this involved required a multilingualism that must feel truly humbling to many of the inhabitants of the twenty-first-century British Isles.[115]

Throughout the twelfth century, the kings of Scots continued to choose wives from families that were among the topmost elite of the cross-Channel empire.[116] This and the fact that nobles of the kingdom retained links into England and northern France facilitated cultural transfer; the court of King William the Lion (1165–1214) was indeed said to be culturally French and French-speaking.[117] Gerald of Wales offered the opinion that marriages between the newcomers and Welsh ruling families were a means by which the former established themselves within the new local and regional societies.[118] The daughter of Gilbert fitz Richard's marriage to Cadwaladr, son of Gruffudd ap Cynan, already mentioned, and the Shropshire magnate Picot de Sai marrying a daughter to Cadwgan ap Bleddyn of Powys in the early twelfth century provide early examples from the upper strata of the phenomenon.[119]

Communication between core and periphery must have been sufficiently normal for peoples to be familiar with one another in ways that absorbed the newcomers into multi-ethnic and multilingual discourse from the start. The movement of peoples across the Irish Sea, for example, is a well-attested phenomenon and linguistic boundaries must therefore have been very permeable.[120] One apparent expression of English and Norman superiority is supplied by the account of the expedition that captured Lisbon in 1147 in which the author puts quarrels among the participants into relief by mentioning that the Scots who took part were amiable souls who caused no trouble, despite the fact that they were supposed to be barbarians.[121] While this suggests that the Suffolk-based author was thoroughly

---

[115] For an appropriately provocative discussion, Elizabeth M. Tyler, 'England and Multilingualism: Medieval and Modern', in Tyler (ed.), *Conceptualizing Multilingualism*, 1–13.

[116] On this subject, see now Jessica A. Nelson, *From Saint Margaret to the Maid of Norway: Queens and Queenship in Scotland, circa 1067–1286*, PhD Thesis, University of London (2006), 16–163.

[117] For a recent assessment of these issues, Sharpe, 'Peoples and Languages', 116–18.

[118] Gerald of Wales, 'Itinerarium Kambrie', in *Opera Omnia*, vi, 91.

[119] See further, Davies, *Age of Conquest*, 102; A. J. Roderick, 'Marriage and Politics in Wales, 1066–1282', *WHR*, iv (1968–9), 3–20, at 4–17.

[120] Julia Crick, '"The English" and "The Irish" from Cnut to John: Speculations on a Linguistic Interface', in Tyler (ed.), *Conceptualizing Multilingualism*, 217–37, and esp. 223–37.

[121] *De Expugnatione Lyxbonensi*, ed. C. W. David (New York, 1936; 2nd edn., New York, 2001), 106–7 (trans., van Houts, *The Normans in Europe*, 273).

schooled in the William of Malmesbury line on the peoples of Britain, and therefore constitutes testimony to its ubiquity, it is important that he was actually using rhetorical irony to set the Scots in counter-point to others who should have known better. What goes unstated is that the entirely anonymous Scots involved were taking part in a western European movement, an expedition that was an offshoot of the Second Crusade.

Another area of exchange is the dynamic interest in the cults of Irish, Welsh, and Scottish saints in monasteries in twelfth-century England. With the extensive knowledge of Bede's *Historia Ecclesiastica* as the great Christian leveller for this subject, the interest is arguably unsurprising. Superiority is expressed only in terms of a condemnation of the quality of the Latin of the accounts of lives and miracles that were being updated, this being done in ways that were different from the analogous critique of Anglo-Saxon saints' lives by the like of Goscelin of Saint-Bertin; the saints were, however, being treated as participants in a common Christian past and in a contemporary updating of its many histories.[122] This awareness of a shared, albeit remote, historical past was of course the foundation for the hijacking of Arthur into the identity of the cross-Channel empire.

When it comes to the techniques of government, the introduction of the writ/brieve into the kingdom of Scots saw an exclusively pre-1066 and post-1066 English documentary form adapted to Scottish circumstances, as was also the case in Normandy when similar documents were introduced there. The process that this involved in Scotland has also been seen as being a top-down one, just as it unquestionably was in Normandy.[123] In the same way, the start of the minting of coin in the kingdom of Scots, while it drew on models drawn from the kingdom of the English, must also be seen as part of increased exchange around north-western Europe and as an element of the standardization of weight standards across that area.[124] The early development of the law of Scotland has been described by Hector MacQueen as 'a legal transplant' and, when treated comparatively with their English equivalents, the legal language of twelfth-century brieves and charters from the kingdom of Scots demonstrate extensive similarities, with differences determined by the context of the two kingdoms.[125] In the text known as *Leges Scotie*, the many borrowings from English texts can be treated, like much else, as cultural transfers from the more southerly kingdom.[126] However, the fact that

---

[122] Robert Bartlett, 'Cults of Irish, Scottish and Welsh Saints in Twelfth-Century England', in Smith (ed.), *Britain and Ireland, 900–1300*, 67–86, at 84–6.

[123] Dauvit Broun, 'The Adoption of Brieves in Scotland', in Marie Therese Flanagan and Judith A. Green (eds), *Charters and Charter Scholarship in Britain and Ireland* (Basingstoke/New York, 2005), 164–83, and esp. 165, 178–9. For Normandy, see Chap. 4.

[124] Ian Blanchard, 'Lothian and Beyond: The Economy of the "English Empire" of David I', in R. H. Britnell and J. Hatcher (eds), *Progress and Problems in Medieval England: Essays in Honour of Edward Miller* (Cambridge, 1996), 23–45; Stringer, 'State-Building', 55.

[125] H. L. MacQueen, *Common Law and Feudal Society in Medieval Scotland* (Edinburgh, 1993), 264–6; John Hudson, 'Legal Aspects of Scottish Charter Diplomatic in the Twelfth Century: A Comparative Approach', *ANS*, xxv (2003), 121–38.

[126] Alice Taylor, '*Leges Scocie* and the Lawcodes of David I, William the Lion and Alexander II', *SHR*, lxxxviii (2009), 207–88, at 243–6.

David I brought monks from Tiron to Selkirk and Kelso makes him a participant in the religious dynamic of Mathieu Arnoux's 'Grande Ouest', not of any dominant culture that might be labeled Norman or English.[127]

The anticipatory association of David's son Henry in kingship, with the use of the phrase *rex designatus* in two St Andrews's charters, might be seen as an importation from the practice of the Capetian kings of France, yet it might equally well be an individual scribe's way of expressing a practice adopted by Henry I for his son William and copied by David.[128] Church architecture draws on a wide range of inspiration that demonstrates a determination to show that the Scottish kingdom was every bit as up-to-date as anywhere else. The abbey church of Dunfermline obviously displays features derived from Durham cathedral, but there are other influences such as Waltham Abbey also at work. And while the west front of the abbey church of Kelso might have drawn on imagery from the Empire, the possibility that these influences were mediated through the great new churches of East Anglia in no way diminishes the basic point; Kelso was 'an exercise in architectural individualism' that demonstrates cultural transfer in which autonomy and choice played the predominant role.[129] The changes in aristocratic titles also reflect practices that were being disseminated across the whole of the medieval West, yet there was significant continuity within the *regnum Scottorum*.[130] Historical writing such as Turgot's *Life* of St Margaret incorporated genealogical information about the dukes of Normandy and an apparent reference to Dudo of Saint-Quentin's *Historia Normannorum*, as if to position her life in relation to the dynasty that ruled the cross-Channel empire.[131] And a further element in the analysis is the burgeoning twelfth-century history of 'Scottish' saints like St Andrew, St Kentigern, and St Columba, and the continuous history of less well-known more local cults. The author of a recent study observes that 'these saints even attracted the patronage of Anglo-French newcomers'; in terms of the analysis developed throughout this book, there should be no surprise at all that this happened.[132]

Even if the evidence is sparser, as elsewhere, the writ-charter was adopted by Welsh rulers and creatively adjusted to local circumstances.[133] The wholesale adoption in the first half of the twelfth century of the terms 'Wales' and 'Welsh' to describe the nation and the people has recently been interpreted as an indication of creativity beyond the core of empire and cultural transfer from it. Gerald of

---

[127] Mathieu Arnoux, 'Dynamics et réseaux de l'Eglise régulière dans l'Ouest de la France (fin XIe–XIIe siècle)', in Jacques Dalarun (ed.), *Robert d'Arbrissel et la vie religieuse dans l'Ouest de la France: Actes du colloque de Fontevraud, 13–16 décembre 2001* (Turnhout, 2004), 57–70, and especially at 57–8 and 69–70.

[128] Duncan, *The Kingship of the Scots*, 69–70.

[129] Fawcett, *Architecture of the Scottish Medieval Church*, 18–37, with the quotation at p. 36.

[130] Crouch, *Image of Aristocracy*, 80–3, 153–5.

[131] See the translation of the *Vita Sanctae Margaretae* in Huneycutt, *Matilda of Scotland*, 164.

[132] Matthew H. Hammond, 'Royal and Aristocratic Attitudes to Saints and the Virgin Mary in Twelfth- and Thirteenth-Century Scotland', in Steve Boardman and Eila Williamson (eds), *The Cult of Saints and the Virgin Mary in Medieval Scotland* (Woodbridge, 2010), 61–85, with the quoted comment at 84.

[133] *The Acts of Welsh Rulers, 1120–1283*, ed. Huw Pryce (Cardiff, 2005), 660–4; Insley, 'Political Culture', 142–50.

Wales, and indeed Geoffrey of Monmouth, might treat this change as a humiliating recognition that the British would never reverse their defeat of half a millennium earlier by the Anglo-Saxons, let alone overcome the Normans, but their conscious selection as the identifiers of choice by Welsh rulers and clergy smacks more of a positive assertiveness and agency within the new culture of the twelfth century; once more we have a warning to treat so-called literary sources cautiously.[134] Even if, in comparison to Maine or Scotland, the potential for a crushing military intervention from England must always have been a necessary element in all calculations, within *pura Wallia* the agency and autonomy to react to, and benefit from, the empire's resources was ever present. On a subject such as religious patronage and monastic change in twelfth-century Wales on both sides of the ethnic divide, there is nowadays an emphasis on collaboration and careful adjustment, rather than brutal change.[135]

The acceptance of the papacy's role as a corrective and legitimating authority, albeit one whose judgments could be disputed, had a profound effect throughout the history of the cross-Channel empire and beyond. One aspect of empire, the *cause célèbre* of the Canterbury–York primacy dispute, was the reason for numerous journeys to Rome and raised issues across the whole of the British Isles, the crucial point being the way in which individuals and institutions from beyond the core found their voice against hegemonic power to defend and justify local and regional interest. The celebrated case of the resistance of the churches of the *regnum Scottorum* to the archbishop of York's attempts to establish the primacy set out in the 1072 Windsor agreement are a crucial manifestation of this.[136] Yet even this episode should not be seen as part of a simple confrontation between core and periphery. It was, for example, King Alexander I who had invited the Canterbury monk Eadmer to take up the bishopric of St Andrews, presumably thinking an intimate of the late Archbishop Anselm a suitable appointment. What is more, one of the men who gave Eadmer advice, David I's former chaplain and one of the major figures of the twelfth-century Scottish Church, Bishop John of Glasgow, had been a monk of Tiron before migrating to Scotland. Within Wales, we can also find examples where factors other than ethnicity determine behaviour. Thus, within conquered South Wales, Bishop Urban of Llandaf, who had been educated at Worcester, could use papal authority against the newcomers to South Wales and, in doing so, in the Book of Llandaf effectively create a history for his diocese where none had previously existed. And, within the principality of Gwynedd, a Welshman, Bishop Meurig of Bangor (1139–61), could turn to Archbishop Theobald of Canterbury for support against the ruler of Gwynedd, Owain Gwynedd.[137]

---

[134] Huw Pryce, 'British or Welsh? National Identity in Twelfth-Century Wales', *EHR*, cxvi (2001), 775–801, at 784–7.

[135] Brian Golding, 'Trans-border Transactions: Patterns of Patronage in Anglo-Norman Wales', *HSJ*, xvi (2006, for 2005), 27–46, at 37–46.

[136] Broun, *Scottish Independence*, 104–6, 109–16.

[137] John Reuben Davies, 'Aspects of Church Reform in Wales, *c.*1093–*c.*1223', *ANS*, xxx (2008), 85–99, at 90–1. For the wider issues involved in the creation of the Book of Llandaf, see now, John Reuben Davies, *The Book of Llandaf and the Norman Church in Wales* (Woodbridge, 2003), 32–59.

Overall, this was a time that stimulated agency and expression beyond the core with remarkable long-term consequences, most notably in the writing of the *Life* of St David and the first version of the St Andrew legend. As earlier, and at the same time, within the kingdom of the English, institutions reacted to change and new forms of authority by setting down in writing ancient traditions and rights. The regulation of the political relationships between core and periphery was of such importance that, in the course of his legatine visit in 1138–9, Alberic of Ostia, among other things, travelled north to Carlisle to negotiate between Stephen and David I, albeit in the end to little meaningful effect.[138]

Illustrative of another form of the same phenomenon is the migration of peoples into the less populated areas of the British Isles, most notably the Flemings who settled and farmed in Dyfed and Upper Clydesdale.[139] These introduce into the discussion the subject of what Rees Davies has called the 'second tidal wave', the argument for a migration under the umbrella of aristocratic colonization of many English peasants to Wales, Ireland, and, to a lesser extent, the Scottish Lowlands.[140] A broader perspective on this must be the population increase of the eleventh and twelfth centuries and the pressures it placed on rural societies, pressures that fuelled a host of changes, such as the foundation of new towns, the growth of old ones, and the clearance of forest. The proposal therefore that these migrations should be seen as another facet of hegemonic power through the imposition not only of a new aristocratic elite, but also of English-speaking peasantries, has been met with some scepticism. The argument has now been made, for example, that the famous case of Flemish and English settlement in Dyfed did not displace the indigenous population; while there can be no doubt from the surviving record of activity and ethnic and linguistic distinctiveness that the scale of the Flemish settlement there was considerable, the process of Anglicization was much more long term.[141] It and the Upper Clydesdale settlement do, however, keep the cross-Channel dimension in the foreground of the argument. What is undeniable is that the settlers were responsible for the organization of farming, with the Upper Clydesdale group in all likelihood responsible for grazing sheep, and possibly therefore liaising directly with the cloth industry in Flanders. These migrations might have happened without the networks of the cross-Channel empire to shape them; it is, however, hard to think that the two phenomena are entirely unconnected.

As a conclusion to this chapter, it is vital to return to the subject of cultural labelling. With the case having been made for dynamic cultural transfer not only from core to periphery, but for a process that sometimes flowed

---

[138] Richard of Hexham, *De gestis regis Stephani et de Bello Standardo*, in *Chronicles*, iii, 170.

[139] Lauran Toorians, 'Wizo Flandrensis and the Flemish Settlement in Pembrokeshire', *Cambridge Medieval Celtic Studies*, xx (1990), 99–118; Lauran Toorians, 'Twelfth-Century Flemish Settlements in Scotland', in Grant Simpson (ed.), *Scotland and the Low Countries* (East Linton, 1996), 1–14, at 5–10; Oksanen, *Flanders and the Anglo-Norman World*, 213–17.

[140] Davies, *Domination and Conquest*, 12–13; cf. John Gillingham, 'A Second Tidal Wave? The Historiography of English Colonization of Ireland, Scotland and Wales in the 12th and 13th Centuries', in Jan M. Piskorski (ed.), *Historiographical Approaches to Medieval Colonization of East Central Europe* (New York, 2002), 303–27.

[141] David Austin, 'Little England beyond Wales: Re-defining the Myth', *Landscapes*, vi (2005), 30–62.

in the reverse direction, it is evident that descriptors such as 'Norman', 'English', and 'Anglo-Norman' are inadequate. The kingdom of Scots might import charter diplomatic and legal process from England, but the inspiration for monastic change came from beyond the territories of the cross-Channel empire. Archbishop Lanfranc's invention of the device of Canterbury's primacy and the associated primacy of York over the bishops of the kingdom of Scots might well be a use of conventional canon law to reinforce the hegemonic power of empire across the British Isles, but the opportunity to resist what the English archbishops believed to be their implications was provided by a process of change that was European, namely, the increasing assertion of the judicial powers of the papacy. The period did also witness the start of the attempts to claim metropolitan status for the bishopric of St David's. Just as confident bishops and abbots in Normandy—in this case arguably therefore at a cultural periphery—drew on cultural resources of the Ile-de-France to build new churches in an up-to-date style, so did confident communities around the periphery in the British Isles evolve new patterns and practices out of a changing European world.

Hence, what is now known about changes in hunting technique and animal exploitation that took place over the period were, in terms of cultural labelling, conceptually more complicated than the 'Norman package' referred to by Naomi Sykes. With a fascinating range of evidence drawing on archaeological sites from across northern France as well as southern Europe, but with only three of them actually being located in Normandy and two in the lands of the kingdom of Sicily, it looks as if change must be pan-European, rather than 'Norman'.[142] As in studies of the castle, the notion of 'An Aristocratic World View?' would surely be a helpful approach; the great tower, the *donjon*, in an insular historiography often seen as something quintessentially Norman, as well as its location in the landscape, must arguably be seen as a European-wide process of change, with personal, local, and regional differences affecting every building.[143]

That there was so much specific responsiveness to the power and culture of the cross-Channel empire across northern and western France and the British Isles demonstrates beyond doubt the persuasiveness that its hard and soft power exercised. But at the same time the empire itself must be located within the major changes of the twelfth century. In an extreme form, this argument can become a counter-factual one since, given that by definition European change was all pervasive, and given the demonstrable capacity of the pre-1066 English kingdom to be responsive to changes and cultures from across the Channel, it is acceptable to speculate how much would have happened either if Harold had won the Battle of Hastings or if the battle had not taken place. I suspect that most aspects of religious change, of aristocratic codes of behaviour, and of changes in hunting technique

---

[142] Naomi Sykes, 'Zooarchaeology of the Norman Conquest', *ANS*, xxvii (2005), 185–97, and esp. at 193–5; Naomi Sykes, *The Norman Conquest: A Zooarchaeological Perspective*, British Archaeological Reports International Series 1656 (Oxford, 2007), *passim*, and for methodological issues, see 7–8, 94–8.

[143] For a survey, Oliver Creighton, 'Castle Studies and the European Medieval Landscape: Traditions, Trends and Future Research Directions', *Landscape History*, xxx (2009), 5–20, at 6–8, 10–12.

would have crossed the Channel without any assistance being needed from an invading army and a dynamic empire. On the other hand, it is inconceivable that they would have been transmitted in the form in which they were channelled by the cross-Channel empire.

For all that change can readily be associated with the forces of hegemony and cultural transfer, it is vital finally to observe that resistance to change was deeply entrenched everywhere. In part this is because the empire itself was born plural and remained plural beneath the unifying drive of cross-Channel dynamism; in short, it was from the start multicultural, and remained so. But it is also because of circumstances linked to different traditions and economic conditions. The practices of killing political enemies and of capturing and selling of men, women, and children into slavery, for example, persisted across parts of Wales, Scotland, and Ireland in ways that disappeared (as it turned out temporarily) from England.[144] Regional difference within England was also considerable, beautifully—if not very accurately—indicated by the Abingdon historian who was impressed that his abbey had acquired a shoulder blade of St Wilfrid from northern England because, so he thought, there were not many churches in that part of the world.[145]

Hegemony and cultural transfer are therefore surely appropriate terms to describe the relationship of core and periphery, with the boundaries between the two of them sometimes being hard to define. They give agency to the peoples of Wales, Scotland, and Ireland in ways that other terms do not. The multiple and diverse networks that existed across the British Isles and northern and western France were truly remarkable and enduring dynamic. Politics and war might disrupt them, and even destroy some of them, but the phenomenon to place in the foreground is the capacity for recovery and reproduction. Yet when it comes to cultural transfer what was ultimately transferred was mostly a culture of power; there were ways of doing things within the empire in terms of methods of rule, exploitation, and aristocratic lifestyle that appealed to elites around the periphery because they seemed more effective, worthy of being copied, and prestigious. But in the end we need to remember that there were a multitude of channels of influence that we can scarcely know about and whose impact is usually hidden from us. What was it, for example, that propelled Robert d'Aunay, 'born in Normandy', so we are told, to travel north and become a monk at Whitby and then a hermit at Hood? We have here another one of those ordinary lives that might not have taken the course they did but for the existence of the cross-Channel empire, and which were one of its essential components.[146] While so much that was local and regional remained unchanged, the networks of empire were omnipresent.

---

[144] John Gillingham, 'The Beginnings of English Imperialism' and 'Conquering the Barbarians: War and Chivalry in Twelfth-Century Britain', in *The English*, 14–15, and 41–58, at 45–6; John Gillingham, 'Women, Children and the Profits of War', in Nelson, Reynolds, and Johns (eds), *Gender and Historiography*, 61–74, at 64–5, 71–3; David Wyatt, *Slaves and Warriors in Medieval Britain and Ireland, 800–1200* (Leiden/Boston, 2009), 337–94.
[145] *Historia Ecclesie Abbendonensis*, 68–9.
[146] *The Foundation History of the Abbeys of Byland and Jervaulx*, ed. Burton, 6.

6
Empire: From Beginning to End

The collapse of the cross-Channel empire is an unusual case in the history of empires. Its end came not as a result of the subjected peoples loosening the imperialists' grip and reasserting agency and identity, but because the founding core failed. Furthermore, the end came suddenly and apparently as a surprise to almost all who were involved.

The construction of life-stories is as relevant to understanding the end of empire as it is to understanding its history. However, the absence of anything approaching a full-scale prosopographical study of the cross-Channel secular aristocracy for the period from 1154 to 1204, combined with the huge increase in the volume of usable evidence, makes this a more daunting task than for the period up until 1154. Despite the outstanding work of the past twenty years, aspects of which have been based on methodologies similar to those of this book, the task of converting what we know about individual lives into life-histories is, inevitably, a harder one. For this reason, this chapter, more than any of the others, is an argument built around probabilities. It is, however, a logical corollary of all that has gone before. It applies the same political and social science framework to the period between 1154 and 1204 that has shaped the rest of the book.

If we accept as a starting point the modern consensus that the empire was still a going concern on the day that Richard the Lionheart received his fatal wound outside the castle of Chalus-Chabrol in Poitou on 26 March 1199, the end of empire becomes a straightforward failure of hard power. The creation by Henry II in 1154 of the huge territorial complex that is usually known as the Angevin or Plantagenet Empire and the material increase in the power and resources of the Capetian kings after 1180 unquestionably made a difference, but, as will continue to be argued, much remained the same within the cross-Channel empire. Whatever the arguments that can both be adduced in favour of long-term decline and the price of empire becoming too high, the surrender of Rouen to Philip Augustus on 24 June 1204 and the failure of the attempted fight-back at Bouvines on 27 July 1214 must ultimately be attributed to inadequate leadership on the part of King John and an inability on his part to deploy resources effectively in ways that had previously been successful in the hands of his predecessors.[1]

---

[1] At the heart of a huge literature, John Gillingham, *Richard I* (New Haven, CT/London, 1999) is not only a magisterial guide to Richard's life, but also a convenient guide to the author's many other publications on the subject. The essays in S. D. Church (ed.), *King John: New Interpretations* (Woodbridge, 1999) illustrate all aspects of the consensus. Even Daniel Power, who emphasizes just

The presumption within John Gillingham's statement that 'in 1198–9 Richard was winning the war against Philip (Augustus)' is that if only there had been, say, another William Rufus or Henry I around in 1199 to go into action against the formidable Philip Augustus, the cross-Channel empire would have lasted longer than it did; the war still had to be won, but someone more capable than John could presumably have done it.[2] However, when this presumption is transferred into a social constructionist framework and into a long-term analysis of the history of the cross-Channel empire, it is also a statement that failure was systemic. The system that had sustained empire for over 130 years had been found wanting because it was ultimately dependent on the individual at its centre. Whatever the strength of the contextual arguments that can be made to explain the collapse, a ruler had appeared who was no longer capable of acting as the clearing-house to process the multiple forces and tensions that had up until this point both held the empire together and at times threatened to pull it apart.

As a narrative from the feverish last years of empire, there is none better than the story of William Marshal, who, on hearing of Richard's death, dashed out of Rouen in the evening into the suburbs to the priory of Notre-Dame du Pré to tell Archbishop Hubert Walter of Canterbury the terrible news and to discuss with him what should be done, in the process disturbing the archbishop as he was getting ready for bed.[3] In persuading Hubert that John was a preferable successor to the childless Richard than Arthur of Brittany, their deceased brother Geoffrey's son, the Marshal was actually behaving just like the great cross-Channel magnates of earlier generations who have featured so often in this book; he was a member of the empire's topmost elite facing an imperial crisis and taking steps aimed at producing a solution. That the Marshal couched his arguments in terms of the general interest cannot disguise what his early thirteenth-century biographer elsewhere had to acknowledge, namely, that his reasoning was to an extent self-serving since John was already his lord in Ireland. It is also a narrative constructed entirely in terms of John's and Arthur's personal qualities that left out the many complexities that the respective claims to succession of uncle and nephew involved.[4] However, unlike Earl Rannulf II of Chester and King David I in earlier times, the Marshal was to live to see the consequences of his manoeuvring. Hence, his biographer, informed of course by hindsight, had the archbishop warn him that he was making the worst mistake of his life.[5]

---

how much ground still had to be regained after the losses of 1193–9, concludes his essay with the comment that 'his [i.e., John's] own errors must account for their failure to defend Normandy for their duke'; 'King John and the Norman Aristocracy', 117–36, at 136.

[2] Gillingham, *Richard I*, 348.

[3] *History of William Marshal*, ed. A. J. Holden, with English translation by S. Gregory and historical notes by D. Crouch, 3 vols, Anglo-Norman Text Society, Occasional Publications Series, nos. 4–6 (London, 2004–06), ii, 92–7, ll. 11,844–908.

[4] *History of William Marshal*, ii, 16–17, ll. 10,312–40; J. C. Holt, 'The *Casus Regis*: The Law and Politics of Succession in the Plantagenet Dominions, 1185–1247', in Holt, *Colonial England, 1066–1215*, 307–26.

[5] *History of William Marshal*, ii, 94–7, ll. 11,903–7.

For all the embellishments of the story-telling, this narrative does illustrate one of the more well-established orthodoxies about the final period of the empire's history, namely that it was the leading members of the cross-Channel aristocracy who were the duchy's staunchest defenders in its last years. The lives of the Marshal himself, Robert IV, earl of Leicester, and Rannulf III, earl of Chester, whose second marriage in 1200 to Clemence de Fougères was, like his first one in 1189 to Arthur's widowed mother Constance, duchess of Brittany, specifically designed to continue to support his interests around the strategically crucial borders of Brittany and Normandy, epitomize this point.[6] Cross-Channel estates might have been broken up and the number of truly great cross-Channel families might have been reduced, but there was still an imperial elite in place to defend the empire, as there had been from the beginning. It is also now argued that the bishops of Normandy, some of whom were once seen as a subversive force that tended to favour Philip Augustus, remained loyal to the end.[7] And, with so many other cross-Channel networks in place, there were a very large number of people with a vested interest in the empire's continuation.

THE BEGINNING

To make the creation of empire an act of power and human agency, as I have done, means that the two main landmarks in its making are firstly, the charter dating from 1046 or early 1047 recording the presence at Rouen of Bishop Ivo of Sées and Count Hugh IV of Maine, and secondly, the two charters of the Conqueror's father, Duke Robert the Magnificent, in which the title *rex* appears alongside the name of the future king Edward the Confessor, with it also being used in a confirmation of William's which was added to one of them.

Given Bishop Ivo's secular status as lord of Bellême, with lands stretching across the region where the interests of the counts of Maine and Anjou and of the dukes of Normandy intersected and were prone to come into conflict, and Count Hugh's well-founded anxieties about the aggressive intentions against Maine of Count Geoffrey Martel of Anjou, the first of the charters can plausibly be interpreted as the first indication we have that the young Duke William of Normandy and those around him were contemplating an intervention against the hegemony exercised by the counts of Anjou over the county of Maine.[8] The second set of charters is a clear

---

[6] See the classic chapter 'The Loss of Normandy and its Consequences', first published in 1961, J. C. Holt, *The Northerners: A Study in the Reign of King John*, 2nd edn. (Oxford, 1992), 143–74; Daniel Power, 'Les dernières années du régime angevin en Normandie', in Martin Aurell and Noël-Yves Tonnerre (eds), *Plantagenêts et Capétiens: confrontations et héritages* (Turnhout, 2006), 163–92, at 163–4; Power, *The Norman Frontier*, 74–5; Richard Eales, 'Ranulf (III), Sixth Earl of Chester and First Earl of Lincoln', *ODNB*; Kathleen Thompson, 'L'aristocratie anglo-normande en 1204', in *Normandie et Angleterre*, 179–87.

[7] Jörg Peltzer, 'The Angevin Kings and Canon Law: Episcopal Elections and the Loss of Normandy', *ANS*, xxvii (2005), 169–84, at 177–82; Daniel Power, 'The Norman Church and the Angevin and Capetian Kings', *JEH*, lvi (2005), 205–34.

[8] *RADN*, no. 107, with the suggestion of the charter's significance and its likely place of issue made in Bates, 'The Conqueror's Adolescence', 9. The date of 1046 proposed there may need to be

statement of commitment to the cause of the future king Edward the Confessor, without, of course, there being at the date of the confirmations any certainty that he would become king. Whatever the nature of the negotiations that took place after 1042 between William and Edward the Confessor—as already indicated their exact nature can be left on one side in this book—the investment made by the Norman ducal court in Edward's kingship in advance of his invitation to return to England and his peaceful succession to kingship that followed unquestionably supplied the rationale for William's interest in the kingdom of the English, and for whatever offers Edward may have made to him.[9]

To reject the idea that the making of empire was 'a continuous and consistent process' that began in the ninth century is not to argue that the period before William the Conqueror's birth was not of indispensable importance within the process. The duchy as created in the tenth and early eleventh centuries supplied a stable base and the intellectual and cultural resources necessary to the making of empire. In terms of the process leading into the making of empire, the reign of Duke Richard II (996–1026), William the Conqueror's grandfather, was a decisive period of change, and not just because asylum was given to the future King Edward and his brother and sister. Even if Richard had often relied on Scandinavian warriors to assist him in his wars, the reign led—probably accidentally—to the severance of the duchy's close political links to the North Sea peoples from whom a significant, if ultimately unverifiable, proportion of its elite were descended. It was also the time of the earliest journeys to southern Italy and when a Norman ruler established significant links across Europe in a way that none of his predecessors had done. In particular, the contact with Pope Benedict VIII in 1016, the provision of military assistance in southern Italy to the enemies of the Byzantine Empire, and the establishment of networks of patronage that linked Richard and his court to religious sites as far afield from Normandy as Mount Sinai and Jerusalem marked a dramatic change from previous times.[10]

---

amended. Strictly speaking the limits are the death of Bishop Hugh of Evreux (20 April 1046) and the death of Abbot Gradulf of Saint-Wandrille (6 March 1047). A further factor is the unknown length of the hostilities that preceded the revolt of Count Guy of Brionne that was defeated at the Battle of Val-ès-Dunes. With Count Guy among the *signa*, a date of 1046 may be more likely, but one of early 1047 cannot be ruled out. For political context, see further, Kathleen Thompson, 'Family and Influence to the South of Normandy in the Eleventh Century', *JMH*, xi (1985), 215–26; Gérard Louise, *La seigneurie de Bellême, X^e–XIIe siècles*, 2 vols, Le Pays Bas-Normand, nos. 199–202 (1990–1), i, 355.

[9] *RADN*, nos. 73, 85, 111. See further, S. D. Keynes, 'The Æthelings in Normandy', *ANS*, xiii (1991), 173–205, at 186–99; Elisabeth van Houts, 'Edward and Normandy', in Richard Mortimer (ed.), *Edward the Confessor: The Man and the Legend* (Woodbridge, 2009), 63–76. See also *RADN*, no. 76.

[10] For the 1016 bull, *Papsturkunden, 896–1046*, ed. Harald Zimmermann, 2 vols, Denkschriften des Osterreichischen akademie der Wissenschaft phil-hist. klasse, (Vienna, 1984–5), ii, 959–61, no. 505. For the military assistance, *Rodvlfi Glabri Historiarvm Libri Quinque*, ed. and trans. John France, OMT (Oxford, 1989), 96–101. For the patronage, *inter alia, Rodvlfi Glabri Historiarvm Libri Quinque*, 36–7; Hugh of Flavigny, *Chronicon, MGH, Scriptores*, viii, 393; *Miracula sanctae Catharinae Rotomagensis*, ed. A Poncelet, *Analecta Bollandiana*, xxii (1903), 423–38, at 428; *Inventio et miracula sancti Vulfranni*, ed. J. Laporte, Société de l'Histoire de Normandie, Mélanges, xiv (Rouen and Paris, 1938), 35. For convenient French translations of some of the accounts of Richard's patronage, Michel

The treaties that were being made between Frankish elites and leaders of Viking war-bands from at least 826 onwards, and possibly from earlier than that, all involved a measure of reciprocity and sometimes went as far as creating alliances between the parties.[11] The formalities and the informalities of the grant to Rollo by King Charles the Simple, conventionally described as the Treaty of Saint-Clair-sur-Epte and usually dated to 911, made the people who came to call themselves the *Normanni* into fully paid-up participants in the politics and cultural life of the *regnum Francorum*.[12] Furthermore, the relationship thus created was multifaceted. While rivalry bred of familiarity surely fed Dudo of Saint-Quentin's readiness to poke fun at the Franks with the anecdote that has one of Rollo's warriors topple King Charles the Simple backwards in the ceremonial confirmation of Saint-Clair-sur-Epte, the situation could also produce violence and war, as, most dramatically, with the murder of Rollo's son William Longsword in 942 at Picquigny-sur-Somme, west of Amiens, at the hands of another of the territorial rulers of northern France, Count Arnulf of Flanders, and the invasions, after William's murder, of the territory that eventually became Normandy.[13]

That he was a more prosaic historian than Dudo makes William of Jumièges's mid-eleventh-century comment that the French had always envied the Normans very important, especially if, as seems likely, it was written in the late 1050s before the great conquests had happened.[14] Alongside it must, however, be set an anecdote inserted by an anonymous author, in all probability in the later eleventh century, into the *Gesta Normannorum Ducum* that William had initiated, of a possibly fictitious visit of Duke Robert I to Constantinople during his pilgrimage to Jerusalem. Here Robert is made to describe himself as 'one of the most distinguished princes and magnates of the Franks' (*de summis Francorum principibus seu optimatibus unum*) after the Emperor had mistakenly believed him to be the king of the Franks, thereby demonstrating the prestige that came from Normandy's location within the kingdom of the Franks.[15] With Richard II's role within the politics of the French kingdom being portrayed by William of Jumièges as that of a

---

de Boüard (ed.), *Documents de l'Histoire de la Normandie* (Toulouse, 1972), 82–5. There is a vast secondary literature on the early migrations to southern Italy. For a survey and appraisal, G. A. Loud, *The Age of Robert Guiscard* (Harlow, 2000), 60–6.

[11] Pierre Bauduin, *Le monde franc et les Vikings* (Paris, 2009), *passim*, with Normandy analysed as a special case at 347–51. The argument is also succinctly and effectively made in Janet L. Nelson, 'Normandy's Early History since *Normandy before 1066*', in *Normandy and Neighbours*, 3–15, at 8–9. Also important is Simon Coupland, 'From Poachers to Gamekeepers: Scandinavian Warlords and Carolingian Kings', *EME*, vii (1998), 85–114 (reprinted in Simon Coupland, *Carolingian Coinage and the Vikings: Studies on Power and Trade in the 9th Century* (Aldershot, 2007), Chap. 12).

[12] On several relevant issues, Nicholas Vincent, 'Some Effects of the Dynastic Alliances between England and France', in Gazeau and Genet (eds), *La France et les îles Britanniques: un couple impossible?*, 59–74, at 60–1, 68–73.

[13] Dudo of Saint-Quentin, *De Moribus et Actis primorum Normanniae Ducum*, ed. Jules Lair (Caen, 1865), 168–9 (= Dudo of St Quentin, *History of the Normans*, trans. Eric Christiansen (Woodbridge, 1998), 49).

[14] *GND*, ii, 142–3.

[15] *GND*, i, lxi–lxv; ii, 82–3; Elisabeth van Houts, 'Normandy and Byzantium in the Eleventh Century', *Byzantion*, lv (1985), 544–59, at 556–7 (reprinted in *History and Family Traditions*, Chap. 1).

consistent supporter of King Robert the Pious (996–1031), and as someone who tried to maintain harmony between the warring rulers of northern French territorial principalities, the breach that occurred, in all probability in 1052, between William the Conqueror and King Robert's son, King Henry I, shattered a long-standing symbiotic political relationship that had, since Richard II's day, provided legitimizing support for the designation of the young William the Conqueror as the future duke and military support in 1047 at the Battle of Val-ès-Dunes.[16]

Given the events of recent and contemporary times, the appearance in the second half of the eleventh century of statements of a well-known kind that proclaimed the Normans to be a people with exceptional military prowess is hardly a surprise. Among less frequently quoted examples, Abbot John of Fécamp (1028–78), one of the great figures of the duchy's intellectual elite, in *c*.1050 in a letter to Pope Leo IX described the Normans as a people who were outstandingly warlike, and, in the early 1080s, the thesis of Normandy as a province pre-eminent over its neighbours and of the Normans as a people with remarkable conquests to their credit was set out in a text written at Le Mont Saint-Michel.[17] In their contemporary terms these are utterly conventional formulations that articulated the standard classical notion of *gens* as filtered through that basic textbook, the *Etymologies* of Isidore of Seville. In modern terms, they are a social construct of the most basic kind. They were manifestly a framework that educated monks and clerks saw that they must adopt to represent success and even, perhaps, a role for those who they called the Normans as God's chosen people. But this does not mean that we should interpret the legacy of what they wrote in terms of 'his [i.e., Wace's] culture's accepted truths', or a 'master narrative', or to demonstrate that 'all the territory's native inhabitants... were born into *Normanitas* as they were born into Normandy'.[18] While membership of a common ethnic identity was beyond any doubt a central influence on behaviour in that it supplied a political structure of obligation and consultation that was essential to the making of empire, the process of imperial creation and continuation shows how it drew on multiple interests and aspirations; individual actions were much more nuanced, calculated, and self-centred to be lumped together in any simplified framework. For this reason, anxiety, debate and even opposition, both individual and collective, were a part of the creative process of the making and continuation of empire alongside acquisitiveness and ambition. Kings and great aristocrats, for example, were expected to listen to homilies on the moralities of

---

[16] *GND*, ii, 22–5, 33–9; *Rodvlfi Glabri Historiarvm Libri Quinque*, 204–5; Bates, *Normandy before 1066*, 65–8.

[17] *PL*, cxliii, col. 798; 'Introductio monachorum' in 'De miraculis in Monte Sancti Michaelis patratis', in *Chroniques latines du Mont Saint-Michel (IXe–XIIe siècle)*, ed. Pierre Bouet and Olivier Desbordes (Caen and Avranches, 2009), 202–3 (*illustrum uirorum animosissimorumque militum populositate, ut testimonio sunt Cenomannicus pagus, Anglica regna, Campania Apulia, Calabria, Sicilia aliaque plura ab eis armis adquisita diuersis temporibus*). On the date of the text, see 151.

[18] Cf. Ashe, *History and Fiction*, 78; Rebecca L. Slitt, 'The Two Deaths of William Longsword: Wace, William of Malmesbury and the Norman Past', *ANS*, xxxiv (2012), 193–208, at 194; Webber, *Norman Identity*, 38.

their actions and their responsibilities.[19] The extent to which they took notice was, of course, a matter for them.

The cross-Channel empire's ideologically plural composition was not just a factor in the history of the British Isles. It was entrenched within the political discourse of the French kingdom from the beginning. Thus, a diploma of the King Philip I (1060–1108) dated 1079, in all likelihood written under the supervision of the French king's chancellor, and confirmed by both Philip and William, placed their crosses alongside each other on the parchment, indicating equal status.[20] But a diploma dealing with property within Normandy and confirmed by William explicitly stated that the ruler of Normandy was a *comes*; kingship was a personal dignity that had no place in Normandy.[21] And in the world of practical politics, William and many others were to learn the meaning of imperial overstretch by as early as 1069, when the recently acquired dominance over Maine was overthrown at exactly the same moment that rebellions in England and invasions from Denmark and Scotland combined to put the conquest of the English kingdom in peril. In the mind and on the battle-field, the problems of empire were present from the beginning.

If preceding events had not done so, the wars between the Conqueror's sons brought home to Normandy the price of empire. Its articulation in the early twelfth century by the poet Serlo, in his verdict on the supposedly supine defenders of Bayeux in 1105, might even be thought to belong in a tradition that links him, in his unsophisticated way, to Edmund Burke and the modern critics of the Iraq war.[22] And Orderic, writing about the same period in the later 1130s, observed that the Normans who had prided themselves on conquests in England and Apulia were now bewailing their miserable fate.[23] In terms of popular memory, Wace's story of the still barren ground at the place where the four citizens of Caen had betrayed Robert Curthose must surely have made the same point to many who passed that busy place; one of the most effective of all life-stories in terms of the communication of popular memory into the literary sources, it must, for Wace, who associated himself closely with Caen, have been a constant presence. It is also notable that he characterized William the Conqueror's seizure of Maine as an illegitimate act, an infringement of the just claims of the rightful heirs.[24] That he wrote in this way may be a reflection of the fact that his patron Henry II was a descendant of the counts of Anjou whom William had pushed aside. Although seeming to be an ethical criticism of the dukes of Normandy, what it actually did was portray Henry II as having righted a wrong; Wace was a clever man with a strong sense of the complexities of the past, the present, and the future, who does not deserve to be labelled as representative of any ending of something called *Normanitas*. To think in such terms also devalues a robust and resilient Norman identity.

---

[19] See Chaps. 3 and 4.
[20] *Regesta*, no. 28 (*Recueil des actes de Philippe Ier, roi de France, (1059–1108)*, ed. Maurice Prou (Paris, 1908), no. XCIV); cf. Bates, 'Normandy and England', 864.
[21] *Regesta*, no. 198 (*et comiti qui pro tempore fuerit*).
[22] See Chap. 2 for the themes of this paragraph.
[23] OV, vi, 58–61.   [24] *Roman de Rou*, 304–5, ll. 9,717–20.

It is also necessary to recognize that when writers in England, Wales, southern Italy, and Normandy wrote about the exceptional military prowess of the Normans, they were coming at the subject from a different direction from those writing in Normandy. William of Malmesbury, Henry of Huntingdon, and, to a lesser extent, the author of the *Brut y Twysogyon* were writing from the perspective of its subjects, peoples who had been defeated, or were threatened with defeat. Yet at the same time, they were also celebrating the achievements of an empire in which they were participants. However, for all that critical and anxious voices were raised, the ultimate determinant of events was the power of the cross-Channel elite and the continuing dynamism of a robust and resilient empire that offered reward for those who continued to seek it. To state again the necessary obvious, the core of the history of the beginning and end of empires is usually the history of hard power and the capacity to continue to mobilize it convincingly.

THE END

After 1154, Normandy's special place within the cross-Channel empire was acknowledged and celebrated in a host of ways with, for example, the Empress living out the remaining years of her life until her death in 1167 near Rouen at the priory of Notre-Dame du Pré and she and her husband financing the construction of the first stone bridge across the Seine at Rouen.[25] In 1162 the bodies of Dukes Richard I and Richard II were translated into new tombs in the abbey of Fécamp in Henry II's presence, and in 1183 his eldest son, the Young King Henry, was buried, as he had requested, in Rouen cathedral alongside several of his ancestors.[26] It is possible that the holder of a Norman *comté* was regarded as having a status at court superior to that of an English earl.[27] Many recent publications make it clear that the cross-Channel elites were still at the heart of the new territorial complex created by Henry II and that cross-Channel networks both remained in place and continued to be dynamic. Henry II spent much more time proportionately in Normandy than anywhere else.[28] In an elegant metaphor—'the hinge on which the Angevin Empire swung'—Lindy Grant has vividly expressed what many others since Haskins have said about Normandy in the second half of the twelfth century.[29]

---

[25] RT (D), i, 367–8; (H), 232–3.   [26] RT (D), i, 336–7; ii, 121; (H), 212–13.
[27] Nicholas Vincent, 'Did Henry II Have a Policy towards the Earls?', in Chris Given-Wilson, Ann Kettle, and Len Scales (eds), *War, Government and Aristocracy in the British Isles, c.1150–1500: Essays in Honour of Michael Prestwich* (Woodbridge, 2008), 1–25, at 24.
[28] Thus, 'Cela nous donne une indication de l'étroitesse des liens qui continuaient à unir l'Angleterre et la Normandie après 1154'; Nicholas Vincent, 'Les Normands de l'entourage d'Henri II Plantagenêt', in *Normandie et Angleterre*, 75–88, at 78–84, with the quotation at 80. See also Vincent, 'Did Henry II Have a Policy towards the Earls?', 15–17.
[29] Grant, *Architecture and Society*, 8; Haskins, *Normans in European History*, 85–6; Holt, 'End of the Anglo-Norman Realm', 243–6 (*Magna Carta and Medieval Government*, 44–7); Musset, 'Quelques problèmes', 301 n. 53; François Neveux, *La Normandie des ducs aux rois X^e–XIIe siècle* (Rennes, 1998), 569.

All of them were, of course, either anticipating or are re-stating an opinion of John Le Patourel's. As already noted, despite regarding the civil war between Stephen and the Empress Matilda as 'a real break', he always stressed very firmly the continuities across that turbulent time and was working on a sequel to *The Norman Empire* when he died.[30]

Although notably different opinions have been expressed about the relative integration of, and the extent of regional diversity within, the Angevin/Plantagenet Empire, there is certainly plentiful evidence for the continuation of an evolving cross-Channel integration involving Normandy and England over the period from 1154 to 1204 in, for example, the creation in 1180 of an 'official' exchange rate between pounds sterling and the *livres angevins* that had displaced Rouen money as the duchy's coinage and in the way in which the returnable writs of the Common Law seemingly developed in parallel with the writs that appear in the *Très Ancien Coutumier*.[31] At the lower social levels that are very important to my argument, the rapid adoption on both sides of the Channel of the cult of the murdered Archbishop Thomas Becket is another important sign of the continuing relationship. That the majority of the dedications are in Upper Normandy in the region around Rouen is suggestive of a response connected to the family networks of the Beckets, rather than being a generalized Norman response, fits very well with this book's argument; once more, it is the cross-Channel dynamic expressed in diverse and multiple ways through the lives and activities of individuals that matters.[32] Also striking is the construction in the mid-twelfth century of near-identical churches at St Margaret-at-Cliffe in Kent and Creully, which is between Bayeux and Caen, two places that had the same lord. There are also notable similarities between the churches at Foulognes and Patrixbourne (Kent), both held by the Patric family.[33] The records prepared in 1204 of lands confiscated in England from relatively minor cross-Channel landowners show very well just how many individuals and families had a stake in the continuation of empire.[34]

An undoubted sign of business as usual is that cross-Channel estates continued to be created into the later twelfth century, and even into the early thirteenth. Thus,

---

[30] See Chap. 5. For the sequel, Holt, 'John Le Patourel', 595–6.

[31] For a survey of the issues, see Gillingham, 'Problems of Integration', 102–35. On specific issues, Barrie Cook, '*En monnaie aiant* cours: The Monetary System of the Angevin Empire', in Barrie Cook and Gareth Williams (eds), *Coinage and History in the North Sea World, c.500–1200: Essays in Honour of Marion Archibald* (Leiden/Boston, 2006), 617–86, at 624–5, 626–41, 669–72. For the general significance of the 1180 reform in England, Allen, *Mints and Money*, 378–9. On the writs, Jean Yver, 'Le bref anglo-normand', *Revue d'histoire du droit: Tijdschrift voor Rechtsgeschiedenis*, xxix (1961), 313–30. For 'imperial acts' in general, Holt, 'End of the Anglo-Norman Realm', 227–8 (*Magna Carta and Medieval Government*, 27–8).

[32] Raymonde Foreville, 'Le culte de Saint Thomas Becket en Normandie: enquête sur les sanctuaires anciennement placés sous le vocable du martyr de Cantorbéry', in Raymonde Foreville (ed.), *Thomas Becket* (Paris, 1975), 135–52, at 139–41; Ursula Nilgen, 'Thomas Becket en Normandie', in Bouet and Neveux (eds), *Les Saints dans la Normandie médiévale*, 189–204, at 195–200.

[33] Berg and Jones, *Norman Churches in the Canterbury Diocese*, 85–6, 90, plates 15 and 16. For other examples of cross-Channel architectural similarity, Grant, *Architecture and Society*, 228–9.

[34] Tony K. Moore, 'The Loss of Normandy and the Invention of *Terre Normannorum*, 1204', *EHR*, cxxv (2010), 1071–1101, at 1090–1.

William de Mandeville, earl of Essex (1166–89), a man whose lands were mostly located in England, not only conscientiously built up an estate in Normandy after marriage to Hawise, countess of Aumale in 1180, but was also prominent in the defence of the duchy's frontier. And Guérin de Glapion, a Norman of relatively humble origins, constructed a cross-Channel estate by acquiring lands in England in the 1190s and 1200s.[35] Monasteries with relatively small cross-Channel landholdings continued to adjust them by exchanging property on one side of the Channel for property on the other.[36] And the non-Norman counts of Perche, initially promoted by Henry I, and with extensive lands beyond the frontiers of Normandy, seem to provide an example of French lords exploiting English estates to maintain an aristocratic lifestyle in France, without apparently ever crossing the Channel.[37] Count Geoffrey of Perche indeed seems to have utilized his role in the negotiation of the Treaty of Le Goulet between John and Philip Augustus (22 May 1200) to secure a major increment from John of his English property; in other words, he looks like those figures of earlier times, Earl William II de Warenne and Rannulf II, earl of Chester, who had sought opportunistically to use their massive power to exploit the anxieties of the cross-Channel empire's rulers.[38] And in another case, a long-established cross-Channel family from the southern frontier lands of Normandy made a cross-Channel comeback in the 1190s and 1200s in the person of Gilbert II de Laigle.[39] In a reverse of this process, a great family of the Ile-de-France, the lords of Montfort-l'Amaury, who had acquired the *comté* of Evreux by marriage, were adeptly integrated into the social framework of the cross-Channel empire and eventually separated from their landholdings in the Ile-de-France.[40]

The expansion of imperial space that followed the intervention in Ireland in 1169 included the creation of networks that linked the new conquests to both England and Normandy. Thus, Bertram III de Verdun and his sons Thomas and Nicholas de Verdun used their enhanced wealth and status, with Bertram founding the Cistercian abbey that was eventually established in 1179 at Croxden (Surrey), to which the first monks came from the Norman abbey of Aunay-sur-Odon, a house to which he also made grants. It is even possible that Nicholas was involved in the final failed defence of Château Gaillard in 1203; certainly the family's history is not just one of expansion into Ireland, but also of a battle to hold onto the end to a network of landholdings across northern France and the British Isles.[41] Of the

---

[35] Power, 'Henry, Duke of the Normans', 87–96; *The Norman Frontier*, 284–5; 'Guérin de Glapion, Seneschal of Normandy (1200–01): Service and Ambition under the Plantagenet and Capetian Kings', in Vincent (ed.), *Records, Administration and Aristocratic Society*, 153–85, at 155, 162, 170–1; Thomas K. Keefe, 'Mandeville, William de, third earl of Essex (*d.*1189)', *ODNB*.

[36] *Chartes du prieuré de Longueville*, no. XXV.

[37] Kathleen Thompson, 'Les seigneuries anglaises et françaises des comtes de Perche (1100–1226)', in Aurell and Boutoulle (eds), *Les seigneuries dans l'espace Plantagenêt*, 61–75, at 63–4, 66.

[38] Thompson, *Power and Border Lordship*, 139–40.

[39] Kathleen Thompson, 'The Lords of Laigle: Ambition and Insecurity on the Borders of Normandy', *ANS*, xviii (1996), 177–99, at 192–5.

[40] Power, *The Norman Frontier*, 228–31.

[41] Mark S. Hagger, *The Fortunes of a Norman Family: The De Verduns in England, Ireland and Wales, 1066–1316* (Dublin, 2001), 39, 45, 57, 60–1, 208.

conquerors of lands in Ireland, not only was 'Strongbow' (Richard fitz Gilbert, earl of Pembroke) active in Normandy in the midst of these campaigns, so too was Hugh de Lacy, who not only defended Verneuil for Henry II in 1173–4, but also founded a priory at Fore, Westmeath, as a dependency of the Norman abbey of Saint-Taurin of Evreux.[42]

The process of the creation of new networks also extended across France, with the already-mentioned Constance, the sole heir of Conan IV, who was Duke of Brittany until his abdication in 1166, and therefore to the cross-Channel estate held from soon after 1066 in turn by the three brothers, Counts Alan the Red (d.1093) and the Black (d.1098), and Stephen (d.1135), being forced into marriage with Henry II's third son Geoffrey.[43] As already noted in Chapter 5, this expansion southwards of a pre-existing cross-Channel estate made strategic sense in the context of the expanded empire because it consolidated Henry's power around Nantes and the mouth of the river Loire. But, in the long term, with this union being the only one of the marriages of Henry II's sons to have produced children by 1199, not for the first time—but this time for the last time—a marriage alliance designed to stabilize, for reasons that were both unforeseeable and accidental, produced the opposite result when, in 1199, some parts of the Angevin Empire opted for Constance's and Geoffrey's son Arthur in preference to John. Viewed systemically, not only was the concentration of power on one individual an issue of central importance, but so too were the human reproductive processes. The marriage also shows how the creation of the Angevin/Plantagenet empire meant that political life was no longer contained within the cross-Channel empire or northern France. The more extensive records available, notably the continuous sequence of Pipe Rolls of the English Exchequer, enable us to grasp some of the financial burdens that the new territorial complex involved Henry's unsuccessful campaign in 1159 to add the county of Toulouse to his territories required heavy tax-raising in both England and Normandy for a campaign that surely cannot have been of much direct interest to most of the inhabitants of either of them.[44] While the networks that bound Normandy and England together remained robust ones, the context in which they operated had changed.

The young William Marshal, like Orderic before him, but in a very different milieu, went from relatively unpromising circumstances in England to Normandy to make his life there. While in the military household of William II de Tancarville, hereditary chamberlain of the dukes of Normandy, a cross-Channel landowner, but one whose estates were mostly in Normandy, he is said to have proposed a visit home to England. Be warned, William de Tancarville said to his protégé, it is a backwater in which he should not stay for long: 'for it was in no way a fitting place to stay, except for the minor gentry and those who had no wish to travel the world'.

---

[42] *CDF*, nos. 312–17; Rory Masterson, 'The Church and the Anglo-Norman Colonisation of Ireland: A Case Study of the Priory of Fore', *Ríocht na Midhe*, xi (2000), 58–70; Arlene Hogan, *The Priory of Llanthony Prima and Secunda in Ireland, 1172–1541* (Dublin, 2008), 65–6.
[43] Everard, *Brittany and the Angevins*, 34–47.
[44] For the taxes raised, Amt, *The Accession of Henry II*, 183–6; RT (D), i, 320–1; (H), 202.

Northern France was the place to be.[45] If reflective of general attitudes among the knightly classes, it points to the centrality of Normandy and northern France to the lives of the aspiring; although he was considered to be English, his career was made in northern France.[46] His modern biographer has commented that, although when he had become a great cross-Channel magnate with lands in Normandy, England, Wales, and Ireland, he recruited the majority of his following from his English estates, 'the bare facts of his itinerary in the 1190s demonstrate that he loved Normandy'.[47] To describe the Marshal as a devoted servant of the cross-Channel empire might be going too far, but to see him as a consistent participant in its affairs is certainly correct. In his early seventies, he was still in the saddle—so we are told—to inspire the troops to victory over the invaders from France at the Battle of Lincoln in 1217.[48] And, although the passage is a garbled one bizarrely referring to the period before 1066, Gervase of Tilbury's observation, written in the early thirteenth century, that it was the custom among the greatest nobles of England to send their sons to be brought up in France may well reflect the same cross-Channel cultural world and its significance for the political elite.[49]

With individuals from England making careers in Normandy in the second half of the twelfth century, of whom the most important were William fitz Ralph, seneschal of Normandy from 1178 to 1200, who came from Derbyshire, and was responsible for the routine management of the duchy's financial and judicial administration, and Geoffrey of Repton, who was mayor of Caen in 1200 and had been resident in the town since at least 1186, as mentioned in Chapter 1, there is an argument to the effect that Normandy had long ceased to be the dynamic centre of empire by the later twelfth century.[50] And when the future King John was given lands in Normandy that from 1189 came to include the *comté* of Mortain, significant periods of residence notwithstanding, his active role within the duchy was small and his entourage usually consisted of individuals from his lands on the north of the Channel or at most with cross-Channel possessions.[51] There also appears to be evidence that ethnicity was seen as a corrosive force in the defence of the duchy. Thus, the Anonymous of Béthune commented on the Englishness of Saer de Quincy and Robert fitz Walter, who were responsible for the surrender without a fight of the important castle of Le Vaudreuil in 1203.[52] However, while based primarily in England and (in Saer's case) Scotland as well, both were extremely well connected at the highest levels of the cross-Channel elite. Once

---

[45] *History of William Marshal*, i, 78–9, ll. 1,526–50, with the quotation at ll. 1,538–40.
[46] For William as ethnically English, *History of William Marshal*, i, 264–7, ll. 5,214–15.
[47] Crouch, *William Marshal*, 150–2, with the quotation at 151.
[48] *History of William Marshal*, ii, 332–3, ll. 16,597–16,624.
[49] Gervase of Tilbury, *Otia Imperialia: Recreation for an Emperor*, ed. and trans. S. E. Banks and J. W. Binns, OMT (Oxford, 2002), 474–5; cit., Robert Bartlett, *England under the Norman and Angevin Kings, 1075–1225* (Oxford, 2000), 490.
[50] Musset, 'Quelques problèmes', 293–4; Jean-Marie, *Caen*, 237.
[51] Nicholas Vincent, 'Jean, comte de Mortain: le futur roi et ses domaines en Normandie, 1183–1199', in *1204*, 37–59.
[52] Anonymous of Béthune, *Histoire des ducs de Normandie et des rois d'Angleterre*, ed. Francisque Michel, Société de l'Histoire de France (Paris, 1840), 130.

more it is a question of what an ethnic descriptor actually meant; with so much evidence suggesting that identity was often described in terms of place of residence, we must be careful before interpreting this material as showing a disengagement by 'the English' from the defence of Normandy.[53]

Whatever the significance of this evidence and of these particular life-stories, they are surely heavily outweighed in their overall significance by what is known about the continuing involvement in the government of Normandy of individuals based in Normandy and of the cross-Channel rewards they were continuing to enjoy.[54] The Marshal's life and the commitment of so many others to the defence of Normandy can make us wonder, the requirements of loyalty and service notwithstanding, how far many of the individuals who at first sight seem to have come from England were actually returning to defend the homeland as well as to preserve a cross-Channel landholding. It is surely reasonable to suggest that, if Normandy had not fallen to Philip Augustus in 1204, or, indeed if the war against him had been won and the cross-Channel empire had survived for a lot longer, this same evidence would be used to argue for a deployment of resources and people across the whole of the cross-Channel empire that was integrative and notably efficient.

It is actually surely unsurprising that, more than one hundred years after the foundation of the cross-Channel empire, individuals from both sides of the Channel were involved in its management. While most would be descendants of earlier settlers in England from either Normandy or other parts of northern France, some might truly be of English descent; the empire's ideologically plural foundations did after all make such participation possible, and arguably to be expected. Richard fitz Nigel, author in the late 1170s and 1180s of *The Dialogue of Exchequer*, saw past and present in exactly these terms, writing—somewhat cold-bloodedly, it must be said—that, after 1066, William the Conqueror had decreed that the English had no right to inherit property they might claim to have held before 1066, but that they could prosper by loyal service to their conquerors.[55] However, one index that can be used to measure what might be termed 'English' participation in the cross-Channel empire,, namely, the amount of land in Normandy granted to English monasteries, shows that the quantity involved was very small indeed.[56] In other words, an awful lot of people and institutions in Normandy had a lot to lose if the cross-Channel empire failed. And furthermore, it must be a mistake to impose a narrowly nationalistic assessment on the

---

[53] See Chap. 2. [54] See Power, 'Les dernières années', 174–9.
[55] Richard fitz Nigel, *Dialogus de Scaccario: The Dialogue of the Exchequer, and Constitutio Domus Regis, The Disposition of the King's Household*, ed. and trans. Emilie Amt and S. D. Church, OMT (Oxford, 2007), 82–3; John Hudson, 'Administration, Family and Perceptions of the Past in Late Twelfth-Century England: Richard fitz Nigel and the Dialogue of the Exchequer', in Paul Magdalino (ed.), *The Perception of the Past in Twelfth-Century Europe* (London/Rio Grande, 1992), 75–98, at 87–8.
[56] Nicholas Vincent, 'The English Monasteries and Their French Possessions', in Dalton, Insley, and Wilkinson (eds), *Cathedrals, Communities and Conflict*, 221–39, at 221–7. For a specific example, Nicholas Vincent, 'A Collection of Early Norman Charters in the British Library: The Case of Jeremiah Holmes Wiffen', *Cahiers Léopold Delisle*, liii (2004), 21–45, at 43–5.

history of an ethnically plural empire.⁵⁷ To do so is also to ignore a general pattern in the history of empires whereby, alongside the continuing dominance of an elite mostly drawn from the homeland, participation broadens out through the opportunism of the defeated and—of central importance in this case—the victors and descendants take on the new identities that follow logically from the evolutionary processes implicit in the empire's ethnic plurality.

If, as was done soon after the collapse of 1204, and is often done nowadays, John's use of non-Norman mercenaries to defend Normandy is seen as a prelude to the end of empire and the rapid surrender of the heartlands of the duchy that were unaccustomed to war, then it needs to be kept in mind that the arrival of a large force of Flemings was deemed by all who wrote about that episode to have been a significant part of the explanation for Stephen's failed military campaign in the duchy in 1137, and that the presence of non-Norman troops in William Rufus's and Henry I's campaigns in Normandy against Robert Curthose was the subject of comment and criticism.⁵⁸ Resentment there might have been in 1204, but earlier generations in Normandy had seen it all before.

Another long-term perspective on the cross-Channel empire is supplied by the history of state finance. While William of Malmesbury's interpretation of the prodigy of the conjoined twins as signifying that the defence of Normandy constituted an unsustainable drain on England's resources appears distinctly melodramatic when we know that the empire was going to last for another eighty years after the passage was written, more prosaic commentaries from the late twelfth century on the same subject, such as Ralph of Coggeshall's to the effect that no one could remember such extortionate taxation as Richard the Lionheart's during the five years between 1194 and 1199, can be checked against extensive financial records.⁵⁹ And on the basis of a meticulous study, one of the latest commentators has written:

> After over thirty years of careful husbandry of demesne revenue, Richard (in 1194) appears to have undone his father's work virtually overnight.⁶⁰

At the same time, he doubled revenue almost in an instant. Over the longer time span of the late twelfth and early thirteenth century, the pattern is one of the selling of assets under Richard, a relative relaxation of the financial demands in John's early years, followed by revenue-raising on a quite unprecedented scale between 1208 and 1212 as a prelude to the counter-offensive that failed at Bouvines.⁶¹ In Normandy, revenue-raising showed a quite astonishing inventiveness that has led to comparison with the economic stimuli that has been seen in modern times to be

---

⁵⁷ See also Mathieu Arnoux, 'Conclusion', in *Normandie et Angleterre*, 359–63, at 362–3; Power, *Norman Frontier*, 74–9.

⁵⁸ For John's use of mercenaries, Holt, 'End of the Anglo-Norman Realm', 265 (with special reference to the advice given to Henry III by a citizen of Caen in 1227) (*Magna Carta and Medieval Government*, 65); Power, 'King John and the Norman Aristocracy', 132–4. For 1137, Crouch, *The Reign of King Stephen*, 66–7; King, *King Stephen*, 74–5. For 1105, see Chap. 4.

⁵⁹ Ralph of Coggeshall, *Chronicon Anglicanum*, ed. Joseph Stevenson, Rolls Series (London, 1875), 93.

⁶⁰ Nick Barratt, 'The English Revenues of Richard I', *EHR*, cxvi (2001), 635–56, with the quotation at 649.

⁶¹ See also Nick Barratt, 'The Revenue of King John', *EHR*, cxi (1996), 835–55.

associated with infrastructure investment during wartime. Although this may be so, it is also impossible not to think in terms of desperation and short-term fixes as other possible interpretations. As in England, what was done in Normandy was ultimately based on the selling of assets and the raising of exceptional taxation through forced loans and tallages.[62] Someone might well have quietly mentioned that the money was running out. Certainly many people would have experienced the generally deflationary economic impact of taxation of this kind.[63]

Writing before 1204, Ralph of Coggeshall did indeed express the sentiment that John was to be praised for bringing peace in 1200 by the Treaty of Le Goulet, although—of course—with the ability later to reflect that pacific intentions had turned out to be an abject surrender that led rapidly to catastrophic defeat (and more taxation).[64] If he had had the language of Joseph Nye at his disposal, he might well have expressed his opinions in terms of a failure of hard power. What his changing opinions certainly reflect are the dilemmas that went with increasing external pressure on an empire that had always had its weaknesses.

In all this, the reactions of contemporaries to Richard the Lionheart—in parallel indeed to the earlier treatment of William Rufus—can be read as the medieval equivalents of those jingoistic portrayals of a hero of empire with which the nineteenth and twentieth centuries were very familiar. Like Rufus's Westminster Hall, the construction of the great castle of Château Gaillard above Les Andelys on the Seine is therefore perhaps yet another *folie de grandeur* of empire.[65] It is indeed arguable that the empire could not have afforded either of them on a long-term basis if they had not both met their accidental deaths. In their careers, however, we are also back to display and reward as the foundations of successful warrior kingship. And we can obtain some idea of what the cost of Rufus's and Henry I's kingship had been from the alienation of the lands of the English royal demesne, a subject of which a study by Judith Green demonstrated that it was both extensive and largely directed towards prominent members of the lay aristocracy whom the kings needed to reward. This process inevitably also led to the need to devise new and innovative methods of taxation in compensation for capital losses.[66]

A further perspective on this situation is provided by the history of prophecy. Thus, while prophecies forecasting the end of the cross-Channel empire appear in

---

[62] Vincent Moss, 'The Norman Fiscal Revolution, 1193–8', in W. M. Ormrod, M. Bonney, and R. Bonney (eds), *Revolutions and Self-Sustained Growth: Essays in European Fiscal History, 1130–1830* (Oxford, 1999), 38–57; Vincent Moss, 'The Defence of Normandy 1193–8', *ANS*, xxiv (2003), 145–61.

[63] J. L. Bolton, 'The English Economy in the Early Thirteenth Century', in Church (ed.), *King John: New Interpretations*, 27–40, at 36–40. Note in particular: 'Henry III's military ineptitude . . . may have been just what an uncertainly expanding and commercialising economy needed' (40).

[64] Ralph of Coggeshall, 101. See further, D. A. Carpenter, 'Abbot Ralph of Coggeshall's Account of the Last Years of King Richard and the First Years of King John', *EHR*, cxiii (1998), 1210–30, at 1219–20; cf. John Gillingham, 'Historians without Hindsight: Coggeshall, Diceto and Howden on the Early Years of John's Reign', in Church (ed.), *King John: New Interpretations*, 1–26, at 7–9, 22–3.

[65] Dominique Pitte, 'Château Gaillard dans la défense de la Normandie orientale (1196–1204)', *ANS*, xxiv (2002), 163–75.

[66] Judith A. Green, 'William Rufus, Henry I and the Royal Demesne', *History*, lxiv (1979), 337–52.

the twelfth century in William of Malmesbury, Geoffrey of Monmouth, and John of Cornwall, at the same time, Robert of Torigni and Wace, writing in Normandy, deliberately suppressed such prophecies.[67] If prophecy represents the expression of what is either wished for or feared, then the contrast between what was written to the north and south of the Channel surely spotlights the mixture of anxiety and resilience that are at the heart of the history of the Normans and empire. And alongside this is the whole range of supposed prophecies and damning verdicts by monastic and clerical writers on rulers whose vainglorious display dazzled them, and whose failure ultimately demanded an explanation. To examine this well-known material is not the subject of this book.[68] I will merely observe that for them, God's will did indeed express itself in curious ways; the rulers could therefore be portrayed as either heroes or tyrants. Hence, yet again, the importance of reading the so-called literary sources carefully and at times sceptically.

In psychoanalytic theory and in terms of some of the reasons advanced as to why nations and empires fail, organizations become disabled by their primitive responses to anxiety and fear. An excessively narrow concentration of power within too small a group and maladaptive defence mechanisms that, in psychoanalytical terms, can be termed paranoid or schizoid result in poor decision-making and boundaries that are less permeable by both the actual and the virtual.[69] With this in mind, it is arguably striking how far many of John's actions appear to conform to earlier patterns of behaviour, yet to have had dramatically different results.

His second marriage to Isabella of Angoulême in 1200, for example, involved the divorce of a childless wife from one of the great families of the cross-Channel empire in favour of a wife—a child as it happens—from one of the great aristocratic families of Poitou who was related to many of the ruling houses of Christendom. Manifestly what John was trying to accomplish was an increase of his influence in a potentially unstable region and to elevate his personal standing from the base of the secure foundation of the cross-Channel empire. That the result was a disaster, with Isabella's previous betrothed, Hugh IX de Lusignan, appealing to Philip Augustus as John's overlord for his lands in France, might suggest that it was tactics rather than the strategy that was at fault; what was after all a conventional strategy that might even have been a good idea was executed without due care.[70] Let us remember not only the barely noticed verdict of the author of the Anglo-Saxon Chronicle on Henry I's organization of the Empress Matilda's marriage to the young Count Geoffrey of Anjou, but also that John's father's rapidly organized marriage to the great heiress Eleanor of Aquitaine actually created the Angevin/

---

[67] See Chap. 2.
[68] For the latest version of the arguments for Angevin/Plantagenet oppression, Maïté Billoré, 'Y a-t-il une "oppression" des Plantagenêt sur l'aristocratie en Normandie à la veille de 1204?', in Martin Aurell and Noël-Yves Tonnerre (eds), *Plantagenêts et Capétiens: confrontations et héritages* (Turnhout, 2006), 145–61.
[69] See Anton Obholzer and Vega Zagier Roberts (eds), *The Unconscious at Work: Individual and Organizational Stress in the Human Services* (London/New York, 1994; and subsequently reprinted many times).
[70] See now Nicholas Vincent, 'Isabella of Angoulême: John's Jezebel', in Church (ed.), *King John: New Interpretations*, 165–219, at 166–84.

Plantagenet empire. Henry I and Henry II rode out criticism and opposition; John could not.

A further difference between earlier times and the first years of the thirteenth century is brought into focus by the way in which Henry I allowed the young William Clito his freedom, just as his father and two brothers had done to Edgar the Ætheling. The truly royal, it seems, should be treated as such, no matter how potentially dangerous they might be; as we have seen, after nineteen years of conflict, Ailred of Rievaulx could write of the descendants of the Old English royal line that included the descendants of King Stephen and the Empress as the 'holy family'. Admittedly both Robert Curthose and King Stephen were imprisoned and William the Conqueror and Henry I have reputations for keeping people shut away for very long periods, but there is nothing to resemble the circulation of stories to the effect that Arthur of Brittany had been murdered in 1203 or the subsequent associated hounding of William de Briouze and the deaths by starvation at Windsor in 1211 of his wife and young son. Viewed as aspects of the phenomena of empire, the parallels with the atrocities and use of torture associated with the fading in the twentieth century of the great colonial empires is notable. To work, hard power must be both effective and convincing; John's rule after 1204 witnessed a mounting crescendo of criticism that suggests that it was ceasing to be either.

For all that this book's argument is that, subject to the eventual results of systematic and intensive prosopographical study, the networks of the cross-Channel empire remained resilient to the end, the obvious great change after 1154 must be that the elites of the cross-Channel empire were no longer as fully in control of their destinies as they had been before. Political life could be thrown into confusion by events a long way away. Henry II's sons were ready to turn to Louis VII and Philip Augustus for support in ways that no one before 1154 had done and the Capetian kings could make a legitimate case for intervention in ways that had not previously been possible. For all that the rulers of the Angevin/Plantagenet empire still favoured Rouen with extravagant buildings, there were now other centres to dramatize and patronize.[71] And within the British Isles, a Welsh ruler, Owain Ewynedd, could make contact with the French king, and ask for help, in a way that had not happened before 1154.[72] The centre of gravity of power truly had shifted in people's minds. The Treaty of Le Goulet, as we have seen, was interpreted as weakness on John's part, whereas his father's homage to Louis VII fifty years earlier was seen by Robert of Torigni as a joyous event, a triumph.[73]

Although they might disagree on details, all historians would certainly agree that, with the advent of Philip Augustus in 1180 and the subsequent enhancement of the power and resources of the Capetian kings, a change in the balance of power, in both

---

[71] Fanny Madeline, 'Rouen and its Place in the Building Policy of the Angevin Kings', in Hicks and Brenner (eds), *Society and Culture in Medieval Rouen*, 65–99, at 69–74, 82–91.
[72] Huw Pryce, 'Owain Gwynedd and Louis VII: The Franco-Welsh Diplomacy of the First Prince of Wales', *WHR*, xix (1998), 1–28.
[73] Gillingham, 'Historians without Hindsight', 7–9, 22–3; RT (D), i, 255; (H), 162.

perception and actuality, occurred. Yet someone taking a long-term systemic view might suggest that all followed in a logical chain that went back to 1063 and the takeover of the county of Maine of that year, and then passed through a series of linked events that included a series of succession disputes, the failure of a count of Maine to produce a male heir to succeed him in 1110, and Henry I's perceived mistake of marrying his daughter to a count of Anjou. It was an empire whose faultlines kept coming to the surface. For all that, however, it was around for a good long time. And it sustained loyalty of most of the political elite to the end. It is of this final point that we should take especial note.

IDENTITY AND THE END OF EMPIRE

Even if Gerald of Wales's comment, written in c.1200, that the English were 'in their own land the slaves of the Normans, and the most worthless of slaves' is interpreted as referring only to the kings as Normans, because of what was invested in this kingship, it must still be seen a statement of a dominance of rule by an imperial elite that, in terms of the shorthand language of ethnicity, he must have conceived of as being Norman. Furthermore, the notion that the kings either were Normans or were of Norman descent was one that was repeated by numerous writers.[74] This does not mean that many among the individuals who had settled in England should be denied a plural and, in all likelihood, a mutable ethnicity that encompassed being in some (or indeed many or all) respects English; it does mean that they were the subjects of an empire that was regarded as being an empire of the Normans. Gerald certainly did also have a clear sense of the existence of a strong Norman identity that was present in his own day, since he thought his contemporary Normans boastful and arrogant.[75]

While the speech supposedly made by Richard de Luci to Henry II in 1157 defending Battle Abbey's exemption from episcopal authority as a symbol of Norman domination against 'the stratagems of the English' may never have been made, it does show that an author in all probability writing in the later decades of the twelfth century thought that an expression of such sentiments in favour of a continuing Norman superiority was credible theatre appropriate for display before the most powerful men and women of the imperial elite.[76] Another likely expression of this continuing domination is found in Thomas of Monmouth's account of the miracles of the murdered boy William of Norwich, in all probability completed

---

[74] *In terra sua Normannorum serui sunt Anglici et serui uilissimi*, in Giraldus Cambrensis, *De invectionibus*, ed. W. S. Davies, *Y Cymmrodor*, xxx (1920), 93; John Gillingham, ' "Slaves of the Normans"? Gerald de Barri and Early Regnal Solidarity in Early Thirteenth-Century England', in Pauline Stafford, Janet L. Nelson, and Jane Martindale (eds), *Law, Laity and Solidarities: Essays in Honour of Susan Reynolds* (Manchester/New York, 2001), 160–71; cf. Bartlett, *Gerald of Wales*, 12–20, 91–4. For other examples of the usage, Gillingham, 'Problems of Integration', 93.

[75] For references, Gillingham, ' "Slaves of the Normans?" ', 168.

[76] *The Chronicle of Battle Abbey*, ed. Eleanor Searle, OMT (Oxford, 1980), 182–3. On the composition of the Battle Chronicle, Nicholas Vincent, 'King Henry II and the Monks of Battle: The Battle Chronicle Unmasked', in Richard Gameson and Henrietta Leyser (eds), *Belief and Culture in the Middle Ages: Studies Presented to Henry Mayr-Harting* (Oxford, 2001), 264–86, at 280–1.

in the 1170s, with the description of the waters between England and Continental Europe as 'the Norman sea' (*mare illud Normannicum*); it was the political elite who controlled the sea lanes.[77] And one final manifestation of the same phenomena is the row that broke out when some men described as Normans, whose place of origin is not made clear, claimed the right to strike the first blow at the Battle of Lincoln in 1217 fought against the invasion of England by Louis, Philip Augustus's son. The quarrel was only defused by the intervention of William Marshal's son, who is specifically said to have been born in Normandy.[78]

Historical writing in later twelfth-century Normandy has been characterized as symptomatic of 'the cultural ephemerality of *Normanitas*' or as 'nostalgia for a glorious past'.[79] Leaving aside for a moment whether we should continue even to use the word *Normanitas*, these assessments are understandable as a reflection of a perceived decline. But on another more appropriate standard of values, they can be seen as products of the organic processes typical of the history of empires. All empires cease to expand and thereafter have a long period of relative stability that can be characterized by a struggle to hold the empire together. When so much evidence points to the continuing resilience of cross-Channel networks and structures, it surely makes sense to interpret this historical writing in these terms.

A regular theme in the twelfth-century literary sources draws attention to Normandy as the place of origin of the diaspora of the Normans. In particular, Normandy is frequently written about in paternal or maternal terms in a range of sources ranging from the early-twelfth-century *Gesta Tancredi* of Ralph de Caen, written by a native of Normandy in all probability in Jerusalem, and referring to 'the unique glory of the fatherland',[80] to the *De Expugnatione Lyxbonensi*'s account of the capture of Lisbon in 1147, which is often argued to have been written in Suffolk.[81] The same theme is also present in Orderic Vitalis, Henry of Huntingdon, and the anonymous Rouen poem presented to Count Geoffrey of Anjou.[82] A variant thereof must surely be Orderic's reworking of his source for the events of the First Crusade, the *Historia Ierosolimitana* of Baudri of Bourgueil, in which he has the duke of Apulia and son of Robert Guiscard Roger Borsa treat the duke of Normandy, Robert Curthose, on his way to the First Crusade as his natural lord

---

[77] Thomas of Monmouth, *The Life and Miracles of William of Norwich*, ed. A. Jessopp and M. R. James (Cambridge, 1896), 178–9.
[78] *History of William Marshal*, ii, 312–13, ll. 16,204–24.
[79] Ashe, *Fiction and History*, 67; Shopkow, *History and Community*, 115–17.
[80] *Radulphi Cadomensis Tancredus*, ed. d'Angelo, 24 (*patriae suae gloriam prerogarent*) (*The Gesta Tancredi of Ralph of Caen: A History of the First Crusade*, ed. and trans. Bernard S. Bachrach and David S. Bachrach (Aldershot, 2005), 45). For comment on Ralph's treatment of identity, Natasha Hodgson, 'Reinventing Normans as Crusaders? Ralph of Caen's *Gesta Tancredi*', ANS, xxx (2008), 117–32, and esp. 126–7.
[81] *generis nostri mater Normannia*, *De Expugnatione Lyxbonensi*, 108–9 (translated, *Normans in Europe*, 273). For the text's authorship and discussion of identity, H. Livermore, 'The "Conquest of Lisbon" and its Author', *Portuguese Studies*, vi (1990), 1–16.
[82] OV, vi, 456–7 (*unde sue matris oculi crebro lacrimantur*); HH, 714–15 (*clarissimi Normannigene*). For the Rouen poem, see Chap. 1.

(*utpote naturalem dominum*);[83] similar considerations must explain his apparently more bizarre statement elsewhere that Robert de Grandmesnil, abbot of Saint-Evroult, was the natural lord of Robert Guiscard.[84]

The unique formulation of phrases that include the word *Normananglus* in the Warenne Chronicle, written in the second half of the 1150s, supplies a notably original statement of the notion of the two peoples as participants in empire.[85] The idea is also one that appears in the *Policraticus* of John of Salisbury, which was being written at almost the same time as the Warenne Chronicle, where the Normans and English are said to be united in a multifaceted confederation (*quia ibi Anglos et Normannos, quos iam multiplex confederatio uniuit*).[86] While a joint participation in empire is also as we saw in Chapter 2, implied by Henry of Huntingdon, Robert of Torigni, and Ailred of Rievaulx, none of them go as far as the Warenne Chronicle's author. When statements such as 'the triumph of Englishness' and, indeed, any assessment drawn from the knowledge that the empire was going to fail within half a century, are disregarded, it is a usage that encapsulates an evolution over almost a century from the empire's plural beginnings and an enduring sense of the two powerful identities at its heart, with the Norman being fuelled by the continuing dynamism of the cross-Channel world and the English by the ideological plurality present from the beginning. That the Warenne Chronicle's usage consistently places 'Norman' first must, however, surely reflect the continued domination of the cross-Channel elite. But it does allow for the flexibility of personal identity and cases such as, for example, a hypothetical, but entirely likely, individual who regarded himself or herself as being a full-blooded Norman residing permanently in England. The author was also capable of thinking of Normandy and England acting in unison. Thus, for example, after his account of the Battle of Brémule (1119), he commented that 'all of Normandy and England were elated with unexpected joy'.[87] However, given the peoples were hardly equal partners, it is probably no surprise that the formulation did not catch on. And given the already observed propensity of many writers to construct identity in terms of place of birth and place of residence, it cut against the grain of deeply entrenched literary norms. His contemporary John of Salisbury, for example, clearly wrote in terms of the inhabitants of England as being English and those of Normandy as being Norman, with Robert Curthose's crossings to England being described in terms of the invasion of a different kingdom from the one he was theoretically ruling, yet another demonstration of how contemporary mechanisms for expressing identity were inadequate in the face of a situation where power enforced plurality.[88]

---

[83] OV, v, 34–5. [84] OV, ii, 98; cf. Chibnall, *The World of Orderic Vitalis*, 125–6.
[85] For a convincing discussion of the word and its significance, *The Warenne (Hyde) Chronicle*, lxiii–lxviii.
[86] *Ioannis Saresberiensis episcopi Carnotensis Policratici*, ii, 616.
[87] *The Warenne (Hyde) Chronicle*, 78–9.
[88] *Ioannis Saresberiensis episcopi Carnotensis Policratici*, ii, 614. For John and identity, see Ilya Afanaseyev, '*In gente Britanniarum, sicut quaedam nostratum testatur historia*...: National Identity and Perceptions of the Past in John of Salisbury's *Policraticus*', *JMH*, xxxviii (2012), 278–94, at 282–3.

Over the period as a whole, an increasing emphasis on conflict and distrust between Normans and French is present in historical writing in Normandy. However the many meetings between Henry II and his sons and Louis VII and Philip Augustus are assessed, this enhancement of a long-established theme must reflect tensions and anxiety.[89] Wace, for example, at the very start of his *Roman de Rou* provides Henry II and Queen Eleanor with a lengthy homily on the consistently treacherous behaviour of the French and their aim to remove the Normans from Normandy, a subject to which he regularly returns.[90] Written approximately two decades later between 1180 and 1194, the *Roman des Franceis* of Andrew de Coutances, inspired by Wace's *Roman de Brut*, recently characterized as 'virulent anti-French propaganda', sets out a whole range of slanders, including, for example, an amusing subversion of the adoption of the Charlemagne legend as set out in the *Chanson de Roland*. But, although written in Normandy, it makes no mention of the Normans; instead the great 'historical' figure set up against Charlemagne is Arthur.[91] The place that Arthur might have taken in so-called Planatgenet/Angevin propaganda is a notably controversial subject, its content being double-edged and the link to the rulers' courts unproven. Yet its extraordinarily prolific introduction into the literary world of the cross-Channel empire must be testimony to an enduringly robust imperial identity and confidence; it is remarkable just how much Arthurian material was reproduced in Normandy, starting with Wace's *Roman de Brut*.[92]

From the time of Robert of Torigni, there exists both a continuation of writing on Norman identity and its insertion within a new framework with a predominantly imperial theme. The unfinished *Draco Normannicus* and other poems written by Stephen of Rouen not only adapted Wace's *Roman de Brut* into an extraordinary, and unfinished, poetic statement of red-blooded Norman superiority that included a prescription for future glories involving Norman independence and the conquest of France, it also had an embassy from the Emperor Frederick Barbarossa place him and Henry II on the same level and—of course—above the kings of France. It has him claim Brittany as Rollo's successor and compares Henry's courage with that of his predecessors, mentioning, for example, that, like William Rufus, he had set out to cross the Channel in rough weather.[93] And later, but before 1204, the *Gesta Normannorum Ducum* was adapted into a new vernacular history that concentrated mostly on the genealogies of the great Norman families already set out by Robert of Torigni, but which, after 1204, created new eulogies of the Norman past to set alongside a Franco-Norman present.[94] In this there was undoubtedly a realistic reappraisal of a historical role, but there is also yet another demonstration of a

---

[89] See, for example, Jean Dunbabin, 'Henry II and Louis VII', and John Gillingham, 'Doing Homage to the King of France', in Harper-Bill and Vincent (eds), *Henry II: New Interpretations*, 47–62, 63-84; Gillingham, 'The Meetings of the Kings of France and England', *passim*; Vincent, 'Some Effects of the Dynastic Alliances', 68–74.

[90] *Roman de Rou*, 2–3, part I, ll. 5–6, 43–69.

[91] Crouch, '*Roman des Franceis*', 178, 181, 182.

[92] Aurell, *The Plantagenet Empire*, 144–61, covers many issues.

[93] Stephen of Rouen, *Draco Normannicus*, in *Chronicles*, ii, 707, 720, 760–1.

[94] Gregory Fedorenko, 'The Thirteenth-Century *Chronique de Normandie*', *ANS*, xxxv (2013), 163–80, at 171–8.

flexible situational construct reworked as circumstances changed. A final manifestation of a continuingly robust Norman identity is provided by the poet Ambroise, who was in all probability from the Evrecin region of Normandy. Writing an account of the Third Crusade between 1194 and 1199, he explained the tensions between the natives and the northerners during Richard I's and his army's visit to the kingdom of Sicily on the grounds that the former had always hated the Normans because they had been conquered by them. And in a variant on the Normans versus French theme, he also wrote of King Philip Augustus's jealousy because it was Richard who carried out the successful attack on Messina.[95]

The relationship between the cross-Channel empire and the conquests in southern Italy conforms to a classic Weberian 'ideal type' of diaspora, as set out at the start of Chapter 2. The most obviously relevant features after the decline of the intense period of the eleventh-century migration and conquest are a sense of empathy and co-responsibility across settlements and a continued sense in the south of a link to the homeland. A situation of this kind must lie behind comments made in the second half of the twelfth century by the anonymous author, often referred to as Hugo Falcandus, who suggested that Roger II of Sicily (1101–54, and from 1130, king of Sicily) retained a special affection for those with the same ethnic origins as himself. That widely travelled man, John of Salisbury, also noted that Roger gave a special welcome to foreigners.[96] The number of individuals in the south who still drew attention to their Norman or French origins in the mid-twelfth century was also considerable, even if manifestly in decline.[97] The movement of information and ideas across the diaspora is further evidence of exchanges to which we cannot assign names or dates; just to read Orderic's *Historia* is a straightforward demonstration of this for the first decades of the twelfth century. It is notable, for example, that material deriving ultimately from Dudo of Saint-Quentin was apparently known to Anna Comnena and that the Arab geographer al-Idrīsī, who was commissioned by King Roger, apparently had special information about the tides of the river Orne at Caen and wrote enthusiastically about the charms and prosperity of Bayeux.[98] The relatively early appearance in the south of the new Norman hero King Arthur in the mosaic pavement in the cathedral at Otranto in Apulia, which is dated to between 1163 and 1166, is

---

[95] *The History of the Holy War: Ambroise's Estoire de la guerre sainte*, ed. Marianne Ailes and Malcolm Barber (Woodbridge, 2011), 39, 42–3.

[96] *La Historia o Liber de regno Sicilie e la Epistola ad Petrum Panormitane ecclesie Thesaurium di Ugo Falcando*, ed. G. B. Siragusa (Rome, 1897), 6 (translated, *The History of the Tyrants of Sicily by 'Hugo Falcandus', 1154–69*, trans. G. A. Loud and T. E. J. Wiedemann (Manchester, 1998), 58); *The Historia Pontificalis of John of Salisbury*, ed. M. Chibnall (London, 1956), 66.

[97] G. A. Loud, 'How "Norman" was the Norman Conquest of Southern Italy?', *Nottingham Medieval Studies*, xxv (1981), 13–34, at 20–5 (reprinted in *Conquerors and Churchmen in Norman Italy*, Chap. 2); Ménager, 'Pesanteur et étiologie', 194–6.

[98] G. A. Loud, 'Anna Komnena and her Sources for the Normans of Southern Italy', in Ian Wood and Graham Loud (eds), *Church and Chronicle in the Middle Ages: Essays presented to John Taylor* (London, 1991), 41–57, at 53 (*Conquerors and Churchmen in Norman Italy*, Chap. 13); Al-Idrīsī, *La première géographie de l'Occident*, trans. P. Jaubert and ed. Henri Bresc and Annliese Nef (Paris, 1999), 424–5.

another sign of vigorous cultural contact, as also may be the introduction into England of fallow deer and some hunting rituals.[99]

This material foregrounds the limitations of a historiography that poses the question of change in southern Europe solely in black-and-white terms such as 'how Norman were the principalities of southern Italy and Sicily and the subsequent kingdom of Sicily?'; to which, on my terms, the answer must be that they were both exceptionally Norman and scarcely Norman at all. The initial transformative stages were dominated by people who had come from Normandy and neighbouring regions, but once new units of power had been established, as in northern Europe, the descendants of the original migrants expressed their identity in relation to these new societies and became less readily disposed to welcome newcomers from the north, particularly potentially disruptive ones, while at the same time maintaining an infrastructure that facilitated the process of movement and made the society accessible to them. In the early stages, this had consisted of a welcome for useful soldiers and churchmen and a fresh base for those who were exiled from Normandy, or had felt it desirable to leave the duchy; this latter created an interesting symbiotic process since it actually encouraged movement between north and south, as well as migration.[100] But for the twelfth century, the subject is readily illustrated with many well-known examples, some of which, as is equally well known, turned out badly.[101] It is notable that, even in the three main late-eleventh- and early-twelfth-century histories of the southern Italian conquests, reference to the *gens Normannorum* fades away within each one of them as the ethnic plurality of the conquests evolved.[102]

However the truly remarkable cultural achievements of the southern conquests are interpreted, one central point is that, as in the northern Europe ones, the new rulers legitimated themselves as the successors to previous powers, in both secular and religious terms.[103] Ideologically therefore, the Normans were programmed to disappear at the same time that the act of conquest ensured that their memory would endure and that the social networks connecting them to northern Europe sustained what can legitimately be termed a Norman diaspora. In contrast to the North, however, the conquest of the southern Italian territories was gendered masculine; women did not move across the diaspora as they did across the northern European empire and the wealthiest members of the new elites intermarried with the survivors of the old ones as did not happen in England. An event such as Roger

---

[99] For the pavement, Loud, 'The Kingdom of Sicily and the Kingdom of England', 551; Alban Gautier. *Arthur* (Paris, 2007), 222, 228. For fallow deer and hunting rituals, Sykes, *Zooarchaeological Perspective*, 76–80, 96.

[100] See now, Ewan Johnson, 'The Process of Norman Exile into Southern Italy', in Laura Napran and Elisabeth van Houts (eds), *Exile in the Middle Ages: Selected Proceedings from the International Medieval Congress, University of Leeds, 8–11 July 2002* (Turnhout, 2002), 29–38.

[101] For some examples, Loud, 'Kingdom of Sicily', 550–1.

[102] Marie-Agnès Lucas-Avenel, 'La *Gens Normannorum* en Italie du Sud d'après les chroniques normandes du XIe siècle', in Véronique Gazeau, Pierre Bauduin, and Yves Modéran (eds), *Identité et Ethnicité: concepts, débats historiographiques, exemples (IIIe–XIIe siècle)* (Caen, 2008), 233–64, at 256–64.

[103] Most recently, Jeremy Johns, *Arabic Administration in Norman Sicily: The Royal Dīwān*, (Cambridge, 2002), with the argument set out at 1–7; Annliese Nef, *Conquérir de gouverner la Sicile islamique aux XIe et XIIe siècles* (Rome, 2011), 1–13, 22–44, 237–301, 429–76, 585–632.

II's legislation in 1140 to the effect that the money known as *romesine*, originally based on Rouen money, should no longer circulate within the kingdom of Sicily is just one of many steps that separated the new rulers from their northern European origins, but across the whole panoply of change, it must be an event of relatively minor significance.[104]

As the twelfth century progressed—and as is to be expected—the cross-currents of interests and loyalties cut across the diaspora. Thus, Orderic, while recording the exploits of the Normans in southern Italy enthusiastically in his interpolations into the *Gesta Normannorum Ducum*, became more critical of the new southern Italian rulers in the *Historia Ecclesiastica* and stopped inserting material at all after 1130. Subsequently, an awareness of Normandy's history as the centre of a diaspora continued to be expressed within the duchy by, as already noted, Robert of Torigni and others.[105] Equally, however, the political and cultural differences between northern and southern Europe could be dramatically expressed, as when, for example, in response to Roger II's use of the papal schism of the 1130s to make himself a king, the Norman cleric Arnulf, then archdeacon of Sées and subsequently bishop of Lisieux (1141–81), described Roger, who was after all the first generation descendant of a man who had actually lived in Normandy, as a tyrant, 'the successor of Dionysius', and 'the purchaser of the empty name of king'.[106]

The southern Italian evidence reinforces this book's argument of a continuing strong Norman identity in the twelfth century. In making such an argument, however, it needs to be kept very clearly in mind that the frameworks for this assertion are those of an empire and a diaspora, both of which by definition assume, according to specific circumstances, an intermittent dilution and reinforcement of identity among many of the participants as time and generations pass. As in the North, the end came through a succession dispute and the failure of hard power that culminated in the kingdom of Sicily passing in 1194 into the hands of the Emperor Henry VI of Hohenstaufen (1190–7) and subsequently of his son Frederick II. Just as in England and Normandy after 1204, these conquests severed the link between political power and the enduring phenomenon of the diaspora. In both northern Europe and southern Europe the ultimate determinant of identity was hard power, or rather, its failure.

It is my hope that this book's arguments will convince its readers that the word *Normanitas* should never be used again. When it was first used, as it was by the late R. Allen Brown, the usage had a vague inclusiveness that was attractive and appealing.[107] But it has since become so deeply entrenched in the literature that

---

[104] L. Travaini, *La monetazione nell'Italia normanna* (Rome, 1995), 295–9. For a translation of the legislation, Hubert Houben, *Roger II of Sicily: A Ruler between East and West*, trans. Graham A. Loud and Diane Milburn (Cambridge, 2002), 159.

[105] Olivier Guyotjeannin, 'L'Italie méridionale vue du royaume de France', in Giosuè Musca (ed.), *Il Mezzogiorno normanno-svevo visto dall'Europa e dal mondo mediterraneo* (Bari, 1999), 143–75, at 147–52. See also the classic essay by E. M. Jamison, 'The Sicilian Norman Kingdom in the Mind of Anglo-Norman Contemporaries', *PBA*, xxiv (1938), 237–85, at 242–57.

[106] 'In Girardum Englolismensium Invectia', *MGH Libelli de Lite*, iii (Hanover,1897), 107.

[107] See Chap. 1.

it has acquired meanings that have gone far beyond the original intention, and which can appear to give the word a concreteness that simply cannot be justified. Within the analytical frameworks of situational constructionism, of empire, and of the diaspora, all of which posit elements of flexibility, subjectivity, and adjustment, it just does not have the precision of meaning to deal with factors influenced by context, circumstances, and change. By the same token, the supposed 'triumph' of Englishness was no triumph at all. This is because English identity never had to re-emerge; its continuation was made certain by the way in which the empire was created. It is also surely the case that triumph cannot be the word to describe the outcome of a process that involved so terrible a human catastrophe as occurred in and after 1066.[108] At the extreme of this discussion, a statement like there being 'no guarantee of the survival of English identity after the Conquest' is utterly misguided.[109] The survival of English identity was, in fact, not only guaranteed, but certain within an empire which was born plural. The issue was the terms on which it survived and evolved; it is on to this subject that attention should be focused.

On the eve of the empire's collapse in 1204, its rulers were the descendants of the conquerors of 1066. In terms of hierarchy, power resided with the same elite that it had always done. Their most powerful members spoke French as a first language, and perhaps as an only language. They intermarried with men and women of equivalent status who also spoke French.[110] They were heavily involved in the continuation of the cross-Channel empire and were expecting to draw profit from it. Their cultural influence spread deeply into society. As the twelfth century passed, and although the arguments are complex ones, the language of the law appears to have been predominantly French. The long-term influence in England of the French language was a profound and enduring one among the elite.[111]

Manifestly the processes of change over time meant that the local and regional became the dominant forces in many lives. In terms of personal identity, many who had once thought of themselves as Normans, Flemings, Bretons, or French, or whatever, would have come to regard themselves primarily as English. However, for pretty much everyone there were still two principal *gentes* within the kingdom of the English, one of whom was the *Angli* and the other the *Normanni* or *Franci*. The passage in the *Dialogue of the Exchequer* that mentions that, at the time of writing in the 1170s and 1180s, it had become impossible to distinguish between French and English is seriously misleading in relation to the history of empire, and indeed to the history of the English kingdom, unless evaluated carefully. It refers to the free classes who would be called upon to give evidence in the hundred courts.[112] As such it is reflective of the massive changes within local and regional societies that had

---

[108] For 'the triumph of Englishness', Thomas, *English and Normans*, 71.
[109] For the statement, Hadley, 'Ethnicity and acculturation', 246.
[110] For succinct surveys, Bartlett, *England under the Norman and Angevin Kings*, 486–90; Thomas, *English and Normans*, 377–90; Short, *Manual of Anglo-Norman*, 14–35.
[111] P. A. Brand, 'The Languages of the Law in Later Medieval England', in D. A. Trotter (ed.), *Multilingualism in Later Medieval Britain* (Woodbridge, 2000), 63–76, at 65–6; cit. Sharpe, 'Peoples and Languages', 13–14, 110 n. 295.
[112] Richard fitz Nigel, *Dialogus de Scaccario*, 82–3.

taken place since 1066, but, even as written, it acknowledges the existence within the kingdom of two distinct peoples. It does not encompass the dominant imperial elite. Furthermore, the celebrated episode involving the supposed anti-Englishness of Richard I's justiciar William de Longchamp is best viewed as a mixture of resentment at a clumsy political outsider and of the machinations of the future King John, rather than as an outbreak of anti-Norman English xenophobia.[113]

Although the literary sources describe the invaders of Ireland after 1169 as English, this does not mean that this is indicative of how the individuals who took part in the conquest and settlement regarded their personal identity.[114] It is clear, for example, that one of the main contemporary writers on whose testimony we rely, the author of *La Geste des Engleis en Yrlande* (formerly known as *The Song of Dermot and the Earl*), was using the term *Angli* to signify people living in the kingdom of the English. Thus, Henry II is described as 'the English king of England' and elsewhere as 'the duke of Normandy'.[115] And like authors such as Turgot in his *Life of St Margaret* or the author of the *Life of Gruffudd ap Cynan*, the author of *La Geste*—who, of course, wrote in French with an audience in the imperial elite in mind—also inserted passages about the history of the cross-Channel empire into the narrative, devoting, for example, a substantial passage to Strongbow's defence of Gisors for Henry II during the great revolt of 1173–4.[116] The evidence of writ-charters and other documents again demonstrates ethnic plurality and multilingualism and, in all likelihood, the hegemonic role of the French language.[117]

The history of identity and the end of empire is, therefore, best interpreted as a reflection of changing times that has much in common with the history of other historical empires. It fits with the history of a cross-Channel elite ready to defend the empire to its end and reluctant to give up after the collapse of 1204. It also fits with the history of an elite that for the most part remained socially exclusive to the end.

THE EMPIRE OF THE NORMANS

At the heart of this book are the histories of two continuing strong identities, the English and the Norman. The apparent paradox between this continuation and the evolution in England and the British Isles of new relationships and new individual and collective identities is actually not a paradox at all. It might look like a dilution of what has unhelpfully come to be called *Normanitas*, but it was, in fact, no such thing. It reflects the facts both that the empire was

---

[113] Thomas, *English and Normans*, 327–32; Gillingham, *Richard I*, 227–9.
[114] Above all, John Gillingham, 'The English Invasion of Ireland', in *The English*, 145–60, at 151–8.
[115] *The Deeds of the Normans in Ireland: La Geste des Engleis en Yrlande*, ed. Evelyn Mullaly (Dublin, 2002), 11, 121 (ll. 2,677, 2,680).
[116] *The Deeds of the Normans in Ireland*, 126–7, ll. 2,860–95.
[117] Gillingham, 'The English Invasion of Ireland', 153 ('Undoubtedly if we turn from chronicles to charters, any idea that the "adventus" was purely an English phenomenon disappears at once'); Sharpe, 'Peoples and Languages', 49–59, 115–16, with references to the spread of French as a language of communication across ethnic boundaries in Ireland at 115 n. 309.

created as a plurality and remained so to the end and that the two identities have continued from the end of empire to the present day. If inevitability in history is possible—and the adoption of a social science framework carries within it both the dangers and the opportunities implicit in this assumption—then the course of events was an inevitable evolutionary organic consequence of the phenomenon of empire and of the ideological principles that underlay this particular empire. And since inevitability in history is rarely possible, but certain outcomes are likely, the history of the cross-Channel empire must actually be seen as a rich tapestry of human agency operating around a complex, but ultimately definable, framework of norms, scripts, and rules. That this particular empire would fail seems to me always to have been a strong likelihood. But how, why, and when were all relatively unpredictable.

If ethnicity and empire must be associated, as they often are, then my phrase of choice is the empire of the Normans. This is because it associates the phenomenon of empire with the identity of the dominant *gens*, but does not make the cultural link between ethnicity and empire that is implied by the phrase 'the Norman Empire/empire'. The connection between empire and ethnicity that I do want to make is ultimately one that focuses on the power of the ruling elite and the changes that occurred because of the interactions between them and the multiple peoples and cultures with which they came into contact. The identities that existed within this process of change must make the empire of the Normans a descriptive simplification, but it is the best we have because it does at least home in on the predominant group. It also focuses on the centrality of Normandy as a place of memory to which emotional attachment was felt, and as the place on which the majority of transimperial networks converged right to the end. That its role was in certain respects exploitative, if not indeed parasitic, strengthens this argument further.

There is a strong temptation to plump for the 'Anglo-Norman Empire' as a solution to the problems of definition.[118] It deals effectively with territorial composition of an empire in which Normandy and England were always distinct entities. It also encompasses the multiple influences in play and the many instances of cultural fusion that occurred. And, of course, it also allows for the flexibility and mutability of personal identity in ways that dovetail exceedingly well with the central arguments of this book. Yet, it is not to be used lightly and without reflection. It is after all a modern way out of a cul-de-sac and not an ethnic identifier that has any significant place in the twelfth-century evidence. The author of the Warenne Chronicle did not obtain many disciples.[119] It has all the weaknesses of a compromise and not many of the strengths. It sidelines too much the history of power, the fact that the takeover of England's wealth was so extraordinarily comprehensive and the culture of the imperial elite so dominant. The empire of the Normans is preferable.

The phrases 'European change' and 'Europeanization' must be kept in the mix. Above all, they make the experience of empire one that relates it to the wider

---

[118] The phrase is used in Bartlett, *Making of Europe*, 47.
[119] Note the unexplained reference in the Ledger Book of Stoneleigh Abbey; Bates, 'Normandy and England', 878.

processes of change that affected medieval Europe, some of which can also be described in terms of a twelfth-century Renaissance. They reject the fallacies whereby cultural change is identified as Norman and by which all change is connected to the Norman Conquest and the processes that followed it. They restore the history of the duchy of Normandy to its rightful place within these processes of change and they recognize the agency of the various kingdoms and principalities of the British Isles in relation to the European continent. The danger, as has been recognized, is that they can be too vague and do not therefore allow for the agency of the regional and the local.[120] Ultimately, the answer can only be to operate on a case-by-case basis, a process that might seem tiresome, but which is the only safeguard against simplified labelling. It acknowledges the existence of multilayered change and human agency and choice, phenomena whose analysis my use of the term empire facilitates.

The empire's frequent crises and its proneness to disruption through accident could be used to justify David Crouch's classifications of it as 'the great artificial condominium of the kingdom of England and the duchy of Normandy which had existed under the Conqueror' and 'a continuation of the sort of tributary over-kingship which had been a political feature of western Europe since the end of the Roman Empire'.[121] There might ultimately here be something like a reference back to F. W. Maitland's 'a certain thoughtlessness or poverty of ideas'.[122] The empire was born philosophically conventional and it remained so. It failed to extract itself from the conceptual problems present at its creation and it paid the price. What existed might ultimately be thought to be based on hard power. And this—arguably—was not enough. Yet if we reflect further on Maitland's words, we must ponder the fact that the cross-Channel empire lasted for rather a long time. The sociological framework of early medieval warrior kingship, the skilful exploitation of resources and opportunities, and the simple human capacity to recover from setbacks played a central part in notable—if always morally controversial—achievements.

The argument set out throughout this book in favour of the use of the term empire is based ultimately on written and architectural rhetoric, on an elite dedicated to the empire's continuation and therefore possessed of an imperial ethos, on a continuing imperial dynamic, and on a cultural influence within and beyond the core that transcended the limitations implied by the phrases 'great artificial condominium' and 'tributary over-kingship'. It accepts philosophical conventionality, but it ultimately proposes that such a formulation is too limited to do justice to the hierarchical strength and ethos, historical significance, political sophistication, and sheer creativity of what I want to call an empire. Peter Heather's characterization of the Norman Conquest of England as 'small-scale elite transfer' has merit because of the contrasts drawn with earlier migrations and the absence of disruption to existing structures in

---

[120] See the reflections by Huw Pryce, 'Welsh Rulers and European Change', 38–40, with the neat insertion of the word 'perhaps' into a variant of one of Rees Davies's statements at 39 (cf. Davies, *First English Empire*, 170: 'Anglicization may be interpreted as the distinctively insular version of this process of Europeanization'); Arnoux, 'Dynamics et réseaux', 57–8, 69–70.
[121] Crouch, *The Reign of King Stephen*, 14, 15. [122] For Maitland, see Chap. 4.

the conquered lands because of the overall control that was maintained.[123] But I doubt that the phrase does justice to the continuing cross-Channel dynamism that is a theme of this book; the use of the word 'transfer' implies a one-directionality that is easily disprovable. A framework that might be brought into play is the phrase 'archaic globalization' that does allow for the dissemination of values, but in ways that lack the full paraphenalia of modern empires.[124] If its use involves rejection of the term empire, however, it creates unsolvable difficulties in relation to earlier empires, above all, the Roman. Like 'artificial condominium' and 'small-scale elite transfer' it helps to define terms and reflect on the nature of power. But—ultimately—my argument is couched in a model of a universal human phenomenon and, for this reason, the use of the term empire is a valid one.

It is perfectly possible to have both a 'first English Empire' and an 'empire of the Normans' in existence at the same time. The first is a categorization that limits its focus to the history of the English state and of the British Isles. The second introduces the continental dimension, while at the same time recognizing that after 1066 the new rulers took on the ideological and political apparatus within England and the British Isles that they believed they had inherited from their predecessors. Just as Henry of Huntingdon did, it makes the empire of the Normans an episode in the history of the English people. The start-date of the first English empire must therefore be placed in the tenth century in the reign of Æthelstan, and not in 1093.[125] The changes that occurred after 1093 undoubtedly gave the continuing English empire a distinctive history after that date, but in what ways it was distinctive in relation to what might have happened if Harold had been the winner in 1066 can only be speculated about. It is surely probable that, if the political ambitions of the English kings had been concentrated much more single-mindedly on the British Isles than was the case after 1066, then hegemonic power would have been advanced more energetically. For these reasons I doubt the validity of opinions that suggest that the Continental empires strengthened the powers of the English kings within the British Isles. In all probability, they did not do so because the rulers were so occupied south of the Channel.

On the other hand, Rees Davies apparently believed that the interest of the rulers of the cross-Channel empire in the British Isles was intermittent:

> Neither John nor his predecessors of course had a policy for, or even a vision of, the British Isles as such. The centre of gravity of their ambitions and anxieties, and those of their political elites, were primarily European and English. Within such a world the outer zones of the British Isles were generally of secondary interest.[126]

---

[123] Heather, *Empires and Barbarians*, 23, 298–9, 327, 350–1, 614.
[124] C. A. Bayly, ' "Archaic" and "Modern" Globalization in the Eurasian and African Arena, c.1750–1850', in A.G. Hopkins (ed.), *Globalization in World History* (London, 2002), 47–73. See also Miri Rubin, *The Global 'Middle Ages'*, The Reuter Lecture, 2007 (University of Southampton, 2008), esp. 4–6, 20–3.
[125] Molyneaux, 'Why Were Some Tenth-Century English Kings?', 77–82, proposes similar arguments.
[126] Davies, *The First English Empire*, 18.

While 'of secondary interest' is undoubtedly justified, it is actually as good as certain that they had no choice but to concentrate their activities where they did. To suggest that William the Conqueror, his two sons, and Henry II had no policy towards the kingdom of the Scots and the various Welsh rulers therefore seems to me to be misguided. The networks established, above all by Henry I and David I, were to have the most fundamental long-term importance and they maintained something close to an equilibrium that sustained the long-term survival of the cross-Channel empire. The creation of the imperial infrastructure was from the beginning a mechanism that envisaged a continuation of imperial power within the British Isles. If this is not policy, I do not know what is.

The sequel that must follow on from this book is an examination of its arguments that is built on the creation of many more life-stories for the whole period from 1066 to 1204 than have featured here. This examination must be cross-Channel in its focus and ethos. In arguing for powerful cross-Channel networks and a continuing dynamism, as well as for change and political turbulence being disturbances that shook but did not, until the end, seriously threaten the infrastructure of empire, it sets up the case for an analysis based on all available evidence for every individual in order to balance the significance in their lives of the local, the regional, the national, and the imperial. This involves the classic process of collecting information on the location of lands, marriages, the careers of siblings, lords, and religious patronage in which others have already engaged within carefully, and appropriately defined, limits. It must unlock the enormous richness of those archives in Normandy and northern France that remain unexplored. And above all, it requires that an analytical framework be created for analysing the material collected. The case studies set out throughout this book suggest how this might be done. It is crucial to unearth the stories beneath the surface. Prosopography is but the starting point. The creation of life histories is what matters. By this means the disconnected historiographies mentioned in Chapter 1 can be moulded into a whole.

As to the argument that maritime empires are intrinsically weaker than land-based ones, I do not think that it applies in this case.[127] This is partly because the distances involved in cross-Channel communication were (and are) relatively short ones, but it also relies on the point that no attempt was ever made seriously to disrupt the empire's cross-Channel lines of communication. The technologies of military power did not encompass this possibility. The problem was, in fact, land-based, namely Normandy's accessibility on all frontiers to invasion by hostile powers. The cost of defending Normandy throughout the history of the empire has often been alluded to. By taxing so heavily the rulers of the cross-Channel empire had from the 1180s to seek for the first time the consent of their subjects.[128] To say that this leads directly to Magna Carta and parliamentary representation is of course too deterministic. But the speculative juxtaposition of this particular 'what if?' with that of an English monarchy inheriting from a victorious King Harold II, a man who would have been able to deploy a quite extraordinary

---

[127] See Chap. 2.
[128] J. R. Maddicott, *The Origins of the English Parliament, 924–1327* (Oxford, 2010), 97–105, 119–26.

charismatic military reputation, and then nurturing the massive landed resources that he would have controlled is at least grounds for thought. This could have been the foundation for an English state of an authoritarian kind very different from the one that did evolve.

This book has argued that the history of the empire of the Normans was a creative one and an exploitative one after the fashion of many empires. It foregrounds empire as a political science model and bases its argument around this framework. It makes power and human agency creative forces and relegates that of ethnicity, while not totally embracing a social constructionist approach. In the end the book's theme is that national histories and national identities do matter, but not as self-contained frameworks of analysis. It is a history of the Normans, the English, the French, the Welsh, the Scots, and the Irish, all of whom are happily still with us.[129] Since it makes no bones about empire being exploitative, it is entirely legitimate to analyse some aspects of the history of England during this period as those of a colony, but within the history of an empire that was born and died plural.

On the basis of my analysis, the period from 1066 to 1204 must be a very important period in English, British, French, and European history. Although my argument is ultimately one based on the creative powers of the phenomenon of empire, it is intended to make it in the most humane way possible. The achievement is one of all the peoples involved in the history of the empire of the Normans, both victors and vanquished, of all who participated and shaped the new world that emerged out of the crucible of conquest and violence. This book does make the case for there having been a Norman achievement. But it is not the Norman achievement in which earlier generations believed.

---

[129] Anthony D. Smith, *The Nation in History* (Hanover, NH, 2000), 61–77.

Bibliography

PRIMARY SOURCES

Les actes de Guillaume le Conquérant et de la reine Mathilde pour les abbayes caennaises, Mémoires de la Société des Antiquaires de Normandie 37, ed. L. Musset (Caen, 1967).
Actes des comtes de Flandre, 1071–1128, ed. F. Vercauteren (Brussels, 1938).
The Acts of Welsh Rulers, 1120–1283, ed. Huw Pryce (Cardiff, 2005).
Actus Pontificum Cenomannensis in Urbe Degentium, ed. G. Busson and A. Ledru, Société des Archives Historiques du Maine (Le Mans, 1902).
AILRED OF RIEVAULX, *De Genealogia Regum Anglorum*, in *PL*, cxcv, cols. 711–38.
——*Relatio de Standardo*, in *Chronicles*, iii, 185–9, 192–3.
——*The Historical Works*, trans. Jane Patricia Freeland and Marsha L. Dutton, Cistercian Fathers Series, no. 56 (Kalamazoo, 2005).
AL-IDRĪSĪ, *La première géographie de l'Occident*, trans. P. Jaubert and ed. Henri Bresc and Annliese Nef (Paris, 1999).
The Anglo-Saxon Chronicle: A Collaborative Edition. 17: The Annals of St Neots with 'Vita Primi Sancti Neoti', ed. David N. Dumville and Michael Lapidge (Cambridge, 1984).
The Anglo-Saxon Chronicle: A Collaborative Edition. Volume 6: ms. D, ed. G. P. Cubbin (Cambridge, 1996).
The Anglo-Saxon Chronicles, trans. and ed. Michael Swanton (London, 2000).
ANONYMOUS OF BÉTHUNE, *Histoire des ducs de Normandie et des rois d'Angleterre*, ed. Francisque Michel (Paris, 1840).
Basset Charters, c.1120 to 1250, ed. William T. Reedy, Pipe Roll Society, new ser., l (London, 1995, for 1989–91).
BAUDRI OF BOURGUEIL, 'Baudri of Bourgueil, "To Countess Adela"', trans. Monika Otter, *Journal of Medieval Latin*, xi (2001), 60–141.
'The *Brevis Relatio de Guillelmo nobilissimo comite Normannorum* written by a Monk of Battle Abbey', ed. Elisabeth M. C. van Houts, *Camden Miscellany*, 5th ser., x (Cambridge, 1997) (reprinted in Elisabeth M. C. van Houts, *History and Family Traditions*, Chap. 7).
BRUNO, 'De Bello Saxonico', ed. F. Schmale, in *Quellen zur Geschichte Kaiser Heinrich IV* (Darmstadt, 1963).
Brut y Tywysogyon or the Chronicle of the Princes, Peniarth MS 20 Version, trans. Thomas Jones (Cardiff, 1952).
Brut y Tywysogyon or the Chronicle of the Princes, Red Book of Hergest Version, trans. Thomas Jones (Cardiff, 1955).
Calendar of Documents preserved in France Illustrative of the History of Great Britain and Ireland, ed. J. H. Round (London, 1899).
The Carmen de Hastingae Proelio of Guy Bishop of Amiens, ed. F. Barlow, OMT (Oxford, 1999).
Le Cartulaire de l'abbaye bénédictine de Saint-Pierre-de-Préaux (1034–1227), ed. Dominique Rouet (Paris, 2005).
Cartulaire de l'abbaye de Saint-Vincent du Mans, ed. R. Charles and M. le vicomte Menjot d'Elbenne (Le Mans, 1913).
Le cartulaire du chapitre cathédral de Coutances, ed. Julie Fontanel (Saint-Lô, 2003).

Cartularium Abbathiae de Whiteby, ed. J. C. Atkinson, 2 vols, Surtees Society, vols lxix, lxii (1879–81).
Cartulary of the Abbey of Mont-Saint-Michel, ed. K. S. B. Keats-Rohan (Donnington, 2006).
Charters and Custumals of the Abbey of Holy Trinity Caen, ed. Marjorie Chibnall, British Academy Records of Social and Economic History, new series, v (Oxford, 1982).
Charters and Custumals of the Abbey of Holy Trinity Caen, Part 2: The French Estates, ed. John Walmsley, British Academy Records of Social and Economic History, new series, xxii (Oxford, 1994).
The Charters of King David I, ed. G. W. S. Barrow (Woodbridge, 1999).
'Charters of the Earldom of Hereford, 1095–1201', ed. David Walker, *Camden Miscellany*, xxii, Camden, 4th ser., i (1964).
Charters of the Honour of Mowbray, 1107–1191, ed. Diana E. Greenway, British Academy Records of Social and Economic History, new series, vol. i (Oxford, 1972).
Charters of the Redvers Family and the Earldom of Devon, 1090–1217, ed. Robert Bearman, Devon and Cornwall Record Society, new series (Exeter, 1994).
Chartes du prieuré de Longueville, ed. Paul Le Cacheux, Société de l'Histoire de Normandie (Rouen, 1934).
The Chronicle of Battle Abbey, ed. Eleanor Searle, OMT (Oxford, 1980).
Chronicle of John of Worcester, ed. R. R. Darlington and P. McGurk, vols ii and iii, OMT (Oxford, 1995–8).
Chronicle of Melrose, ed. Alan Orr Anderson and Marjorie Ogilvie Anderson (London, 1936).
The Chronicle of Melrose Abbey: A Stratigraphic Edition. I. Introduction and Facsimile, ed. Dauvit Broun and Julian Harrison, Scottish History Society (Woodbridge, 2007).
Chronicle of Robert of Torigni, Abbot of the Monastery of St Michael-in-Peril-of the Sea, in *Chronicles*, vol. iv.
'Chronicon Sancti Huberti Andaginensis', ed. L. Bethmann and W. Wattenbach, MGH, *Scriptores*, viii, 565–630.
Chronique de Robert de Torigni, abbé du Mont-Saint-Michel, suivie de divers opuscules historiques de cet auteur et de plusieurs religieux de la même abbaye, ed. Léopold Delisle, 2 vols, Société de l'Histoire de Normandie (Rouen, 1872–3).
'Chronique de Sainte-Barbe-en-Auge', in Mathieu Arnoux (ed.), *Des clercs au service de la réforme*, Bibliotheca Victorina, vol. xi (Turnhout, 2000), 275–93.
Chroniques latines du Mont Saint-Michel (IXe-XIIe siècle), ed. Pierre Bouet and Olivier Desbordes (Caen and Avranches, 2009).
Councils and Synods, with other Documents relating to the English Church, I: A.D. 871–1204, ed. D. Whitelock, M. Brett, and C. N. L. Brooke, 2 vols (Oxford, 1981).
De Expugnatione Lyxbonensi, ed. C. W. David (New York, 1936; 2nd edn., New York, 2001).
Die Gesetze der Angelsachsen, ed. F. Liebermann, 3 vols (Halle, 1903–16).
Die Krezzugsbriefe aus dem Jahren, 1088–1100, ed. H. Hagenmeyer (Innsbruck, 1901).
Diplomatic Documents Preserved in the Public Record Office, ed. Pierre Chaplais, i (1101–1272) (London, 1964).
Documents de l'Histoire de la Normandie, ed. Michel de Boüard (Toulouse, 1972).
Domesday Book, seu Liber Censualis Willelmi Primi regis Angliae, 2 vols, ed. Abraham Farley (London, 1783).
Domesday Monachorum of Christ Church, Canterbury, ed. D. C. Douglas (London, 1944).
DUDO OF SAINT-QUENTIN, *De Moribus et Actis primorum Normanniae Ducum*, ed. Jules Lair (Caen, 1865).
——*History of the Normans*, trans. Eric Christiansen (Woodbridge, 1998).

EADMER, *Historia Nouorum in Anglia*, ed. Martin Rule, Rolls Series (London, 1884).
Early Yorkshire Charters, vols iv–xii, ed. C. T. Clay, Yorkshire Archaeological Society Record Series, (Wakefield, 1935–65).
The Ecclesiastical History of Orderic Vitalis, ed. and trans. Marjorie Chibnall, 6 vols, OMT (Oxford, 1969–80).
Encomium Emmae Reginae, ed. Alistair Campbell, with a supplementary introduction by Simon Keynes, Camden Classic Reprints, 4 (Cambridge, 1998).
English Episcopal Acta II: Canterbury, 1162–1190, ed. C. R. Cheney and B. E. A. Jones (Oxford, 1986).
English Lawsuits from William I to Richard I, ed. R. C. van Caenegem, 2 vols, Selden Society, vols cvi–cvii (London, 1990–1).
'*Epistulae Fiscannenses*: lettres d'amitié, de gouvernement et d'affaires', ed. J. Laporte, *Revue Mabillon*, xliii (1953), 5–31.
Facsimiles of English Royal Writs to A.D. 1100 presented to V. H. Galbraith, ed. T. A. M. Bishop and P. Chaplais (Oxford, 1957).
The Foundation History of the Abbeys of Byland and Jervaulx, ed. Janet Burton, Borthwick Texts and Studies, no. 35 (York, 2006).
'Fulcoii Belvacensis epistolae', ed. M. Colker, *Traditio*, x (1954), 191–273.
GEFFREI GAIMAR, *Estoire des Engleis (History of the English)*, ed. and trans. Ian Short (Oxford, 2009).
GEOFFREY GROSSUS, 'Vita Beati Bernardi Tironiensis', *PL*, clxii, cols. 1367–1446 (trans. Ruth Harwood Cline, *The Life of the Blessed Bernard of Tiron/Geoffrey Grossus* (Washington, DC, 2009)).
GEOFFREY OF MONMOUTH, *The History of the Kings of Britain*, ed. Michael D. Reeve and trans. Neil Wright (Woodbridge, 2007).
GERALD OF WALES, *Giraldus Cambrensis, Opera Omnia*, ed. J. S. Brewer, J. F. Dimock, and G. F. Warner, 8 vols, Rolls Series (London, 1861–91).
—— *De invectionibus*, ed. W. S. Davies, *Y Cymmrodor*, xxx (1920), 1–248.
GERVASE OF TILBURY, *Otia Imperialia: Recreation for an Emperor*, ed. and trans. S. E. Banks and J. W. Binns, OMT (Oxford, 2002).
The Gesta Guillelmi of William of Poitiers, ed. and trans. R. H. C. Davis and Marjorie Chibnall, OMT (Oxford, 1998).
The Gesta Normannorum ducum of William of Jumièges, Orderic Vitalis, and Robert of Torigni, ed. and trans. Elisabeth M. C. van Houts, 2 vols, OMT (Oxford, 1992–5).
Gesta Stephani, ed. and trans. K. R. Potter and R. H. C. Davis, OMT (Oxford, 1976).
The Gesta Tancredi of Ralph of Caen: A History of the First Crusade, ed. and trans. Bernard S. Bachrach and David S. Bachrach (Aldershot, 2005).
GOSCELIN OF SAINT-BERTIN, *Historia maior sancti Augustini*, *Acta Sanctorum*, ed. D. Papebroch, May, vi (Antwerp, 1688), 374–95.
The Great Roll of the Pipe for the Thirty-First Year of King Henry I, Michaelmas 1130, ed. Judith Green, Pipe Roll Society, new series, vol. lvii (2012).
Guglielmo di Puglia, Le Gesta di Roberto il Guiscardo, ed. Francesco de Rosa (Cassino, 2003).
Guibert de Nogent, Autobiographie, ed. E.-R. Labande (Paris, 1981).
Guibertus abbas S. Mariae Nogenti, Gesta Dei per Francos, ed. R. B. C. Huygens, Corpus Christianorum Continuatio Medievalis, no.127A (Turnhout, 1996) (*The Deeds of God through the Franks: A Translation of Guibert of Nogent's* 'Gesta Dei per Francos', trans. R. Levine (Woodbridge, 1997)).
HENRY, ARCHDEACON OF HUNTINGDON, *Historia Anglorum: The History of the English People*, ed. and trans. Diana Greenway, OMT (Oxford, 1996).

Historia Ecclesie Abbendonensis: The History of the Church of Abingdon, vol. ii, ed. and trans. John Hudson, OMT (Oxford, 2002).
Historia et Cartularium monasterii sancti Petri Gloucestriae, ed. W. H. Hart, 3 vols, Rolls Series (London, 1863–7).
La Historia o Liber de regno Sicilie e la Epistola ad Petrum Panormitane ecclesie Thesaurium di Ugo Falcando, ed. G. B. Siragusa (Rome, 1897), 6 (trans., *The History of the Tyrants of Sicily by 'Hugo Falcandus', 1154–69*, trans. G. A. Loud and T. E. J. Wiedemann (Manchester, 1998)).
Historians of the Church of York and its Archbishops, ed. J. Raine, 2 vols, Rolls Series (London, 1879–94).
History and Politics in Late Carolingian and Ottonian Europe: The 'Chronicle' of Regino of Prüm and Adalbert of Magdeburg, trans. and annotated by Simon MacLean (Manchester, 2009).
The History of the Holy War: Ambroise's Estoire de la guerre sainte, ed. Marianne Ailes and Malcolm Barber (Woodbridge, 2011).
History of William Marshal, ed. A. J. Holden, with English translation by S. Gregory and historical notes by D. Crouch, 3 vols, Anglo-Norman Text Society, Occasional Publications Series, nos. 4–6 (London, 2004–6).
HUGH OF FLAVIGNY, *Chronicon*, MGH, *Scriptores*, viii, 280–502.
HUGH THE CHANTER, *The History of the Church of York, 1066–1127*, ed. Martin Brett, C. N. L. Brooke, and Michael Winterbottom, OMT (Oxford, 1990).
'In Girardum Englolismensium Invectia', MGH *Libelli de Lite*, iii (Hanover, 1897), 81–108.
Inventio et miracula sancti Vulfranni, ed. J. Laporte, Société de l'Histoire de Normandie, Mélanges, xiv (Rouen and Paris, 1938).
JOHN OF SALISBURY, *Ioannis Saresberiensis episcopi Carnotensis Policratici sive de Nugis Curialium et Uestigiis Philosophorum Libri VIII*, ed. C. C. I. Webb, 2 vols (Oxford, 1909).
——*Historia Pontificalis: Memoirs of the Papal Court*, ed. Marjorie Chibnall, OMT (Oxford, 1986).
Letters of Lanfranc, Archbishop of Canterbury, ed. and trans. Helen Clover and Margaret Gibson, OMT (Oxford, 1979).
Liber Confortatorius of Goscelin of Saint Bertin, ed. C. H. Talbot, in *Analecta Monastica: textes et études sur la vie des moines au moyen âge*, ed. M. M. Lebreton *et al* (Rome, 1955) (trans. Goscelin of St Bertin, *The Book of Encouragement and Consolation (Liber confortatorius)*, trans. Monika Otter (Cambridge, 2004)).
Liber Eliensis, ed. E. O. Blake, Camden, 3rd ser., xcii (1962) (trans. *Liber Eliensis: A History of the Isle of Ely from the Seventh Century to the Twelfth*, trans. Janet Fairweather (Woodbridge, 2005)).
Life of Christina of Markyate: A Twelfth Century Recluse, ed. and trans. C. H. Talbot (Oxford, 1959; reprinted, 1987).
Life of King Edward who rests at Westminster, attributed to a monk of Saint-Bertin, ed. Frank Barlow, 2nd edn., OMT (Oxford, 1992).
Life of St Anselm by Eadmer, ed. and trans. R. W. Southern, OMT (Oxford, 1972).
Llandaff Episcopal Acta, 1140–1287, ed. David Crouch, South Wales Record Society (Cardiff, 1988).
Memorials of Saint Edmund's Abbey, ed. Thomas Arnold, Rolls Series, 3 vols (London, 1890–96).
Miracula sanctae Catharinae Rotomagensis, ed. A. Poncelet, *Analecta Bollandiana*, xxii (1903), 423–38.

Newington Longueville Charters, ed. H. E. Salter, Oxfordshire Record Society, iii (1921).
Papsturkunden, 896–1046, ed. Harald Zimmermann, 2 vols, Denkschriften des Osterreichischen akademie der Wissenschaft phil-hist.klasse (Vienna, 1984–5).
Papsturkunden in England, ed. W. Holtzmann, 3 vols (Berlin, 1930–52).
Patrologia cursus completus, series Latina, ed. J.-P. Migne, 221 vols (Paris, 1844–65).
The Peterborough Chronicle, 1070–1154, ed. Cecily Clark, 2nd edn. (Oxford, 1970).
The Peterborough Chronicle, ed. Dorothy Whitelock, Early English Manuscripts in Facsimile, iv (Copenhagen, 1954).
'QUADRIPARTITUS': 'The Prefaces of "Quadripartitus"', trans. Richard Sharpe, in George Garnett and John Hudson (ed.), *Law and Government in Medieval England and Normandy: Essays in Honour of Sir James Holt* (Cambridge, 1994), 148–72.
Radulphi Cadomensis Tancredus, ed. Edoardo d'Angelo, Corpus Christianorum, Continuatio mediaevalis, vol. ccxxxi (Turnhout, 2011).
Recueil des actes de Henri II, roi d'Angleterre et duc de Normandie, ed. L. Delisle and E. Berger, 4 vols (Paris, 1909–27).
Recueil des actes de Philippe Ier, roi de France (1059–1108), ed. Maurice Prou (Paris, 1908).
Recueil des actes des ducs de Normandie de 911 à 1066, ed. Marie Fauroux, Mémoires de la Société des Antiquaires de Normandie 36 (Caen, 1961).
Regesta Regum Anglo-Normannorum, 1066–1154, 3 vols (i, ed. H. W. C. Davis, Oxford 1913; ii, ed. Charles Johnson and H. A. Cronne, Oxford 1956; iii, ed. H. A. Cronne and R. H. C. Davis, Oxford, 1968).
Regesta Regum Anglo-Normannorum: The Acta of William I (1066–1087), ed. David Bates (Oxford, 1998).
RICHARD FITZ NIGEL, *Dialogus de Scaccario: The Dialogue of the Exchequer, and Constitutio Domus Regis, The Disposition of the King's Household*, ed. and trans. Emilie Amt and S. D. Church, OMT (Oxford, 2007).
RICHARD OF HEXHAM, *De gestis regis Stephani et de Bello Standardo*, in *Chronicles*, iii, 170.
Rodvlfi Glabri Historiarvm Libri Quinque, ed. and trans. John France, OMT (Oxford, 1989).
ROGER OF HOWDEN, *Chronica Rogeri de Houedene*, ed. W. Stubbs, 4 vols, Rolls Series (London, 1868–71).
Sancti Anselmi Opera Omnia, ed. F. S. Schmitt, 6 vols (Edinburgh, 1938–51).
SERLO OF BAYEUX, 'Quae monachi quaerunt' and 'De capta Bajocensium civitate', in *The Anglo-Latin Satirical Poets and Epigrammists of the Twelfth Century*, 2 vols, ed. T. H. Wright, Rolls Series (London, 1872), 202–7, 241–51.
STEPHEN OF ROUEN, *Draco Normannicus*, in *Chronicles*, vol. ii.
Stoke by Clare Cartulary: BL Cotton Appx. xxi, ed. Christopher Harper-Bill and Richard Mortimer, 3 vols, Suffolk Records Society (Woodbridge, 1982–4).
SYMEON OF DURHAM, *Libellus de Exordio atque Procursu istius, hoc est Dunhelmensis Ecclesie*, ed. and trans. David Rollason, OMT (Oxford, 2000).
THOMAS OF MONMOUTH, *The Life and Miracles of William of Norwich*, ed. A. Jessopp and M. R. James (Cambridge, 1896).
Two of the Saxon Chronicles Parallel, ed. Charles Plummer, 2 vols (Oxford, 1892–9).
Vie de Christina de Markyate, ed. and trans. Paulette L'Hermite-Leclercq and Anne-Marie Legras, 2 vols, Sources d'histoire médiévale, 35 (Paris, 2007).
Vita Griffini filii Conani: The Medieval Life of Gruffudd ap Cynan, ed. Paul Russell (Cardiff, 2005).
Vita Lanfranci, ed. Margaret Gibson, in D'Onofrio (ed.), *Lanfranco di Pavia*, 661–715.

Vita Sanctae Margaretae, trans. in Huneycutt, *Matilda of Scotland* (Woodbridge, 2003), 161–78.

WACE, *Wace's Roman de Brut: A History of the British*, trans. Judith Weiss, Exeter Medieval English Texts and Studies (Exeter, 1999).

——*History of the Norman People: Wace's Roman de Rou*, trans. Glyn S. Burgess (Woodbridge, 2004).

The Warenne (Hyde) Chronicle, ed. Elisabeth M. C. van Houts and Rosalind C. Love, OMT (Oxford, 2013).

WILLIAM OF MALMESBURY, *Early History of Glastonbury: An Edition, Translation and Study of William of Malmesbury's 'De Antiquitate Glastonie Ecclesie'*, ed. John Scott (Woodbridge, 1981).

——*Historia Novella: The Contemporary History*, ed. Edmund King and trans. K. R. Potter, OMT (Oxford, 1998), 32–3, 72–3.

—— *Gesta regum Anglorum: The History of the English Kings*, ed. and trans. R. A. B. Mynors, M. Winterbottom, and R. M. Thomson, 2 vols, OMT (Oxford, 1998–9).

—— *Gesta pontificum Anglorum: The History of the English Bishops*, ed. and trans. M. Winterbottom and R. M. Thomson, 2 vols, OMT (Oxford, 2007).

——*William of Malmesbury: Saints' Lives*, ed. and trans. M. Winterbottom and R. M. Thomson, OMT (Oxford, 2002).

WILLIAM OF NEWBURGH, *The History of English Affairs, Book I*, ed. P. G. Walsh and M. J. Kennedy (Warminster, 1988).

SECONDARY SOURCES

ABELS, Richard, 'Sheriffs, Lord-Seeking and the Norman Settlement of the South-East Midlands', *ANS*, xix (1997), 21–50.

ABRAMS, Lesley, 'Diaspora and Identity in the Viking Age', *EME*, xx (2012), 17–38.

ACEMOGLU, Daron, and ROBINSON, James A., *Why Nations Fail: The Origins of Power, Prosperity and Poverty* (London, 2012).

ADAM, J.-L., 'Le prieuré de Saint-Pierre de la Luthumière à Brix', *Revue catholique de Normandie*, ii (1892), 174–92.

AFANASEYEV, Ilya, '*In gente Britanniarum, sicut quaedam nostratum testatur historia*...: National Identity and Perceptions of the Past in John of Salisbury's *Policraticus*', *JMH*, xxxviii (2012), 278–94.

AIRD, William M., *St. Cuthbert and the Normans: the Church of Durham, 1071–1153* (Woodbridge, 1998).

—— *Robert Curthose, Duke of Normandy, c.1050–1134* (Woodbridge, 2008).

AIRLIE, Stuart, 'The Aristocracy', in Rosamond McKitterick (ed.), *The New Cambridge Medieval History*, vol. ii: *c.700–c.900* (Cambridge, 1995–2005), 431–50.

—— *Power and its Problems in Carolingian Europe* (Farnham and Burlington, VT, 2012).

ALBU, Emily, *The Normans in their Histories: Propaganda, Myth and Subversion* (Woodbridge, 2001).

ALLEN, Martin, *Mints and Money in Medieval England* (Cambridge, 2012).

ALLEN, Richard, 'Avant Lanfranc. Un réexamen de la carrière de Mauger, archevêque de Rouen (1037–1054/55)', in Julia Barrow and Véronique Gazeau (eds), *Autour de Lanfranc (1010–2010): réforme et réformateurs dans l'Europe du Nord-Quest (XIe–XIIe siècles)*, forthcoming.

AMT, Emilie, *The Accession of Henry II in England: Royal Government Restored, 1149–1159* (Woodbridge, 1993).

ANDRIEU-GUITRANCOURT, Pierre, *Histoire de l'Empire normand et de sa civilisation* (Paris, 1952).
ARNOUX, Mathieu, 'Conclusion', in *Normandie et Angleterre*, 359–63.
—— 'Dynamics et réseaux de l'Eglise régulière dans l'Ouest de la France (fin XIe-XIIe siècle)', in Jacques Dalarun (ed.), *Robert d'Arbrissel et la vie religieuse dans l'Ouest de la France: Actes du colloque de Fontevraud, 13–16 décembre 2001* (Turnhout, 2004), 57–70.
—— 'L'événement et la conjuncture. Hypothèses sur les conditions économiques de la conquête de 1204', in *1204*, 227–38.
—— and MANEUVRIER, Christophe, 'Deux abbayes de la Basse-Normandie: Notre-Dame du Val et le Val Richer', *Le Pays Bas-Normand*, nos. 237–8 (2000).
ASHE, Laura, *Fiction and History in England, 1066–1200* (Cambridge, 2007).
AUBÉ, Pierre, *Les Empires normands d'Orient, XIe-XIIIe siècle* (Paris, 1985; 2nd edn., Paris, 1991).
AURELL, Martin, *The Plantagenet Empire, 1154–1224*, trans. David Crouch (Harlow, 2007).
—— and BOUTOULLE, Frédéric (eds), *Les seigneuries dans l'espace Plantagenêt (c.1150–c.1250)* (Bordeaux, 2009).
AUSTIN, David, 'Little England beyond Wales: Re-defining the Myth', *Landscapes*, vi (2005), 30–62.
AYERS, Brian, 'Building A Fine City: The Provision of Flint, Mortar and Freestone in Medieval Norwich', in David Parsons (ed.), *Stone: Quarrying and Building in England, AD 43–1525* (Chichester, 1990), 217–28.
—— 'The Urban Landscape', in Rawcliffe and Wilson (eds), *Medieval Norwich*, 1–28.
BABCOCK, Robert S., 'Rhys ap Tewdwr, King of Deheubarth', *ANS*, xvi (1994), 21–35.
—— 'The Irish Sea Province and the Accession of Henry I', in Fleming and Pope (eds), *Henry I and the Anglo-Norman World*, 39–62.
BACHRACH, Bernard S., 'William Rufus' Plan for the Invasion of Aquitaine', in Richard P. Abels and Bernard S. Bachrach (eds), *The Normans and their Adversaries at War: Essays in Memory of C. Warren Hollister* (Woodbridge, 2001), 31–63.
BACHRACH, David S., *Religion and the Conduct of War, c.300–1215* (Woodbridge, 2003).
BAGGE, Sverre, *Kings, Politics and the Right Order of the World in German Historiography, c.950–1150* (Leiden, 2002).
BARLOW, Frank, *William I and the Norman Conquest* (London, 1965).
—— *The English Church, 1000–1066*, 2nd edn, (London/New York, 1979).
—— *The English Church, 1066–1154* (London, 1979).
—— *William Rufus*, 2nd edn. (New Haven, CT/London, 2000).
BARRATT, Nick, 'The Revenue of King John', *EHR*, cxi (1996), 835–55.
—— 'The English Revenues of Richard I', *EHR*, cxvi (2001), 635–56.
BARROW, Julia, 'Origins and Careers of Cathedral Canons in Twelfth-Century England', *Medieval Prosopography*, xxi (2000), 23–40.
—— 'Clergy in the Diocese of Hereford in the Eleventh and Twelfth Centuries', *ANS*, xxvi (2004), 37–53.
BARTHÉLEMY, Dominique, *La chevalerie* (Paris, 2007).
—— 'The Chivalric Transformation and the Origins of Tournament as seen through Norman Chroniclers', *HSJ*, xx (2009, for 2008), 141–60.
BARTLETT, Robert, *Gerald of Wales, 1146–1223* (Oxford, 1982).
—— *The Making of Europe: Conquest, Colonisation and Cultural Change, 950–1350* (London, 1994).
—— 'Cults of Irish, Scottish and Welsh Saints in Twelfth-Century England', in Brendan Smith (ed.), *Britain and Ireland, 900–1300: Insular Responses to Medieval European Change* (Cambridge, 1999), 67–86.

—— *England under the Norman and Angevin Kings, 1075–1225* (Oxford, 2000).
—— 'Heartland and Border: The Mental and Physical Geography of Medieval Europe', in Pryce and Watts (eds), *Power and Identity*, 23–36.
BARTON, Richard E., *Lordship in the County of Maine, c.890–1160* (Woodbridge, 2004).
—— 'Henry I, Count Helias of Maine and the Battle of Tinchebray', in Fleming and Pope (eds), *Henry I and the Anglo-Norman World*, 63–90.
BATES, David, 'The Character and Career of Odo, Bishop of Bayeux (1049/50–1097)', *Speculum*, l (1975), 1–20.
——*Normandy before 1066* (London/New York, 1982).
—— 'The Origins of the Justicarship', *ANS*, iv (1982), 1–12, 167–71.
—— 'The earliest Norman writs', *EHR*, c (1985), 266–84.
—— 'A Neglected English Charter of Robert Curthose, Duke of Normandy', *(BI)HR*, lix (1986), 121–4.
—— 'Normandy and England after 1066', *EHR*, civ (1989), 851–80.
—— 'The Rise and Fall of Normandy, *c.*911–1204', in *England and Normandy*, 19–35.
—— 'Les chartes de confirmation et les pancartes normandes du règne de Guillaume le Conquérant', in M. Parisse, P. Pégeot, and B.-M. Tock (eds), *Pancartes monastiques des XIe et XIIe siècles* (Turnhout, 1998), 95–109.
——*Re-ordering the Past and Negotiating the Present in Stenton's 'First Century'*, Stenton Lecture 1999 (University of Reading, 2000).
—— 'The Conqueror's Adolescence', *ANS*, xxv (2003), 1–18.
—— 'William the Conqueror and His Wider Western World', *HSJ*, xv (2006, for 2004), 73–87.
—— 'The Conqueror's Earliest Historians and the Writing of his Biography', in Bates, Crick, and Hamilton (ed.), *Writing Medieval Biography, 750–1250*, 129–41.
—— 'William the Conqueror, William fitz Osbern and Chepstow Castle', in Rick Turner and Andy Johnson (eds), *Chepstow Castle: Its History and Buildings* (Logaston Press, 2006), 15–22, 274–5.
—— 'The Representation of Queens and Queenship in Anglo-Norman Royal Charters', in Paul Fouracre and David Ganz (eds), *Frankland: Essays in Honour of Dame Jinty Nelson* (Manchester, 2008), 285–303.
—— 'Anger, Emotion and a Biography of William the Conqueror', in Nelson, Reynolds, and Johns (eds), *Gender and Historiography*, 21–33.
—— 'Robert of Torigni and the *Historia Anglorum*', in Roffe (ed.), *The English and Their Legacy*, 175–84.
——and CURRY, Anne (eds), *England and Normandy in the Middle Ages* (London/Rio Grande, 1994).
——and CRICK, Julia, and HAMILTON, Sarah (eds), *Writing Medieval Biography, 750–1250: Essays in honour of Professor Frank Barlow* (Woodbridge, 2006).
——and LIDDIARD, Robert (eds), *East Anglia and its North Sea World in the Middle Ages* (Woodbridge, 2013).
BAUDUIN, Pierre, *La première Normandie (X^e-XIe siècles). Sur les frontières de la haute Normandie: identité et construction d'une principauté* (Caen, 2004).
—— 'Les modèles anglo-normands en questions', in Raffaele Licinio and Francesco Violante (eds), *Nascita di un regno. Poteri signorili, istituzioni feudali e strutture sociali nel Mezzogiorno normanno (1130–1194)* (Bari, 2008), 51–97.
——*Le monde franc et les Vikings* (Paris, 2009).

BAXTER, Stephen, 'The Representation of Lordship and Land Tenure in Domesday Book', in Hallam and Bates (eds), *Domesday Book*, 73–102.
—— *The Earls of Mercia: Lordship and Power in Late Anglo-Saxon England* (Oxford, 2007).
—— 'Lordship and Labour', in Crick and van Houts (eds), *A Social History of England*, 98–114.
—— 'The Making of Domesday Book and the Languages of Lordship in Conquered England', in Tyler (ed.), *Conceptualizing Multilingualism*, 271–308.
BAYLÉ, Maylis (ed.), *L'architecture normande au Moyen Age*, 2 vols (Caen and Condé-sur-Noireau, 1997).
BAYLY, C. A., '"Archaic" and "Modern" Globalization in the Eurasian and African Arena, *c.*1750–1850', in A. G. Hopkins (ed.), *Globalization in World History* (London, 2002), 47–73.
—— *The Birth of the Modern World, 1780–1914* (Oxford, 2004).
BEARMAN, Richard, 'Baldwin de Redvers: Some Aspects of a Baronial Career in the Reign of King Stephen', *ANS*, xviii (1996), 17–45.
—— 'Revières, Baldwin de, earl of Devon (*c.*1095–1155)', *ODNB*.
BEECH, George, 'Aquitanians and Flemings in the Refoundation of Bardney Abbey (Lincolnshire) in the Later Eleventh Century', *HSJ*, i (1989), 73–90.
BENHAM, J. E. M., 'Anglo-French Peace Conferences in the Twelfth Century', *ANS*, xxvii (2005), 52–67.
BERG, Mary, and JONES, Howard, *Norman Churches in the Canterbury Diocese* (Stroud, 2009).
BERKHOFER III, Robert F., *Day of Reckoning: Power and Accountability in Medieval France* (Philadelphia, PA, 2004).
BIENVENU, Jean-Marc, 'L'ordre de Fontevraud et la Normandie au XIIe siècle', *AN*, xxv (1985), 3–15.
BINNS, Alison, *Dedications of Monastic Houses in England and Wales, 1066–1216* (Woodbridge, 1989).
BISSON, Thomas N., *The Crisis of the Twelfth Century: Power, Lordship and the Origins of European Government* (Princeton, NJ/Oxford, 2009).
BLACKER, Jean, '"Ne vuil sun livre translater": Wace's Omission of Merlin's Prophecies from the *Roman de Brut*', in Ian Short (ed.), *Anglo-Norman Anniversary Essays*, Anglo-Norman Text Society, Occasional Publications Series, no. 2 (London, 1993), 49–59.
—— 'Where Wace Feared to Tread: Latin Commentaries on Merlin's Prophecies in the Reign of Henry II', *Arthuriana*, vi (1995), 36–52.
BLAIR, John, *Anglo-Saxon Oxfordshire* (Stroud, 1995).
BLAKELY, Ruth M., *The Brus Family in England and Scotland, 1100–1295* (Woodbridge, 2005).
BLANCHARD, Ian, 'Lothian and Beyond: The Economy of the "English Empire" of David I', in R. H. Britnell and J. Hatcher (eds), *Progress and Problems in Medieval England: Essays in Honour of Edward Miller* (Cambridge, 1996), 23–45.
BÖKER, Hans J., 'The Bishop's Chapel at Hereford Cathedral and the Question of Architectural Copies in the Middle Ages', *Gesta*, xxxvii (1998), 44–54.
BOLTON, J. L., 'The English Economy in the Early Thirteenth Century', in Church (ed.), *King John: New Interpretations*, 27–40.
BOUET, Pierre, 'Orderic Vital, lecteur critique de Guillaume de Poitiers', in C. E. Viola (ed.), *Medievalia Christiana, xie–xiiie siècles. Hommage à Raymonde Foreville de ses amis, ses collègues et ses anciens élèves* (Paris, 1989), 25–50.

―― 'Les Normands, le nouveau people élu', in Pierre Bouet and François Neveux (eds), *Les Normands en Méditerranée dans le sillage des Tancrède* (Caen, 1994), 239–52.

―― and NEVEUX, François (eds), *Les Saints dans la Normandie médiévale* (Caen, 2000).

―― and GAZEAU, Véronique (eds), *La Normandie et l'Angleterre au Moyen Age* (Caen, 2003).

BOUGY, Catherine, 'L'Image des ducs de Normandie dans le *Roman de Rou* de Wace et dans le *Roman du Mont Saint-Michel* de Guillaume de Saint-Pair', in Glyn S. Burgess and Judith Weiss (eds), *Maistre Wace: A Celebration: Proceedings of the International Colloquium held in Jersey, 10–12 September 2004*, Société Jersiaise (2006), 73–90.

BOUVRIS, Jean-Michel, 'Pour une étude prosopographique des familles nobles d'importance moyenne en Normandie au XIe siècle: l'exemple du lignage des Dastin', *Revue de l'Avranchin et du Pays de Granville*, lxi (1984), 65–101.

BRETT, Martin, 'John of Worcester and His Contemporaries', in R. H. C. Davis and J. M. Wallace-Hadrill (eds), *The Writing of History in the Middle Ages: Essays Presented to Richard William Southern* (Oxford, 1981), 101–26.

―― 'The Use of Universal Chronicle at Worcester', in Jean-Philippe Genet (ed.), *L'historiographie médiévale en Europe* (Paris, 1992), 277–85.

―― 'Gundulf and the Cathedral Communities of Canterbury and Rochester', in Eales and Sharpe (eds), *Canterbury and the Norman Conquest*, 15–25.

―― 'David (*d*.1137 × 9), bishop of Bangor', *ODNB*.

BRINDLE, Steven, 'The Keep at Conisbrough Castle, Yorkshire', *Château Gaillard*, xxv (2012), 61–74.

BROOKE, Z. N., and BROOKE, C. N. L., 'Hereford Cathedral Dignitaries in the Twelfth Century: Supplement (*Conventio* between Roger, Earl of Hereford, and William de Braose, his Brother-in-Law (1148–1154))', *Cambridge Historical Journal*, viii (1944–6), 179–85.

BROOKS, Nicholas, 'Why is the Anglo-Saxon Chronicle about Kings?', *ASE*, xxxix (2011), 43–70.

BROUN, Dauvit, 'The Adoption of Brieves in Scotland', in Marie Therese Flanagan and Judith A. Green (eds), *Charters and Charter Scholarship in Britain and Ireland* (Basingstoke/New York, 2005), 164–83.

―― *Scottish Independence and the Idea of Britain from the Picts to Alexander III* (Woodbridge, 2007).

―― et al. (eds), *The Reality behind Charter Diplomatic in Anglo-Norman Britain* (Glasgow, 2011).

BROWN, R. Allen, *The Normans* (Woodbridge, 1984).

BUC, Philippe, *The Dangers of Ritual: Between Early Medieval Texts and Social Scientific Theory* (Princeton, NJ, 2001).

BÜHRER-THIERRY, Geneviève, '"Just Anger" or "Vengeful Anger"? The Punishment of Blinding in the Early Medieval West', in Barbara H. Rosenwein (ed.), *Anger's Past: The Social Uses of Emotion in the Middle Ages* (Ithaca, NY/London, 1998), 75–91.

BURBANK, Jane, and COOPER, Frederick, *Empires in World History: Power and the Politics of Difference* (Princeton, NJ, 2010).

BURKE, Peter, *History and Social Theory*, 2nd edn. (Cambridge and Malden, MA, 2005).

BURR, Vivien, *Social Constructionism*, 2nd edn. (London, 2003).

BURTON, Janet, *The Monastic Order in Yorkshire, 1069–1215* (Cambridge, 1999).

―― '*Fundator Noster*: Roger de Mowbray as a Founder and Patron of Monasteries', in Emilia Jamroziak and Janet Burton (eds), *Religious and Laity in Western Europe, 1000–1400: Interaction, Negotiation and Power* (Turnhout, 2006), 23–39.

CAMPBELL, James, 'Some Twelfth-Century Views of the Anglo-Saxon Past', reprinted in James Campbell, *Essays in Anglo-Saxon History* (London/Ronceverte, WV, 1986), 209–28.

―― 'Norwich before 1300', in Rawcliffe and Wilson (eds), *Medieval Norwich*, 29–48.

CANOSA, Rosa, *Etnogenesi normanne e identità variabilii. Il retroterra cultural dei Normanni d'Italia fra Scandinavia e Normandia* (Turin, 2009).

CARPENTER, D. A., 'Abbot Ralph of Coggeshall's Account of the Last Years of King Richard and the First Years of King John', *EHR*, cxiii (1998), 1210–30.

―― *The Struggle for Mastery: Britain, 1066–1284* (Oxford, 2003).

CASTIÑEIRAS, Manuel, '*Didacus Gelmiras*, Patron of the Arts. Compostela's Long Journey: from the Periphery to the Center of Romanesque Art', in Manuel Castiñeiras (ed.), *Compostela and Europe: The Story of Diego Gelmirez* (Santiago de Compostela and Milan, 2010), 32–97.

CHANDLER, Victoria, 'Warenne, William (III) de, third earl of Surrey (*d*.1148)', *ODNB*.

CHIBNALL, Marjorie (as Marjorie Morgan), *The English Lands of the Abbey of Bec* (London, 1946).

―― 'Mercenaries and the *Familia Regis* under Henry I', *History*, lxii (1977), 15–23, reprinted in Strickland (ed.), *Anglo-Norman Warfare*, 84–92.

―― *The World of Orderic Vitalis* (Oxford, 1984).

―― 'L'ordre de Fontevrault en Angleterre au XIIe siècle', *Cahiers de civilisation médiévale*, xxix (1986), 41–7.

―― *The Empress Matilda: Queen Consort, Queen Mother, and Lady of the English* (Oxford, 1991).

―― 'Monastic Foundations in England and Normandy, 1066–1189', in *England and Normandy*, 37–49.

―― *The Debate on the Norman Conquest* (Manchester, 1999).

―― 'Les Normands et les saints anglo-saxons', in Bouet and Neveux (eds), *Les Saints dans la Normandie médiévale*, 259–68.

―― 'The Relations of Saint Anselm with the English Dependencies of the Abbey of Bec 1079–1093', in *Spicilegium Beccense I. Le Bec-Hellouin and Paris, 1959*, 521–30, reprinted in *Piety, Power and History in Medieval England and Normandy* (Aldershot/Burlington VT, 2000), Chap. 9.

―― 'Matilda [Matilda of Boulogne] (*c*.1103–1152), queen of England', in *ODNB*.

―― 'Introduction', in Dalton and White (eds), *King Stephen's Reign*, 1–9.

CHURCH, S. D. *The Household Knights of King John* (Cambridge, 1999).

―― (ed.), *King John: New Interpretations* (Woodbridge, 1999).

CLANCY, Thomas O., 'A Gaelic Polemic Quatrain from the Reign of Alexander I, ca.1113', *Scottish Gaelic Studies*, xx (2000), 88–96.

CLARKE, Howard B., 'The Identity of the Designer of the Bayeux Tapestry', *ANS*, xxxv (2013), 119–39.

COATES, Alan, *English Medieval Books: The Reading Abbey Collections from Foundation to Dispersal* (Oxford, 1999).

COHEN, Robin, *Global Diasporas: An Introduction*, 2nd edn. (London/New York, 2008).

COLLEY, Linda, 'What Is Imperial History Now?', in David Cannadine (ed.), *What Is History Now?* (Basingstoke/New York, 2002), 132–47.

―― 'The Difficulties of Empire: Present, Past and Future', *HR*, lxxix (2006), 367–82.

COOK, Barrie, 'Foreign Coins in Medieval England', in Lucia Traviaini (ed.), *Moneta Locale, Moneta Straniera: Italia ed Europa XI-XV secolo* (Milan, 1999), 231–84.

—— 'En monnaie aiant cours: The Monetary System of the Angevin Empire', in Barrie Cook and Gareth Williams (eds), *Coinage and History in the North Sea World, c.500–1200: Essays in Honour of Marion Archibald* (Leiden/Boston, 2006), 617–86.

CORDERO CARRETE, F. R., 'De los esponsales de una hija de Guillermo el Conquistador con un "Rey de Galicia"', *Cuadernos de Estudios Gallegos*, vii (1952), 55–78.

COUPLAND, Simon, 'From Poachers to Gamekeepers: Scandinavian Warlords and Carolingian Kings', *EME*, vii (1998), 85–114; reprinted in Simon Coupland, *Carolingian Coinage and the Vikings: Studies on Power and Trade in the 9th Century* (Aldershot, 2007), Chap. 12.

COWDREY, H. E. J., 'Bishop Ermenfrid of Sion and the Penitential Ordinance following the Battle of Hastings', *JEH*, xx (1969), 225–42.

—— 'Pope Gregory VII and the Anglo-Norman Church and Kingdom', *Studi Gregoriani*, ix (1972), 79–114; reprinted in Cowdrey, *Popes, Monks and Crusaders*, Chap. 9.

—— 'The Anglo-Norman *Laudes Regiae*', *Viator*, xii (1981), 37–78; reprinted in Cowdrey, *Popes, Monks and Crusaders*, Chap. 8.

—— *Popes, Monks and Crusaders* (London, 1984).

—— 'The Gregorian Reform in the Anglo-Norman Lands and Scandinavia', *Studi Gregoriani*, xiii (1989), 321–52; reprinted in Cowdrey, *Popes and Church Reform*, Chap. 7.

—— 'The Papacy and the Berengarian Controversy', in R. B. C. Huygens and F. Niewöhner (eds), *Auctoritas und Ratio. Studien zu Berengar von Tours* (Wiesbaden, 1990), 109–38; reprinted in Cowdrey, *Popes and Church Reform*, Chap. 6.

—— 'Lanfranc, the Papacy and Canterbury', in D'Onofrio (ed.), *Lanfranco di Pavia, 439–500; reprinted in Cowdrey, Popes and Church Reform*, Chap. 10.

—— *Popes and Church Reform in the 11th Century* (Aldershot/Burlington, 2000).

—— *Lanfranc: Scholar, Monk and Archbishop* (Oxford, 2003).

COWNIE, Emma, *Religious Patronage in Anglo-Norman England, 1066–1135*, Royal Historical Society Studies in History (Woodbridge, 1998), 193–200.

CRICK, Julia, *The Historia Regum Britannie of Geoffrey of Monmouth*, iii. *A Summary Catalogue of Manuscripts* (Cambridge, 1989).

—— '"The English" and "The Irish" from Cnut to John: Speculations on a Linguistic Interface', in Tyler (ed.), *Conceptualizing Multilingualism*, 217–37.

—— and VAN HOUTS, Elisabeth (eds), *A Social History of England, 900–1200* (Cambridge, 2011).

CROOKS, Peter, 'State of the Union: Perspectives on English Imperialism in the Late Middle Ages', *P&P*, no. 212 (2011), 3–42.

CROUCH, David, *The Beaumont Twins: The Roots and Branches of Power in the Twelfth Century* (Cambridge, 1986).

—— *The Image of Aristocracy in Britain, 1000–1300* (London/New York, 1992).

—— 'Normans and Anglo-Normans: A Divided Aristocracy?', in *England and Normandy*, 51–67.

—— 'The March and the Welsh Kings', in King (ed.), *The Anarchy*, 255–89.

—— 'From Stenton to McFarlane: Models of Societies of the Twelfth and Thirteenth Centuries', *TRHS*, 6th. ser., v (1995), 179–200.

—— 'Robert of Gloucester's Mother and Sexual Politics in Norman Oxfordshire', *HR*, lxxii (1999), 323–31.

—— *The Reign of King Stephen, 1135–1154* (Harlow, 2000).

—— *The Normans: The History of a Dynasty* (London/New York, 2002).

—— *William Marshal*, 2nd edn. (Harlow, 2002).

—— 'Beaumont, Henry de, first earl of Warwick (*d.*1119)', *ODNB*.

—— 'Clare, Richard de (*d*.1136)', *ODNB*.
—— 'Nest (*b*. before 1092, *d.c*.1130)', *ODNB*.
—— 'Robert, first earl of Gloucester (*b*. before 1100, *d*.1147)', *ODNB*.
—— 'Robert, second earl of Leicester (1104–1168)', *ODNB*.
—— 'Vere, Aubrey (III), de, count of Guînes and earl of Oxford (*d*.1194)', *ODNB*.
—— *The Birth of Nobility: Constructing Aristocracy in England and France, 900–1300* (Harlow, 2005).
—— 'King Stephen and Northern France', in Dalton and White (eds), *King Stephen's Reign*, 44–57.
—— 'Between Three Realms: The Acts of Waleran II, Count of Meulan and Worcester', in Vincent (ed.), *Records, Administration and Aristocratic Society*, 75–90.
—— 'Chivalry and Courtliness: Colliding Constructs', in Peter Coss and Christopher Tyerman (eds), *Soldiers, Nobles and Gentlemen: Essays in Honour of Maurice Keen* (Woodbridge, 2009), 32–48.
—— *The English Aristocracy, 1070–1272: A Social Transformation* (New Haven, CT/London, 2011).
—— and THOMPSON, Kathleen (eds), *Normandy and Its Neighbours, 900–1250: Essays for David Bates* (Turnhout, 2011).
DALTON, Paul, '*In neutro latere*: The Armed Neutrality of Rannulf II, earl of Chester in King Stephen's Reign', *ANS*, xiv (1992), 39–59.
—— *Conquest, Anarchy and Lordship: Yorkshire, 1066–1154* (Cambridge, 1994).
—— 'Eustace fitz John and the Politics of Anglo-Norman England: The Rise and Survival of a Twelfth-Century Royal Servant', *Speculum*, lxxi (1996), 358–83.
—— and WHITE, Graeme (eds), *King Stephen's Reign, 1135–1154* (Woodbridge, 2008).
—— and INSLEY, Charles and WILKINSON, Louise J. (eds), *Cathedrals, Communities and Conflict in the Anglo-Norman World* (Woodbridge, 2011).
DANIÉLO, Sébastien, 'Land, Family and Depredation: The Case of St Benet of Holme's Manor of Little Melton', *ANS*, xxxi (2009), 49–63.
DAVIES, John Reuben, *The Book of Llandaf and the Norman Church in Wales* (Woodbridge, 2003).
—— 'Aspects of Church Reform in Wales, *c*.1093–*c*.1223', *ANS*, xxx (2008), 85–99.
—— 'Cathedrals and Cults of Saints in Eleventh- and Twelfth-Century Wales', in Dalton, Insley and Wilkinson (ed.), *Cathedrals, Communities and Conflict*, 99–115.
DAVIES, Kerrith, 'The Count of the Cotentin: Western Normandy, William of Mortain, and the Career of Henry I', *HSJ*, xxii (2012, for 2010), 123–40.
DAVIES, R. R., *Conquest, Coexistence, and Change, Wales, 1063–1415* (Oxford, 1987).
—— *Domination and Conquest: The Experience of Ireland, Scotland and Wales, 1100–1300* (Cambridge, 1990).
—— *The Matter of Britain and the Matter of England: An Inaugural Lecture Delivered before the University of Oxford on 29 February 1996* (Oxford, 1996).
—— *The First English Empire: Power and Identities in the British Isles, 1093–1343* (Oxford, 2000).
—— 'The Medieval State: The Tyranny of a Concept?', *Journal of Historical Sociology*, xvi (2003), 280–300.
DAVIES, Sean, *Welsh Military Institutions, 633–1283* (Cardiff, 2004).
DAVIS, R. H. C., *The Normans and Their Myth* (London, 1976).
—— 'Domesday Book: Continental Parallels', in Holt (ed.), *Domesday Studies*, 15–39.
—— *King Stephen*, 3rd edn. (London, 1990).

DAVY, Gilduin, 'Autour de la restauration de l'ordre: les justifications juridiques de la bataille de Tinchebrai dans "l'Histoire ecclésiastique" d'Orderic Vital', in *Tinchebray*, 21–34.
DE BOÜARD, Michel, *Guillaume le Conquérant* (Paris, 1984).
DECAËNS, Joseph, 'Le château de Falaise', in Baylé (ed.), *L'architecture normande*, ii, 305–9.
DIXON, Philip, 'The Influence of the White Tower on the Great Towers of the Twelfth Century', in Impey (ed.), *The White Tower*, 243–75.
D'ONOFRIO, G. (ed.), *Lanfranco di Pavia e L'Europa del secolo XI nel IX centenario della morte* (Rome, 1993).
DOUGLAS, David C., *William the Conqueror: The Norman Impact upon England* (London, 1964).
—— *The Norman Achievement* (London, 1969).
—— *The Norman Fate, 1100–1154* (London, 1976).
—— *The Normans* (London, 2002).
DOWNHAM, Clare, 'England and the Irish-Sea Zone in the Eleventh Century', *ANS*, xxvi (2004), 55–73.
DUFFY, Seán, 'Henry II and England's Insular Neighbours', in Harper-Bill and Vincent (eds), *Henry II: New Interpretations*, 129–53.
DUMAS, Françoise, 'Les monnaies normandes des Xe-XIIe siècles avec un répertoire', *Revue numismatique*, xxi (1979), 84–140.
DUMVILLE, David N., 'An Early Text of Geoffrey of Monmouth's *Historia Regum Britanniae* and the Circulation of Some Latin histories in Twelfth-Century Normandy', *Arthurian Literature*, iv (1985), 1–36; reprinted in Dumville, *Histories and Pseudo-Histories*, Chap. 14.
—— 'Celtic-Latin Texts in Northern England, *c*.1150–*c*.1250'; reprinted in Dumville, *Histories and Pseudo-Histories*, Chap. 11.
—— *Histories and Pseudo-Histories of the Insular Middle Ages* (Aldershot, 1990).
—— 'Anglo-Saxon Books: Treasure in Norman Hands?', *ANS*, xvi (1994), 83–99.
DUNBABIN, Jean, 'Geoffrey of Chaumont, Thibaud of Blois and William the Conqueror', *ANS*, xvi (1994), 101–16.
—— 'Henry II and Louis VII', in Harper-Bill and Vincent (eds), *Henry II: New Interpretations*, 47–62.
DUNCAN, A. A. M., 'Yes, the Earliest Scottish Charters', *SHR*, lxxviii (1999), 1–38.
—— *The Kingship of the Scots, 842–1292: Succession and Independence* (Edinburgh, 2002).
EALES, Richard, 'Local Loyalties in Norman England: Kent in Stephen's Reign', *ANS*, viii (1986), 88–108.
—— 'Ranulf (III), sixth earl of Chester and first earl of Lincoln', *ODNB*.
—— and SHARPE, Richard (eds), *Canterbury and the Norman Conquest: Churches, Saints and Scholars, 1066–1109* (London/Rio Grande, 1995).
EDGINGTON, SUSAN, 'Pagan Peverell: an Anglo-Norman Crusader', in P. W. Edbury (ed.), *Crusade and Settlement: Papers read at the First Conference for the Study of the Crusades and the Latin East, and presented to R. C. Smail* (Cardiff, 1985), 90–3.
ESDERS, Stefan, 'Regionale Selbstbehauptung zwischen Byzanz und dem Frankenreich: Die *inquisitio* der Rechtsgewohnheiten Istriens durch die Sendboten Karls des Großen und Pippins von Italien', in Stefan Esders and Thomas Scharff (eds), *Eid und Wahrheitsuche. Studien zu rechttlichen Befragungspraktiken im Mittelalter und früher Neuzeit, Gesellschaft, Kultur und Schrift Mediävistiche Beiträge*, vii (1999), 49–112.
EVERARD, Judith A., 'The Foundation of an Alien Priory at Linton, Cambridgeshire', *Proceedings of the Cambridge Antiquarian Society*, lxxxvi (1997), 169–74.
—— *Brittany and the Angevins: Province and Empire, 1158–1203* (Cambridge, 2000).

FALQUE REY, Emma, *Historia Compostellana* (Turnhout, 1988).
FARRER, W., 'An Outline Itinerary of Henry I', *EHR*, xxxiii (1919), 303–82, 507–79.
FAWCETT, Richard, *The Architecture of the Scottish Medieval Church, 1100–1560* (New Haven, CT/London, 2011).
FEDORENKO, Gregory, 'The Thirteenth-Century *Chronique de Normandie*', *ANS*, xxxv (2013), 163–80.
FENTON, Kirsten A., *Gender, Nation and Conquest in the Works of William of Malmesbury* (Woodbridge, 2008).
FERGUSON, Niall, *Empire: How Britain Made the Modern World* (London, 2003).
——*Civilization: The West and the Rest* (London, 2011).
FERNIE, Eric, *The Architecture of Norman England* (Oxford, 2000).
——'Three Romanesque Great Churches in Germany, France and England, and the Discipline of Architectural History', *Architectural History*, liv (2011), 1–22.
FLAMBARD HÉRICHER, Anne-Marie, and GAZEAU, Véronique (eds), *1204: la Normandie entre Plantagenêts et Capétiens* (Caen, 2007).
FLANAGAN, Marie Therese, *Irish Society, Anglo-Norman Settlers, Angevin Kingship: Interactions in Ireland in the Late Twelfth Century* (Oxford, 1989).
——'Clare, Richard fitz Gilbert de [*called* Strongbow], second earl of Pembroke (*c.*1130–1176)', *ODNB*.
FLEMING, Donald F., 'Landholding by *milites* in Domesday Book: A Revision', *ANS*, xiii (1991), 83–98.
——and POPE, Janet M. (eds), *Henry I and the Anglo-Norman World: Studies in Memory of C. Warren Hollister*, *HSJ*, special volume, xvii (2006).
FLEMING, Robin, *Kings and Lords in Conquest England* (Cambridge, 1991).
FOLZ, Robert, *The Concept of Empire in Western Europe from the Fifth to the Fourteenth Century*, trans. Sheila Ann Ogilvie (London, 1969).
FOOT, Sarah, 'The Historiography of the Anglo-Saxon "Nation-State"', in Len Scales and Oliver Zimmer (eds), *Power and Nation in European History* (Cambridge, 2005), 125–42.
——*Æthelstan, The First King of England* (New Haven, CT/London, 2011).
FOREVILLE, Raymonde, 'Le culte de Saint Thomas Becket en Normandie: enquête sur les sanctuaires anciennement placés sous le vocable du martyr de Cantorbéry', in Foreville (ed.), *Thomas Becket* (Paris, 1975), 135–52.
FRAME, Robin, *The Political Development of the British Isles, 1100–1400* (Oxford, 1990).
FRASER, James E., 'Early Medieval Europe: The Case of Britain and Ireland', in D. Bloxham and A. D. Moses (eds), *The Oxford Handbook of Genocide Studies* (Oxford, 2010), 259–79.
FREEMAN, Edward. A., *The History of the Norman Conquest of England: Its Causes and Its Results*, 6 vols (Oxford, 1867–79).
FREEMAN, Elizabeth, *Narratives of a New Order: Cistercian Historical Writing in England, 1150–1220* (Turnhout, 2002).
GABRIELE, Matthew, 'The Provenance of the *Descriptio qualiter Karolus Magnus*: Remembering the Carolingians in the Entourage of King Philip I (1060–1108) before the First Crusade', *Viator*, xxxix (2008), 93–117.
GALBRAITH, V. H., 'The Making of Domesday Book', *EHR*, lvii (1942), 160–77.
GAMESON, Richard, 'English Book Collections in the Late Eleventh and Early Twelfth Centuries: Symeon's Durham and its Context', in David Rollason (ed.), *Symeon of Durham: Historian of Durham and the North* (Stamford, 1998), 230–5.

—— *The Manuscripts of Early Norman England (c.1066–1130)*, British Academy Postdoctoral Fellowship Monograph (Oxford, 1999).
GARDINER, Mark, 'Shipping and Trade between England and the Continent during the Eleventh Century', *ANS*, xxii (2000), 71–93.
GARNETT, George, '*Franci* et *Angli*: The Legal Distinctions between Peoples after the Conquest', *ANS*, viii (1985), 109–37.
—— 'Coronation and Propaganda: Some Implications of the Norman Claim to the Throne of England in 1066', *TRHS*, 5th ser., xxxvi (1986), 91–116.
—— 'The Third Recension of the English Coronation *Ordo*: The Manuscripts', *HSJ*, xi (2003, for 1998), 43–71.
—— *Conquered England: Kingship, Succession, and Tenure, 1066–1166* (Oxford, 2007).
GAUTIER, Alban, *Arthur* (Paris, 2007).
—— 'Comment Harold prêta serment: circonstances et interprétations d'un rituel politique', *Cahiers de civilisation médiévale*, lv (2012), 33–56.
GAZEAU, Véronique, 'Les abbés bénédictins de la Normandie ducale', *ANS*, xxvi (2004), 75–86.
—— *Normannia Monastica (X^e-XIIe siècle): Princes normands et abbés bénédictins; Prosopographie des abbés bénédictins*, 2 vols (Caen, 2007).
—— and GREEN, Judith (eds), *Tinchebray 1106–2006: Actes du colloque de Tinchebray (28–30 septembre 2006)*, Le Pays Bas-Normand (Flers, 2009).
—— and GENET, Jean-Philippe (eds), *La France et les îles Britanniques: un couple impossible?* (Paris, 2012).
GEARY, Patrick J., 'Ethnic Identity as a Situational Construct in the Early Middle Ages', *Mitteilungen der Anthropologischen Gesellschaft in Wien*, cxiii (1983), 15–26.
—— *The Myth of Nations: The Medieval Origins of Europe* (Princeton, NJ/Oxford, 2002).
GEM, Richard, 'The Bishop's Chapel at Hereford: The Roles of Patron and Craftsman', in Sarah Macready and F. H. Thompson (eds), *Art and Patronage in the English Romanesque*, Society of Antiquaries of London, Occasional Paper (new series), viii (1986), 87–96.
—— 'Canterbury and the Cushion Capital: A Commentary on Passages from Goscelin's *De Miraculis Sancti Augustini*', in Neil Stratford (ed.), *Romanesque and Gothic: Essays for George Zarnecki*, 2 vols (Woodbridge, 1987), 83–101.
GERGEN, Kenneth J., *An Invitation to Social Constructionism*, 2nd edn. (London, 2008).
GIBSON, Margaret, 'The Image of Lanfranc', in D'Onofrio (ed.), *Lanfranco di Pavia*, 21–8.
GILCHRIST, Roberta, *Medieval Life: Archaeology and the Life Course* (Woodbridge, 2012).
GILLINGHAM, John, 'William the Bastard at War', in Christopher Harper-Bill, Christopher Holdsworth, and Janet L. Nelson (eds), *Studies in Medieval History presented to R. Allen Brown* (Woodbridge, 1989), 141–58; reprinted in Strickland (ed.), *Anglo-Norman Warfare*, 143–60.
—— 'The Beginnings of English Imperialism', *Journal of Historical Sociology*, v (1992), 392–409; reprinted in Gillingham, *The English*, 3–18.
—— 'The Context and Purposes of Geoffrey of Monmouth's *History of the Kings of Britain*', *ANS*, xiii (1992), 99–118; reprinted in Gillingham, *The English*, 19–39.
—— 'Conquering the Barbarians: War and Chivalry in Twelfth Century Britain', *HSJ*, iv (1993), 67–84; reprinted in Gillingham, *The English*, 41–58.
—— '1066 and the Introduction of Chivalry into England', in George Garnett and John Hudson (eds), *Law and Government in Medieval England and Normandy: Essays in Honour of Sir James Holt* (Cambridge, 1994), 31–55; reprinted in Gillingham, *The English*, 209–31.

―――'Henry of Huntingdon and the Twelfth-Century Revival of the English Nation', in S. Forde, L. Johnson, and A. Murray (eds), *Concepts of National Identity in the Middle Ages*, Leeds Texts and Monographs (Leeds, 1995), 75–101; reprinted in Gillingham, *The English*, 123–44.

―――'Gaimar, the Prose *Brut* and the making of English History', in Jean-Philippe Genet (ed.), *L'Histoire et les nouveaux publics dans l'Europe médiévale* (Paris, 1997), 165–76; reprinted in Gillingham, *The English*, 113–22.

―――'Historians without Hindsight: Coggeshall, Diceto and Howden on the Early Years of John's Reign', in Church (ed.), *King John: New Interpretations*, 1–26.

―――*Richard I* (New Haven, CT/London, 1999).

―――*The English in the Twelfth Century: Imperialism, National Identity and Political Values* (Woodbridge, 2000).

―――'"Slaves of the Normans"? Gerald de Barri and Early Regnal Solidarity in Early Thirteenth-Century England', in Pauline Stafford, Janet L. Nelson, and Jane Martindale (eds), *Law, Laity and Solidarities: Essays in Honour of Susan Reynolds* (Manchester and New York, 2001), 160–71.

―――*The Angevin Empire*, 2nd edn. (London, 2001), 59–60.

―――'A Second Tidal Wave? The Historiography of English Colonization of Ireland, Scotland and Wales in the 12th and 13th Centuries', in Jan M. Piskorski (ed.), *Historiographical Approaches to Medieval Colonization of East Central Europe* (New York, 2002), 303–27.

―――'Problems of Integration within the Lands Ruled by the Norman and Angevin Kings of England', in Werner Maleczek (ed.), *Fragen der Politischen Integration in Mittelalterlichen Europa*, Vorträge und Forschungen, vol. lxiii (Ostfildern, 2005), 85–135.

―――'Doing Homage to the King of France', in Harper-Bill and Vincent (eds), *Henry II: New Interpretations*, 63–84.

―――'Holding to the Rules of War (*Bellica Iura Tenentes*): Right Conduct before, during, and after Battle in the Eleventh Century', *ANS*, xxix (2007), 1–15.

―――'At the deathbeds of the kings of England, 1066–1216', in Brigitte Kasten (ed.), *Herrscher- und Fürstentestamente im Westeuropäischen Mittelalter* (Cologne, Weimar and Vienna, 2008), 509–30.

―――'The Meetings of the Kings of France and England, 1066–1204', in *Normandy and Neighbours*, 17–42.

―――'Women, Children and the Profits of War', in Nelson, Reynolds, and Johns (eds), *Gender and Historiography*, 61–74.

GOLDING, BRIAN, 'The Coming of the Cluniacs', *ANS*, iii (1981), 65–77, 208–12.

―――*Conquest and Colonisation: The Normans in Britain, 1066–1100* (London, 1994; rev. edn., 2001).

―――'Trans-border Transactions: Patterns of Patronage in Anglo-Norman Wales', *HSJ*, xvi (2006, for 2005), 27–46.

GRANT, Alexander, 'Lordship and Society in Twelfth-Century Clydesdale', in Pryce and Watts (eds), *Power and Identity*, 98–124.

GRANT, Lindy, 'Architectural Relationships between England and Normandy, 1100–1204', in *England and Normandy*, 117–29.

―――*Architecture and Society in Normandy, 1120–1270* (New Haven, CT/London, 2005).

―――'Les relations culturelles et artistiques entre le sud-ouest de la Normandie et le Maine autour de 1106', in *Tinchebray*, 235–47.

GREEN, Judith A., 'William Rufus, Henry I and the Royal Demesne', *History*, lxiv (1979), 337–52.

―――*The Government of England under Henry I* (Cambridge, 1986).

—— 'King Henry I and the Aristocracy of Normandy', in *La 'France Anglaise' au Moyen Age: actes du 111ᵉ congrès national des sociétés savantes* (Paris, 1988), 161–73.

—— 'Unity and Disunity in the Anglo-Norman State', *HR*, lxii (1989), 115–34.

—— 'Aristocratic Loyalties on the Northern Frontier of England, *c.*1100–1174', in Daniel Williams (ed.), *England in the Twelfth Century: Proceedings of the 1988 Harlaxton Symposium* (Woodbridge, 1990), 83–100.

—— *The Aristocracy of Norman England* (Cambridge, 1997).

—— 'The Piety and Patronage of Henry I', *HSJ*, x (2001), 1–16.

—— *Henry I, King of England and Duke of Normandy* (Cambridge, 2006).

—— 'Networks and Solidarities at the Court of Henry I Beauclerc', in David Bates, Véronique Gazeau et al. (eds), *Liens personnels, réseaux, solidarités en France et dans les îles Britanniques (XIᵉ–XXᵉ siècle)* (Paris, 2006), 113–26.

—— 'King Henry I and Northern England', *TRHS*, 6th ser, xvii (2007), 35–55.

—— 'Henry I and the Origins of the Civil War', in Dalton and White (eds), *King Stephen's Reign*, 11–26.

—— —— 'La bataille de Tinchebray: un tournant dans l'histoire de la Normandie et de l'Angleterre', in *Tinchebray*, 47–60.

—— 'Duchesses of Normandy in the Eleventh and Twelfth Centuries', in *Normandy and Neighbours*, 43–59.

—— 'Henri Iᵉʳ entre Angleterre et Normandie', in Gazeau and Genet (eds), *La France et les îles Britanniques*, 29–41.

GREENWAY, Diana E. et al. (eds), *John Le Neve: Fasti ecclesiae Anglicanae, 1066–1300*, 10 vols (London, 1968–2005).

—— 'Authority, Convention and Observation in Henry of Huntingdon's *Historia Anglorum*', *ANS*, xviii (1996), 105–21.

GROSSE, Rolf, *Saint-Denis zwischen Adel und König: Die Zeit vor Suger (1053–1122)* (Stuttgart, 2002).

GUILMIN, Maxime, 'Un exemple de réseau relationnel de l'aristocratie anglo-normande, les Paynel et leur entourage (milieu du XIᵉ siècle-début du XIIᵉ siècle)', in *Tinchebray*, 221–34.

GUYOTJEANNIN, Olivier, 'L'Italie méridionale vue du royaume de France', in Giosuè Musca (ed.), *Il Mezzogiorno normanno-svevo visto dall'Europa e dal mondo mediterraneo*, (Bari, 1999), 143–75.

HADLEY, D. M., 'Ethnicity and Acculturation', in Crick and van Houts (eds), *A Social History of England*, 235–46.

HAGGER, Mark S., *The Fortunes of a Norman Family: The De Verduns in England, Ireland and Wales, 1066–1316* (Dublin, 2001).

—— 'The Norman *Vicomte*, *c.*1035–1135: What Did He Do?', *ANS*, xxix (2007), 65–83.

—— 'The Earliest Norman Writs Revisited', *HR*, lxxxii (2009), 181–206.

—— 'Secular Law and Custom in Ducal Normandy, *c.*1000–1144', *Speculum*, lxxxv (2010), 827–67.

HALLAM, Elizabeth, and BATES, David (eds), *Domesday Book* (Stroud, 2001).

HALSALL, Guy, *Warfare and Society in the Barbarian West, 450–900* (London, 2003).

HAMILTON, Sarah, *The Practice of Penance, 900–1050*, Royal Historical Society Studies in History (Woodbridge, 2001).

HAMMERSLEY, Martyn, and ATKINSON, Paul, *Ethnography: Principles and Practice*, 3rd edn. (London, 2007).

HAMMOND, Matthew H., 'Ethnicity and the Writing of Medieval Scottish History', *SHR*, lxxxv (2006), 1–27.

—— 'Royal and Aristocratic Attitudes to Saints and the Virgin Mary in Twelfth- and Thirteenth-Century Scotland', in Steve Boardman and Eila Williamson (eds), *The Cult of Saints and the Virgin Mary in Medieval Scotland* (Woodbridge, 2010), 61–85.

HARPER-BILL, Christopher, and VINCENT, Nicholas (eds), *Henry II: New Interpretations* (Woodbridge, 2007).

HARRISON, Stuart, and NORTON, Christopher, 'Lastingham and the Architecture of the Benedictine Revival in Northumbria', *ANS*, xxxiv (2012), 63–103.

HASKINS, C. H., *The Normans in European History* (London/Boston/New York, 1916).

—— *Norman Institutions*, (Cambridge, MA, 1918).

HAYWARD, P. A., 'Translation-Narratives in Post-Conquest Hagiography and English Resistance to the Norman Conquest', *ANS*, xxi (2000), 67–93.

HEATHER, Peter J., 'Ethnicity, Group Identity and Social Status in the Migration Period', in Ildar H. Garipzanov, Patrick J. Geary, and Przemyslaw Urbanczyk (eds), *Franks, Northmen and Slavs: Identities and State Formation in Early Medieval Europe* (Turnhout, 2008), 17–49.

—— *Empires and Barbarians: Migration, Development and the Birth of Europe* (London, 2009).

HESLOP, T. A., 'The Canterbury Calendars and the Norman Conquest', in Eales and Sharpe (eds), *Canterbury and the Norman Conquest*, 53–85.

—— *Norwich Castle Keep* (Norwich, 1994).

—— 'Regarding the Spectators of the Bayeux Tapestry: Bishop Odo and His Circle', *Art History*, xxxii (2009), 223–49.

HEYWOOD, Stephen, 'Stone Building in Romanesque East Anglia', in Bates and Liddiard (eds), *East Anglia and its North Sea World*, 256–69.

HICKS, Leonie v., 'Coming and Going: The Use of Outdoor Space in Norman and Anglo-Norman Chronicles', *ANS*, xxxii (2010), 40–56.

—— and BRENNER Elma (eds.), *Society and Culture in Medieval Rouen* (Turnhout, 2013).

HILEY, David, 'Thurstan of Caen and Plainchant at Glastonbury: Musicological Reflections on the Norman Conquest', *PBA*, lxxii (1986), 57–90.

HILLABY, Joe, 'Jewish Colonisation in the Twelfth Century', in Patricia Skinner (ed.), *The Jews in Medieval Britain: Historical, Literary and Archaeological Perspectives* (Woodbridge, 2003), 15–40.

HILLGARTH, J. N., *The Problem of a Catalan Mediterranean Empire, 1229–1324*, EHR Supplement, no. 8 (London, 1975).

HILLION, Yannick, 'Arnaud et Hoël, deux évêques du Mans au service de Guillaume le Conquérant', *Annales de Bretagne et des pays de l'Ouest*, cx (2003), 49–77.

HINGST, Amanda Jane, *The Written Word: Past and Place in the Work of Orderic Vitalis* (Notre-Dame, IN, 2009).

HODGSON, Natasha, 'Reinventing Normans as Crusaders? Ralph of Caen's *Gesta Tancredi*', *ANS*, xxx (2008), 117–32.

HOLLAND, Martin, 'Dublin and the Reform of the Irish Church in the Eleventh and Twelfth Centuries', *Peritia*, xiv (2000), 111–60.

—— 'The Synod of Dublin in 1080', in Seán Duffy (ed.), *Medieval Dublin III* (Dublin, 2002), 81–94.

HOLLISTER, C. W., 'The Anglo-Norman Civil War: 1101', *EHR*, lxxxviii (1973), 315–34; reprinted in *Monarchy and Magnates*, 77–96.

—— 'Normandy, France and the Anglo-Norman *regnum*', *Speculum*, li (1976), 202–42; reprinted in *Monarchy and Magnates*, 17–57.

—— 'The Taming of a Turbulent Earl: Henry I and William of Warenne', *Réflexions historiques*, iii (1976), 83–91; reprinted in *Monarchy and Magnates*, 137–44.

—— 'The Rise of Administrative Kingship', *American Historical Review*, lxxx (1978), 868–91; reprinted in *Monarchy and Magnates*, 171–89.

—— 'Henry I and the Anglo-Norman Magnates', *ANS*, ii (1980), 93–107, 184–8; reprinted in *Monarchy and Magnates*, 223–45.

—— *Monarchy, Magnates and Institutions in the Anglo-Norman World* (London/Ronceverte, WV, 1986).

—— *Henry I*, edited and completed by A. Clark Frost (New Haven, CT/London, 2001).

—— 'Warenne, William (II) de, second earl of Surrey (*d*.1138)', *ODNB*.

—— and KEEFE, T. K., 'The Making of the Angevin Empire', *Journal of British Studies*, xii (1973), 1–25; reprinted in *Monarchy and Magnates*, 247–71.

HOLT, J. C., 'Politics and Property in Early Medieval England', *P&P*, no. 57 (1972), 3–52; reprinted in Holt, *Colonial England*, 113–59.

—— 'The End of the Anglo-Norman Realm', *PBA*, lxi (1975), 223–65; reprinted in Holt, *Magna Carta and Medieval Government*, 23–65.

—— *What's in a Name? Family Nomenclature and the Norman Conquest*, Stenton Lecture, University of Reading (1981); reprinted in Holt, *Colonial England*, 179–96.

—— 'Feudal Society and the Family: Notions of Patrimony', *TRHS*, 5th ser., xxxiii (1983), 193–220; reprinted in Holt, *Colonial England*, 197–221.

—— 'John Le Patourel, 1909–81', *PBA*, lxxi (1985), 583–96.

—— *Magna Carta and Medieval Government* (London, 1985).

—— (ed.), *Domesday Studies: Papers Read at the Novocentenary Conference of the Royal Historical Society and the Institute of British Geographers, Winchester, 1986* (Woodbridge, 1987).

—— '1086', in Holt (ed.), *Domesday Studies*, 41–64.

—— *The Northerners: A Study in the Reign of King John*, 2nd edn. (Oxford, 1992).

—— 'The Treaty of Winchester 1153', in King (ed.), *The Anarchy*, 291–316; reprinted in Holt, *Colonial England*, 271–90.

—— *Colonial England, 1066–1215* (London, 1997).

—— 'The *Casus Regis*: The Law and Politics of Succession in the Plantagenet Dominions, 1185–1247', in Holt, *Colonial England*, 307–26.

HOME, Malasree, 'Déjà Vu: The Complexity of the Peterborough Chronicle', in Alice Jorgensen (ed.), *Reading the Anglo-Saxon Chronicle: Language, Literature and History* (Turnhout, 2010), 67–90.

HOOFNAGLE, Wendy Marie, 'Charlemagne's Legacy and Anglo-Norman *Imperium* in Henry of Huntingdon's *Historia Anglorum*', in Matthew Gabriele and Jane Stuckey (eds), *The Legend of Charlemagne in the Middle Ages: Power, Faith and Crusade* (New York, 2008), 77–94.

HOOPER, Nicholas, 'Edgar the Ætheling: Anglo-Saxon prince, rebel and crusader', *ASE*, xiv (1985), 197–214.

HOUBEN, Hubert, *Roger II of Sicily: A Ruler between East and West*, trans. Graham A. Loud and Diane Milburn (Cambridge, 2002).

HOWE, Stephen, 'The Slow Death and Strange Rebirths of Imperial History', *Journal of Imperial and Commonwealth History*, xxix (2001), 131–41.

HUDSON, Benjamin, 'William the Conqueror and Ireland', *Irish Historical Studies*, xxix (1994), 145–58.

HUDSON, John, 'Administration, Family and Perceptions of the Past in Late Twelfth-Century England: Richard fitz Nigel and the Dialogue of the Exchequer', in Paul

Magdalino (ed.), *The Perception of the Past in Twelfth-Century Europe* (London/Rio Grande, 1992), 75–98.

—— 'Legal Aspects of Scottish Charter Diplomatic in the Twelfth Century: A Comparative Approach', *ANS*, xxv (2003), 121–38.

—— 'The Fate of Earl Waltheof and the Idea of Personal Law in England after 1066', in *Normandy and Neighbours*, 223–35.

—— *The Oxford History of the Laws of England*, vol. II: *871–1216* (Oxford, 2012).

HUNEYCUTT, Lois L., *Matilda of Scotland: A Study in Medieval Queenship* (Woodbridge, 2003).

HUNTINGTON, Joanna, 'David of Scotland: "Vir tam necessarius mundo"', in Steve Boardman, John Reuben Davies, and Eila Williamson (eds), *Saints' Cults in the Celtic World* (Woodbridge, 2009), 130–45.

HYAMS, Paul R., '"No Register of Title": The Domesday Inquest and Land Adjudication', *ANS*, ix (1987), 127–41.

—— 'The Jews in Medieval England, 1066–1290', in Alfred Haverkamp and Hanna Vollrath (eds), *England and Germany in the High Middle Ages* (Oxford, 1996), 173–92.

—— *Rancor and Reconciliation in Medieval England* (Ithaca, NY/London, 2003).

IMPEY, Edward, 'La demeure seigneuriale en Normandie entre 1125 et 1225 et la tradition anglo-normande', in Baylé (ed.), *L'architecture normande*, i, 219–41.

—— 'The Seigneurial Residence in Normandy, 1125–1225: An Anglo-Norman Traditon?', *Medieval Archaeology*, xliii (1999), 45–73.

—— (ed.), *The White Tower* (New Haven, CT/London, 2008).

—— and MCNEILL, John, 'La grande salle des ducs de Normandie à Caen', in G. Meirion-Jones (ed.), *La demeure seigneuriale du monde plantagenêt (XIe-XVIe siècles): salles, chambres et tours* (Rennes, 2013), 95–131.

INNES, Matthew, 'Land, Freedom and the Making of the Medieval West', *TRHS*, 6th ser., xvi (2006), 39–74.

INSLEY, Charles, 'Kings, Lords, Charters, and the Political Culture of Twelfth-Century Wales', *ANS*, xxx (2008), 133–53.

—— 'The Family of Wulfric Spott: an Anglo-Saxon Mercian Marcher Dynasty?', in Roffe (ed.), *The English and Their Legacy*, 115–28.

IRVINE, Susan, 'The Production of the Peterborough Chronicle', in Alice Jorgensen (ed.), *Reading the Anglo-Saxon Chronicle: Language, Literature and History* (Turnhout, 2010), 49–66.

JAMISON, E. M., 'The Sicilian Norman Kingdom in the Mind of Anglo-Norman Contemporaries', *PBA*, xxiv (1938), 237–85.

JAMROZIAK, Emilia, *Rievaulx Abbey and Its Social Context, 1132–1300: Memory, Locality, and Networks* (Turnhout, 2005).

JEAN-MARIE, Laurence, 'Anthroponymie caennaise et origine géographique des caennais (XIe-milieu au XIVe siècle)', *AN*, xlviii (1998), 33–65.

—— 'La population de Caen XIe-XVe siècles', *AN*, xlix (1999), 115–37.

—— *Caen aux XIe et XIIe siècles: espace urbain, pouvoirs et société* (Cormeilles-le-Royal, 2000).

JOHNS, Jeremy, *Arabic Administration in Norman Sicily: The Royal Dīwān* (Cambridge, 2002).

JOHNS, Susan M., *Noblewomen, Aristocracy and Power in the Twelfth-Century Anglo-Norman Realm* (Manchester/New York, 2003).

—— 'Nest of Deheubarth: Reading Female Power in the Historiography of Wales', in Nelson, Reynolds, and Johns (eds), *Gender and Historiography*, 91–100.

JOHNSON, Ewan, 'The Process of Norman Exile into Southern Italy', in Laura Napran and Elisabeth van Houts (eds), *Exile in the Middle Ages: Selected Proceedings from the International Medieval Congress, University of Leeds, 8–11 July 2002* (Turnhout, 2004), 29–38.

——'Origin Myth and the Construction of Medieval Identities: Norman Chronicles 1000–1100', in Richard Corradini, Rob Meens, Christina Pössel, and Philip Shaw (eds), *Texts and Identities in the Early Middle Ages*, Forschungen zur Geschichte des Mittelalters (Vienna, 2006), 153–64.

JONES, Michael, 'The House of Brittany and the Honour of Richmond in the Late Eleventh and Twelfth Centuries: Some New Charter Evidence', in Karl Borchardt and Enno Bünz (eds), *Forschungen zur Reichs-, Papst- und Landesgeschichte: Peter Herde zum 65. Geburstag von Freunden, Schülern und Kollegen*, 2 vols (Stuttgart, 1998), i, 161–73.

——'Conan (IV), duke of Brittany (*c*.1135–1171)', *ODNB*.

JOUET, Roger, *Et la Normandie devint française* (Paris, 1983).

——'Avant-propos: Faut-il commémorer 1204?', in *1204*, 3–8.

JOYCE, Patrick, 'The Return of History: Post-Modernism and the Politics of Academic History in Britain', *P&P*, no. 158 (1998), 207–35.

KEATS-ROHAN, Katharine S. B., 'The Devolution of the Honour of Wallingford, 1066–1148', *Oxoniensia*, liv (1989), 311–18.

——'William I and the Breton Contingent in the Non-Norman Conquest, 1066–1087', *ANS*, xiii (1991), 157–72.

——'Le rôle des Bretons dans la politique de colonisation normande de l'Angleterre (vers 1042–1135)', *Mémoires de la Société d'Histoire et d'Archéologie de Bretagne*, lxxiv (1996), 181–215.

——*Domesday People: A Prosopography of Persons Occurring in English Documents, 1066–1166. 1. Domesday Book* (Woodbridge, 1999).

——*Domesday Descendants: A Prosopography of Persons Occuring in English Documents, 1066–1166* (Woodbridge, 2002).

——'Alan Rufus (*d*.1093)', *ODNB*.

——'Les Bretons en Angleterre au XIIe siècle', in Joëlle Quaghebeur and Bernard Merdrignac (eds), *Bretons et Normands au Moyen Age: Rivalités, malentendus, convergences* (Rennes, 2008), 263–80.

KEEFE, Thomas K., 'Mandeville, William de, third earl of Essex (*d*.1189)', *ODNB*.

KEMPSHALL, Matthew, *Rhetoric and the Writing of History, 400–1500* (Manchester/New York, 2011).

KENNEDY, Paul, *The Rise and Fall of the Great Powers: Economic Change and Military Conflict from 1500 to 2000* (London, 1988).

KERR, Berenice, *Religious Life for Women c.1100–c.1350: Fontevraud in England* (Oxford, 1999).

KERSHAW, Paul J. E., *Peaceful Kings: Peace, Power and the Early Medieval Political Imagination* (Oxford, 2011).

KEYNES, Simon, 'The Crowland Psalter and the Sons of Edmund Ironside', *Bodleian Library Record*, xi (1985), 359–70.

——'The Æthelings in Normandy', *ANS*, xiii (1991), 173–205.

——'Giso, Bishop of Wells', *ANS*, xix (1997), 203–71.

——'Rosalind, 'Earl Godwine's Ship', *ASE*, xxxviii (2009), 185–223.

——and LOVE, Rosalind, 'Earl Godwine's Ship', *ASE*, xxxviii (2009), 185–223.

KING, Edmund, 'The Foundation of Pipewell Abbey, Northamptonshire', *HSJ*, ii (1990), 167–77.

——(ed.), *The Anarchy of King Stephen's Reign* (Oxford, 1994).
——'Stephen, Count of Mortain and Boulogne', *EHR*, cxv (2000), 271–96.
——'Brian fitz Count (*c*.1090–*c*.1149)', *ODNB*.
——'The Accession of Henry II', in Harper-Bill and Vincent (eds), *Henry II: New Interpretations*, 24–46.
——*King Stephen* (New Haven, CT/London, 2010).
KNOWLES, David, BROOKE, C. N. L., and LONDON, Vera C. M. (eds), *The Heads of Religious Houses: England and Wales, 940–1216* (Cambridge, 1972).
KOZIOL, Geoffrey, 'The Dangers of Polemic: Is Ritual Still an Interesting Topic for Historical Study?', *EME*, xi (2002), 367–88.
KWARTENG, Kwasi, *Ghosts of Empire: Britain's Legacies in the Modern World* (London, 2011).
LACK, Katherine, *Conqueror's Son: Duke Robert Curthose, Thwarted King* (Stroud, 2007).
——'The De Obitu Willelmi: Propaganda for the Anglo-Norman Succession, 1087–88', *EHR*, cxxiii (2008), 1417–56.
——'Robert Curthose: Ineffectual Duke or Victim of Spin?', *HSJ*, xx (2009, for 2008), 110–40.
LAINÉ, Stéphane, 'La bataille de Varaville (1057): examen critique des récits médiévaux', *Bulletin de la Société des Antiquaires de Normandie*, lxvii (2009, for 2008), 257–88.
LAPIDGE, M. T., 'The Welsh-Latin Poetry of Sulien's Family', *Studia Celtica*, viii/ix (1973–4), 68–106.
LARKIN, Edward, 'Diaspora and Empire: Towards a New Synthesis?', *Diasporas: A Journal of Transnational Studies*, xv (2010, for 2006), 167–84.
LAWSON, M. K., *The Battle of Hastings, 1066* (Stroud, 2002).
LE PATOUREL, John, 'The Plantagenet Dominions', *History*, l (1965), 289–308 (*Feudal Empires*, Chap. 8).
——*Norman Barons* (Hastings and Bexhill Branch of the Historical Association, 1966) (*Feudal Empires*, Chap. 6).
——*Normandy and England, 1066–1144*, The Stenton Lecture 1970 (University of Reading, 1971) (*Feudal Empires*, Chap. 7).
——*The Norman Empire* (Oxford, 1976).
——'The Norman Conquest, 1066, 1106, 1154?', *ANS*, i (1979), 103–20, 216–20.
——*Feudal Empires. Norman and Plantagenet*, ed. Michael Jones (London, 1984).
——'Angevin Successions and the Angevin Empire' (*Feudal Empires*, Chap. 9).
LE SAUX, Françoise H. M., *A Companion to Wace* (Cambridge, 2005).
LECKIE, Jr., R. William, *The Passage of Dominion: Geoffrey of Monmouth and the Periodization of Insular History in the Twelfth Century* (Toronto/Buffalo/London, 1981).
LEMESLE, Bruno, *La société aristocratique dans le Haut-Maine (XIe-XIIe siècles)* (Rennes, 1999).
LEMOINE DESCOURTIEUX, Astrid, 'La ville fortifiée de Verneuil-sur-Avre et son complexe castral aux XIIe et XIIIe siècles', in Jean-Paul Hervieu, Gilles Désiré dit Gosset, and Eric Barré (eds), *Construire, reconstruire, aménager le château en Normandie*, Congrès des societies historiques et archéologiques en Normandie, ix (Caen, 2004), 51–70.
LETOUZEY-RÉTY, Catherine, 'L'organisation seigneuriale dans les possessions anglaises et normandes de l'abbaye de la Trinité de Caen au XIIe siècle', *AN*, lv (2005), 213–45, 291–332.
——'Entre Angleterre et Normandie: la politique de conversion des redevances de l'abbaye de la Trinité de Caen (XIIe–XIIIe siècle), in Laurent Feller (ed.), *Calculs et rationalités dans la seigneurie médiévale: les conversions de redevances entre XIe et XVe siècles* (Paris, 2009), 73–108.

LEWIS, C. P., 'The Domesday Jurors', *HSJ*, v (1993), 17–45.
—— 'Gruffudd ap Cynan and the Normans', in Maund (ed.), *Gruffudd ap Cynan*, 61–77.
—— 'Warenne, William (I) de, first earl of Surrey', *ODNB*.
—— 'The Invention of the Manor in Norman England', *ANS*, xxxiv (2012), 123–50.
LICENCE, Tom, 'History and Hagiography in the Late Eleventh Century: The Life and Work of Herman the Archdeacon, Monk of Bury St Edmunds', *EHR*, cxxiv (2009), 516–44.
—— 'Herbert Losinga's Trip to Rome and the Bishopric of Bury St Edmunds', *ANS*, xxxiv (2012), 151–68.
LIEBERMAN, Max, *The Medieval March of Wales: The Creation and Perception of a Frontier, 1066–1283* (Cambridge, 2010).
—— 'The Medieval "Marches" of Normandy and Wales', *EHR*, cxxv (2010), 1357–81.
LIEVEN, Dominic, 'Empire, History and the Contemporary Global Order', *PBA*, cxxxi (2005), 127–56.
LIVERMORE, H., 'The "Conquest of Lisbon" and its Author', *Portuguese Studies*, vi (1990), 1–16.
LOPRETE, Kimberly A., *Adela of Blois: Countess and Lord (c.1067–1137)* (Dublin, 2007).
LOUD, Graham A., 'How "Norman" was the Norman Conquest of Southern Italy?', *Nottingham Medieval Studies*, xxv (1981), 13–34; reprinted in Loud, *Conquerors and Churchmen*, Chap. 2.
—— 'The *Gens Normannorum*—Myth or Reality', *ANS*, iv (1982), 104–16, 204–9; reprinted in Loud, *Conquerors and Churchmen*, Chap. 1.
—— 'Anna Komnena and her Sources for the Normans of Southern Italy', in Ian Wood and Graham Loud (eds), *Church and Chronicle in the Middle Ages: Essays Presented to John Taylor* (London, 1991), 41–57; reprinted in Loud, *Conquerors and Churchmen*, Chap. 13.
—— *Conquerors and Churchmen in Norman Italy* (Aldershot, 1999).
—— *The Age of Robert Guiscard* (Harlow, 2000).
—— 'The Kingdom of Sicily and the Kingdom of England, 1066–1266', *History*, lxxxviii (2003), 540–67.
—— *The Latin Church in Norman Italy* (Cambridge, 2007).
LOUISE, Gérard, *La seigneurie de Bellême, X^e-XIIe siècles*, 2 vols, Le Pays Bas-Normand, nos. 199–202 (1990–1).
LUCAS-AVENEL, Marie-Agnès, 'La *Gens Normannorum* en Italie du Sud d'après les chroniques normandes du XIe siècle', in Véronique Gazeau, Pierre Bauduin, and Yves Modéran (eds), *Identité et Ethnicité: concepts, débats historiographiques, exemples (IIIe-XIIe siècle)* (Caen, 2008), 233–64.
—— 'Le récit de Geoffroi Malaterra ou la légitimation de Roger, Grand Comte de Sicile', *ANS*, xxxiv (2012), 169–92.
LUSCOMBE, David, 'Hugh (*d.*1164), Abbot of Reading and Archbishop of Rouen', *ODNB*.
MCCRANK, L. J., 'Norman Crusaders in the Catalan Reconquest', *JMH*, vii (1981), 67–82.
MACLEAN, Simon, 'Recycling the Franks in Twelfth-Century England: Regino of Prüm, the Monks of Durham and the Alexandrine Schism', *Speculum*, lxxxvii (2012), 649–81.
MACQUEEN, H. L., *Common Law and Feudal Society in Medieval Scotland* (Edinburgh, 1993).
MADDICOTT, J. R., *The Origins of the English Parliament, 924–1327* (Oxford, 2010).
MADELINE, Fanny, 'Rouen and its Place in the Building Policy of the Angevin Kings', in Hicks and Brenner (eds), *Society and Culture*, 65–99.

MANN, Michael, *The Sources of Social Power: I. A History of Power from the Beginning to 1760 AD; II. The Rise of Classes and Nation States, 1760–1914* (Cambridge, 1986–93).
—— *Incoherent Empire* (London, 2003).
MARRITT, Stephen, 'Coincidences of Names, Anglo-Scottish Connections and Anglo-Saxon Society in the Late Eleventh Century', *SHR*, lxxxiii (2004), 150–70.
MARSHALL, P. J., *The Making and Unmaking of Empires: Britain, India and America, c.1750–1783* (Oxford, 2005).
MARTEN, Lucy, 'The Rebellion of 1075 and Its Impact in East Anglia', in C. Harper-Bill (ed.), *Medieval East Anglia* (Woodbridge, 2005), 168–82.
MARTINDALE, Jane, 'Aimeri of Thouars and the Poitevin Connection', *ANS*, vii (1985), 224–45.
—— 'Succession and Politics in the Romance-speaking World, c. 1000–1140', in Michael Jones and Malcolm Vale (eds), *England and Her Neighbours, 1066–1453: Essays in Honour of Pierre Chaplais* (London/Ronceverte, WV, 1989), 19–41.
MASON, Emma, *St Wulfstan of Worcester, c.1008–1095* (Oxford, 1990).
MASON, J. F. A., 'Barons and Their Officials in the Later Eleventh Century', *ANS*, xiii (1991), 243–62.
MATHIEU, Marguerite, 'Le manuscrit 162 d'Avranches et l'édition princeps des *Gesta Roberti Wiscardi* de Guillaume d'Apulie', *Byzantion*, xxiv (1954), 111–30.
MATTHEW, D. J. A., *The Norman Monasteries and Their English Possessions* (Oxford, 1962).
—— 'Mont Saint-Michel and England', in Dom. J. Laporte (ed.), *Millénaire monastique du Mont Saint-Michel, tom i: Histoire et vie monastique* (Paris, 1966), 677–702.
—— *Britain and the Continent, 1000–1300* (London, 2005).
MAUDUIT, Christophe, 'Les pouvoirs anglais et l'abbaye de Montebourg (XIe-XIIIe siècles)', in Bernard Bodinier (ed.), *Les Anglais en Normandie: Actes du 45e congrès organisé par la fédération des sociétés historiques et archéologiques de Normandie* (Louviers, 2011), 127–33.
MAUND, Kari L., *Gruffudd ap Cynan: A Collaborative Biography* (Woodbridge, 1996).
—— 'Gruffudd, grandson of Iago: *Historia Gruffud vab Kenan* and the Construction of Legitimacy', in Maund (ed.), *Gruffudd ap Cynan*, 109–16.
—— 'Owain ap Cadwgan: A Rebel Revisited', *HSJ*, xiii (2004, for 1999), 65–74.
—— *Princess Nest of Wales: Seductress of the English* (Stroud, 2007).
MAYR-HARTING, Henry, 'Charlemagne, the Saxons, and the Imperial Coronation of 800', *EHR*, cxi (1996), 1113–33.
—— 'Liudprand of Cremona's Account of His Legation to Constantinople (968) and Ottonian Imperial Strategy', *EHR*, cxvi (2001), 539–56.
MAZEL, Florian, *Féodalités, 888–1180* (Paris, 2010).
MÉNAGER, L.-R., 'Pesanteur et étiologie de la colonisation normande de l'Italie', 'Appendice: Inventaire des familles normandes et franques émigrés en Italie mériodionale et en Sicile (XIe-XIIe siècles)', and 'Additions à l'inventaire des familles normandes et franques émigrés en Italie mériodionale et en Sicile', in Ménager, *Hommes et institutions de l'Italie normande* (London, 1981), Chap. 4.
MOESGAARD, Jens Christian, 'Two Finds from Normandy of English Coins of the Norman Kings (1066–1154)', *Numismatic Chronicle*, cliv (1994), 209–13.
MOLYNEAUX, George, 'Why Were Some Tenth-Century Kings Presented as Rulers of Britain?', *TRHS*, 6th ser., xxi (2011), 59–91.
MOMMSEN, Wolfgang J., *Theories of Imperialism* (London, 1981).
MOOERS CHRISTELOW, Stephanie, 'Patronage in the Pipe Roll of 1130', *Speculum*, lix (1984), 282–307.
—— 'The Division of Inheritance and the Provision of Non-Inheriting Offspring among the Anglo-Norman Elite', *Medieval Prosopography*, xvii (1994), 3–43.

MOORE, R. I., 'Ranulf Flambard and Christina of Markyate', in Samuel Fanous and Henrietta Leyser (eds), *Christina of Markyate: A Twelfth-Century Holy Woman* (London/New York, 2005), 138–42.

MOORE, Tony K., 'The Loss of Normandy and the Invention of *Terre Normannorum*, 1204', *EHR*, cxxv (2010), 1071–1101.

MORGAN (CHIBNALL), Marjorie, *The English Lands of the Abbey of Bec* (Oxford, 1946).

MORILLO, Stephen, 'A General Typology of Transcultural Wars—The Early Middle Ages and Beyond', in H.-H. Kortüm (ed.), *Transcultural Wars from the Middle Ages to the 21st Century* (Berlin, 2006), 29–42.

MORTIMER, Richard, 'The Beginnings of the Honour of Clare', *ANS*, iii (1981), 119–41, 220–1.

——'Clare, Baldwin de (*fl.* 1130–1154)', *ODNB*.

——'Clare, Gilbert de (*d.*1117)', *ODNB*.

——'Clare, Richard de (1030 × 35–1087 × 90)', *ODNB*.

——'Clare, Roger de, second earl of Hertford (*d.*1173)', *ODNB*.

——(ed.), *Edward the Confessor: The Man and the Legend* (Woodbridge, 2009).

Moss, Vincent, 'Normandy and England in 1180: The Pipe Roll Evidence', in *England and Normandy*, 185–95.

——'The Norman Fiscal Revolution, 1193–8', in W. M. Ormrod, M. Bonney, and R. Bonney (eds), *Revolutions and Self-Sustained Growth: Essays in European Fiscal History, 1130–1830* (Oxford, 1999), 38–57.

——'The Defence of Normandy 1193–8', *ANS*, xxiv (2003), 145–61.

MÜNKLER, Herfried, *Empires: The Logic of World Domination from Ancient Rome to the United States* (Cambridge, UK/Malden, MA, 2007).

MURRAY, A. V., 'Money and Logistics in the Forces of the First Crusade: Coinage, Bullion, Service and Supply, 1096–99', in J. H. Pryor (ed.), *Logistics of Warfare in the Age of the Crusades* (London, 2006), 229–49.

MUSSET, Lucien, 'Quelques problèmes posés par l'annexion de la Normandie au domain royal français', in R.-H. Bautier et al. (eds), *La France de Philippe Auguste* (Paris, 1982), 291–309.

——'Barfleur, plaque tournante de l'Etat anglo-normand', *Annuaire des cinq départements de la Normandie*, cxli (1983), 51–7.

——'La pierre de Caen: extraction et commerce, XIe–XVe siècles', in Odette Chapelot and Paul Benoit (eds), *Pierre et métal dans le bâtiment au Moyen Age* (Paris, 1985; repr., 2001), 219–35.

——'Un empire à cheval sur la mer: les périls de mer dans l'Etat anglo-normand d'après les chartes, les chroniques et les miracles', in Alain Lottin, Jean-Claude Hocquet, and Stéphane Lebecq (eds), *Les Hommes et la Mer dans l'Europe du Nord-Ouest de l'Antiquité à nos jours*, *Revue du Nord*, numéro 1 spécial hors série—collection Histoire (1986), 413–24.

——'Y eut-il une aristocratie d'affaires commune aux grandes villes de Normandie et d'Angleterre entre 1066 et 1204?', *Etudes normandes*, xxxv, no. 3 (1986), 7–19.

——'Le mécenat des princes normands au XIe siècle', in X. Barret I. Altet (ed.), *Artistes, artisans et production artistique au Moyen Age*, 3 vols (Paris, 1986–90), ii, 121–33.

——'Réflexions sur les moyens de paiement en Normandie au XIe et XIIe siècle', in Lucien Musset, Jean-Michel Bouvris, and Véronique Gazeau (eds), *Aspects de la société et de l'économie dans la Normandie mediévale (Xe-XIIIe siècles)*, Cahiers des Annales de Normandie, no. 22 (Caen, 1989), 65–89.

—— 'Essai sur le peuplement de la Normandie (VIe–XIIe siècle)', in L. Musset, *Nordica et Normannica: Recueil d'études sur la Scandinavie ancienne et médiévale, les expéditions des Vikings et la fondation de la Normandie* (Paris, 1997), 389–402.
NEF, Anniliese, *Conquérir de gouverner la Sicile islamique aux XIe et XIIe siècles* (Rome, 2011).
NELSON, Janet L., 'Kingship and Empire in the Carolingian World', in Rosamond McKitterick (ed.), *Carolingian Culture: Emulation and Renovation* (Cambridge, 1994), 52–87.
——*Charlemagne and the Paradoxes of Power*, Reuter Lecture 2005 (Southampton, 2006).
—— 'Henry Loyn and the Context of Anglo-Saxon England', Henry Loyn Memorial Lecture for 2006, *HSJ*, xix (2007), 154–70.
—— 'Frankish Identity in Charlemagne's Empire', in Ildar H. Garipzanov, Patrick J. Geary, and Przemyslaw Urbanczyk (eds), *Franks, Northmen and Slavs: Identities and State Formation in Early Medieval Europe* (Turnhout, 2008), 71–83.
—— 'Normandy's Early History since *Normandy before 1066*', in *Normandy and Neighbours*, 3–15.
——, REYNOLDS, Susan, and JOHNS, Susan M. (eds), *Gender and Historiography: Studies in the History of the Earlier Middle Ages in Honour of Pauline Stafford* (London, 2012).
NEVEUX, François, *La Normandie des ducs aux rois X^e-XIIe siècle* (Rennes, 1998).
——*L'Aventure des Normands (VIIIe–XIIIe siècle)* (Paris, 2006), translated into English as *A Brief History of the Normans: The Conquests that Changed the Face of Europe*, trans. Howard Curtis (London, 2008).
NIGHTINGALE, Pamela, 'The Evolution of Weight-Standards and the Creation of New Monetary and Commercial Links in Northern Europe from the Tenth to the Twelfth Century', *Economic History Review*, 2nd ser., xxxviii (1985), 192–210; reprinted in Nightingale, *Trade, Money, and Power in Medieval England* (Aldershot/Burlington VT, 2007), Chap. 4.
NILGEN, Ursula, 'Thomas Becket en Normandie', in Bouet and Neveux (eds), *Les Saints dans la Normandie médiévale*, 189–204.
NIP, Renée, 'The Political Relations between England and Flanders (1066–1128)', *ANS*, xxi (1999), 145–67.
NORTON, Christopher, *Archbishop Thomas of Bayeux and the Norman Cathedral at York*, Borthwick Papers, no. 100 (York, 2001).
NYE Jr., Joseph S., *Soft Power: The Means to Success in World Politics* (New York, 2004).
O'BRIEN, Bruce R., 'From *Morðor* to *Murdrum*: The Preconquest Origin and Norman Revival of the Murder Fine', *Speculum*, lxxi (1996), 321–5.
——*God's Peace and King's Peace: The Laws of Edward the Confessor* (Philadelphia, 1999).
O'KEEFFE, Tadgh, *Romanesque Ireland: Architecture and Ideology of the Twelfth Century* (Dublin, 2003).
OBHOLZER, Anton, and ROBERTS, Vega Zagier (eds), *The Unconscious at Work: Individual and Organizational Stress in the Human Services* (London/New York, 1994; and subsequently reprinted many times).
OGBORN, Miles, *Global Lives: Britain and the World, 1550–1800* (Cambridge, 2008).
OKSANEN, Elijas, *Flanders and the Anglo-Norman World, 1066–1216* (Cambridge, 2012).
ORAM, Richard, *David I: The King Who Made Scotland* (Stroud, 2004).
PALMER, J. J. N., 'The Conqueror's Footprints in Domesday Book', in Andrew Ayton and J. L. Price (eds), *The Medieval Military Revolution: State, Society and Military Change in Medieval and Early Modern Europe* (London/New York, 1995), 23–44.
—— 'War and Domesday Waste', in Strickland (ed.), *Armies, Chivalry and Warfare*, 256–75.
—— 'The Wealth of the Secular Aristocracy in 1086', *ANS*, xxii (2000), 279–91.

PARSONS, Timothy H., *The Rule of Empires: Those Who Built Them, Those Who Endured Them, and Why They Always Fall* (Oxford, 2010).

PELTZER, Jörg, 'Henry II and the Norman Bishops', *EHR*, cxix (2004), 1202–29.

—— 'The Angevin Kings and Canon Law: Episcopal Elections and the Loss of Normandy', *ANS*, xxvii (2005), 169–84.

PÉPIN, Guilhelm, 'Les couronnements et les investitures des ducs d'Aquitaine (XIe–XIIe siècle)', *Francia*, xxxvi (2009), 35–65.

PERCIVAL, John, 'The Precursors of Domesday: Roman and Carolingian Land Registers', in P. H. Sawyer (ed.), *Domesday Book: A Reassessment* (London, 1985), 5–27.

PFAFF, Richard W., 'Lanfranc's Supposed Purge of the Anglo-Saxon Calendar', in Timothy Reuter (ed.), *Warriors and Churchmen in the High Middle Ages: Essays Presented to Karl Leyser* (London/Rio Grande, 1992), 95–108.

PHILPOTT, Mark, 'Some Interactions between the English and Irish Churches', *ANS*, xx (1998), 187–204.

PICHOT, Daniel, *Le Bas-Maine du Xe au XIIIe siècle: étude d'une société* (Laval, 1995).

PITHOIS, Claude, *Brix, berceau des rois d'Ecosse* (Condé-sur-Noireau, 1980).

PLANT, Richard, 'Architectural Developments in the Empire north of the Alps: The Patronage of the Imperial Court', in Nigel Hiscock (ed.), *The White Mantle of Churches. Architecture, Liturgy, and Art around the Millennium* (Turnhout, 2003), 29–56.

——'Ecclesiastical Architecture *c*.1050 to *c*.1200', in Christopher Harper-Bill and Elisabeth van Houts (eds), *A Companion to the Anglo-Norman World* (Woodbridge, 2003), 215–53.

——'Romanesque East Anglia and the Empire', in Bates and Liddiard (eds), *East Anglia and its North Sea World*, 270–86.

PLASSMANN, Alheydis, *'Origo gentis': Identitäts- und Legitimitätsstiftung in früh- und hochmittelalterlichen Herkunftserzählunge* (Berlin, 2006).

PORTER, Bernard, *Absent-Minded Imperialists: Empire, Society and Culture in Britain* (Oxford, 2004).

——'Cutting the British Empire Down to Size', *History Today*, lxii, no. 10 (2012), 22–9.

PÖSSEL, Christina, 'The Magic of Early Medieval Ritual', *EME*, xvii (2009), 111–25.

POTTS, Cassandra, '*Atque unum et diversis gentibus populum effecit*: Historical Tradition and Norman Identity', *ANS*, xviii (1996), 139–52.

POWER, Daniel, *The Norman Frontier in the Twelfth and Thirteenth Centuries* (Cambridge, 2004).

——'The Norman Church and the Angevin and Capetian Kings', *JEH*, lvi (2005), 205–34.

——'Les dernières années du régime angevin en Normandie', in Martin Aurell and Noël-Yves Tonnerre (eds), *Plantagenêts et Capétiens: confrontations et héritages* (Turnhout, 2006), 163–92.

——'Henry, Duke of the Normans (1149/50–1189)', in Harper-Bill and Vincent (eds), *Henry II: New Interpretations*, 85–128.

——'Guérin de Glapion, Seneschal of Normandy (1200–01): Service and Ambition under the Plantagenet and Capetian Kings', in Vincent (ed.), *Records, Administration and Aristocratic Society*, 153–85.

——'Le régime seigneurial en Normandie (XIIe-XIIIe s.)', in Aurell and Boutoulle (eds), *Les seigneuries dans l'espace Plantagenêt*, 117–36.

POWICKE, F. M., *The Loss of Normandy, 1189–1204: Studies in the History of the Angevin Empire*, 2nd edn. (Manchester, 1961).

PRESTWICH, J. O., 'The Military Household of the Norman Kings', *EHR*, xcvi (1981), 1–37; reprinted in Strickland (ed.), *Anglo-Norman Warfare*, 93–127.

PRYCE, Huw, 'Owain Gwynedd and Louis VII: The Franco-Welsh Diplomacy of the First Prince of Wales', *WHR*, xix (1998), 1–28.

—— 'British or Welsh? National Identity in Twelfth-Century Wales', *EHR*, cxvi (2001), 775–801.

—— and WATTS, John (eds), *Power and Identity in the Middle Ages: Essays in Memory of Rees Davies* (Oxford, 2007).

—— 'Welsh Rulers and European Change, c.1100–1282', in Pryce and Watts (eds), *Power and Identity*, 37–51.

—— 'The Normans in Welsh History', *ANS*, xxx (2008), 1–18.

RAWCLIFFE, Carole, and WILSON, Richard (eds), *Medieval Norwich* (London/New York, 2004).

REIMITZ, Helmut, '*Omnes Franci*: Identifications and Identities of the Early Medieval Franks', in Ildar H. Garipzanov, Patrick J. Geary, and Przemyslaw Urbanczyk (eds), *Franks, Northmen and Slavs: Identities and State Formation in Early Medieval Europe* (Turnhout, 2008), 51–68.

REUTER, Timothy, 'Plunder and Tribute in the Carolingian Empire', *TRHS*, 5th. ser., xxxv (1985), 75–94; reprinted in Janet L. Nelson (ed.), *Medieval Polities and Modern Mentalities* (Cambridge, 2006).

REYNOLDS, Susan, *Kingdoms and Communities in Western Europe* (Oxford, 1984).

—— 'Fiefs and Vassals in Scotland: A View from the Outside', *SHR*, lxxxii (2003), 176–93.

—— 'Empires: A Problem of Comparative History', *HR*, lxxix (2006), 151–65.

—— 'Secular Power and Authority in the Middle Ages', in Pryce and Watts (eds), *Power and Identity*, 11–22.

—— *Before Eminent Domain: Towards a History of the Expropriation of Land for the Common Good* (Chapel Hill, NC, 2010).

RICHARD, C., 'Notice sur l'ancienne bibliothèque des Echevins de la ville de Rouen', in *Précis Analytique des Travaux de l'Académie Royale des Sciences, Belles-Lettres et Arts de Rouen* (Rouen, 1845), 127–82.

RIDEL, Elisabeth, *Les navires de la Conquête: construction navale et navigation en Normandie à l'époque de Guillaume le Conquérant* (Cully, 2010).

RIDYARD, Susan J., '*Condigna Veneratio*: Post-Conquest Attitudes to the Saints of the Anglo-Saxons', *ANS*, ix (1987), 179–206.

—— *The Royal Saints of Anglo-Saxon England* (Cambridge, 1988).

RILEY-SMITH, Jonathan, *The First Crusaders, 1095–1131* (Cambridge, 1997).

ROCHE, Thomas, 'The Way Vengeance Comes: Rancorous Deeds and Words in the World of Orderic Vitalis', in Susanna A. Throop and Paul R. Hyams (eds), *Vengeance in the Middle Ages: Emotion, Religion and Feud* (Farnham/Burlington VT, 2010), 115–36.

ROFFE, David, 'Domesday Book and Northern Society: A Reassessment', *EHR*, cv (1990), 310–36.

—— 'From Thegnage to Barony: Sake and Soke, Titles and Tenants-in-Chief', *ANS*, xii (1990), 157–76.

—— *Domesday: The Inquest and the Book* (Oxford, 2000).

—— (ed.) *The English and their Legacy, 900–1200: Essays in Honour of Ann Williams* (Woodbridge, 2012).

—— 'Hidden Lives: English Lords in post-Conquest Lincolnshire and Beyond', in Roffe (ed.), *The English and Their Legacy*, 205–28.

ROLLASON, David, 'Symeon's Contribution to Historical Writing in Northern England', in David Rollason (ed.), *Symeon of Durham: Historian of Durham and the North* (Stamford, 1998), 1–13.

ROSE, R. K., 'Cumbrian Society and the Anglo-Norman Church', in Stuart Mews (ed.), *Religion and National Identity: Papers Read at the Nineteenth Summer Meeting of the Twentieth Winter Meeting of the Ecclesiastical History Society* (Oxford, 1982), 119–35.

ROTHSCHILD, Emma, *The Inner Life of Empires: An Eighteenth-Century History* (Princeton, NJ/Oxford, 2011), 300.

ROUET, Dominique, 'Le patrimoine anglais et l'Angleterre vus à travers les actes du cartulaire de Saint-Pierre de Préaux', in *Normandie et Angleterre*, 99–116.

ROUND, J. H., 'The Family of Ballon and the Conquest of South Wales', in *Studies in Peerage and Family History* (Westminster, 1901), 181–215.

—— 'Clare, Walter de (*d*.1137/8?)' (*rev*. C. Warren Hollister), *ODNB*.

ROWLANDS, I. W., 'The Making of the March: Aspects of the Norman Settlement in Dyfed', *ANS*, iii (1981), 142–57.

—— '"Warriors Fit for a Prince": Welsh Troops in Angevin Service, 1154–1216', in John France (ed.), *Mercenaries and Paid Men: The Mercenary Identity in the Middle Ages* (Leiden/Boston, 2008), 207–30.

RUBINSTEIN, Jay C., 'The Life and Writings of Osbern of Canterbury', in Eales and Sharpe (eds), *Canterbury and the Norman Conquest*, 27–40.

—— 'Eadmer (Edmer) of Canterbury', *ODNB*.

SANDS, H., BRAUN, H., and LOYD, L. C., 'Conisbrough and Mortemer', *Yorkshire Archaeological Journal*, xxxii (1936), 147–59.

SCALES, Len, 'Bread, Cheese and Genocide: Imagining the Destruction of Peoples in Medieval Western Europe', *History*, xcii (2007), 284–300.

SCHMITT, Jean-Claude, *The Holy Greyhound: Guinefort, Healer of Children since the Thirteenth Century* (Cambridge, 1983).

SEARLE, Eleanor, *Predatory Kinship and the Creation of Norman Power, 840–1066* (Berkeley/London, 1988).

SEELEY, J. R., *The Expansion of England*, ed., with an introduction by John Gross (Chicago/London, 1971).

SHARPE, Richard, 'The Setting of St Augustine's Translation, 1091', in Eales and Sharpe (eds), *Canterbury and the Norman Conquest*, 1–13.

—— 'King Harold's Daughter', *HSJ*, xix (2008, for 2007), 1–27.

—— 'Peoples and Languages in Eleventh- and Twelfth-Century Britain and Ireland: Reading the Charter Evidence', in Broun et al. (eds), *The Reality behind Charter Diplomatic*, 1–119.

—— et al., *English Benedictine Libraries: The Shorter Catalogues*, Corpus of British Medieval Library Catalogues, 4 (London, 1996).

SHOPKOW, Leah, *History and Community: Norman Historical Writing in the Eleventh and Twelfth Centuries* (Washington, DC, 1997).

SHORT, Ian, 'Patrons and Polyglots: French Literature in Twelfth-Century England', *ANS*, xiv (1992).

—— 'Literary Culture at the Court of Henry II', in Harper-Bill and Vincent (eds), *Henry II: New Interpretations*, 335–61.

—— *Manual of Anglo-Norman*, Anglo-Norman Text Society, Occasional Publications Series no. 7 (London, 2007).

SIRANTOINE, Hélène, 'Memoria construida, memoria destruida: La identidad monárquica a través del recuerdo de los emperadores de *Hispania* en los diplomas de los soberanos

castellanos y leonese (1065–1230)', in José Antonio Jara Fuente, Georges Martin, and Isabel Alfonso Antón (eds), *Construir la identidad en la Edad Media. Poder y memoria en la Castilla de los siglos VII al XV* (Cuenca, 2010), 225–47.
——*Imperator Hispaniae: les idéologies impériales dans le royaume de León (IXe–XIIe siècles)* (Madrid, 2012).
Six, Manon, 'De la Vicomtesse Emma et son entourage', *Tabularia 'Etudes'*, iv (2004), 79–103 (<http://www.unicaen.fr/mrsh/craham/revue/tabularia>).
——'The Burgesses of Rouen in the Late Twelfth and Early Thirteenth Centuries', in Hicks and Brenner (eds), *Society and Culture*, 247–78.
Slitt, Rebecca L. 'The Two Deaths of William Longsword: Wace, William of Malmesbury and the Norman Past', *ANS*, xxxiv (2012), 193–208.
Smith, Anthony D., *The Nation in History* (Hanover, NH, 2000).
Smith, Brendan, 'The Frontiers of Church Reform in the British Isles, 1170–1230', in David Abulafia and Nora Berend (eds), *Medieval Frontiers: Concepts and Practices*, (Aldershot/Burlington VT, 2002), 239–53.
Smith, Julia M. H., *Province and Empire: Brittany and the Carolingians* (Cambridge, 1992).
——'*Fines Imperii*: The Marches', in Rosamond McKitterick (ed.), *The New Cambridge Medieval History*, vol. ii: *c.700–c.900* (Cambridge, 1995), 169–89.
——*Europe after Rome: A New Cultural History* (Oxford, 2005).
Smith, Marc H., 'Aux origines incertaines de l'écriture gothique, entre Angleterre et Normandie', in Jean-Paulle Hervieu, Emmanuel Poulle, and Philippe Manneville (eds), *La place de la Normandie dans la diffusion des savoirs: Du livre manuscript à la bibliothèque virtuelle* (Rouen, 2006), 79–94.
Sønnesyn, Sigbjørn Olsen, *William of Malmesbury and the Ethics of History* (Woodbridge, 2012).
Southern, R. W., *Saint Anselm and his Biographer* (Cambridge, 1963).
——'Aspects of the European Tradition of Historical Writing: 4. The Sense of the Past', *TRHS*, 5th ser., xxiii (1973), 246–63; reprinted in Robert Bartlett (ed.), *History and Historians: Selected Papers of R.W. Southern* (Oxford, 2004), 66–83.
Spear, David, 'The Norman Empire and the Secular Clergy, 1066–1204', *Journal of British Studies*, xxi (1982), 1–10.
——'Power, Patronage and Personality in the Norman Cathedral Chapters, 911–1204', *ANS*, xx (1998), 205–21.
——*The Personnel of the Norman Cathedrals during the Ducal Period, 911–1204* (London, 2006).
Stafford, Pauline, *Queen Emma and Queen Edith* (Oxford, 1997).
——'Writing the Biography of Eleventh-Century Queens', in Bates, Crick, and Hamilton (eds), *Writing Medieval Biography*, 99–109.
——'Archbishop Ealdred and the D Chronicle', in *Normandy and Neighbours*, 135–56.
Stephenson, David, 'Madog ap Maredudd: *Rex Powissensium*', *WHR*, xxiv (2008), 1–28.
——'The "Resurgence" of Powys in the Late Eleventh and Early Twelfth Centuries', *ANS*, xxx (2008), 182–95.
Strevett, Neil, 'The Anglo-Norman Civil War of 1101 reconsidered', *ANS*, xxvi (2004), 159–75.
Strickland, Matthew, 'Securing the North: Invasion and the Strategy of Defence in Twelfth-Century Anglo-Scottish Warfare', *ANS*, xii (1990), 177–98; reprinted in Strickland (ed.), *Anglo-Norman Warfare*, 208–29.
——(ed.), *Anglo-Norman Warfare: Studies in Late Anglo-Saxon and Anglo-Norman Military Organisation and Warfare* (Woodbridge, 1992).

—— *War and Chivalry: The Conduct and Perception of War in England and Normandy, 1066–1217* (Cambridge, 1996).

—— (ed.), *Armies, Chivalry and Warfare in Medieval Britain and France: Proceedings of the 1995 Harlaxton Symposium* (Stamford, 1998).

—— 'Provoking or Avoiding Battle? Challenge, Judicial Duel, and Single Combat in Eleventh- and Twelfth-Century Warfare', in Strickland (ed.), *Armies, Chivalry and Warfare*, 317–43.

—— 'Killing or Clemency? Ransom, Chivalry and Changing Attitudes to Defeated Opponents in Britain and Northern France, 7–12th centuries', in Hans-Henning Kortüm (ed.), *Krieg im Mittelalter* (Berlin, 2001), 93–122.

—— 'Henry I and the Battle of the Two Kings: Brémule, 1119', in *Normandy and Neighbours*, 77–116.

STRINGER, Keith J., *The Reign of Stephen: Kingship, Warfare and Government in Twelfth-Century England* (London/New York, 1993).

—— 'State-Building in Twelfth-Century Britain: David I, King of Scots, and Northern England', in J. C. Appleby and Paul Dalton (eds), *Government, Religion and Society in Northern England, 1000–1700* (Stroud, 1997), 40–62.

SUPPE, F. C., *Military Institutions on the Welsh Marches: Shropshire, AD 1066–1300* (Woodbridge, 1994).

SYKES, Naomi, 'Zooarchaeology of the Norman Conquest', *ANS*, xxvii (2005), 185–97.

—— *The Norman Conquest: A Zooarchaeological Perspective* (Oxford, 2007).

TABUTEAU, Emily Zack, 'The Role of Law in the Succession to England and Normandy, 1087', *HSJ*, iii (1991), 141–69.

—— 'Punishments in Eleventh-Century Normandy', in Warren C. Brown and Piotr Górecki (eds), *Conflict in Medieval Europe: Changing Perspectives on Society and Culture* (Aldershot/Burlington, VT, 2003), 131–49.

TANNER, Heather J., 'Queenship: Office, Custom or Ad Hoc? The Case of Queen Matilda III of England (1135–1152)', in Bonnie Wheeler and John Carmi Parsons (eds), *Eleanor of Aquitaine: Lord and Lady* (New York, 2002), 133–58.

—— *Families, Friends and Allies: Boulogne and Politics in Northern France and England, c.879–1160* (Leiden and Boston, 2004).

TATTON-BROWN, Tim, 'La pierre de Caen en Angleterre', in Baylé (ed.), *L'architecture normande*, 305–14.

TAYLOR, Alice, '*Leges Scocie* and the lawcodes of David I, William the Lion and Alexander II', *SHR*, lxxxviii (2009), 207–88.

—— 'Historical Writing in Twelfth- and Thirteenth-Century Scotland: The Dunfermline Compilation', *HR*, lxxxiii (2010), 1–25.

THOMAS, Hugh M., *The English and the Normans: Ethnic Hostility, Assimilation, and Identity, 1066-c.1220* (Oxford, 2003).

—— 'The Significance and Fate of the Native English Landholders of 1086', *EHR*, cxviii (2003), 303–33.

THOMAS, Mark G., STUMPF, Michael P. H., and HÄRKE, Heinrich, 'Evidence for an Apartheid-Like Social Structure in Early Anglo-Saxon England', *Proceedings of the Royal Society B*, no. 273 (2006), 2651–7.

THOMPSON, Kathleen, 'Robert of Bellême Reconsidered', *ANS*, xiii (1991), 263–86.

—— 'William Talvas, Count of Ponthieu, and the Politics of the Anglo-Norman Realm', in *England and Normandy*, 169–84.

—— 'The Lords of Laigle: Ambition and Insecurity on the Borders of Normandy', *ANS*, xviii (1996), 177–99.

―――― *Power and Border Lordship in Medieval France: the County of Perche, 1000–1226*, Royal Historical Society Studies in History (Woodbridge, 2002).
―――― 'Queen Adeliza and the Lotharingian Connection', *Sussex Archaeological Collections*, cxl (2002), 57–64.
―――― 'L'aristocratie anglo-normande en 1204', in *Normandie et Angleterre*, 179–87.
―――― 'Affairs of State: The Illegitimate Children of Henry I', *JMH*, xxix (2003), 129–51.
―――― 'Bellême, Robert de, earl of Shrewsbury and count of Ponthieu', *ODNB*.
―――― 'L'héritier et le remplaçant: le rôle du frère puîné dans la politique anglo-normande (1066–1204)', in *Tinchebray*, 93–101.
―――― 'Les seigneuries anglaises et françaises des comtes de Perche (1100–1226)', in Aurell and Boutoulle (eds), *Les seigneuries dans l'espace Plantagenêt*, 61–75.
―――― 'Being the Ducal Sister: The Role of Adelaide of Aumale', in *Normandy and Neighbours*, 61–76.
―――― 'The Arrival of the Tironensians: Twelfth-Century Monastic Foundations in the British Isles', *Nottingham Medieval Studies*, lv (2011), 79–103.
THOMSON, R. M., 'William of Malmesbury's Carolingian Sources', *JMH*, vii (1981), 321–37; reprinted in Thomson, *William of Malmesbury* (rev. edn., Woodbridge, 2003), 137–53.
TOORIANS, Lauran, 'Wizo Flandrensis and the Flemish Settlement in Pembrokeshire', *Cambridge Medieval Celtic Studies*, xx (1990), 99–118.
―――― 'Twelfth-Century Flemish Settlements in Scotland', in Grant Simpson (ed.), *Scotland and the Low Countries* (East Linton, 1996), 1–14.
TRAVAINI, L., *La monetazione nell'Italia normanna* (Rome, 1995).
TURNER, Ralph V., 'Les contacts entre l'Angleterre normanno-angevine et la Sicile normande', *Etudes normandes*, no. 3 (1986), 39–55.
TYLER, Elizabeth M. (ed.), *Conceptualizing Multilingualism in Medieval England, c.800–c.1250* (Turnhout, 2011).
―――― 'England and Multilingualism: Medieval and Modern', in Tyler (ed.), *Conceptualizing Multilingualism*, 1–13.
URBANSKI, Charity, 'Apology, Protest and Suppression: Interpreting the Surrender of Caen (1105)', *HSJ*, xix (2008, for 2007), 137–53.
URRY, John, *Mobilities* (Cambridge, 2007).
URRY, William, 'The Normans in Canterbury', *AN*, viii (1958), 119–38.
―――― *Canterbury under the Angevin Kings* (London, 1967).
VAN EICKELS, Klaus, '*Homagium* and *Amicitia*: Rituals of Peace and their Significance in the Anglo-French Negotiations of the Twelfth Century', *Francia*, xxiv (1997), 133–40.
―――― *Vom inszenierten Konsens zum systematisierten Konflikt: Die englische-französischen Beziechengen und ihre Wahrnehmung an der Wende vom Hoch- zum Spätmittelalter* (Stuttgart, 2002).
VAN HOUTS, Elisabeth, 'The *Gesta Normannorum Ducum*: a History without an End', *ANS*, iii (1981), 106–18, 215–20.
―――― 'The Adaptation of the *Gesta Normannorum Ducum* by Wace and Benoît', in M. Gosman and J. Van Os (eds), *Non Nova, sed Nove: Mélanges de civilisation médiévale dédiées à Willelm Noomen*, (Groningen, 1984), 115–24; reprinted in van Houts, *History and Family Traditions*, Chap. 11.
―――― 'Normandy and Byzantium in the Eleventh Century', *Byzantion*, lv (1985), 544–59; reprinted in van Houts, *History and Family Traditions*, Chap. 1.
―――― 'The Ship List of William the Conqueror', *ANS*, x (1988), 159–83; reprinted in van Houts, *History and Family Traditions*, Chap. 6.

—— 'Latin Poetry and the Anglo-Norman Court 1066–1135: the *Carmen de Hastingae Proelio*', *JMH*, xv (1989), 103–32; reprinted in van Houts, *History and Family Traditions*, Chap. 9.
—— 'The Norman Conquest through European Eyes', *EHR*, cx (1995), 832–53; reprinted in van Houts, *History and Family Traditions*, Chap. 8.
—— 'The Trauma of 1066', *History Today*, xlvi, no. 10 (1996), 9–15.
—— 'The Memory of 1066 in Written and Oral Traditions', *ANS*, xix (1997), 167–79.
—— *History and Family Traditions in England and the Continent, 1000–1200* (Aldershot, 1999).
—— *Memory and Gender in Medieval Europe, 900–1200* (Basingstoke and London, 1999).
—— (ed. and trans.), *The Normans in Europe*, Manchester Medieval Sources (Manchester/New York, 2000).
—— 'The Echo of the Conquest in the Latin Sources: Duchess Matilda, Her Daughters, and the Enigma of the Golden Child', in Pierre Bouet, Brian Levy, and François Neveux (eds), *The Bayeux Tapestry: Embroidering the Facts of History* (Caen, 2004), 135–53.
—— 'The Warenne View of the Past, 1066–1203', *ANS*, xxvi (2004), 103–21.
—— 'Gender, Memories and Prophecies in Medieval Europe', in Werner Verbeke, Ludo Milis, and Jean Goossens (eds), *Medieval Narrative Sources. A Gateway into the Medieval Mind* (Louvain, 2005), 21–36.
—— 'Edward and Normandy', in Richard Mortimer (ed.), *Edward the Confessor: The Man and the Legend* (Woodbridge, 2009), 63–76.
—— 'Intermarriage in Eleventh-Century England', in *Normandy and Neighbours*, 237–70.
—— 'Rouen as another Rome in the Twelfth Century', in Hicks and Brenner (eds), *Culture and Society*, 101–24.
VAN TORHOUDT, Eric, 'L'"énigme" des origines de l'abbaye de Montebourg: une question de methode?', in Pierre Bouet et al. (eds), *De Part et d'Autre de la Normandie médiévale: Recueil d'études en hommage à François Neveux*, Cahiers des Annales de Normandie (Caen, 2009), 331–46.
VAUGHN, Sally N., 'Charles Homer Haskins', in Clyde N. Wilson (ed.), *The Dictionary of Literary Biography*, vol. 47: *American Historians, 1866–1912* (Detroit, 1986), 122–44.
—— 'Charles Homer Haskins (1870–1937)', in Helen Damico and Joseph B. Zadavil (eds), *Medieval Scholarship: Biographical Studies on the Formation of a Discipline*, vol. 1: *History* (New York/London, 1995), 169–84.
VINCENT, Nicholas, 'Isabella of Angoulême: John's Jezebel', in Church (ed.), *King John: New Interpretations*, 165–219.
—— 'King Henry II and the Monks of Battle: The Battle Chronicle Unmasked', in Richard Gameson and Henrietta Leyser (eds), *Belief and Culture in the Middle Ages: Studies presented to Henry Mayr-Harting* (Oxford, 2001), 264–86.
—— 'Les Normands de l'entourage d'Henri II Plantagenêt', in *Normandie et Angleterre*, 75–88.
—— 'A Collection of Early Norman Charters in the British Library: The Case of Jeremiah Holmes Wiffen', *Cahiers Léopold Delisle*, liii (2004), 21–45.
—— 'The Strange Case of the Missing Biographies: The Lives of the Plantagenet Kings of England, 1154–1272', in Bates, Crick, and Hamilton (eds), *Writing Medieval Biography*, 237–57.
—— 'Jean, comte de Mortain: le futur roi et ses domaines en Normandie, 1183–1199', in *1204*, 37–59.
—— 'Did Henry II Have a Policy towards the Earls ?', in Chris Given-Wilson, Ann Kettle, and Len Scales (eds), *War, Government and Aristocracy in the British Isles, c.1150–1500: Essays in Honour of Michael Prestwich* (Woodbridge, 2008), 1–25.

—— (ed.) *Records, Administration and Aristocratic Society in the Anglo-Norman Realm: Papers Commemorating the 800th Anniversary of King John's Loss of Normandy* (Woodbridge, 2009).
—— 'More Tales of the Conquest', in *Normandy and Neighbours*, 271–301.
—— 'The English Monasteries and their French Possessions', in Dalton, Insley, and Wilkinson (eds), *Cathedrals, Communities and Conflict*, 221–39.
—— 'Some Effects of the Dynastic Alliances between England and France', in Gazeau and Genet (eds), *La France et les îles Britanniques*, 59–74.
WARD, Jennifer C., 'Royal Service and Reward: the Clare Family and the Crown, 1066–1154', *ANS*, xi (1989), 261–78.
WAREHAM, Andrew, 'The Motives and Politics of the Bigod Family, c.1066–177', *ANS*, xvii (1995), 223–42.
WASSERMANN, Stanley, and Katherine FAUST, *Social Network Analysis: Methods and Applications* (Cambridge, 1994).
WEBB, Nigel M., 'Settlement and Integration: The Establishment of an Aristocracy in Scotland (1124–1214)', *ANS*, xxv (2003), 227–38.
WEBBER, Nick, *The Evolution of Norman Identity, 911–1154* (Woodbridge, 2005).
—— 'England and the Norman Myth', in Julia Barrow and Andrew Wareham (eds), *Myth, Rulership, Church and Charters: Essays in Honour of Nicholas Brooks* (Aldershot/Burlington VT, 2008), 211–28.
WEBBER, Teresa, 'Script and Manuscript Production at Christ Church, Canterbury, after the Norman Conquest', in Eales and Sharpe (eds), *Canterbury and the Norman Conquest*, 145–58.
WEILER, Bjørn, 'William of Malmesbury on Kingship', *History*, xc (2005), 3–22.
WEST, Charles, 'All in the Same Boat? East Anglia, the North Sea World and the 1147 Expedition to Lisbon', in Bates and Liddiard (eds), *East Anglia and its North Sea World*, 287–300.
WEST, Francis J., 'The Colonial History of the Norman Conquest', *History*, lxxxiv (1999), 219–36.
WHITE, Graeme J., *Restoration and Reform, 1153–1165: Recovery from Civil War in England* (Cambridge, 2000), 77–122.
—— 'Ranulf (II), fourth earl of Chester (d.1153)', *ODNB*.
WHITE, Stephen D., 'The Beasts who talk on the Bayeux Embroidery: The Fables Revisited', *ANS*, xxxiv (2012), 209–36.
WIGHTMAN, W. E., *The Lacy Family in England and Normandy, 1066–1194* (Oxford, 1966).
WILLIAMS, Ann, *The English and the Norman Conquest* (Woodbridge, 1995).
—— 'Little Domesday and the English: the hundred of Colneis in Suffolk', in Hallam and Bates (eds), *Domesday Book*, 103–20.
—— 'The Cunning of the Dove: Wulfstan and the Politics of Accommodation', in Julia S. Barrow and N. P. Brooks (eds), *St Wulfstan and his World* (Aldershot/Burlington VT, 2005), 23–38.
—— 'Henry I and the English', in Fleming and Pope (eds), *Henry I and the Anglo-Norman World*, 27–38.
WILLIAMS, Gareth, 'Monetary Contacts between England and Normandy, c.973–1180: A Numismatic Perspective', in Jérémie Chameroy and Pierre-Marie Guihard (eds), *Circulations monétaires en Normandie et dans le Nord-Ouest européen (Antiquité-Moyen-Âge)* (Caen, 2012), 173–84.
WILSON, Christopher, 'Abbot Serlo's Church at Gloucester, 1089–1100: Its Place in Romanesque Architecture', in T. A. Heslop and V. A. Sekules (eds), *Medieval Art and Architecture at Gloucester and Tewkesbury*, British Art and Archaeological Association Conference Transactions, vii (1985), 52–83.

WINTERBOTTOM, Michael, 'William of Malmesbury and the Normans', *Journal of Medieval Latin*, xx (2010), 70–7.
WOOLF, Alex, 'Apartheid and Economics in Anglo-Saxon England', in Nick Higham (ed.), *Britons in Anglo-Saxon England* (Woodbridge, 2007), 115–29.
WORMALD, Patrick, *How Do We Know So Much about Anglo-Saxon Deerhurst*, Deerhurst Lecture, 1991 (Deerhurst: Friends of Deerhurst Church, 1991); reprinted in Wormald, *The Times of Bede: Studies in Early English Christian Society and its Historian*, ed. Stephen Baxter (Oxford, 2006), 229–48.
—— *The Making of English Law: King Alfred to the Twelfth Century*, vol 1: *Legislation and its Limits* (Oxford, 1999).
—— 'Germanic Power Structures: The Early English Experience', in Len Scales and Oliver Zimmer (eds), *Power and Nation in European History* (Cambridge, 2005), 105–24.
WRIGHT, Neil, 'The Place of Henry of Huntingdon's *Epistola ad Warinum* in the Text History of Geoffrey of Monmouth's *Historia regum Britannie*: A Preliminary Investigation', in G. Jondorf and D. N. Dumville (eds), *France and the British Isles in the Middle Ages and the Renaissance: Essays by Members of Girton College, Cambridge, in Memory of Ruth Morgan* (Woodbridge, 1991), 71–113.
YARROW, Simon, *Saints and Their Communities: Miracle Stories in Twelfth-Century England* (Oxford, 2006).
YVER, JEAN, 'Le bref anglo-normand', *Revue d'histoire du droit: Tijdschrift voor Rechtsgeschiedenis*, xxix (1961), 313–30.

UNPUBLISHED THESES

ALEXANDER, Alison, *Annalistic Writing in Normandy, c.1050–c.1225*, PhD Thesis, University of Cambridge (2011).
DUJARDIN, Laurent, *Carrières de Pierre en Normandie. Contribution à l'étude historique et archéologique des carrières de pierre à bâtir à Caen (Calvados) et en Normandie aux époques médiévale et moderne*, 3 vols, Thèse de Doctorat de l'Université de Caen (1998).
LETOUZEY-RÉTY, Catherine, *Écrit et gestion du temporal dans une grande abbaye de femmes anglo-normande: la Sainte-Trinité de Caen (XIe-XIIIe siècle)*, Doctoral Thesis, Université de Paris I and University of London (2011).
NELSON, Jessica A., *From Saint Margaret to the Maid of Norway: Queens and Queenship in Scotland, circa 1067–1286*, PhD Thesis, University of London (2006).
WALDMAN, Thomas G., 'Hugh "of Amiens", Archbishop of Rouen (1130–64)', DPhil Thesis, University of Oxford (1970).

WEBSITES

'Domesday—Prosopography of Anglo-Saxon England', <http://www.pase.ac.uk>
'The "Lands of the Normans" in England (1204–1244)', <http://www.hrionline.ac.uk/normans/search>
'The Norman Edge', <http://www.lancs.ac.uk/normanedge>
'The Paradox of Medieval Scotland, 1093–1286', <http://www.poms.ac.uk>
'Prosopography of Anglo-Saxon England', <http://www.pase.ac.uk>
Tabularia: Sources écrites de la Normandie medieval [online journal: <http://www.unicaen.fr/mrsh/craham/revue/tabularia/>]

Index

Aachen, imperial palace chapel 26
Abernethy (Perth and Kinross) 87
Abingdon (Oxfords.), abbey, *Historia* of 23, 31, 41, 159
Ada de Warenne, wife of Henry, son of King David I 134
Adam I de Brus (dép. Manche) 130–1
Adela, countess of Blois-Chartres, daughter of William the Conqueror and Queen Matilda 84, 92, 104
Adelaide, sister of William the Conqueror 84
Adelida, daughter of William the Conqueror and Queen Matilda 84, 85
Adeliza of Louvain, queen of England 116, 147
Adeliza Peverel, wife/widow of Richard de Reviers 15–17, 28, 114
Ælfgar, earl of Mercia 125
Æthelfrith, St 91
Æthelred the Unready, king of England 59
Æthelstan, king of England 20, 88, 188
Ailred of Rievaulx 34, 51–2, 57, 100, 122, 129, 176, 179
Aimeri de Thouars (dép. Deux-Sèvres) 80
Alan Rufus, count of Brittany 107, 109, 137, 138, 138–9, 170
Alan Niger, count of Brittany 107, 137, 170
Alan III, count of Brittany, earl of Cornwall and Richmond 138, 139
Alberic, bishop of Ostia, papal legate 157
Albu, Emily 15
Alençon (dép. Orne) 72, 104, 108
Alexander I, king of Scots 156
Alexander II, pope 76, 82, 83
Alfred of Beverley 53
'alien priories' 148–9
Al-Idrīsī 181
Alton, Treaty of (1101) 102
Alvred d'Epaignes (dép. Eure) 39
Ambrières (dép. Mayenne), castle 146
Ambroise 181
'American Empire' 15
Amiens (dép. Somme) 164
Andrew, St 155, 156
Andrew of Coutances 56, 180
Andrieu-Guitrancourt, Pierre 2–3
Angers (dép. Maine-et-Loire) 44
  abbey of Saint-Serge and Saint-Bacchus 138
Angevin/Plantagenet Empire 5, 6, 10, 125, 141, 160, 167, 168, 170, 175–6, 180
'Anglicization' 9, 157, 187
'Anglo-Norman' 9, 29, 107, 158

'Anglo-Norman Empire' 5, 186
Anglo-Saxon Chronicle 35, 59–60, 69–71, 79, 87, 88, 99, 105, 119, 141, 175
Anjou, county of 56, 105
  counts of 51, 77–8, 119, 138, 140, 162, 166, 177
Anna Comnena 181
Annals of St Neots 60–1
Anonymous of Béthune 171
Anselm, St, abbot of Le Bec and archbishop of Canterbury 30, 39, 45, 46, 47, 156
Anselm, *vicomte of* Rouen 147
Antioch (Turkey) 51, 96
'apartheid' 63
Apulia 43, 49, 51, 73, 96, 166, 181
Aquitaine, duchy of 99, 141
Argentan (dép. Orne) 101, 137
Arnoux, Mathieu 155
Arnulf, archdeacon of Sées and bishop of Lisieux 144, 183
Arnulf I, count of Flanders 164
Arnulf de Montgommery (dép. Calvados) 109–10
Arthur, King 154, 180, 181–2
Arthur, duke of Brittany 161, 162, 170, 176
Arthurian histories 55, 180; *see also* Andrew of Coutances, Geoffrey of Monmouth, Wace.
Ashe, Laura 13
Astronomer, 'Life of Louis the Pious' 90
Athens, Acropolis Museum 20
Aubrey de Coucy-le-Château-Auffrique (dép. Aisne) 86
Aubrey III de Vere (Ver, dép. Manche, or Vair in Ancenis, dép. Loire-Atlantique), count of Guines 147–8
Aunay-sur-Odon (dép. Calvados), abbey 169
Aversa, bishopric of 40
Avranchin 47
Ayers, Brian 38

Babylon 96, 128
Baldwin, abbot of Bury St Edmunds 60
Baldwin de Reviers (dép. Calvados), earl of Devon 16
Baldwin, sheriff of Devon 136
Baldwin son of Clarus, citizen of Rouen 147
Bangor (Gwynedd), bishopric of 124
Bardney (Lincs.), abbey 141
Barfleur (dép. Manche) 10, 31, 60, 105
Barlow, Frank 66, 78, 114
Barnwell (Cambs.), priory 37
Barthélemy, Dominique 18

Index

Bartlett, Robert 9, 12–13
Battle (Sussex), abbey of 38, 177
Baudri of Bourgueil 92, 178
Bauduin, Pierre 11
Bayeux (dép. Calvados) 48, 49, 103, 120, 125, 166, 168, 181
Bayeux Tapestry 23, 37, 86
Bazouches-en-Houlme (dép. Orne) 114
Beaumont (dép. Eure), family 74, 132–3
Bec (-Hellouin), Le (dép. Eure), abbey 30, 39, 45, 50, 53, 54, 55, 56, 135, 136, 137
Beckford (Glos.) 149
Bede 22, 154
Bégard, abbey (dép. Côtes d'Armor) 139
Belinus 56
Benedict VIII, pope 163
Benedict, Master 50; *see also* Matilda of Wallingford.
Benoît de Sainte-Maure 61
Berengar of Tours 85
Berkshire 147
Bernard, abbot of Tiron (dép. Eure-et-Loir) 31
Bertrada, queen of France 146
Bertram de Verdun (dép. Manche) 169
Beroul of Rouen 42
Bertha, daughter of Conan III, duke of Brittany 138
Binham (Norfolk), priory 144
Bisson, Thomas 106
'Blanchelande', Treaty of 78
Boethius 22
Bohemond of Antioch 42–3
Book of Revelations 22, 129
Boulogne (dép. Pas-de-Calais), counts and county of 56, 105, 140
Bouvines (dép. Nord), Battle of (1214) 160, 173
Brémule (dép. Eure), Battle of (1119) 96, 104, 111, 136, 179
Brennius 56
Breteuil (dép. Eure) 112, 133
Bretons 36, 49, 49–50, 79, 80, 86, 125, 139, 140, 184
Brevis Relatio 49
Brian, a count of Brittany 80, 86
Brian fitz Count 50, 105, 147
Brionne (dép. Eure) 136
British Empire 4, 7, 13, 28
British Isles 4–5, 7, 8, 9, 11, 20, 21, 22, 23, 40, 42, 60, 83, 87–8, 91–2, 93–4, 101, 122, 123, 136, 141, 142, 152–7, 158, 159, 166, 169, 176, 185, 187, 188–9
British Museum 20
Brittany 84, 105, 121, 138, 140, 162, 180
   dukes of 80
Brown, R. Allen 6, 183
Brus (Bruce) (dép. Manche), family 130
Brut y Twysygion 21, 97–8, 110, 124–5, 167
Burgundy 149

Burgundians 36, 56
Burke, Edmund 166
Bury St Edmunds (Suffolk), abbey 25, 27, 36, 45–6, 138
Byzantine Empire 26, 43, 89, 163

Cadwaladr ap Gruffudd, king in Wales 125, 136, 153
Cadwgan ap Bleddyn, king of Powys 153
Caen (dép. Calvados) 22, 31, 38, 42, 48, 85, 103, 120, 150, 166, 168, 171, 181
   abbey of La Trinité 76, 85, 92, 148
   abbey of Saint-Etienne 26, 27, 39, 85, 102
   church of Saint-Martin 48
   Salle de l'Echiquier 27
   stone 30, 37, 38–9, 42, 150
Caesar Augustus, emperor 88
Calabria 43, 49, 73, 96
Calixtus II, pope 94
Cambridge 37
'Camp de Beugy, Le', at Sainte-Suzanne (dép. Mayenne) 77
Campbell, James 36, 58
canon law 82
Canterbury 37, 38
   abbey of St Augustine 38
   archbishopric and cathedral 25, 83
   cathedral priory 45, 46
   primacy 83, 88, 153, 156, 158
Carisbrooke (Isle of Wight) 15
Carlisle (Cumbria) 104, 122, 157
Carmen de Hastingae Proelio 35, 79
Carolingian Empire 7, 10, 11, 18, 58, 66, 83, 102, 103
Cassel (dép. Nord), Battle of (1071) 83
Castle Acre (Norfolk), priory 134
Cecilia, daughter of William the Conqueror and Queen Matilda, abbess of La Trinité, Caen 76, 92
Ceredigion 45, 101, 110, 135
Chalus-Chabrol (dép. Haute-Vienne) 160
Channel, English 6, 8, 19, 30–1, 35, 38, 39, 40, 49–50, 61, 66, 67, 80, 99, 110, 117, 148, 149, 150, 151, 159, 168, 171, 172, 175, 178
Channel Islands 3
Chanson de Roland 180
Charlemagne, emperor 21, 26, 62, 89, 103, 133, 180
Charles III the Fat, emperor 102
Charles III the Simple, king of the West Franks 164
Charroux (dép. Allier), abbey 141
Château Gaillard (dép. Eure), castle of 169, 174
Chartres (dép. Eure-et-Loir), abbey of Saint-Père 76
Chausey Islands 31
Chepstow (Gwent) 19

Index

Cherbourg (dép. Manche), college of canons 76
Chibnall, Marjorie 1–2
Childeric III, king of the Franks 103
chivalry 9
Christina of Markyate 44
Chronicle of Melrose 97
Cistercian order 151
Clare, family 110, 135–7
Clemence de Fougères (dép. Ille-et-Vilaine) 162
Cluny, abbey, and Cluniac order 134, 148–9
Clydesdale, Upper 157
Cnut, king of England and king of Denmark 18, 23, 70
Cogges (Oxfords.), priory 115, 149–50
Cohen, Robin 29
coinage 118–19, 168
    Arabic 119
    Byzantine 119
    Frankish/French 119
    Scottish 154
Colchester (Essex), castle 25
Coleman, biographer of St Wulfstan, bishop of Worcester 34
Collectio Lanfranci 82
Colley, Linda 2, 28
Columba, St 155
colonization 8
Conan III, duke of Brittany 138
Conan IV, duke of Brittany 138, 139, 140, 170
Conisbrough (S. Yorks.), castle 135
Conrad II, emperor 69
Constance, duchess of Brittany, daughter of William the Conqueror and Queen Matilda 84
Constance, duchess of Brittany (1181–1201) 138, 140, 162, 170
Constantinople 43, 84, 164
Consuetudines et Iusticie (1091) 102
Cotentin 15, 16, 112, 131
Cownie, Emma 126
Creully (dép. Calvados) 108, 168
Crooks, Peter 4–5
Crouch, David 106, 110, 111, 132, 171, 187
Crowland (Lincs.), abbey 95
Croxden (Surrey), abbey 169
Cumbria 100, 101, 142
Cuthbert, St 86–7, 91

danegeld 30
Dastin, family 47
David I, king of Scots 22, 26, 52, 57, 95, 97, 100, 101, 109, 110, 114, 120, 121–3, 126, 129, 130–1, 145, 155, 156, 157, 161, 189
David (the Scot), bishop of Bangor 124
David, St 157,
Davies, R. R. 4–5, 93, 151, 157, 188–9
Davis, R. H. C. 6, 88, 114
De Bello Saxonico 85
de Boüard, Michel 66

De Expugnatione Lyxbonensi 146, 178
Delisle, Léopold 54
Denmark 44, 166
Derbyshire 171
Devil, the 81
Devon 15, 146
Dialogue of the Exchequer, The 172, 184
Diarmait mac Murchada, king of Leinster 126, 137
diaspora (of the Normans) 9, 29, 42–4, 46, 47, 52, 54–5, 56, 63, 67, 94, 96, 178–9, 181–3
Diego Paláez, bishop of Santiago 85
Dieppe (dép. Seine-Maritime) 31
Dinan (dép. Côtes d'Armor), abbey of Saint-Jacut 138
Dives, river (Normandy) 72
Dol (dép. Ille-et-Vilaine) 84
    archbishop of 138
Domesday Book 18, 19, 33, 35, 36, 40, 41, 74, 88–90, 148
Domfront (dép. Orne) 121
Donnchad (Duncan) II, king of Scots 87, 100
Douglas, D. C. 6, 66
Dover (Kent) 31, 79
Dreux (dép. Eure-et-Loir) 76
Dudo of Saint-Quentin 155, 164, 181
Duncan, A. A. M. 122
Dunfermline (Fife), abbey 155
Durazzo (Durrës, Albania) 42–3
Durham 57, 59, 86–7
    cathedral 25, 57, 100, 142, 155
    Treaty of (1139) 101
Dyfed 157

Eadmer of Canterbury 46, 52, 156
Ealdred, archbishop of York 20, 66–7, 70–1, 83
Early Yorkshire Charters 137
East Anglia 26–7, 86, 134, 138–9, 146, 155
Edgar, king of Scots 97, 100
Edgar the Ætheling 43, 70, 87–8, 100, 176
Edith, queen of England 33–4
Edith Swanneck 139
Edmund, St 30, 45–6, 60, 118, 142
Edward the Confessor, king of England 33–4, 60, 75, 162, 163
    laws of 47, 82
Edward of Salisbury, sheriff of Wiltshire 35
Edwin, earl of Mercia 71, 81, 91
Einhard, 'Life of Charlemagne' 90
Eleanor of Aquitaine, Queen of England, Duchess of Aquitaine and Normandy, Countess of Anjou 175, 180
Ely:
    abbey church/cathedral 25, 26
    Isle of 71
Emma, *vicomtesse* of Rouen 151
Empire, the (German) 25, 150, 155
Encomium Emmae Reginae 23

England, kingdom 1, 3, 9, 10, 13, 14, 19, 20, 22, 23, 25, 29, 30, 31, 36, 37, 38, 40, 41, 49, 52, 56, 57, 58, 60, 62, 65, 71, 74, 78, 79, 80, 85, 86, 89, 90, 91–2, 96, 100, 110, 116, 121, 126, 132, 136, 137, 138, 140, 142, 150, 158, 159, 163, 166, 167, 174, 182
  relationship with Normandy 1, 3, 10–11, 25, 36, 37, 42, 48, 53–5, 58, 60–1, 90–1, 94–5, 99, 104, 105–6, 107–15, 115–20, 126–7, 130–41, 168–71, 172, 174–5
English, the 21, 24, 55, 57–8, 59, 63, 67, 68, 70, 71, 78, 80, 81, 86, 87, 95, 96, 105, 114, 125, 172, 173, 177
  language 31, 44, 47, 91, 105
Eremberge, daughter of Helias, count of Maine 121
'European change' 9, 93–4, 118, 144–5, 158–9, 186–7
Eusebius, bishop of Caesarea 54
Eustace II, count of Boulogne 75
Eustace III, count of Boulogne 112
Eustace de Breteuil (dép. Eure) 49
Eustace fitz John 145
Eva, nun of Wilton and anchoress 44
Evesham (Worcs.), abbey 39
Evreux (dép. Eure)
  abbey of Saint-Taurin 170
  comté of 169
exchequers, English and Norman 116, 117, 149, 170
Exeter (Devon) 72
  castle gate 26

Falaise (dép. Calvados) 22
  castle 85, 118
  Treaty of (1174) 22, 122
Fawdon in Whaddon (Cambs), battle at 79
Fécamp (dép. Seine-Maritime), abbey 115, 149, 167
Fens, the 52
Ferguson, Niall 3, 4
Fernie, Eric 9
feud 74–5
First Crusade 37, 43, 59, 84, 100, 112, 119, 120, 136, 178
Flanders 84, 105, 134, 135, 141, 146, 147, 150, 157
  counts of 75, 80, 125
Fleming, Donald 40
Flemings 80, 86, 125, 141, 147, 157, 173, 184
Folkestone (Kent), priory 151
Fontenay (dép. Calvados), abbey 89
Fontevrault (dép. Maine-et-Loire), abbey of 44, 51
Fore (Westmeeth), priory 170
Forth, river 20, 60, 86, 87, 97
Foulognes (dép. Calvados) 168
Frame, Robin 5

France 13, 20, 93–4, 169, 170, 171, 172, 175
  Capetian kings of 75, 78, 104, 119, 155, 160, 176–7
  kingdom 141, 164–5, 166, 180
Franks, the 58, 164
Frederick I Barbarossa, emperor 62, 180
Frederick II, emperor 183
Frederick, brother of Gerbod, earl of Chester, and Gundrada de Warenne 80
Freeman, E.A. 66
French, the 52, 58, 59, 70, 97, 105, 125, 164, 180, 181, 184
French language 9, 44, 47, 55, 56–7, 63, 84, 153, 184, 185
Fulk IV le Rechin, count of Anjou 78, 121
Fulk V, count of Anjou 104, 121
Furness (Cumbria), abbey 110

Galbraith, V. H. 88
Galicia, kingdom of 85
Gameson, Richard 46–7
Garnett, George 90, 94
Gayton-le-Wold (Lincs.) 139
Gazeau, Véronique 143–4
Geary, Patrick 12
Geffrei Gaimar 53, 56–7, 95, 96, 99
Geoffrey II Martel, count of Anjou 75, 162
Geoffrey III the Bearded, count of Anjou 77, 78
Geoffrey IV Plantagenet, count of Anjou and duke of Normandy 16, 22, 24, 55, 56, 59, 105–6, 114, 121, 122, 130, 140, 141, 175, 178
Geoffrey Boterel II, count of Penthièvre (dép. Côtes d'Armor) 139
Geoffrey de Chaumont-sur-Loire (dép. Loir-et-Cher) 80
Geoffrey de Mandeville, earl of Essex 113
Geoffrey de Mayenne (dép. Mayenne) 77
Geoffrey Malaterra 43, 69
Geoffrey Martel, son of Count Fulk IV le Rechin 121
Geoffrey of Chelsfield (Cambs.) 41
Geoffrey of Monmouth 53–5, 56, 98, 156, 175
Geoffrey of Repton, mayor of Caen 171
Geoffrey, abbot of St Albans 44
Geoffrey, bishop of Coutances (dép. Manche) 43
Geoffrey, count of Perche 169
Geoffrey, duke of Brittany 109, 138, 140, 161, 170
George of Antioch 26
Gerald of Wales 13, 45, 62, 94, 153, 155–6, 177
Gerard, bishop of Sées (dép. Orne) 114
Gerald of Windsor, castellan of Pembroke 45
Gerbod, earl of Chester, brother of Gundrada de Warenne 80, 86, 134
Germany 84, 85, 124, 136
Gervase of Tilbury 171
Gervase, prior of Saint-Céneri-le-Gérei (dép. Orne) 56

Gesta Normannorum Ducum 23, 54, 56, 61, 71, 72, 164, 180, 183
Gesta Stephani 95, 111–12, 136
Geste des Engleis en Yrlande, La 185
Gilbert, abbot of Saint-Etienne of Caen 39
Gilbert II de Laigle (dép. Orne) 169
Gilbert fitz Gilbert (fitz Richard) de Clare ('Strongbow') 136
Gilbert fitz Richard de Clare 110, 135–6, 153
Gillingham, John 14, 18, 57, 78, 161
Giso, bishop of Wells 33
Gisors (dép. Eure) 185
Glastonbury (Som.), abbey 46
Gloucester 20, 89
  abbey of St Peter 37
Godwine, earl of Wessex 33
Golding, Brian 1
Gorron (dép. Mayenne), castle 146
Goscelin of Saint-Bertin 23, 38, 44, 154
Gothic architecture 144
Götterdamerung 129
Gower 109
Grant, Lindy 144, 167
Green, Judith 174
Gregorian Reform 93–4
Gregory VII, pope 84
Grimoald du Plessis-Grimoult (dép. Calvados) 73
Gruffudd ap Cynan, king of Gwynedd 120, 124
Gruffudd ap Llywelyn, king of Gwynedd and of Deheubarth 20, 125
Guérin de Glapion (dép. Orne) 169
Guibert of Nogent 72, 119
Guitmund, monk, later bishop of Aversa 40
Gundrada, wife of William I de Warenne 134, 135
Gunnhild, daughter of King Harold 137, 139
Guy, count of Brionne (dép. Eure) 73
Guy, count of Ponthieu 75
Gwent 18–19
Gwynedd, kingdom of 124, 125, 156

Hagger, Mark 117
Haimo Dentatus 73
Hait, sheriff of Pembroke 45
halls 31, 44, 117
Halsall, Guy 65
Hamelin de Ballon (dép. Sarthe) 36–7, 100
Hamelin de Mayenne (dép. Mayenne) 146
Hamelin de Warenne, earl of Surrey, half-brother of King Henry II 134, 135
'hard power' 4, 18–23, 97, 123
Harold II (Godwineson), king of England 20, 33, 35, 45, 75, 79, 83, 95, 137, 139, 158, 188, 189–90
'Harrying of the North', the 33, 39, 91
Haskins, Charles Homer 2–3, 30, 167
Hastings (Sussex) 31
  Battle of (1066) 18, 19, 33, 65, 66, 70, 72, 78, 79, 83, 90, 158

Hautes-Bruyères (dép. Yvelines), priory 146
Hawise, countess of Aumale (dép. Seine-Maritime) 169
Heather, Peter 12, 187
Helias de La Flèche (dép. Sarthe), count of Maine 103, 120–1
Henry, bishop of Winchester and abbot of Glastonbury 104
Henry, earl of Warwick 109, 133
Henry III, emperor 69
Henry IV, emperor 84
Henry V, emperor 124, 136
Henry VI, emperor 183
Henry I, king of England and duke of Normandy 8, 10, 15, 16, 21, 24, 27, 30, 36, 37, 41, 42, 43, 45, 46, 47, 50, 52, 54, 57, 58, 60, 61, 87, 94, 96, 97–8, 99, 100, 101, 102, 103, 108, 109, 110, 111, 112–13, 116, 119–20, 121, 123, 124, 126–7, 132, 134, 135, 136, 137, 141, 143, 145, 146, 147, 149, 152, 155, 161, 173, 174, 175, 176, 189
  and Normandy 48–9, 103–5, 108, 112–13, 117, 119–20, 126, 143
  arrangements for imperial succession 59–60, 105–6, 108, 121, 141, 146–7, 177
  treatment of Robert Curthose 110–11, 176
  treatment of William Clito 105, 176
Henry II, king of England, duke of Normandy and Aquitaine, count of Anjou 16, 24, 50, 54, 55, 56, 57, 61, 62, 106, 109, 110, 111, 113, 114, 115, 121, 122, 123, 125, 134, 136, 137, 138, 139, 140, 145, 149, 152, 160, 166, 167, 170, 175–6, 177, 180, 185, 189
Henry I, king of France 75, 165
Henry, son of King David I 129, 134, 155
Henry (the Young King), son of King Henry II 109, 167
Henry de Sully, abbot of Fécamp 144
Henry of Huntingdon 21–2, 41, 51–3, 54, 57, 60, 61, 62, 96, 167, 178, 179, 188
Herbert II, count of Maine 77
Herbert of Middlesex, bishop of Conza 43
Hereford 113
Herefordshire 18
Hereward the Wake 56, 95
Herfast, bishop of Thetford 45
Herman, archdeacon and monk of Bury St Edmunds 45–6, 52, 60
Hoel, bishop of Le Mans 48
Hollister, C. Warren 2
Holt, J. C. 88, 89
Holy Land 146
Hood (Byland) (N. Yorks.), abbey 159
households, royal and aristocratic 37, 42, 45, 87, 98–9, 107, 109, 120, 124, 129, 131–2, 137, 140, 170

Hubert, *vicomte* of Sainte-Suzanne (dép. Mayenne) 77
Hubert Walter, archbishop of Canterbury 161
Hugh, archbishop of Rouen 113, 131
Hugh, bishop of Langres 84
Hugh IV, count of Maine 162
Hugh, count of Vermandois 133
Hugh de Lacy (Lassy, dép. Calvados) 170
Hugh IX de Lusignan (dép. Vienne) 175
Hugh Bigod, earl of East Anglia 132
Hugh I, earl of Chester 86
Hugo Falcandus 181
Humphrey de Vieilles (dép. Eure) 133
hundred courts 184
Huntingdon (Cambs.) 52
  earldom of 121, 123

Iberian peninsular, kingdoms of 24
identity 6–7, 12–13, 27, 29, 32, 44, 46–7
  English 13–14, 16, 27, 29, 37, 40–2, 45, 51–2, 57, 58–9, 82, 87, 91, 95–6, 171, 172, 177–85
  Frankish 12–13
  French 184
  Norman 11–13, 16, 27, 29, 36, 40–2, 46, 49, 51–2, 56, 58–9, 61–2, 64, 67, 82, 87, 95–6, 99, 165–7, 171, 177–85
  Scottish 57
Ilbert II de Lacy (Lassy, dép. Calvados) 147
Ile-de-France 144, 158, 169
imperialism 8
Innocent II, pope 97
Iraq, war 166
Ireland 88, 99, 126, 137, 157, 159, 161, 169–70, 171
Irish Sea 88, 137, 153
Isabel, wife of (1) William, son of King Stephen, and (2) Hamelin de Warenne 134, 135
Isabel of Vermandois, wife of (1) Robert, count of Meulan, (2) William II de Warenne 133, 134
Isabella de Montfort-en-Yvelines (dép. Yvelines) 146
Isabella of Angoulême, Queen of England, Duchess of Normandy and Aquitaine, Countess of Anjou 175
Isidore of Seville 72, 82, 165
Isleham (Cambs.), priory 138
Istria 89
Italy 84
  southern, Norman settlement in 13, 26, 42–4, 67, 163, 167
Ivo, bishop of Sées (dép. Orne) 43, 162

Jarrow, re-founded monastery 39
Jepthah, king 76
Jericho 150
Jerome, St 54
Jerusalem 43, 51, 150, 163, 164, 178
  kingdom 121
Jervaulx (N. Yorks.), abbey 139
Jewish communities 150
John, abbot of Fécamp 165
John, bishop of Glasgow 156
John, king of England, duke of Normandy and Aquitaine, count of Anjou 109, 160, 161, 169, 170, 171, 173, 174, 175–6, 185, 188
John of Cornwall 175
John of Salisbury 49, 97, 179, 181
John of Worcester 30, 52, 59, 60, 70, 112
Johnson, Ewan 13

Keats-Rohan, Katharine 40, 42, 78, 140
Kelso (Roxburghshire), abbey 26, 110, 122, 155
Kennedy, Paul 2
Kent 79, 147, 150
Kentigern, St 155
Kershaw, Paul 69
kingship 106–07
Kirkstead, abbey (Lincs.) 139

Lamentations of Jeremiah 96
Lancaster 123
Lanfranc, archbishop of Canterbury 33, 45, 46, 83, 88, 158
Last Judgement, the 22
Latakia (Syria) 119
Latin 63, 69, 154
Laudes Regiae 82, 117
Laval, family 147
Leges Scocie 154
Leicestershire 109
Le Cacheux, Paul 149
Le Goulet (dép. Eure), Treaty of (1200) 169, 174, 176
Le Mans (dép. Sarthe) 49, 72, 77, 99
  abbey of Saint-Pierre de la Couture 47
  abbey of Saint-Vincent 37
  bishopric of 47–8, 77, 87
Le Neubourg (dép. Eure) 49, 109
Le Patourel, John 1–3, 5, 6, 19, 29–30, 64, 98, 107, 120, 151, 168
Le Sap (dép. Orne) 136
Le Val Richer (dép. Calvados), abbey 146
Le Vaudreuil (dép. Eure), castle of 171
Les Andelys (dép. Eure) 174
Leo IX, pope 165
Lewes (Sussex), abbey 134
Lieven, Dominic 2
Lincoln 111
  Battle of (1141) 125
  Battle of (1217) 171, 178
  bishopric of 52
Linton (Cambs.), priory 138
Lisbon 153, 178
Llandaf (Cardiff), bishopric of 142
Loders (Dorset), priory 15
Loire, river 48, 77, 138, 170

Index

London 47, 68, 79, 82, 85
Longueville (dép. Seine-Maritime), priory 149
Lonlay (dép. Orne), abbey 151
Lotharingia 33, 44
Louis VI, king of France 96, 104
Louis VII, king of France 134, 176, 180
Louis, prince, son of King Philip Augustus 178
Louvre, the 20

Mac Bethad mac Findlaích (Macbeth), king of Scots 20
MacQueen, Hector 154
Madog ap Maredudd, king of Powys 125
Mael Coluim (Malcolm) III, king of Scots 87, 91, 100, 123
Mael Coluim (Malcolm) IV, king of Scots 122, 123
Magna Carta 189
Maine, county of 1, 22–3, 35, 36–7, 47–8, 56, 72, 75–6, 77–8, 80, 87, 90, 100, 101, 102, 103, 105, 120–1, 146, 147, 156, 162, 166, 173, 177
Maitland, F. W. 94, 187
Manceaux 125
Manche, Archives Départementales of 15
Mann, Michael 2
Mantes (dép. Yvelines) 84
Marcigni-sur-Loire (dép. Saône-et-Loire), abbey 44, 104
Margam (South Wales), abbey 110
Margaret, St, queen of Scots 57, 87, 100, 122, 155
Marianus Scotus, chronicle of 59
marriage 31, 33, 35–6, 41, 45, 57, 81, 84, 100, 116–17, 121, 133–6, 143, 153, 170, 189
Matilda, the Empress, *domina Anglorum*, countess of Anjou 15, 16, 22, 24, 47, 49, 49–50, 53, 59, 97, 101, 105–6, 108, 113, 121, 122, 124, 125, 129, 133, 135–6, 139, 140, 141, 147, 149, 167, 168, 175
Matilda, daughter of count Fulk V of Anjou and Eremberge 121
Matilda, queen, wife of William the Conqueror 75, 76, 82, 84, 87, 116, 134, 148
Matilda, queen, wife of King Henry I 57, 60, 87, 100, 116, 137
Matilda, queen, wife of Stephen 116
Matilda of Wallingford 49–50, 114
Matthew, count of Boulogne 109
Mayr-Harting, Henry 11
mercenaries 112, 125–6, 173
Merlin, prophecies of 53, 55
Messina (Sicily) 181
Meurig, bishop of Bangor 156
Midlands, English 133
Miles, earl of Hereford 125
Miles Crispin 50
Molyneaux, George 11
Monreale (Sicily), abbey church 26

Mont Saint-Michel, Le (dép. Manche), abbey 47, 55, 62, 115, 149, 150, 165
Montebourg (dép. Manche), abbey of 15–16, 50, 129, 130, 133
Montfort-l'Amaury (dép. Yvelines), lords of 169
Montgommery-Bellême, family of 108, 143
Morgan ab Owain, king of Morgannwg 125
Mortain (dép. Manche), *comté* of 171
Mortemer (dép. Seine-Maritime), castle 135
Mount Sinai 163
murdrum fine 82, 95
Musset, Lucien 3, 10, 30, 38

Nantes (dép. Loire-Atlantique) 138, 140
Napoleon Bonaparte 18
Néhou (dép. Manche) 27
Nelson, Jinty 12, 89
Nest 44–5
New College, Oxford 149
Newington Longueville (Bucks.) 149
Nicholas, archdeacon of Huntingdon, father of Henry of Huntingdon 52
Nicholas de Stuteville (Etoutteville, dép. Seine-Maritime) 145–6
Nicholas de Verdun (dép. Manche) 169
Nicholas, prior of Worcester 34
Nigel d'Aubigny (Saint-Martin d'Aubigny, dép. Manche) 145
Nigel de Monville (dép. Seine-Maritime) 151
Nigel, *vicomte* of the Cotentin 73
Norfolk 27, 36
Normandy, duchy of 3, 5, 9, 11–12, 16, 19, 20, 22, 31, 32, 35, 38, 39, 42, 43, 46, 47–9, 51, 53, 54, 55, 62, 68, 70, 72, 73, 74, 75–6, 80, 82, 83, 89, 96, 100, 103, 104, 108, 110, 114, 121, 124, 125, 128–9, 132, 133, 134, 136, 137, 139, 141, 143–4, 145, 148, 151, 152, 158, 162, 163–7, 167, 171, 173–4, 178, 180
  bishops of 113–14, 162
  relationship with England 10–11, 14–15, 19, 23–5, 26–7, 36–42, 48, 49–51, 54–7, 58, 60–1, 74–5, 86, 92, 94, 99, 101, 103, 104, 105–6, 107, 109, 111–15, 115–20, 126–7, 128–9, 132–7, 141, 143–4, 146–50, 150–1, 152, 167–9, 170, 172, 174–5
  relationship with Scotland 109, 121–2, 130–1
'Normanization' 9, 47
Normanitas 6–7, 61, 64, 165, 178, 183–4, 185
Normans, the 1, 2, 3, 4, 7, 8, 9, 15, 19, 21, 24, 27, 29, 32, 42, 45, 46, 47, 52, 53, 58, 61–2, 66, 73, 86, 88, 94, 96, 97, 99, 177; *see also* identity.
North Sea 26–7, 146
Norwich 36, 38, 85
  castle 118
  cathedral 25, 27
Notre-Dame-du-Pré (dép. Seine-Maritime), priory 50, 161, 167

Nuneaton (Warws.), priory 50–1, 115
Nye, Joseph Jnr 4, 174

Odo, bishop of Bayeux and earl of Kent 69, 70, 74, 85, 86, 107, 108
Ogbourne St. Andrew (Berks.) 50
Ogbourne St. George (Berks.) 50
O'Keeffe, Tadhg 26
Orderic Vitalis 15, 19, 22, 30, 31–2, 33, 35, 36, 39, 40, 43, 47, 48, 49, 51, 52, 53, 61, 62, 68, 71, 73, 74, 77, 80, 81, 94, 96, 99, 102, 107, 108, 110, 112, 120, 125, 126, 128, 133, 152, 166, 170, 178–9, 181, 183
Orne, river (Normandy) 181
Orwell, George 14
Osbern, monk of Canterbury 45, 46, 52
Otranto (Lecce), cathedral 182
Oswald, St, bishop of Worcester and archbishop of York 34
Owain ap Cadwgan ab Bleddyn, king of Powys 97–8, 124
Owain Gwynedd, king of Gwynedd 125, 156, 176
Oxford 36
Oxford Dictionary of National Biography 5

Patrick of Chaworth (Sourches, dép. Sarthe) 100
Palermo (Sicily) 26
Palmer, John 40
Paris 151
Patric, family 168
Patrixbourne (Kent) 168
Paxman, Jeremy 3
Payn Peverel 37–8, 43
Paynel family 146
Pembroke (Pembrokeshire) 45, 110
 earldom of 136
Penitential Ordinance 39, 76, 82
Perche, counts of 105, 169
Peter de Valognes (dép. Manche) 144
Philip, count of Flanders 109
Philip I, king of France 24, 84, 166
Philip II Augustus, king of France 160, 161, 162, 169, 172, 175, 176, 180, 181
Picot de Sai (dép. Orne) 153
Picquigny-sur-Somme (dép. Somme) 164
Pippin III, king of the Franks 103
piracy 30–1
Plantagenet Empire, *see* Angevin/Plantagenet Empire
Poitou 160, 175
Pontefract, honour of 147
Porter, Bernard 14
Pössel, Christina 67
pound sterling 37, 118–19, 168
Power, Daniel 6, 143
Powicke, Sir Maurice 10
Powys, kingdom of 124, 125
Préaux (dép. Eure), abbey of Saint-Léger 85

Préaux (dép. Eure), abbey of Saint-Pierre 37, 39, 133
prophecy 55, 58, 104, 128–9, 174–5
Pseudo-Isidorean Decretals 82

Quadripartitus 23

Ralph, bishop of the Orkneys 51
Ralph II de Tosny (dép. Eure) 112, 146
Ralph, earl of East Anglia 86
Ralph of Caen 178
Ralph of Coggeshall 173, 174
Ralph Paynel 146
Ralph Taisson 73
Ralph the Red de Pont-Echanfray (now Notre-Dame-du-Hamel, dép. Eure) 42–3
Rannulf, bishop of Durham 44
Rannulf II, earl of Chester 111–12, 113, 123, 125, 145, 161, 169
Rannulf III, earl of Chester and duke of Brittany 162
Rannulf, *vicomte* of the Bessin 73
Raymond of Aguilers 119
Reading (Berks.), abbey 54
Reginald, son of William I de Warenne 134
Regino of Prüm 102
Reimitz, Helmut 19–20
Reinfrid, prior of Whitby 39
Remigius, bishop of Lincoln 52
Rennes (dép. Ille-et-Vilaine) 138
 abbey of Saint-Melaine 138
Reviers, family 129, 133
Reuter, Timothy 65
Reynolds, Susan 8
Rhygyfarch ap Sulien 97
Rhys ap Tewdwr, king of Deheubarth 45, 87
Richard, abbot of Montebourg (dép. Manche) 131 note 11
Richard, bishop of Coutances 114
Richard I, count/duke of Normandy 167
Richard II, duke of the Normandy 59, 163, 164–5, 167
Richard I the Lionheart, king of England, duke of Normandy and Aquitaine, count of the Anjou 117, 136, 140, 160, 161, 173, 174, 181, 185
Richard Basset 36
Richard de Luci (Lucé, dép. Orne) 177
Richard de Reviers (dép. Calvados) (d.1060) 76
Richard de Reviers (dép. Calvados) (d.1107) 15–16, 28; *see also* Adeliza, wife of
Richard fitz Gilbert (de Clare) 74, 135, 136
Richard fitz Gilbert de Clare, earl of Pembroke ('Strongbow') 126, 137, 170, 185
Richard fitz Nigel 172
Richard, landholder in the Risle valley 37
Richard 'Palmer', bishop of Syracuse 43
Richmond, honour of 137

Index

Rievaulx (N. Yorks.), abbey of 57, 144–5
Robert Bordet 43
Robert Curthose, duke of the Normans, count of Maine 15, 37, 43, 48, 59, 61, 75, 77, 78, 83, 87, 90, 94, 96, 100, 101–3, 107, 110–11, 112, 120–1, 128, 132, 134, 136, 166, 173, 176, 178, 179
Robert II, count of Flanders 103
Robert, count of Meulan 109, 120, 133, 134, 136
Robert, count of Mortain 74, 84, 86, 87, 133
Robert d'Aunay-sur-Odon (dép. Calvados) 159
Robert de Bellême (dép., Orne), earl of Shrewsbury 101, 110, 121, 125–6, 143
Robert I de Brus (dép. Manche) 130–1
Robert II de Brus) (dép. Manche) 130
Robert de Chesney, bishop of Lincoln 62
Robert de Grandmesnil (dép. Calvados), abbot of Saint-Evroult and abbot of St Eufemia (Calabria) 43, 179
Robert de Lacy (Lassy, dép. Calvados) 147
Robert de Montfort-sur-Risle (dép. Eure) 43
Robert de Sainte-Mère-Eglise (dép. Manche) 16
Robert III de Stuteville (Étoutteville, dép. Seine-Maritime) 145
Robert fitz Walter 171
Robert Guiscard, duke of Apulia 43, 67, 179
Robert, earl of Gloucester 57, 107–8, 108, 110, 113, 125
Robert II, earl of Leicester 50–1, 56, 109, 110, 113, 115, 133
Robert IV, earl of Leicester 162
Robert of Torigni 15, 23, 24, 49, 50, 53–5, 56, 57, 61, 62, 98, 104, 106, 115, 136, 149, 152, 175, 176, 179, 180, 183
Robert the Lotharingian, bishop of Hereford 26
Robert the Magnificent, duke of Normandy 162, 164
Robert II the Pious, king of France 165
Roffe, David 88
Roger the Great Count, count of Sicily 43, 46, 69
Roger II, king of Sicily 26, 56, 181, 182–3, 183
Roger Borsa, count of Apulia 178–9
Roger, earl of Hereford 113
Roger, earl of Warwick 114
Roger de Beaumont (dép. Eure) 39–40, 74, 108, 109, 132–3
Roger de Montbrai (Mowbray) (dép. Manche) 114
Roger de Montgommery (dép. Calvados), earl of Shrewsbury 74, 84
Roger fitz Richard (fitz Gilbert) 135–6, 136
Rollo, count of Rouen 164, 180
Roman Empire 7, 10, 20, 25, 187
Rome 23, 24, 25, 55, 86, 128, 156
    St Peter's 26
Romney (Kent) 79
Rothschild, Emma 28

Rotrou, bishop of Evreux and archbishop of Rouen 114, 144
Rotrou II, count of the Perche 105
Rouen (dép. Seine-Maritime) 24, 42, 55, 115, 128, 134, 147, 150, 151, 160, 161, 162, 167, 168, 176
    abbey of La Trinité-du-Mont 67
    cathedral 167
    church of Saint-Gervais 90
    money of 37, 118–19, 168, 183
    poem 24, 55–6, 128, 178
    Treaty of (1091) 59, 102
Round, J. H. 18
Roxburghshire 143
Rubinstein, Jay 45
Rule of St Benedict 45

Saer de Quincy, earl of Winchester (Cuinchy, dép. Pas-de-Calais) 171
St Albans (Herts.), abbey church 25, 144
St Andrews (Fife), bishopric of 46, 155, 156
St David's (Pembrokeshire) 20, 87, 158
St Eufemia (Calabria), abbey of 43
St Margaret-at-Cliffe (Kent) 168
St Michael's Mount (Cornwall), priory 149
St Neots (Cambs.) 39
Saint-Clair-sur-Epte, Treaty of 164
Saint-Denis, (dép. Seine-Saint-Denis), abbey 19, 60
Saint-Evroult (dép. Orne), abbey 32, 43
Saint-Germain-des-Prés, Paris 89
Saint-Omer (dép. Pas-de-Calais) 134
    Saint-Bertin, abbey of 134, 147
Saint-Sauveur-le-Vicomte (dép. Manche) 130–1
Sainte-Barbe-en-Auge (dép. Calvados), college of canons 146, 149
Sainte-Suzanne (dép. Mayenne) 77
saints' cults, English 142
Samson, royal chaplain, bishop of Worcester 47–8
Savigny (-le-Vieux) (dép. Manche), abbey of 110, 139, 141, 151–2
'Saxo-Norman overlap', the 35
Scandinavia 33
Schama, Simon 3
Scots, the 24, 55–6, 153–4
    kingdom of 57, 97, 100, 117, 129, 143, 145, 153, 154–5, 156–7, 158
Scotland 86, 96–7, 102, 116, 130–1, 149, 153, 159, 166, 171
script 46–7
Second Crusade 38, 114, 134, 146, 154
Second Lateran Council (1139) 94, 97
Seeley, Sir John 14–15
Sées (dép. Orne) 101
    abbey of Saint-Martin 109–10
Seine, river 167, 174
Selkirk (Scottish Borders), abbey 110, 122, 155

Serlo of Bayeux 38–9, 49, 125, 152, 166
sheriffs 32
Short, Ian 9, 57
Sicily 43, 96
    kingdom of 3, 26, 158, 181, 183
Simon of Felsted (Essex) 148
Siward, earl of Northumbria 20
Smith, Julia 8
'soft power' 4, 17, 19, 49, 50, 76, 81–2, 83, 86, 87, 97, 101, 123, 158
Solway Firth 97
Sønnesyn, Sigbjørn Olsen 58
Sourches (dép. Sarthe) 100
Southampton (Hants.) 31
Southern, Sir Richard 14, 58
Soviet Union 8
Spear, David 140, 144
Speyer (Germany), cathedral 25
spielregeln 66
Stamford Bridge, Battle of (1066) 79
Standard, Battle of (1138) 22, 51–2, 123, 130, 145
Stephen, constable of Ceredigion II/26
Stephen, count of Blois-Chartres 84
Stephen, count of Brittany 138, 139, 170
Stephen, king of England and duke of Normandy 15, 16, 17, 101, 104–5, 106, 107–8, 108, 109, 110, 111, 113, 114, 116, 122, 125, 129, 130, 135, 136, 139, 147, 173, 176
Stephen of Rouen 56, 62, 71, 180
Stephen of Whitby 39
Stigand, archbishop of Canterbury 83
Stringer, Keith 5
Stoke-by-Clare (Suffolk), priory 136
Strathcathro (Angus), Battle of (1130) 123
succession to Normandy and England 10, 90, 94–5, 101–3, 105–6, 141, 145, 152, 161
Suffolk 44, 146, 153, 178
Sussex 79
Swavesey (Cambs.), priory 138
Sybil of Conversano, wife of Robert Curthose 43
Sykes, Naomi 158
Symeon of Durham 59

Tarragona (Catalonia) 43
Tay, river 123
Theobald, archbishop of Canterbury 149, 156
Theobald, count of Blois-Chartres 49, 106
Thetford (Norfolk) 36
Thierry, count of Flanders 115
Thimert (dép. Eure-et-Loir) 76
Third Crusade 181
Third Reich 4
Thomas, Hugh 14
Thomas Becket, St, archbishop of Canterbury 71, 168
Thomas de Verdun (dép. Manche) 169
Thomas of Bayeux, archbishop of York 25
Thomas of Monmouth 177–8
Thompson, Kathleen 110

Thomson, Rodney 58
Thurstan, abbot of Glastonbury 46
Tinchebrai (dép. Orne), Battle of (1106) 103, 116, 117, 120, 126
Tiron (dép. Eure-et-Loir), abbey of 110, 122, 149, 155, 156
Toirrdelbach Ua Briain, king of Munster 88
Toki, son of Wigod of Wallingford 35
Tonbridge (Kent) 136
toponyms 41, 42
Tosny (dép. Eure), family 74
Toulouse (dép. Haute-Garonne) 123
    county of 170
trauma 22
Très Ancien Coutumier 168
Turgot, *Life of St Margaret* 155, 185

Ulger, bishop of Angers 97
UN Convention on the Prevention and Punishment of the Crime of Genocide 34
United States of America 3, 8; *see also* 'American Empire'.
Urban, bishop of Llandaf 156
Urry, John 29 and note 8, 131

Val-ès-Dunes (dép. Calvados), Battle of (1047) 73, 165
Valmont (dép. Seine-Maritime), abbey 145
van Houts, Elisabeth 17
Varaville (dép. Calvados), Battle of (1057) 72
Verdun, Treaty of (843) 89
Verneuil (dép. Eure) 170
Vernon (dép. Eure) 27
Verse Chronicle 97
Vexin, French 84
Vita Ædwardi Regis 33–4
Vita Griffini ap Conani 124, 185
Vitalis of Canterbury 37, 38

Wace 15, 48, 55–6, 61–2, 98, 111–12, 112, 152, 165, 166, 175, 180
Waleran, count of Meulan 109, 133
Wales 1, 20, 21, 22, 37, 44–5, 87, 96, 97, 97–8, 100, 101, 108, 113, 117, 124–5, 126, 135, 136, 137, 145, 153, 155–7, 159, 167, 171, 176, 189
Wallingford (Berks.), college of canons 50
Walter de Clare 136
Walter Espec 144
Waltham (Essex), abbey 95, 155
Waltheof, earl 91, 95
Warenne (Hyde) Chronicle 49, 111, 135, 179
Warin, a monk 37
Warwick, church of St Mary 114
Warwickshire 109
Webber, Teresa 46
Welsh, the 21, 24, 55–6, 95
    as auxiliary troops 125–6
    March 143

Index

Wessex 87
Westminster 38, 114
  Hall 25, 27, 38, 85, 174
Whitby (N. Yorks.), abbey 39, 159
White Ship, wreck of 10, 30, 42, 58, 125
White Tower of London 25, 85
Wilfrid, St 159
William Longsword, count of Rouen 164
William I the Conqueror, king of England, duke of Normandy, count of Maine 1, 16, 18, 20, 21, 23, 24, 25, 27, 30, 31, 33, 34, 35, 39, 40, 52, 56–7, 58, 60, 61, 62, 64–92, 99, 100, 101, 102, 105, 107, 110, 113, 116, 123, 125, 126, 132, 134, 141, 162–3, 165, 166, 172, 173, 176, 189
  conquest of Maine (1062–3) 35, 47, 72, 75, 77–9, 80, 87, 90, 101, 162, 166
  Christmas court (1067) 68
  conduct of warfare 72–3, 77–9
  coronation (25 Dec. 1066) 20, 66–7, 70, 79, 80, 81, 83
  crown-wearing at York (1069) 71
  kingship 65–9, 79–82
  religious patronage 60, 76, 84
  treatment of rebellion 73–4, 77–8, 83, 91
William II Rufus, king of England 22, 27, 30, 37, 41, 43, 46, 56, 59, 90, 92, 99, 99–100, 101–2, 107, 108, 109, 110, 112, 119, 120–1, 123, 125, 132, 134, 135, 152, 161, 173, 174, 180
William I the Lion, king of Scots 22, 123, 153
William II, king of Sicily 26
William Clito, son of Robert Curthose, count of Flanders 48, 60, 104, 105–6, 121
William, count of Eu 112
William, count of Evreux 132
William, count of Mortain 108, 112
William d'Aubigny (Saint-Martin d'Aubigny, dép. Manche), *pincerna* 144
William d'Aubigny (Saint-Martin d'Aubigny, dép. Manche), earl of Arundel 147
William de Beauchamp of Elmley (Worcs.) 149
William de Breteuil (dép. Eure) 49, 132
William II de Briouze (dép. Orne) 113
William III de Briouze (dép. Orne) 176
William de Longchamp, bishop of Ely 185
William de Mandeville, earl of Essex 169
William de Saint-Pair 62
William II de Tancarville (dép. Seine-Maritime) 170
William I de Warenne (dép. Seine-Maritime), earl of Surrey 74, 84, 86, 110, 133–4

William II de Warenne (dép. Seine-Maritime), earl of Surrey 110–12, 133, 134, 169
William III de Warenne, (dép. Seine-Maritime), earl of Surrey 134
William IV de Warenne (dép. Seine-Maritime), son of King Stephen 109, 111, 135
William d'Ypres (Belgium) 147
William du Hommet (dép. Manche), constable of Normandy 131
William fitz Osbern 18–19, 70, 74, 83–4, 113, 132, 133
William fitz Ralph, seneschal of Normandy 171
William Maltravers 147
William Marshal, earl of Pembroke 161, 162, 170–1, 172, 178
William of Apulia 55
William of Jumièges 71, 72, 73, 79, 164
William of Malmesbury 4, 10, 18, 21, 26, 34, 35, 39–40, 46, 52, 53, 57–9, 60, 62, 67, 70, 71, 76, 81, 88, 92, 95, 96, 97, 99, 100, 104, 107–8, 119, 125, 126, 128, 129, 153, 154, 167, 173, 175
William of Norwich 177
William of Poitiers 23, 68–70, 71, 72, 73, 77, 79, 80, 81
William of Seacourt (Oxfords.) 41–2
William, prior of Sainte-Barbe-en-Auge 149
William, son of King Henry I 105, 121, 155
William, son of Richard de Reviers and Adeliza Peverel 16
William Talvas, count of Ponthieu 101
Williams, Ann 13, 32
Wilton (Wilts.), abbey 44
Winchester 148
  cathedral 25
  Treaty of (1153) 106, 114–15, 135, 139
Windsor (Berks.) 176
  primacy agreement (1072) 156
Winebald de Ballon (dép. Sarthe) 36–7, 100
Wipo, *Gesta Chuonradi* 69
Woolley (Berks.) 15
Worcestershire 133
writs/writ charters 62, 117, 154, 155, 168, 185
Wulfstan, archbishop of York 70
Wulfstan, St, bishop of Worcester 18, 34–5, 59
Wymondham (Norfolk), priory 144

York
  abbey of St Mary 109, 138, 139, 145
  cathedral church of St Peter 25, 66, 71
  primacy over Scottish Church 153, 156, 158
Yorkshire 33, 130, 134, 138, 145